you all about it.
for now, as I just have time to
mail.

walks home together. She a
the clouds consoling the o
dog house. those were y
derful years and I'll
el them.
in starting on my four
senior year in
they ha

lim H. Husselman 0-17918
P.M., APO 403
master, New York, N.Y.

U S ARMY POSTAL
JAN
23 6
1944
U.S. A.P.O.

VIA AIR MAIL

Mrs Oak Husselman
burn, Indiana

Brandon
er St.
urn,   Indiana

New York City

Miss Mary Brandon
American Red Cross

Mrs Oak Husa
Auburn
Indiana

erbon
ed Cross
0 782
o Postmaster New York, N.Y.

PAR AVION
AIRMAIL
CORREO AEREO

LT. J M PETERSON
F.P.O. SAN FRAN
U.S.S. YORKTOWN

JAN
1944
U.S. A.P.O.

AIR 6
UNITED STATES OF AMERICA

Mrs. George Olinger
Midway Drive
Auburn, Indiana

which they
nderful they
od either. I enlisted
after the beginning!
or. Most all of
west,

Dear Folks:-

Sun
17

ARMY GUY, RED CROSS GAL

The Lives & Letters of Two Small-Town
Hoosiers Who Helped Win World War II

By Barbara Olenyik Morrow with Ellen England

Pale Oak Publishing ❖ Auburn, Indiana

Pale Oak Publishing, Auburn, Indiana

Copyright © 2023 by Barbara Olenyik Morrow and Ellen England

All rights reserved.

No portion of this book may be reproduced in any form without written permission from the publisher or author, except as permitted by U.S. copyright law

ISBN 979-8-9882490-2-3 (hardback)

ISBN 979-8-9882490-1-6 (paperback)

ISBN 979-8-9882490-0-9 (ebook)

Cover design, frontispiece design, and map illustrations by Mary Noelle Itin

Cover and frontispiece images courtesy of Ellen England

Composed in EB Garamond

For it is not Histories that I am writing, but Lives. – Plutarch (c. AD 46-119)

There is properly no history; only biography. – Ralph Waldo Emerson (1803-1882)

There's no reason for history to be boring, absolutely none. It isn't. It's about people. – David McCullough (1933-2022)

Contents

Prologue	IX
A Note on the Letters	XIII
Map of Indiana	XIV
1. BILL AND MARY	1
2. BILL: 1911 - 1942	5
3. BILL: 1942	18
4. BILL: 1942 - 1943	41
5. MARY: 1910 - 1943	73
6. MARY: 1943	88
7. BILL: 1943 - 1944	124
8. MARY: 1943 - 1944	149
9. MARY: 1944	176
10. BILL: 1944	204
11. BILL: 1944	221
12. BILL: 1944	240
13. MARY: 1944	255

14. BILL: 1944 - 1945	292
15. MARY: 1945	311
16. BILL: 1945	330
17. MARY: 1945	346
18. BILL: 1945	375
19. BILL AND MARY	387
Epilogue	400
Acknowledgments	402
Selected Bibliography and Index	406
About the Authors	417

Prologue

A TRUCK PULLED UP in front of Ellen England's home in Richmond, California, in the mid-1980s, and movers unloaded an antique armchair, boxes of carefully wrapped crystal glassware, and other heirlooms shipped from the Midwest. They were from Ellen's widowed mother, Mary Brandon Husselman, who having recently sold the family home was downsizing to a smaller residence in her hometown of Auburn, Indiana. Mary, then in her seventies, had decided it was time to divide keepsakes between her two daughters. Given that Ellen lived half a continent away, a truck bearing the treasures had been dispatched west.

Among the delivered items was a cedar chest filled with photo albums and a gray shirt box. A note taped atop the box identified the contents as "Bill's War Letters." When Ellen removed the lid, she saw a pile of old letters that her father, Bill Husselman, had written to his parents while serving stateside and in northwest Europe with the U.S. Army in World War II. Never having seen the letters or even aware that they existed, Ellen quickly read a few and thought to herself, "Oh, this looks interesting. Maybe someday I'll have a chance to get to them." But Ellen – married, working as a programmer analyst for the University of California library system, and strapped for time – returned the letters to the box and carried on with her busy life.

Some twenty-five years later, having retired and moved with her husband back to Auburn, Ellen set about doing what librarians do, organizing by date the jumbled collection of letters. As she began reading the correspondence chronologically, she was emotionally drawn into and fascinated by her father's tale of wartime service. Deciding that the letters merited sharing – with family members, at the very least – Ellen began transcribing all 296 of them, a task that engaged her for seven months and concluded in February 2012.

But more work loomed, as she would soon learn. In another cardboard box, in an upstairs closet in the Auburn home of Ellen's older sister, Anne Thomas, were more letters, 209 to be exact. During World War II, their mother, at the time unmarried, had been an American Red Cross worker in Italy. Just as Bill Husselman's parents had lovingly saved his wartime correspondence, the Brandon family had done likewise with Mary's letters from overseas.

In 1994, upon Mary's death, Anne discovered those letters among the family belongings. Anne dutifully saved them but chose not to read them, fearing memories of her mother would make her sad. Ellen's project – the transcribing of their father's correspondence – prompted Anne one evening to deliver to her sister-turned-family-archivist the cardboard box bearing Mary's letters. Thoroughly delighted, but also surprised to learn more correspondence existed, Ellen launched into another round of transcription. This time she worked from handwritten pages that still bore her mother's scent: "I could smell her perfume."

Newspaper headlines and obituaries confirm what is evident by observation: The World War II generation is fast disappearing, with surviving veterans now well into their high nineties and older. The last American president to have fought in that war, George H. W. Bush, died in November 2018 at age ninety-four. When veterans today manage to attend anniversary ceremonies – such as those commemorating the 1941 Pearl Harbor attack, which launched the United States into World War II, and the 1944 D-Day invasion, which began the liberation of western Europe from Nazi Germany – their presence carries a poignancy. The public understands that these veterans, many clutching canes or sitting in wheelchairs with blankets draped across their laps, may not live long enough to witness the next commemoration.

Statistics put an even finer point on what has been and continues to be lost. Of the sixteen million American men and women who put on

PROLOGUE

uniforms during World War II, just under one million were still alive in 2015, the 70th anniversary of the war's end in 1945. Three years later, in 2018, about half a million WWII vets remained, and by 2022, the number had shrunk to less than 200,000. With an average of 180 U.S. veterans dying every day, demographers estimate that in 2025 – the 80th anniversary of the war's conclusion – only about 60,000 will be alive; in 2035, fewer than 600. The last World War II veteran is expected to pass away in 2043, according to U.S. government estimates.

With each veteran's passing comes another reality: Stories go untold. That's not to say personal narratives from World War II vets and others who contributed to the war effort do not exist. Many men and women wrote their memoirs, which they shared with family and friends. Others published books. Still others offered oral histories. But many more said little about their wartime experiences – not upon their return from service, not in their waning years. They saw the war for what it was, something in their past, and they chose not to revisit it. As noted by Kimberly Guise, senior curator and curatorial affairs director at The National WWII Museum in New Orleans, some vets kept quiet because of too-painful memories, others because they "considered their story insignificant when compared with those who lost their lives."

But stories untold do not necessarily mean stories lost. As Ellen England and her sister learned, letters – whether stuffed in a cedar chest or squirreled away in an upstairs closet – can provide a rich "in-the-moment" account of an individual's wartime experience. Through such letters one can encounter the highly personal, as when Mary Brandon wrote from Italy saying she needed more stockings, mascara, even brassieres. Likewise, letters can shed light on war's comical side, as when Bill Husselman, still stateside, wrote his parents about soldiers hiding in wall lockers and under bunks and even "hanging from fire escapes" to avoid dreaded kitchen duty. Then, too, letters can tug at the heart: "I am rather lonesome," Bill wrote at one point, "as all of my buddies have gone."

Beyond that, wartime letters can connect readers to 1940s-era pop culture and to the colloquialisms and regional expressions of the time ("Swell," "Miss you like sixty," "Got het up"). They can familiarize readers with military jargon (PX, APO, JAG). And they can reveal for readers the pejorative slang so pervasive during the war years – when words such as Japs, Jerries, and Heinies were shorthand for America's enemies.

In 2018, curator Guise wrote an article highlighting The National WWII Museum's archival collection of mail from men and women in uniform, and her article referred to war correspondence as "time capsules in envelopes." That apt phrase applies here. This book is a collection of time capsules, straight from the pens and pencils of two Midwesterners who grew up in the same era, among the same friends, in the same small town. One a man, one a woman, the two did not go looking for their place on the world stage; international events brought war into their lives and compelled them to cross an ocean to try to defeat tyranny as best they could.

Patriotism and a sense of duty inspired one to serve the country. Patriotism and adventure motivated the other. Never did their paths cross overseas, never did their duties – wildly different – overlap. But they were united by the ethic of teamwork, sacrifice, determination, and courage, the same ethic that propelled millions of Americans in the early 1940s to adjust the course of their lives and vigorously defend freedom.

The time capsules in the ensuing pages are from Bill Husselman and from Mary Brandon. Two voices, hundreds of letters, thousands of words. One family's story – in fragile envelopes, preserved.

A Note on the Letters

IN PREPARING THIS BOOK, I exercised my editorial judgment when deciding which of Bill Husselman's and Mary Brandon's letters to include in their entirety, to excerpt, or to omit. With Ellen England's guidance, I tried to allow the voice of Bill and of Mary to come through clearly, while also avoiding much of the redundancy that inevitably appeared in four years' worth of correspondence. To aid storytelling, I also tried to contextualize the letters so readers might better understand what was happening militarily, politically, and culturally throughout the war.

Bill's letters generally were grammatically correct and did not require much editing. Mary's style was more freeform, with arbitrary capitalizations and punctuation, and sometimes with ungrammatical turns of phrase, no doubt caused by interruptions as she tried to write. With Ellen's permission, I made only minor changes, sometimes inserting commas to aid the reader, and correcting – only very rarely – a simple misspelling. In all other cases, I inserted the Latin adverb *sic* in brackets when odd or erroneous spellings appeared.

Also for the reader's benefit, I sometimes made paragraph breaks when a paragraph ran long. I also made use of ellipses to help – as noted earlier – the story's pacing and to not bog down the reader with too many hometown references or repetitious topics (as in Mary's requests for clothing items or Bill's queries about DeKalb County legal proceedings). In most, but not all, cases, I included the terms of endearment that appeared at the close of each letter – the "Love, Bill," the "All my Love, Mary," and the various iterations.
   – Barbara Olenyik Morrow

Indiana

Chapter One

BILL AND MARY

*D*EAR FOLKS:
I'M PRACTICALLY IN *the Army. I passed all the physical examinations OK and have only the intelligence test to take. I imagine it would be pretty hard to flunk that one....*

WITH HIS TRADEMARK DIRECTNESS, William "Bill" Husselman wrote those words on April 1, 1942. He posted his letter from Fort Benjamin Harrison in Indianapolis, where he had arrived two days earlier to finalize his enlistment in the military. Sixteen million Americans would eventually serve in the armed forces during World War II, and he was about to become one of them.

Thirty-one years old and single, Bill was leaving behind a comfortable life as he swore an oath to the Constitution and slipped into uniform that spring. He was uprooting himself from a modestly furnished farmhouse east of Auburn, Indiana, where he lived with his parents and his maternal grandmother. Likewise, he was stepping away from a law practice that bore the family name and that he and his father successfully operated. The Auburn firm was a stone's throw from the DeKalb County Courthouse, in the state's rural northeast corner, not far from the Ohio and Michigan state lines.

Intelligent and well-read, Bill had entertained thoughts well before April 1942 that military service might be in his future. The fall of France to Nazi Germany in June 1940, followed by Chancellor Adolf Hitler's orders to aerial bomb Great Britain and to invade the Soviet Union, had led many Americans – their isolationist feelings notwithstanding – to recognize that the United States might be drawn into Europe's conflict. On December 7, 1941, with the Japanese attack on Pearl Harbor, all doubts were erased. Congress declared war on Japan, followed by Germany and its Axis partner Italy declaring war on the U.S., and Bill weighing his options. Rather than wait to be drafted, he volunteered for military duty. On March 30, he headed to "Ft. Ben."

Bill arrived at a time when newspaper headlines were grim, and more disturbing news was in the making. German U-boats were sinking tankers along America's Atlantic seaboard, French Jews were being deported by trainloads to a camp in Nazi-occupied Poland, and Japanese soldiers were about to herd defeated U.S and Filipino troops on a sixty-mile journey that became known as the Bataan Death March. If Bill was rattled by the headlines or had second thoughts about enlisting, he did not inform his parents. In lawyerly fashion, he stuck to reporting the basics in that first letter home: "About the worst discomfort I've suffered to date is in shaving. We have poor aluminum mirrors and most of us are already entitled to wound stripes." Three days later, more basics, with Bill telling his parents: "I have my clothes [uniform], shots, etc. My arm got pretty sore from the shots." He closed with candor: "I am impatient to be sent on. . . . There is a lot of plain waiting for something to happen."

Back in Auburn, a petite thirty-one-year-old teacher named Mary Brandon was, if not impatient, at least restless that spring. As music supervisor in Auburn's four public schools, she filled her days teaching children how to sing, directing the high school operettas, and organizing festivals that showcased hundreds of student-musicians in a gym packed with admiring townsfolk. When not at school, she volunteered by rolling bandages for the American Red Cross, one of countless ways citizens on the home front supported the war effort.

Yet despite her busy schedule, Mary, unmarried and living with her parents, wrestled with an urge to contribute more. Her restlessness intensified as more men from Auburn and neighboring towns donned uniforms and as women nationwide signed up for noncombat duty in the Women's Army Auxiliary Corps (WAAC, later WAC) and the Women Accepted for Volunteer Emergency Service (WAVES). In the spring of 1943, a year after Bill Husselman's enlistment and as he continued his stateside training, Mary's restlessness led her to apply for a job with the Red Cross, with a goal to serve overseas. The multistep selection process was rigorous. But Mary – mature, outgoing, and college-educated – was just the sort of young woman the Red Cross wanted to boost troop morale in theaters of war. After passing all the tests and securing the position, she traveled in late July to Washington, D. C. There, on the wooded campus of American University, she began two weeks of intense instruction in everything from Red Cross procedures to military organization and courtesy. On August 6, after only a week in the nation's capital, Mary didn't mince words when writing her parents: "They say if we think we are busy now we don't know the half of what it will be overseas."

What she and others *did* know is that the war already was exacting a terrible price. In the thirteen months between the Pearl Harbor attack and January 1943, some 60,000 American servicemen, Auburn "boys" among them, had died. By the time Mary reached Washington that summer, the casualty list had lengthened and more families had reasons to mourn. Gone were husbands, fathers, brothers, sweethearts. Lost were soldiers, seamen, airmen, Marines.

Yet for all the grieving and all the bracing for bad news, no family – not Bill's, not Mary's, not anyone's – wanted to fixate on harm that might come to a loved one answering the call to duty. Neither did men and women in uniform want to entertain dark thoughts about their fate. By mid-1943, "Oh, What a Beautiful Mornin'," from the acclaimed new Broadway musical *Oklahoma!*, was emerging as one of the most popular tunes of the wartime era. The song's uplifting lyrics – "I've got a beautiful feelin' everything's going my way" – spoke to people's nostalgia for simpler times and to hopes that all would turn out right, that good would triumph over evil.

Whatever lyrics looped in Bill's and Mary's head, whatever tunes the two hummed, by late autumn 1943 each had moved closer to an overseas departure date. When the appointed day finally arrived, each boarded crowded troopships and sailed into submarine-infested waters. Each headed for distant shores where blood had been shed and bloodier battles would be fought.

The two had no timetable for returning home. They likewise had no assurance that they would return with body and mind intact or, more ominously, ever come back. But still they went. And if from time to time they rooted for beautiful mornings, if they leaned into comforting thoughts that everything would go their way, why not? And who – *who?* – was inclined to blame them?

Asked by President Franklin D. Roosevelt in 1940 to become the "great arsenal of democracy," U.S. industries and businesses responded quickly, especially after Pearl Harbor, to produce necessities of war. Rieke Metal Products, a major Auburn employer, did its part to help the war effort and hasten the day when Bill and Mary - and millions of others in uniform - could return home. (William H. Willennar Genealogy Center, Eckhart Public Library)

Chapter Two
BILL: 1911 - 1942

*W*EDNESDAY NIGHT
APRIL 1, 1942

Dear Folks:

... We arrived at Ft. Benj. Harrison about 6 o'clock. We were fed at the mess hall & then given cots in the barracks. Nothing more happened that night, except they turned the lights out at 9:00 so there was nothing to do but go to bed. They got us up at about 5:20 and taught us to make beds, army style. Then we had to sweep out and mop the barracks.

Incidentally, the barracks here are two story frame buildings and there are about 30 men quartered on each floor. It is just a big room with a bathroom off of one end and a couple of orderly rooms off the other. There is no furniture except cots. ...

They make quite a lot of work just to keep us occupied. Today we mopped about 3 times and washed the windows inside and out. Just to keep us from being idle too much. ...

IN HIS NEW ROLE as citizen-turned-soldier, Bill Husselman found life turned upside-down in the spring of 1942. For him, no more rising in the morning to a satisfying breakfast prepared by his doting mother. No more heading with his father to their second-floor law office in the Auburn State Bank building. No more serving as president of the local Lions Club or golfing at the country club or performing in hometown plays. The Army needed him to learn the art of warfare. With war escalating, he needed to learn fast.

Born in Auburn in 1911, Bill grew up in a family with a limited – though not inconsequential – martial tradition. One of his paternal ancestors had been a German Hessian mercenary hired by Britain's King George III to fight American colonists during the Revolutionary War. According to family lore, the ancestor reportedly defected, joined the 8th Virginia Regiment of the Continental Army, and after the war remained in the new country, changing his name from "Yorrick Healshliman" to one he considered less German-sounding – George Husselman. Four generations later, Bill's father, Oak Husselman, registered for military service in 1917 upon the United States' entry into World War I (also known as the Great War). But that conflict's conclusion a year later, on November 11, 1918, spared Oak from ever putting on a uniform, a welcome development given his responsibilities as breadwinner, husband, and father.

Bill greatly admired his father, especially his intellect. Oak was a voracious reader who, as Bill recalled, "would get interested in a particular field and stick with it for months. At one time it might be philosophy, or history, or archeology or art." Though Oak would make lawyering his career, his path into the profession was anything but direct. Born in 1888 in Wichita, Kansas, he moved at age twelve to Auburn and soon became best friends with Bill Hebel, the son of a well-to-do local grocer. The Hebel family liked Oak and, recognizing his unfortunate circumstances (both his mother and his stepmother died in his youth), invited him regularly into their home. The Hebels' mentoring likely influenced Oak to enroll, with their son, at Indiana University in Bloomington in the fall of 1907.

Sigma Chi, Class of 1908. Oak is in the back row, far left.

Oak enjoyed his freshman year, especially his membership in Sigma Chi fraternity. But when a tight-fisted uncle reneged on financing his education, as the promised repayment for summers that Oak had labored on the uncle's farm, he quit college and returned to Auburn. Knowing he had to earn a living, Oak worked first in a factory, then studied to become a machinist, then bought and successfully operated a newsstand. In 1912, Bill Hebel's father, John, having been elected to serve as DeKalb County Clerk, asked Oak to be his deputy. Oak viewed the clerk's office as a place where he could learn to become a lawyer, a well-founded assumption in an era before formal law schooling was required. In 1915, after taking correspondence courses to augment his on-the-job training, Oak was admitted to the Indiana Bar. Soon afterwards, he opened a law office in Auburn, where he continued to practice until his death at age sixty-five in 1953.

Oak was not, in son Bill's estimation, "cut out to be a trial lawyer as he lacked the thespian or histrionic qualities that requires. He was incapable of being bombastic." Oak was talented, however, at working out compromises between litigants, aided by his sound legal reasoning and, as Bill put it, natural ability to "smooth out ruffled feathers." Early in his career, Oak bought a set of abstract books and records and incorporated DeKalb Abstract & Title Company, a business that served him well in his practice of real estate law. "He was probably regarded by the bar as a whole to be the best real estate lawyer in the county," Bill wrote years after Oak's death. That assessment aside, Oak received a top-tier rating for legal ability and integrity from Martindale-Hubbell, the national legal directory that rates lawyers based on the opinions of their colleagues.

Bill's admiration for his father matched his fondness for his mother, Blanche, who proved herself in many ways to be Oak's equal. She also was a reader, her tastes tending toward fiction, and Bill recalled that his mother spoke and wrote "practically perfect English." Oak liked to tease Blanche by deliberately using wrong verb forms, something that – according to Bill – "always got a rise out of her." Born on a DeKalb County farm in 1889, Blanche Cattell grew up and attended school in Garrett, a railroad town five miles west of Auburn where her father owned a pool hall and later a livery stable. Her middle name was "Adell," prompting her friends – aware of her quick temper and feistiness – to refer to her as "Blanche Adell t'Hell Cattell." Though she stood only five feet and one-half inch tall, she played forward on the Garrett High School girls basketball team, when the game itself was new and growing in popularity.

Blanche, fourth from left, with her teammates, 1906.

How Blanche met Oak, who was older by a year, is not clear. Nor is much known about their courtship. But the two married – Blanche at age twenty, Oak at twenty-one – on Nov. 13, 1909. When Oak accepted the job of deputy county clerk in 1912, he soon found himself in charge of the office, due to Clerk John Hebel's frequent absences because of poor health. Committed to helping her husband advance in his career, Blanche served as Oak's deputy for two years.

THE COUPLE HAD ONLY one child, the reason being – according again to family lore – that Blanche had a hard labor and that Oak vowed never to put his wife through such an ordeal again. Their brown-eyed infant, William Henry Husselman, was born at home at 7:35 a.m. on March 10, 1911. His name was likely a nod to Oak's friend, Bill Hebel, and to other Henrys in the Husselman lineage. A few days after his birth, Bill went into convulsions, prompting his worried parents to consult two doctors, one of whom administered castor oil. A time-honored remedy for constipation, the castor oil, in Bill's later telling, "fixed me up," no doubt to his and his family's relief.

Bill's arrival came as Auburn itself was coming of age. The community had evolved from an 1830s-pioneer settlement into a village, then a town, then an incorporated city in 1900. Though Auburn's 3,400 residents enjoyed a degree of prosperity as the twentieth century dawned, the city still had no paved streets, the electric system was primitive, and outhouses handled sewage. Water came courtesy of private wells with hand pumps.

It was that newfangled contraption – the automobile – that spurred Auburn's economic growth in the decade before Bill's birth. Hoosier entrepreneurs, along with those in Michigan and Ohio, were fast making the Midwest the heart of the new automobile industry, and by the early 1900s four Auburn companies had jumped into the car-making business. One firm, the Auburn Automobile Company, quickly flourished.

"The big increase in the volume of business in the Auburn Automobile Co. . . . is demanding the enlargement of their quarters," reported the weekly newspaper, the *Auburn Courier*, on April 21, 1910. "The company finds itself overwhelmed with orders, last week's shipments exceeding those of any other week since the inception of the institution."

1910 Auburn (Willennar Genealogy Center)

Within a relatively short time, at least twenty-four different makes of autos would be produced in Auburn, earning the community the nickname "Little Detroit." The success of the city's fledgling car companies helped lure other industries to the area, which in turn energized the citizenry and fueled even more expansion. As the *Auburn Courier* declared on May 12, 1910, "The building boom is still on in Auburn, all the contractors having all and more construction work that they can do."

The era's leading citizen was Charles Eckhart, a Pennsylvania native and Civil War veteran who settled in the area in the 1870s, built a successful carriage-making business, and supported his entrepreneurial sons, Frank and Morris, in founding the Auburn Automobile Company. Eckhart's business acumen made him wealthy. His civic-mindedness matched his wealth. When the industrialist Andrew Carnegie offered in 1909 to donate $12,500 for a library in Auburn, as part of his philanthropic effort to build free public libraries throughout the English-speaking world, Eckhart tendered the city a better offer. He bankrolled the project himself, and in January 1911 presented the community with a handsome two-story brick library located a few blocks from the courthouse square.

Charles Eckhart, c. 1911 (Willennar)

Eckhart Public Library (Willennar Genealogy Center)

In rapid succession, Eckhart also donated money for a fountain on the library grounds, a YMCA building, and a community park bearing his name. Not to be outdone, citizens rallied elected officials to showcase progress in another way: In July 1911, just four months after Bill's birth, construction began on the ornate glass-domed DeKalb County Courthouse, still in use more than a century later and still admired by visitors today.

Newly constructed courthouse (Willennar Genealogy Center)

Bill grew up within walking distance of the courthouse and library. His birthplace was a small home on Phillip Street, southwest of the town square. Before long, his family moved to a duplex just off North Main Street, where car company executives and other moneyed residents owned fashionable homes. At the time, as Bill recalled years later, Main was "the only street in town that was paved for any considerable distance and was used by the Auburn Automobile Company as a road testing ground for their cars."

Bill's first set of wheels

Young Bill viewed test-driving as a "very glamorous profession," especially since he and his family typically traversed the town on their feet, not in a motorized vehicle. When his mother, who was competent at handling rigs from having grown up in the livery business, wanted to visit her kinfolk on area farms, she would borrow a horse-and-buggy and have Bill accompany her. With her child in tow, Blanche – still strong-willed and spirited – presumably traveled at a reasonable speed, unlike in her youth when she gamely raced boys on the Auburn-Garrett Road.

In 1916, as the nation edged toward entering World War I, the Husselman family moved again. Bill, who was five years old at the time, viewed his new residence as "a real palace" compared to the family's earlier dwellings. Located at 327 West Eleventh Street, the house featured a first-floor living room, formal dining room, music room, and kitchen, with three bedrooms and a bathroom upstairs. It was adjacent to Harrison School, an aging two-story brick building with a belfry where Bill attended grades one through five.

Bill in front of the family's new home on West Eleventh Street.

The school grounds served as Bill's extended backyard, and he regularly joined neighborhood youth there to play baseball, a game he enthusiastically embraced. Oak, a baseball lover who had played the sport in high school, kept his son well-supplied with balls and bats, worked with him on hitting and fielding, and took him to major-league games in Chicago, where the two rooted for the White Sox. In spite of Oak's coaching and encouragement, Bill, by his own admission, "lacked coordination" and displayed no innate athletic ability. Moreover, he had little appetite for rough-and-tumble competition. "When I was six I had my first fight – really a wrestling match with a kid a few months younger – he being only five," Bill recalled years later. "He was a stout little fellow and promptly put me down and sat on me. This not only embarrassed me but gave me a life-long conviction that fighting was not my cup of tea."

Physical competitions aside, Bill was smart and twice was promoted ahead of his classmates, making him thirteen years old when he entered Auburn High School in the fall of 1924. With his interests veering toward the arts and all matters cerebral, he played violin in the school orchestra, served on the newspaper and yearbook staffs, performed in plays, and participated actively in the History Club, where he was remembered for his forceful arguments. In his sophomore year, he was class president; the next two years, class treasurer.

Bill with his sweetheart Opal

Though he courted a girl named Opal Knott, he never socialized with classmates in ways his parents had envisioned. Indeed, soon after moving into the Eleventh Street house, Oak and Blanche arranged for hardwood floors to be installed on the first level so that, when Bill was older, he could invite friends over for dancing. Alas, as Bill later noted, "I'm afraid I never cooperated."

IN THE FALL OF 1928, Bill followed in Oak's footsteps and attended Indiana University. Like his father, he also pledged Sigma Chi fraternity. How actively Bill participated in the Greek social scene isn't known, but he did represent his fraternity in an intramural debating contest. He also served one year as a manager for IU's basketball team. Though no war was in the offing and though Bill had no desire for a military career, he did what IU required of all able-bodied males: He completed two years of coursework in the Reserve Officers Training Corps (ROTC), a nationwide program designed to prepare college men to become military officers. Upon fulfilling that requirement, Bill concentrated on his undergraduate studies and gained admittance to IU's law school. By the time he earned his law degree in June 1933, he had amassed several honors, including serving as president of his law class and being elected to the Order of the Coif, the highest scholastic honor a law student could receive.

Despite millions of Americans being out of work in 1933 – the prosperity and partying of the "Roaring Twenties" had given way to the Great Depression – Bill found employment as legal counsel for a mortgage company in Fort Wayne, Indiana. He commuted back and forth to Auburn, living with his parents who by then had moved to a farm several miles east of town on the Auburn-Butler road. After a year, Bill left the mortgage company to form Husselman & Husselman, a DeKalb County-based partnership with his father. The business officially took effect on January 1, 1935.

Bill as a young attorney

The following year, Bill ran for DeKalb County Prosecutor on the Democratic ticket, pledging in a campaign ad to "cooperate in the enforcement and administration of the great recovery programs" begun under President Franklin D. Roosevelt's "New Deal." He unseated the incumbent Republican prosecutor by 313 votes and spent the next two years overseeing criminal cases ranging from the commonplace (transients charged with drunkenness) to at least one headline-grabber involving an itinerant handyman accused of murdering an elderly woman. In 1938, as Roosevelt's popularity ebbed, Democratic candidates nationwide suffered losses in the midterm elections. DeKalb County Democrats were no exception. Bill was booted out.

Returning to private practice full-time, Bill remained active in civic life. Along with his membership and eventual leadership in organizations ranging from the DeKalb County Bar Association to the Indiana University Alumni Association, he supported local theater and appeared in amateur productions large and small. One of his more memorable performances came in the mid-1930s when, in the stylish Court Theatre on Auburn's town square, he played the lead in *Big Hearted Herbert*, a Broadway comedy about a domineering Indiana businessman and his fictional family.

Joining Bill in that cast was Mary Brandon, a high school classmate who – like him – had returned to Auburn after college. Throughout the 1930s the two moved in the same social circles, largely because the musically talented Mary organized many of Auburn's arts programs. Pretty and vivacious, Mary caught the eye of many Auburn men, Bill among them. But the bespectacled attorney sensed that Mary had no interest in him beyond friendship, and thus the two never dated. For his part, Bill – shy, serious-minded, and seemingly content to live at home – displayed no urgency to find a wife. As he inched toward age thirty, bachelorhood seemed to suit him.

What did not suit him was news from across the Atlantic. Hitler's 1938 land grab in Czechoslovakia and his army's 1939 invasion of Poland, followed by Nazi Germany's occupation of countries across northwest Europe, compelled Bill to monitor overseas developments closely. Like most Americans, he also tracked the U.S. government's shift in policy from neutrality to preparedness. When Congress passed legislation in September 1940 requiring men between the ages of twenty-one and thirty-five to register for a military draft, Bill complied – one of nearly 2,600 DeKalb County men to register that autumn. Within months, he began chairing Auburn's USO (United Service Organization) drive, part of a new nationwide effort to raise money for "morale and recreation services" for an American military not yet combat-ready. Soon he also was chairing the local Red Cross drive to raise funds for Europe's victims of Nazi aggression, their plight growing ever more dire.

Bill at the family farmhouse, Christmas Day 1939

When the December 7, 1941 attack on Pearl Harbor made any neutrality talk moot, Bill immediately wrote U.S. Senator Frederick Van Nuys of Indiana, asking about the possibility of joining the Judge Advocate General's Department, the legal arm of the U.S. Army. When Bill had registered for military service in 1940, he had been classified as 1-B due to "internal hemorrhoids," a rating that did not make him completely ineligible but did place him in the "limited service" pool. In his December 11 letter to Van Nuys, Bill expressed his desire to serve the country and noted that his "physical disqualification is not of such nature as to interfere with performance of any duties of that [legal] branch." Van Nuys' office immediately forwarded the letter to proper authorities. Within a week, the senator received the Army's blunt response: "Since Mr. Husselman states that he has been classified as 1-B . . . it is impracticable to authorize his enlistment or induction in the Army at this time."

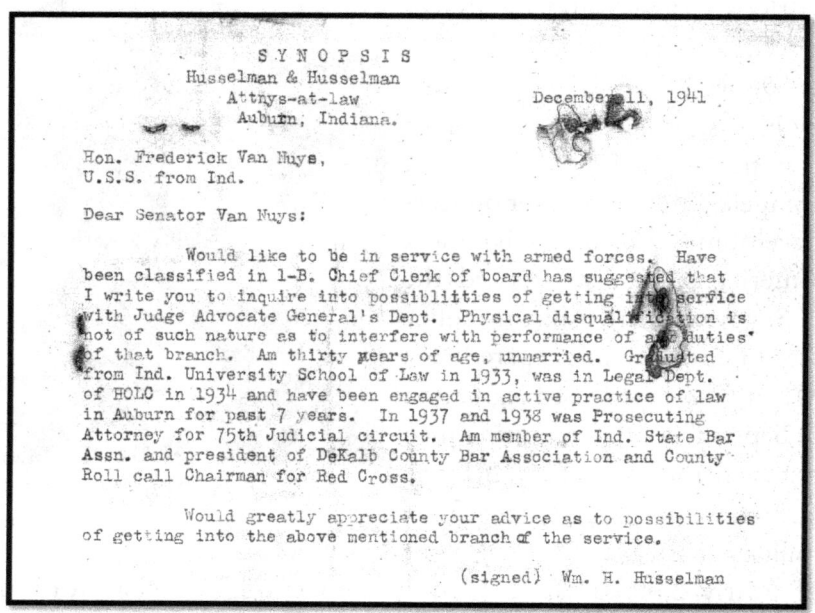

A synopsis of Bill's December 11, 1941 letter to U.S. Senator Van Nuys. The stains are due to a fire at the government facility where Bill's military personnel file was stored. (National Personnel Records Center, National Archives, St. Louis)

Disappointed but undeterred, Bill arranged at his own expense to have the hemorrhoids surgically removed in January 1942. By mid-March, he had satisfied DeKalb County's selective service board that he was fit for enlistment, and that board forthwith instructed the Fort Wayne recruiting office to receive him. His "troubles," as Bill would refer to his hemorrhoids, were no more.

And soon there was no more time to waste. By month's end he was packing a small bag, saying goodbye to family and friends, and reporting to the Fort Benjamin Harrison Reception Center in Indianapolis for induction into the United States Army. He wasn't one to fool himself. He understood that his life was about to change, though to what extent and in what direction he could not foresee. Nonetheless, he had chosen to become part of America's fighting force, and from the outset he appeared determined to put on as brave a face as possible. "The enlisted men are in good spirits and their morale is high," he informed his parents in his first letter posted from "Ft. Ben."

Surely not lost on Blanche and Oak was the poignancy of his next sentence: "They say that in the barracks where draftees are quartered some of the boys cry themselves to sleep."

Chapter Three
BILL: 1942

*W*EDNESDAY NIGHT
APRIL 8, 1942

Dear Folks:
I have been assigned to – of all places – the Air Corps. About 300 of us were shipped out of Ft. Harrison yesterday by train and brought to Jefferson Barracks, about 14 miles from St. Louis. This is just an assignment center for the air corps and we will only be held here for from three to six weeks – thank God! . . . We (five of us) are living in a tent with an open door. A bitter cold rain has been falling all day. A small coke stove is in the tent but it won't work, so we've really been in a bad way all day. I'm writing this with the winter overcoat on. Strangely enough, none of us have caught colds. . . .

IF BILL HUSSELMAN knew little about Jefferson Barracks before arriving there in April 1942, he likely soon got a cram course in the post's storied history. Established in 1826 on the west bank of the Mississippi River, Jefferson Barracks was at one point the largest military post in the United States, and it remained a major Army installation well into the twentieth century, with soldiers in the Mexican-American War, Civil War, Spanish-American War, and World War I having passed through its gates. Passing through, too, were a host of military leaders who later rose to national prominence, among them Zachary Taylor, Robert E. Lee, and Ulysses S. Grant. Even Dwight D. Eisenhower, who in 1942 was about to take command of U.S. Army operations in Europe, had a connection to the base. He reported there in 1911 before starting his West Point cadetship.

After nearly a century of hard use, Jefferson Barracks might reasonably have been targeted for closure when World War I ended in 1918. But the Army, increasingly aware of aviation's importance in modern warfare, began envisioning the military post as a basic training center for its aviation arm, the Air Corps. By February 1941 that vision had materialized and in the spring of 1942, in the wake of Pearl Harbor, raw "air" recruits were pouring into the post, a raw Private Husselman among them.

Former Jefferson Barracks post exchange (PX)

Bill's assignment surprised him. While still at Fort Benjamin Harrison, he had assumed that of the Army's three branches – ground, air, and services of supply – he would be in ground forces, and he had told his parents as much: "I'll probably end up in an infantry company." He based his prediction on his poor eyesight, writing in a follow-up letter, "I am not qualified for any sort of flying, of course." But while the Air Corps needed flying personnel (pilots, bombardiers, navigators and gunners), it also needed men who could be trained quickly and successfully as mechanics, radio operators, weather forecasters, and other aviation-related technicians. In January 1942, shortly before Bill's enlistment, the War Department had been informed that nearly half of the draftees assigned to the corps in 1941 had lacked the intelligence necessary for specialized technical training, threatening to jeopardize the corps' overall mission. Bill's scores, on tests taken at "Ft. Ben," showed he possessed the requisite smarts. Thus, into the Air Corps and to Jefferson Barracks he went.

Jefferson Barracks Military Post, 1826-1946. Today the buildings are part of a National Historic District. (Photos by author)

He arrived at the post as the U.S. Army, in its entirety, was feverishly engaged in catch-up. World War I had left Americans with little appetite to intervene further in Europe's problems, and throughout the 1920s and 1930s Congress responded to the nation's isolationist sentiment by starving the military (Army and Navy) of funds. When Germany attacked Poland on September 1, 1939, signaling the start of World War II, the Army was in such an emaciated condition that it would have been hard-pressed to defend even the continental United States, much less engage in a global conflict. In stark contrast to Germany's modern war machine, the U.S. Army ranked seventeenth in size and combat-effectiveness, behind nations such as Portugal and Romania. A rightfully alarmed Congress sought in 1940 to expand the military's skeletal ranks by instituting the draft, a mobilization that paid dividends, though slowly at first, given that more than forty of every one hundred men were rejected by the Army for physical or psychiatric reasons. That rejection rate, as the acclaimed military history writer Rick Atkinson noted in his book *An Army at Dawn*, was "a grim testament to the toll taken on the nation's health by the Great Depression."

Compounding the Army's prewar problems were too few professional officers capable of leading new recruits. Moreover, the Army was saddled with broken-down equipment and weaponry, much of it of World War I vintage. To reinvigorate the entire organization, President Roosevelt had tapped a distinguished World War I veteran, George C. Marshall, to be Army Chief of Staff in 1939 – on the same infamous September day that World War II began. Under Marshall's direction, the Army would grow from a moribund force of fewer than 200,000 active-duty soldiers into a well-trained and well-equipped host of eight million, one of the largest armies in history. But in early 1942, the Army was still getting its footing, and the learning curve, for all involved, was steep.

Bill (serial number 15101477) spent his first days at Jefferson Barracks standing in line for more shots (typhoid, tetanus, and yellow fever) and undergoing more tests and interviews to determine eligibility for various technical schools. His "basic training" began on April 15, exactly one week after his arrival, and as he informed his mother, he prided himself on his opening performance:

We started drill today and are all pretty tired. Sampson, one of the boys, got sick & had to drop out. He is only 25 yrs. old and has been a dirt track race driver for five years, so it seems funny that a 31 year old lawyer could out-last him. I got along pretty well.

Bill continued to do well, largely because the training, in his opinion, was mostly superficial. Writing again four days later, he told his father:

... It seems to me that we are going about the business of fighting this war at a leisurely pace. For instance, here at J.B. you are more or less on duty from 5:15 [A.M.] to 6:00 P.M. (at least) in a normal day when you are not on detail. Yet out of this 12 hours and 45 minutes, you only spend about 5 hours in actual drilling or receiving instruction. They seem to regard the condition of the barracks and the order in which your clothes hang as more important than drill. This is, of course, of some value in instilling discipline, but doesn't seem to me to be of major importance. The actual fighting seems to be proceeding at about the same pace, although they say Wall Street is betting it will end in 1943 (I personally doubt it).

In a letter to his parents a week later, on April 26, Bill expressed more frustration:

... This is a screwy camp. No one seems to think much about the war, or fighting. I believe I've lost condition instead of gaining. Their calisthenics are not nearly so hard as the ones I was doing at home. They drill you six or seven hours a day, but the great bulk of this time is spent in just fooling around and killing time.

The Air Corps would eventually confirm Bill's assessment that its training program was inadequate and would begin addressing the deficiencies in 1943. But in the spring of 1942, amid Japan's attacks and Germany's naked violence, the corps was under intense pressure to compress training and to ship recruits to technical schools as quickly as possible. The result, as Bill discovered, was that he and thousands of Jefferson Barracks men received only bare-bones instruction in certain drills and no practice in the use of weapons. As for his bungled execution of one critical drill, Bill self-deprecatingly explained:

> ... *Yesterday [April 25] we had a gasmask drill. We put on masks and went into a tent where there was a concentration of tear gas. This was fine until they made us take the masks off to prove there was really gas there. We all cried. When they call 'gas!' you are supposed to hold your breath until you get the thing on. If we had really been under attack yesterday I would have been a dead duck, because in my haste, & with my usual grace, I tried to put it on upside down.*

Soon after that "graceless" performance, Bill landed in the base hospital where he remained for ten days recovering from bronchitis. During his first week at Jefferson Barracks, when he had lived in a tent due to camp overcrowding, he had reported feeling "swell." But soon after his transfer into a barracks, which he described as a "consumptive ward with everyone coughing & spitting & sniffling on a 24 hour schedule," he began feeling lousy and sought medical treatment. Admitted to the hospital on April 28, he wrote his parents several times from his infirmary bed, assuring them he was "getting along satisfactorily" and grateful that, unlike healthier patients, he was not required to sweep and mop floors every morning. Bill also reported that his illness had not adversely affected his hemorrhoidectomy, a topic he returned to from time to time in his letters home. Earlier in the month, Bill had asked his father to "tell Mother that I am feeling O.K. & that my 'troubles' are not bothering.... Army life would have been just about impossible without the operation."

Discharged from the infirmary on May 8, Bill completed what remained of his eighteen days of basic training. On May 12, his group – part of the 27th School Squadron – passed inspection, and a day later Bill learned he was to attend Radio School at Scott Field, about thirty miles from Jefferson Barracks on the Illinois side of the Mississippi River. Weeks earlier he had reviewed the Air Corps' list of technical schools for ground personnel and had decided to take the radio aptitude test. "Darned if I didn't qualify," he had written home upon getting the results. "Imagine a lawyer as a radio operator and mechanic!"

Pleased as he was to be finished with his first phase of military life, Bill nonetheless had mixed feelings about his impending shipment. He had no objection to Scott Field's location (the base was closer to

Auburn, presenting the possibility of weekend visits home) and the post had a good reputation – "one of the best," as he would tell his parents. But Bill still harbored hopes of serving in the Judge Advocate General's (JAG) Department, and he was surprised when the Jefferson Barracks post commander informed him on "inspection" day that a JAG school for clerks was being established at the Missouri base. Asked if he would be interested in attending it, Bill said yes, and the commander promised to forward his name to those in charge.

While heartened by that unexpected development, Bill understood fully that lowly privates were in no position to demand that higher-ups act quickly. He also considered it too dicey to seek his name's removal from the Scott Field shipping list, knowing a JAG assignment was not guaranteed. Thus, when shipping orders came through a few days later, Bill packed his belongings and headed for Illinois, ready – albeit reluctantly – to receive radio instruction.

BUILT ACROSS A STRETCH of southern Illinois farm and coal country, Scott Field opened as a training center for World War I pilots when the U.S. War Department had only a handful of airplanes and when aviation's importance to the military was only starting to become known. After the Great War, the government purchased the leased site and repurposed Scott Field as an experimental station for balloonists and for scientists studying the upper atmosphere. By the late 1930s, the War Department, attracted to Scott because of its central U.S. location, began eyeing it as a new home for Army Air headquarters, then housed at Langley Field in Virginia.

But the mounting threat of World War II abruptly upended any relocation plans. The Army instead assigned Scott Field a communications mission, with air corpsmen sent there to learn how to operate and maintain radios at military stations on the ground and aboard aircraft. Initially, Scott's "Radio School" students were expected to master Morse Code and learn the theory of radio and the fundamentals of radio equipment in twenty-two weeks. By the time Bill arrived in mid-May 1942, military urgency dictated that the coursework be compressed to eighteen weeks, a punishing schedule that would not be relaxed until late in the war. If students cursed the rigorous curriculum, they were inspired by the school's motto: Scott prided itself on graduating "the best damned radio operators in the world!"

Scott Field Radio School postcard, 1943. (U.S. Army Air Forces via Wikimedia Commons)

Assigned to Scott's 30th Technical School Squadron, Barracks 772, Bill wasted no time familiarizing himself with the base, a city unto itself with cement roads, school buildings, libraries, three chapels, a 600-bed hospital, a fire department, and a huge mess hall that could accommodate six thousand men. Bill had hoped to start his schooling immediately but, much to his chagrin, he "got a miserable break" and had to spend his first two weeks doing work details, mostly in the kitchen. Not all his assignments were taxing, however, as his May 20 letter to his parents made clear: "This afternoon they had me working in the flower gardens. Tell Grandma she'd be right useful in the Army."

At the end of May, a weekend visit from Oak and Blanche boosted Bill's spirits, especially since it allowed the three of them to enjoy an outing in St. Louis, less than twenty miles away. On Monday, June 1, the visit over, Bill dashed off a note thanking his parents for making the trip by car from Auburn and reminding them that "when you relieve the boredom of a soldier, you are contributing to the National Defense!"

Bill enjoys a weekend in St. Louis with his parents, May 1942.

That same day he officially began Radio School. At week's end, on June 7, he wrote again:

Dear Folks:

Well, I'm a school boy again. I rather enjoy it, but it is tough. They are giving us a pretty stiff course in the physics of Direct Current electricity in 10 days and they have to stuff you pretty fast.

We spend about 6 hours a day in school, not counting the time off for breaks, half of which is spent trying to receive code, and half in theory classes.

It would be fun if they could forget this is Army and not have so many class room rules and regulations.

There have been several B-17s (Flying Fortresses) stopping over here. The radio operator on one spoke before the basic code class. He has been in the Army only 4 months, and in radio only 3. He had no previous experience and did not go to radio school but just studied it himself under radio men at his field. His pay and allowances while flying & not attached to a base amount to over $200.00 a month and he is just a private. He likes it fine, naturally.

I got up at seven this morning to study and have been working hard at it all day (it's now 2 P.M). However, I have my pass in my pocket and think I'll run into town (Belleville) to eat tonight. Just because I can.

It has been terribly hot and humid. Almost unbearable. During the early part of the week I felt rotten, with a cold & some sort of bowel trouble. However, it's all straightened out now and I feel fine. Going to school isn't much of a physical strain. Tuesday I think I'll get KP [Kitchen Police] again, though. Darn it!

One of the boys who came to Scott Field with me didn't get to start to school. His place was taken by one of several Dutch East Indians who came here to go to school. He protested about it and got a seven day pass. [Throughout the war, men from numerous Allied nations, including The Netherlands, trained at Scott Field.]

Our barracks has been on the night shift, ie. we start to school at 2:30 PM and go to 10:20. Tomorrow we shift to the day shift for a month. Start early in the morning & go to 2 something in the afternoon.

I'll like that better, even tho we have to get up at 4:45.

Well, I want to get started so I guess this will be all. I got the package O.K....

Love, Bill

Morse Code training class (Scott Field Yearbook, 1942)

Within days, Bill shared more about his "code" classwork and admitted to finding it difficult, despite working his way up to "eight words per minute." Elaborating on the difficulties, he told his parents: "You have to print the characters in a special way developed by the Army Signal Corps, and this slows you up. After you get to taking code faster than 20 words per minute, they let you use a typewriter. Figuring five characters to the word, eight W.P.M. [words per minute] is pretty fast. That means you have to hear the signal, translate it, and write the character in 1 ½ seconds. Commercial operators receive at speeds of 50 and even faster. You have to pass 16 to pass this course."

Soon he sent another update, though he wrote less about code – and more about potatoes.

Saturday, June 13, 1942

Dear Folks:

Well the first theory course has been completed. Direct Current. We took the final examination Thursday. We covered so much territory in the ten days that I was hopelessly confused. On top of that the exam was one of those speed affairs, 100 questions in 90 minutes, and as usual I didn't get it finished. I didn't figure I had done at all well, but I got a 90, fifth in a class of thirty, at least two of whom were communications men. Nobody failed, two having the minimum passing grade of 70. It is obvious that they try to pass anyone they possibly can & base the grades of the rest on a curve computed from the poorest grade. I'm afraid if my knowledge of DC is worth 90, some of the 70s and 71s don't know too much about it. Well, they need operators badly and have to turn them out some way. The school is good, but too fast.

I am still in 8 wpm in code, but think I'll get along all right. We are now in A.C. [alternating current] in theory. Each course is 10 days.

Well I got K.P. yesterday as anticipated. Marched into the mess hall at 4:15 AM and left at 5 of 9 P.M. Nearly 17 hours. Worked on the serving line during meals and eyed spuds the rest of the time. They peel them with a machine. They are put into a kettle like affair with an abrasive bottom (like sand-paper). They are agitated with [swirling] soapy water until the abrasive bottom has worn off the skins. Obviously if they were left until the eyes were gone there would be little left. So they are peeled by the machine and eyed by hand. The mess takes 7000 pounds a day. About 15 of us worked on this detail. I was less tired than I've ever been after K.P. in spite of the long hours. Got to sit on a stool most of the time, you see. I served fried potatoes at breakfast & few wanted them. At supper I wasn't so lucky. Served kraut. It was hard to serve and popular. This was a tough two hours.

The weather has been terrible. Rain most of the time. I've plans to go to the [St. Louis Cardinals] ball game tomorrow, weather allowing. Right now I'm trying to make up my mind about going to Belleville tonight. My pass is in my pocket & it burns, but the weather is lousy. Maybe I'll just go over to the main PX [post exchange] and have a steak dinner. They are pretty good.

Love, Bill

As he had done at Jefferson Barracks, where he had befriended Jo Ferguson, a Kentucky lawyer who later became that state's attorney general, Bill sought companions to pal around with in his spare time. By mid-June he had made the acquaintance of a furniture businessman from Houston, Texas, and he had high hopes for a budding friendship: "He and I have quite similar tastes and I shouldn't wonder if we would spend quite a lot of time together. He likes fancy meals too. We are talking about going into St. Louis Saturday night and taking in the performance of a light opera company playing there this Summer." Unfortunately, the businessman was soon assigned to a different school shift, limiting opportunities for the two to connect. Undeterred, Bill looked for others who might share his interests.

In the course of his search, he encountered soldiers whose talents and brainpower impressed him – or, as he phrased it for his parents, "You run into funny fellows in the Army." To underscore his point, he shared in a June 21 letter that – at the very moment he was writing – he could hear music coming from a nearby woodworking shop. "There is some fellow in it practicing on a violin. He's almost a Kreisler, too. Plays difficult stuff and makes the fiddle sing," effused Bill, whose own youthful attempts at violin playing had made him familiar with the genius of Friedrich "Fritz" Kreisler, one of the most acclaimed violinists of the twentieth century. In that same letter, Bill described "a little gray haired rather rough spoken fellow named Van Buskirk" who lived in his barracks:

I noticed he just ate up this electrical theory. (He happens to be in my class). Finally he got into a discussion of calculus computations with the instructor, so I got curious and asked him what his business had been. He is an electrical engineer, trained at New York University and was for nine years an experimental engineer in the Bell Telephone laboratories. Imagine trying to teach him the fundamentals of electrical physics! He has become quite a consultant in electrical theory around the barracks.

Not usually one to boast, Bill informed his parents several days later that he had recently taken an alternating current test and received a score of 92. "Funny thing," he reported, "I beat the engineer [Van Buskirk] I told you about by 1% and I think it kind of burns him up."

Meanwhile, with or without a buddy, Bill seldom passed on opportunities to leave the base, especially when nearby St. Louis offered what he most enjoyed and seldom got to experience: high-class musical entertainment and professional baseball. On a Tuesday in late June, he packed into one of seven Army trucks jammed with soldiers and, when the convoy reached St. Louis, he and two radio classmates headed to the "Muny," the city's heralded outdoor theater known for its summer season of light opera productions. There, he took in a performance of *Song of the Flame*, a 1920s-era musical by George

Gershwin and Herbert Stothart, and he left thoroughly satisfied. "The singing was great & the setting's gorgeous," he wrote his parents the next day, adding, "I've paid the piper tho. We didn't get back until 12:30 and had only 4 hours sleep."

Scene from 1942 Muny production of "Song of the Flame." An air-raid warning printed in the program instructed the audience to seek protection under the theater's reinforced concrete pergolas should a hostile plane fly over the city. (Photo by Ruth Cunliff Russell from The Muny Archive)

Several days later, Bill returned to St. Louis, this time for a full-blown "soldier weekend." The two-day outing included a Sunday baseball double-header at Sportsman's Park, where Bill watched the hometown Browns lose twice to the Washington Senators. What seemingly impressed him most, however, was the city's hospitality toward servicemen. In his June 29 letter, he specifically lauded USO [United Service Organization] centers, designed to be GIs' "home away from home." He also spoke approvingly of the sprawling army recreation camp west of downtown in Forest Park, site of the 1904 World's Fair and home to city landmarks such as the zoo, art museum, and "Muny" theater. The camp could accommodate up to 1,500 servicemen, though in keeping with the military's racial segregation policy, only white soldiers were admitted. African-American soldiers were required to stay at a "Negro" camp more than a mile away. That reality aside, Bill detailed the following:

Three of us went into St. Louis Saturday afternoon & didn't come back until [Sunday] night. We stayed out at Tent city, which is maintained in Forest Park., St. L., by the Army to house soldiers on [leave]. You just register like you would at a hotel. They issue you clean bedding and assign you to a tent. The tents have wooden frames and concrete floors, and, of course, are screened. It makes a nice place to stay on summer nights. We bought Military passes for 50 cents that permitted us to ride buses and street cars all we wanted all weekend. Sunday Morning we went to the U.S.O. Service Men's Center in the big auditoriums to clean up. They give you free towels, soap, shaving cream etc. The Center is quite a place. A lot of free pool & billiard tables, ping pong, eats, etc. It is very large – occupies the main portion of a whole floor in that huge building and parts of others.

If anyone tells you the U.S.O. isn't doing a fine job, tell them they're nuts. Some of their centers aren't so necessary, but one like that at St. Louis is really a fine thing.

NEVER FAR FROM BILL'S MIND, even as he attended Radio School, was the possibility of moving into another line of military work. He still hoped that he might attend a JAG school for clerks, though paperwork submitted in his final days at Jefferson Barracks had yet to yield results. With July's arrival, he focused on a different means of advancement – admittance into Officer Candidate School, which he was now eligible to apply for based on his three months of military service and on test scores at his time of induction. Choosing to be proactive, Bill had done some nosing around in June and had identified an OCS where, as he told his parents, "a legal education is a qualification" – namely, a school for military police officers. Getting more information proved challenging, however, with Bill lamenting in a June 21 letter that "I went over to the Orderly Room to try to find out something about the Officers Candidate School I mentioned, but I couldn't get past the corporal at the information desk." Three days later: "I haven't been able to get anywhere filing an application for Officer's training. Every time I go to the Orderly Room they tell me to come back tomorrow."

By July 9, however, just days after enjoying a weekend visit to Auburn, he reported on progress regarding his application and even indulged in a bit of playful overconfidence.

Things have been really developing since I last wrote. I finally managed to get an interview with a squadron officer, and have my papers all signed up for Officers Candidate School. I talked to two different lieutenants about it and each thought my qualifications were fine and that I didn't have much to worry about. I'll be called in in two or three weeks for an interview by the Board, and its decision will determine everything, subject to physical examination. I've at least got over the first hurdle – ie getting the recommendation of the Squadron. So I might <u>possibly</u> be sporting some gold bars within a few months. I took Military Police as first choice, Air Corps Administrative as second and quartermaster's corps as third....

One of the main things the OCS Board examines you in is knowledge of current events. So Bob Irons [another student] and I are going to cram on them with Newspapers, Time, and Newsweek, until we are a couple of walking Press services. If there is anyone in the world who wants to make it as badly as I, he is the man. He too is going in for Military Police as he once was an investigator for the Commercial Credit Company and later worked as a personnel investigator for a defense plant. He is a swell fellow and I wish we would both make the grade and be sent to the same school. I bought a Blitz cloth [polishing cloth] to clean my belt buckle today and showed it to Bob & told him it was to shine my shoulder bars!...

Well, it is about time for school Call, so this will be all for now.
Love, Bill

With war having erupted across the globe, Bill was correct to assume he had lots of news to digest. In early May, just before he arrived at Scott Field, American forces had surrendered their island garrison at Corregidor, at the entrance to Manila Bay, making the Japanese conquest of the Philippines complete. Days later, the Imperial Japanese Navy suffered a strategic setback when U.S. and Australian forces checked an assault in the Battle of the Coral Sea. A month later, the United States scored a decisive victory against Japan in a fierce air-sea battle near the now-famous atoll of Midway.

But the Pacific was hardly the only military hotspot. Half a world away, Hitler's armies had overrun the Crimean Peninsula and were pressing that summer toward Stalingrad in southern Russia. In North Africa, the daring German commander Erwin Rommel, known as the

Desert Fox, had just led Axis troops to victory over the British at the Libyan port of Tobruk and had turned his attention to Egypt, where he hoped to advance to the vital Suez Canal.

Determined to make a good showing before the OCS board, Bill spent all his free time the next two weeks poring over publications in the base library. His friend, Bob Irons, was interviewed on July 22 and, as expected, the board had peppered him with a range of current-events questions, from identifying commanders of aircraft carriers to naming the island in Alaska's Aleutian chain that the Japanese presently occupied. "Irons says it is pretty rugged," Bill wrote his parents upon getting his friend's summary. Bill's interview was scheduled for the next day, July 23, and as he soon recapped for his parents, it diverged sharply from expectations.

July 24, 1942
Dear Folks:

The interview came off yesterday and was quite a lot different than anticipated. Always before, as I've been informed, the Board gives everyone a pretty tough going over, especially on current events. I went in with four others. The Board consisted of a Lt. Col., Major, Captain and Lieutenant. When I went in I was mentally composed, but not physically, and as was often the case when starting an argument to a jury or something, my knees were shaking. It evidently showed through the G.I. pants because the Lt. Col. said "Husselman, you'd better relax before you fall down." All I could do was grin at him & shift my weight. This wasn't a very good start, as poise is one of the things they are supposed to look for.

After that various members of the board questioned the other fellows about their background, experience, etc., but no current events. They just ignored me until toward the end the Lieutenant asked me if I was feeling well when I took the I.Q. I told him no. All of this hadn't taken over ten minutes.

Then the Board went into a whispered conference, told me to remain and dismissed the rest. Then in private they questioned me closely as to my [hemorrhoid] operation, whether I was completely cured, etc. Of course, I insisted I was. Then the Captain said "You understand, of course, it will be up to the medical examiner to decide that." Then they dismissed me.

This whole business was so completely different than the experience of those going before the board at other times, that I have no idea where I stand. I might get called soon, six weeks from now, or more likely, never.

We have no school tomorrow, as they are reorganizing in order to work in a new shift . . . I guess I'll have to come home to keep your electrical equipment running. I'm an expert along those lines, of course. . . .

It's time for school, so I'll have to quit. I don't know just when we can leave the post tomorrow, there being no school. I'm bored and will spend as much time in town as possible, if we don't get KP Sunday.

Love, Bill

As days then weeks passed, with Bill receiving no word regarding his OCS status, his letters home struck a downbeat note. "I'm afraid my OCS has blown up. . . . I haven't heard a thing," he informed his parents on August 9. Two days later: "I am becoming pretty well convinced that I was washed out. I'm afraid I haven't much military bearing." Two weeks later, on August 23 – and exactly a month after his interview – more gloom: "I'm apparently washed up so far as OCS is concerned and am apparently destined to be a radio man of some sort."

The next day, however, he dashed off "breaking" news:

Monday Night, August 24, 1942

Dear Folks:

This afternoon at about 3 o'clock I was awakened by an Orderly Room runner and told to report to a Sergeant Barnes. I did, and was ordered to report to the hospital for an OCS physical examination Wednesday morning [August 26] at 7:30. I knew this would be of interest to you, so decided I'd drop you a line. I doubt very much that I'll pass, on account of my left eye, and possibly my feet, but it is a source of some satisfaction to know I was passed by the OCS Board even if I am rejected by the medical board.

Two days later, on August 26, he wrote home again:

Well, I've had the physical examination and am neither in nor out yet. They red-lined me for being underweight and I have to go back Friday to try to get a waiver. I guess I have to see the Major in charge. I weighed 138 lb stripped on their scales and they say at my age I ought to weigh 146. They said I shouldn't have much trouble getting a waiver, but I haven't much faith in it. I'm afraid other little things like the hemorrhoids, flat feet etc. will militate against getting a waiver for a definite disqualification.

I had no trouble with the eyes. They tested the right eye first and only used a 5 letter group. You can memorize that short a group almost instantly. I might have been able to read the line correctly with the left eye unassisted by memory, but it would have been touch and go. I also had to fake a little with the dentist. I knew they'd object to my over-bite, so I held my lower jaw way out all the time. The Doc was suspicious but finally O.Ked it. It's funny how careless they are about taking you in as a private, where you are bound to take something of a physical beating, and how careful they are when you want to be an Administrative Officer, who takes no beating at all. Boy, if I ever get a commission out of this I'll sure have done it over a rough path. If I should get the waiver, I don't believe I'll be here long....

Love, Bill

EVEN AS BILL SHARED the ups and downs of his OCS application process, he did not dwell exclusively on the topic when writing home. He remembered his mother's June birthday and penned a few lines telling her a package had been mailed. He responded to his father's queries about office legal matters. He also did what was generally considered to be every soldier's right: He complained. Sometimes he griped about much-despised kitchen duty. More often he cursed the sultry weather. "Sweat is running from me in streams," he ended one letter in late July. In another he groused: "The weather is awful. Hot & sticky. They make you wear these heavy fatigues, which soon smell to high Heaven. You usually have to wear a pair two weeks." To his list of nature-related complaints, he added one more – "vicious" flies.

St. Louis remained his go-to place on weekends, and he regularly shared excursion highlights with his parents. He also mentioned the occasional snag, as when he and his engineer friend, Van Buskirk, arrived in the city too late one Saturday night in July: "Tent City was full and no hotels were available, so we were up all night, except from 4 AM on we tried to sleep in chairs in the Y.M.C.A. lobby." A few weeks later, after a long night of classes, he and Van Buskirk returned to St. Louis determined to find an air-conditioned hotel room, which, after some searching, they did. "It [the room] set us back $7.00 but Boy it was worth it," Bill wrote home on August 3. "We laid down at 11 AM for a two hour nap to freshen up a little. I woke up first at exactly 6:15 [PM] so you can figure how tired we were."

Hoping his parents might visit him again, Bill assured them, in that same August letter, that he would book them reservations in an air-conditioned St. Louis hotel so "hot weather shouldn't worry you." He also listed upcoming shows – *Roberta, Wizard of Oz* and *Showboat* – to be performed at the Muny and predicted they would enjoy any entertainment there "for it's the best thing of the sort I've ever seen."

But the visit never took place due to Bill's father, long plagued with kidney and other health problems, becoming ill around that time. The illness was grave enough to keep Oak away from his office for weeks, and a deeply worried Bill wrote home frequently to learn his father's condition. At month's end, Bill was still sending get-well wishes to Oak, expressing concern, and urging his mother to "make him take it easy."

Meanwhile, Bill himself suffered that August – from sleep deprivation. When he began Radio School in June, he had spent his first week on the night shift (2:30 to 10:30 p.m.), a schedule he did not like but tolerated. Next came a multi-week assignment on the day shift (5:30 a.m. to 2:30 p.m.), which he much preferred despite having to arise extra early. At the end of July, Scott Field commanders had reorganized Radio School to add a graveyard shift (11 p.m. to 6:45 a.m.), one to which Bill and his entire squadron were immediately assigned and one that Bill hated. Even so, he was in no position to argue. Competent radio communications men were needed for the 60,000 airplanes that President Roosevelt, in his January "State of the Union" address, had called upon the nation to produce in 1942 and for the 125,000 new planes that the president wanted in 1943. To train ground and air crews for such a rapidly expanding fleet, Scott Field officials had but one choice: funnel more men into more classes around-the-clock.

Calling the overnight shift "murderous" and "horrible," Bill wasted no time detailing the ill effects on him and classmates. "The instructors in the school spend most of their time trying to keep us awake. Last night (or rather this morning at 5 AM) we took the final examination in receivers. I'll bet grades were terrible, as everybody had to have their eyes propped open by that time," he wrote home on July 29, just three days into his new schedule. Two weeks later, he had no better news to report: "Sleep is the thing uppermost in our minds now. We don't seem to adjust to the night-shift very much. Grades in the last phase were terrible. I had an 81 in Circuit Analysis, but so did VanB., the engineer. The last two or three hours of school every night are just wasted." Five days later came more of the same: "The night shift is still pretty tough to take. I get so jittery I can hardly stand it about the last hour. Everyone seems to have the same trouble. Oh well, we only have 45 more days (or rather nights) to go."

Lest he had complained too much and provoked too much worry, Bill struck a different tone when writing his parents near the end of August. In spite of sleepless nights, irregular meal schedules, and beastly heat, he offered up reassurance: "I am feeling fine."

HE DID NOT FEEL "fine," however, about his OCS application, which continued to languish for reasons unclear to him. He also was unsettled by his decision in late August to apply to a school about which he knew very little, other than it went by the name "RL School" and appeared to involve advanced radio training. His parents, upon reading his August 24 letter, may have been unsettled themselves – or, at the very least, perplexed:

Last night I signed an application to go to RL school. I doubt if anything develops from it and am not sure I even want it, but you had to take it or leave it. If I later decide I'm not interested I can talk my way out of the interview. They investigate you very closely on this thru the FBI before making any appointments, as the equipment is highly secret.

His letter two days later offered little clarity:

About 3:30 [in the afternoon] a fellow woke me up and told me they were looking for me at one of the school buildings to interview me about my RL application. I told him to go to H. and went back to sleep. About a half hour later one of my friends from another barracks came into wake me up to tell me the same thing. So I finally decided I couldn't sleep anyway and went over for the interview. I don't think anything will ever come of that, as I have no special qualifications. I haven't much enthusiasm for it anyway.

Three days later, on August 31:
I regret that I applied for RL School. I don't believe I'll get it & doubt if I want it, and it's costing me sleep. I've been ordered to report Wednesday at 8 AM for fingerprinting, which will mean I'll undoubtedly get to bed at least two hours later than usual. Fortunately, Wednesday is our 'day off,' no roll call 'till 10 PM & no calisthenics or inspection, so I can get the sleep back. Trouble is, it is also our only day during the week to go to town.

Bill with Oak during a brief visit home, September 1942.

Given that his experience with his earlier applications – for JAG and for OCS – had taught him not to expect quick answers, Bill tried to brush aside thoughts of RL School and focus on his classes, which by September were rapidly coming to an end. He took advantage of a much-needed Labor Day break to hitch a ride home to see his recovering father. Upon his return, he then began a nonstop round of testing. "We had our last test last night. Maintenance. I made 91 in the course. Friday night we had a test in Tactical Procedure and I made 93 in that course," he wrote home on September 14, a week after Labor Day. On September 20, another update: "Friday night I passed a code check at 20 W.P.M. . . . 20 is a pretty fair speed, as it is all that is required for a commercial operator's license." Days earlier, he had written his folks that "I'm now all thru with the theory phases of the radio school and spend all night taking code and dealing with tactical procedure. We spend about half the night on field sets, operating actual stations scattered over the field, communicating back and forth with each other. It's rather fun."

As graduation grew near, Bill ordered a yearbook, writing his parents on September 21 that "I thought it might be nice to have after the war, as it has pictures of all members of Class 45." Knowing he soon might be restricted to base, he also planned a final trip to St. Louis. In addition, he started putting his gear in order: "Tonight [September 30] I'm going to sew a handkerchief to my barracks bags with my name & number printed on it in ink, which is one of the steps preparatory to shipping. I still haven't the slightest idea where I'm going."

Within two days, some clarification came. He was to proceed to RL School, though his destination remained unknown. "My next address will probably be Florida, altho I understand there is a remote chance it might be California. 99 out of 100 chances it will be Florida, tho," he wrote on Oct. 2. In that same letter, he repeated the mystery that surrounded his new assignment: "They are a lot more particular about your background for RL than for OCS, because you are taught closely kept military secrets there. I am not very enthusiastic about the set-up, but I'm afraid my eyes would keep me from being an operator and RL is probably better than being an ordinary radio mechanic."

Then five days later this:

Oct. 7, 1942

Dear Folks:

I am now a full fledged 'Radio-Operator-Mechanic," according to a diploma I received yesterday at graduation exercises. I celebrated by going over to the main PX for a steak dinner, then on out to the #1 hospital to see Bill Husing [the furniture businessman from Houston] who is a patient there.

Many of the men in class 45 already have shipping orders. Some, I guess, have already left. Van Buskirk is leaving under sealed orders, so he doesn't know where he's going, nor the exact time of departure. The R.L. men have not yet been placed under shipping orders, so we don't have any idea when we leave. If you shouldn't hear from me for several days, think nothing of it as I may be in for a long trip & my letter writing might be restricted when I get there....

I am sending the diploma home in a mailing tube.

Both last night & the night before [I] slept 'round the clock, from 11 PM 'til 11 AM. Great feeling to have so much leisure. I'm scared stiff they'll remember me & put me on work call if I'm around too long, tho.

I've asked some of the boys who are leaving to write me at Auburn, so you can forward their letters. Only way I know of how we can keep in touch.

I guess this is all the news for now.

Love, Bill

With his classwork finished and his affairs in order, Bill continued to lead a leisurely life, telling his parents on October 10: "My sole duty consists of participating in an hour and fifteen minutes of [calisthenics] and athletic games. Otherwise the day is mine. I've had to turn in my bedding, so I don't even have a bed to make. Sleep on a bare mattress and pillow under comforters I swipe off someone else's bed." By then he had confirmation that his OCS application, sidetracked by medical paperwork errors, was still viable. By then, too, he had accepted an invitation from a Scott Field commander to fill out yet another application for a JAG appointment. But given prior military hiccups, he chose not to pin his hopes on what "might be" and to focus instead on his next assignment. "I imagine," his October 10 letter concluded, "I'll be at my next post for about two months. After that I don't think I'll be in the U.S.A. long either. I hope not, for I think we'd better get in and get it over."

As he wrote, tens of thousands of American servicemen were already "in" – fighting fiercely to expel the Japanese from the jungle hell known as Guadalcanal Island, battling for possession of waters in the Pacific's Solomon Islands chain, and running nonstop convoys across the Atlantic and Pacific to protect troopships and tankers. So, too, were American soldiers massing in England and at Hampton Roads, Virginia for the soon-to-come amphibious invasion of North Africa.

Like Bill, however, not everyone was fully "in" yet. Thousands of men were still being drafted and shipped to stateside boot camps. Thousands of others, having been introduced to the rigors of military life, were receiving or – as in Bill's case – about to receive more specialized instruction.

On October 13, 1942, Bill bid farewell to Scott Field. With six months of military service to his credit and with a new assignment awaiting him, he boarded a train that carried him across rolling Illinois prairie, bore him through a slice of southern Indiana, and then comfortably conveyed him through swaths of country he had never before seen. Within days, his parents would receive a postcard he penned en route.

> **Gibson County Service Organization**
> **Princeton, Indiana.**
>
> Tues, Oct 13.
>
> Enroute, and are we going in style! - Not just in Pullmans, but in private compartments, 3 men to each. - Sound-proofed air-conditioned cars.
>
> All for now, as it is too tough to write on a moving train.
>
> Bill

Chapter Four
BILL: 1942 - 1943

Boca Raton, Fla.
Oct. 15, 1942

Dear Folks:
Not having heard from home for two weeks, I thought I'd better write a note & send my address right away. It is on the envelope. Make use of it.
We were on the train about 46 hours. Awfully slow train, but good [accommodations]. Pullman compartments, three men to each. We stopped off for dinner Tues. night at Louisville & ate at a hotel. After that, they had a regular diner on the train.
I mailed you a card while going thru Indiana, by passing it out the window to a very small boy. I'm curious to know whether he posted it. Did he?
We are in a land of sand, orange trees and palm trees, just four or five miles from the ocean. It is pretty hot and pretty wild. The Army has the club house here, an $18,000,000.00 layout, and had we come here a month earlier we would be living there. As it is we are in barracks a good distance away.
My barracks bags haven't arrived yet, so I have no clean clothes, towels or anything. Fortunately I bought a cheap case at Scott Field for toilet things & have a razor and tooth-brush.
I enjoyed the trip quite a lot. We ran thru Georgia in the daytime. Trouble is, you can't see nice homes & things like that from a railroad. Lots of crackers, tho. . . .

I may want my golf clubs later, after figuring the time angles. They have two magnificent 18 hole courses here & I could play for $1.00 per month.

I'll write more later. Right now I'm too tired.

TWO DAYS AFTER LEAVING Illinois and after traveling more than 1,100 miles, Bill Husselman reported for duty at a military base along Florida's Atlantic coast between the resort cities of Palm Beach and Miami. Known as Boca Raton Army Air Field (BRAAF), the base officially opened the day Bill arrived, though troops already had begun assembling there and more were on the way.

To say that the base had been hurriedly built was an understatement. Within months after Pearl Harbor, the government acquired nearly six thousand acres near the sleepy town of Boca Raton, population just over seven hundred. The Army Air Corps, noting Florida's mild winters, the state's flat terrain, and an existing airfield at Boca Raton, had identified the area as an ideal training site and proceeded quickly to relocate residents. It likewise began building four major runways and sending work crews across white-sand fields to erect everything from tarpaper barracks and mess halls to three chapels complete with organs. Left undisturbed were palmettos and shrubs, deemed useful as camouflage against enemy surveillance.

The military also commandeered the luxurious oceanfront Boca Raton Club, the "$18,000,000.00 layout" Bill referenced in his letter. The Club, which since the 1920s had served as a winter destination for the wealthy, consisted of an ornately decorated multistory hotel, two premier golf courses, six tennis courts, swimming pools, beaches, and lushly foliaged grounds. The first trainloads of troops had the good fortune of being housed in the swanky hotel – accommodations that, as Bill's letter pointedly noted, he missed out on by "a month." Even so, for all its one-time elegance, the Boca Raton Club soon succumbed to the changing times. Antiques were packed away in storage, gilded columns were wrapped for protection, and expensive furnishings were replaced with standard-issue army bunks, eight men to a room.

Soon, too, the resort's grounds took a beating as troops dug foxholes on a golf course and practiced maneuvers and pitched tents on once immaculately manicured lawns.

Top, club grounds. Above, club interior with carpet, furnishings, and artwork removed. (Boca Raton Historical Society)

Assigned to BRAAF's 40th Technical School Squadron, Bill arrived at his new post with no clear idea of what he would be doing. Scott Field commanders had told him his new work would entail "closely kept military secrets" and "highly secret" equipment – pronouncements that piqued his curiosity and likely prompted him to wonder if such talk was overblown. But Bill had not been misled nor was the talk hyperbolic. His new training was to be in radar, a then-emerging technology with top-secret military implications.

During the 1930s numerous countries, among them Great Britain, Germany, France, and the United States, had experimented with radio waves to navigate ships and airplanes and to detect objects within limited ranges. War lent urgency to developing better detection devices, and by 1940 – around the time the term RADAR, an acronym for *Ra*dio *D*etection *a*nd *R*anging, was coined – British scientists and military experts started sharing their technical secrets with the United States. Full-scale collaboration ensued, with researchers from both nations working in a window-darkened laboratory, the so-called Rad Lab, at Massachusetts Institute of Technology outside Boston. Their research soon yielded the next generation of radar, specifically airborne radar that enabled pilots to locate enemy targets through heavy cloud cover and on the darkest of nights – and that ultimately gave Allied bombers the precision tool needed to hasten the war's end.

To assess whether scientists were on the right track, Boca Raton became radar's testing site. It was there that new radar equipment was strapped aboard B-17s and other aircraft. It was there, too, that thousands of soldiers were trained in the latest see-in-the-dark technology, with some taught to operate radar instruments on the ground and others aboard planes. Among the trainees arriving at BRAAF in the fall of 1942, around the time Bill did, was Jacob Beser. Within three years, Beser – by then a lieutenant and a radar specialist – would take his place in history as the only crew member to participate in both of the atomic-bomb missions over Japan.

Soldiers receiving radar training (Boca Raton Historical Society)

With "keep quiet" the byword at BRAAF, Bill wasted no time being blunt with his family. "We are strongly enjoined," he informed them a week after his arrival, "to avoid mentioning any detail about the school other than that it is an 'Advanced Radio school,' so I won't be able to tell you anything about it, except that I'll be here only a few weeks." Five days later, on Oct. 27, he repeated as much: "I haven't much to write about, for we are not allowed to discuss the school and are given very little time to get into anything else to talk about." Three days later, the same: "I got the camera and both letters today. I am sorry you sent the camera, for I have no use for it here. Picture taking is taboo at this post."

It was also taboo for Bill to describe his physical surroundings. Thus his letters contained no mention of the barbed-wire fencing around classroom buildings or the guard shacks at entrances. Neither did he mention that note-taking was prohibited, meaning classroom information had to be memorized. Moreover, he dared not divulge what loose talk might cost him. Years later, a soldier who had been stationed at BRAAF told the author Sally Ling, for her 2012 book *Small Town, Big Secrets: Inside Boca Raton Army Air Field During*

World War II, that "discussion of even the word 'radar' off the base was an automatic court-martial."

Yet even as Bill honored military secrecy, he knew how much his parents welcomed his correspondence, and hence he made every effort that autumn to write, at times expansively, about his off-base jaunts. His travels required transportation, and for that his thumb proved useful. "The Army," he explained in an October 22 letter, "usually discourages [hitchhiking], but here there is no other satisfactory way of getting around so there are signs posted on the main highways reading 'Remember, Soldiers Want Rides!'" Having hitchhiked that very afternoon to nearby Delray Beach, he reported that "I not only saw the Atlantic, but dipped my hand in it. I had to look lively to avoid being drenched with a breaker when I did it, too." Not overly impressed with his first ocean sighting, Bill added, "It really looks little different than Lake Michigan."

Boca Raton, with its two bars, a roadside restaurant, and a handful of stores and gas stations, also failed to impress him. Referencing a small hamlet in his home county, Bill described Boca Raton as "about like Corunna, only not quite so big." Yet tiny as the seaside town was, its coastal waters loomed large militarily. On May 8, 1942, five months before Bill arrived in Florida, a German U-564 submarine – one of many Nazi U-boats then prowling America's eastern seaboard – attacked a freighter several miles off Boca Raton's coast. Within two minutes of being torpedoed, the ship sank, resulting in the deaths of fifteen of the thirty-seven crew members.

The attack was no anomaly. Between mid-January and late July 1942, German U-boats traveling in predatory "wolfpacks" sank nearly four hundred tankers and merchant vessels in Navy-protected waters along the East Coast and in the neighboring Gulf of Mexico and Caribbean Sea. Of the ships sent to their watery graves, twenty-four went down off Florida's coast, most within a 150-mile stretch from Boca Raton to Cape Canaveral and often within sight of shore. The monthslong German assault, which resulted in the deaths of some 5,000 Allied seamen and passengers – more than twice the number who died at Pearl Harbor – was eventually checked when the U.S. Navy implemented a long-overdue system of having ships travel in convoys with escorts. Improved air patrols and a government-ordered blackout along the coast also helped trim Allied shipping losses and stem the calamitous death toll. By early August, *Operation Drumbeat* – the Nazi campaign that brought war to America's doorstep – was finally over, though danger still lurked in the mid-Atlantic where German submarines redeployed.

Exactly how much Bill knew about the previous months' coastal perils isn't clear from his letters. He had not been present to hear the booms from detonated torpedoes, see billowing smoke on the horizon, or encounter the dead washed ashore, their bodies coated in oil and tangled in seaweed. He recognized, however, that the atmospherics of Florida were much different, militarily, from that of the Midwest. "I doubt if it is advisable to carry a camera anywhere as this is virtually a war zone, it being so close to the coast," he wrote his parents at one point that October. In another letter, he mentioned visiting the resort town of West Palm Beach, twenty-eight miles north of Boca Raton, and noted that "it seemed pretty dead . . . partly because of the semi-black-out, I suppose. The top half of the streetlights were blacked out, and there were no electric signs going even at the theatres." Months earlier, West Palm Beach's Good Samaritan Hospital was anything but quiet when emergency workers, springing into action following a U-boat attack, treated as many as fifty seamen one night, many of the rescued screaming in agony from their torpedo-blast injuries.

Bill, meanwhile, continued to explore South Florida, highlighting trips to Fort Lauderdale and Miami Beach. He visited the latter one Sunday in early November when a family offered to drive him across the causeway where he saw "miles of beautiful homes, apartments, & hotels." Declaring Miami Beach to be "magnificent," he also observed that the Army had "taken over" much of the place, an observation grounded in fact. In February 1942, an Army Air Corps basic training center and an officer candidate school opened in Miami Beach and quickly became one of the nation's largest. By the war's end, one-fourth of all Army Air officers and one-fifth of the corps' enlisted men had received training there.

While Bill claimed to have seen "thousands of officers" during that weekend outing, one in particular caught his eye – or as he told his parents: "I rather think I saw Clark Gable." In all likelihood he had.

Known as the "King of Hollywood," the forty-one-year-old Gable had put his movie career on hold to join the Air Corps and, just days before Bill's visit, had completed his OCS training in Miami.

Clark Gable, c. 1940 (Wikimedia Commons)

Turning heads wherever he went in the beach city, the screen idol had been motivated to enlist out of both patriotism and grief. His glamorous actress wife – Fort Wayne, Indiana native Carole Lombard – had died months earlier in an airplane crash while en route home from a war bond rally in Indianapolis. Her war sacrifice would lead to a posthumous honor in 1944 when the military launched a cargo vessel bearing her name: the Liberty ship *Carole Lombard*. As for Gable, he would fly at least five combat missions over Europe in 1943, including one over Germany, and his service as a gunner and aerial photographer would earn him the Air Medal and the Distinguished Flying Cross. Notably, the Hollywood star drew the special ire of Hitler, who reportedly had been a big Gable fan before the war. The Führer offered a $5,000 reward to any pilot who shot down the actor's plane.

Despite Miami Beach's many attractions, soldier congestion soon put that city off-limits to Bill and his BRAAF mates. Fortunately, Fort Lauderdale, about twenty miles south of the base, offered enough restaurants, watering holes, and entertainment to make it a desirable destination. When not saddled with weekend KP or other base duties, Bill often thumbed a ride there. On one such visit, he spent a leisurely Sunday afternoon cruising the city's waterways, as he detailed in a lengthy November 9 letter:

Dear Folks:

... Sunday morning there was supposed to be a work call of some sort but it didn't materialize, so we [he and a friend named McSay] left about 9 o'clock for Ft. Lauderdale. We had to wait about a half hour for a ride, but then got one all the way thru in a nice car. Most of your rides are in rattletraps driven by war workers or in trucks, partly because such fellows seem to be more generous to soldiers than the better-off, and partly because they can get gas easier.

They have 30-mile excursion trips thru Florida waters in power boats for $1.00, so we, at heart more tourist than soldier, decided to take one Sunday afternoon. It was very interesting. First we went up New River, which runs thru the city. The Indians gave it that name because it appeared in a single night. It was formerly an underground stream, but broke thru for seven miles one night a couple of hundred years ago.

It is quite wide thru town, but gets down to only thirty or forty feet a little way above. At this point it is sixty to seventy feet deep and has been characterized by Ripley as the deepest river in the world for its length and width. There is a whirlpool where they have never reached bottom, altho it has been sounded to a depth of 185 feet. We went up this stream thru New River Jungles, a very dense forest in swampland where many semitropical plants grow. Many little streams and canals flow into the river. Perhaps you've seen movies of this . . . Remember the out-board motor obstacle races in the Florida Everglades? This is the country. We went thru the edge of Everglades proper, but they are not nearly so wild. There are alligators in these streams, but we didn't see any.

Fort Lauderdale postcard that Bill sent his parents. "It's certainly nice to winter in Florida," he wrote on the back.

Then we returned to town and cruised around Ft. Lauderdale, which was the most interesting part of the trip for me. The city almost outdoes Venice. It has 128 miles of waterways within the city limits and seventy-some bridges. Even so, some homes can only be reached by boat. The town has a normal summer population of around 20,000 and swells to 75,000 in Winter. Where the resort section stands was, until a few years ago (& in some cases I mean only one or two years) a great mangrove swamp along the river. The river is salt at this point, so mangrove trees will grow. They are great soil builders, taking root in three feet or more of salt water & in some way causing the land to rise about them until they no longer can root in the water. Then they die & go down, adding to the land they've created. At Ft. Lauderdale they couldn't wait for nature to take her course, but would go into the swamp, select a suitable tract, and cut down all the Mangroves and every other living thing. Then they would dredge canals thru the piece, leaving everything lay just where it was cut and throwing the soil dredged out on top.

This accounts for the intricate system of waterways. Some of the canals are not over fifty or sixty feet wide, others must be a hundred or more. All are navigable by good sized yachts. The islands made in that manner now have the most magnificent homes upon them. Many of them must have cost considerably in excess of $100,000 just to build, without figuring the cost of reclamation. This process is evidently not too expensive, as dredging here is easy. Even in the most exclusive sections, I understand the lots only cost about 100.00 per front foot. The guide mentioned the names of the owners of the larger houses. Most were big names from the big cities, but one was owned by that attorney, Green, of Champaign Ill. with whom I held a conference at So. Bend some years ago.

Then there are many small homes along the waterways owned by ordinary folks. They are small but pretty. Nearly all buildings here are of the same construction, no matter what the size – building blocks faced with cement or stucco. This white facing never cracks or gets dirty in Florida. These canals & the river are full of swell boats, cabin cruisers, etc.

The down town section is typical of any town of the size except for the number and size of the hotels, theatres, bars, etc. Everything in a Florida town's business section is white, too.

Ft. L. is much the most attractive & interesting place I've seen in Florida, and I'd certainly advise anyone wintering in Florida to try there. I forgot to mention the landscaping on these islands. As I mentioned, all vegetation is destroyed in their building, so all plant life you find is transplanted, grass, trees, shrubs and all. Florida is only semi-tropical, but will sustain many tropical plants when transplanted.

So the yards are full of great [coconut] palms, Royal Palms, Australian pine, banana trees, orange trees, tropical flowers and ferns, and other species too numerous to mention. All of this is hard to describe, but I hope I've given you some idea of what it is like....

Love, Bill

ON NOVEMBER 8, 1942, as Bill was enjoying his tropical excursion via motorboat, waves of American and British troops under the command of then-Lieutenant General Eisenhower landed on beaches in French Morocco and Algeria. British soldiers had been fighting in North Africa since the summer of 1940, first against Italian troops, then against German forces who came to the aid of their beleaguered Axis partner. The launch of *Operation Torch*, code name for that day's amphibious invasion, signalled the United States was finally and fully committed to putting boots on the ground in the bloody clash across the Atlantic. The invasion also meant Germany's formidable Wehrmacht – its army, navy, and air force – was about to be tested by the combined power of an Anglo-American army.

Cheering the much-anticipated invasion and all that it portended, Bill began speculating on how it might affect him. A week later, in a November 16 letter to his parents, he outlined possibilities:

Now here is my present situation: I am supposed to graduate this coming Saturday. In all likelihood I'll have to take one more course, but it only lasts a week, so in two weeks I'll probably be completely done with this school business. I may leave here immediately, or be kept around some time. (Hope it's soon, for graduates catch the dickens in the way of K.P. & work call). The next trip might possibly be overseas, & under such circumstances that I couldn't communicate with you....

The point to all of this is that if you shouldn't hear from me for, say, two weeks, don't worry but conclude that I've shipped out of the country. Under such circumstances don't be surprised if you don't hear from me for four or five months. If I should go overseas don't worry because I'm afraid they'll never let me fly with my eyes & I'll be stuck with maintenance work. That would be about as safe as anything in the army.

Three days later, Bill wrote home again, saying he had been given the option to remain permanently at BRAAF as an instructor but had declined the offer. "I don't think," he explained, "it's much of a job for an able bodied man in war time for one thing, and I believe a fellow has a better time of it when assigned to a combat unit. Everybody has a job to work at there and nobody has time for the Comic Opera instructions and parades these Administrative Officers entertain themselves with here."

Graduating as expected on Saturday, November 21, Bill promptly began another week of specialized training. Even as he returned to the classroom, however, he took time to recap his weekend graduation celebrations, confident his parents would find the summary entertaining.

Monday, Nov. 23, 1942
Dear Folks:
Well we graduated Saturday as per schedule & threw a big graduation party in Ft. Lauderdale Saturday night. We had to stand a personal inspection and couldn't get away until late, so we had taxis from Ft. L. waiting for us at the gate. We had dinner at the Pioneer House, twenty-one attending. Had a swell meal, and only six-bits too. Then we adjourned to one of the town's popular bars where we had a private balcony reserved, and drank ourselves into a proper state of confusion.

We had four rooms at the Boulevard Hotel & stayed there the remainder of the night, i.e., four rooms-full of us stayed there. We are not supposed to stay away from the post all night, but we got away with it OK. (I think!) This hotel is a small resort hotel, very nice. Fancy furniture, swell beds, rooms open onto a patio; regular Hollywood set up. And a room for two set us back exactly $3.00. If I was going to be here long I would certainly insist that you came down for awhile.

Our principal entertainer was a character named Szymanski, who, as you can easily guess is of Polish origin, altho he is called "Murphy" by some of the non-coms in this squadron who haven't education enough to spell "Szymanski." He is a blondy, in his early twenties, and a screw-ball if I ever saw one. He claims he once had a Great Dane named "Brutus" who apparently had a perfectly amazing set of vocal chords. One of his favorite pastimes is imitating Brutus' stirring basso, particularly when stimulated by the strains of "The Whistler & His Dog." We will suddenly start whistling the tune & no matter where he is or who is around, at a certain place he'll "give out" with his remarkable imitation. He even did it at inspection the other day with officers around (but oh, so softly!). Then he has a number of fifteen cent tin whistles from which he gets the most amazing results. He entertains us with everything from the Hootchi Cootchi Dance to Wagner. One of the most mournful things I've ever heard is his interpretation of "The Funeral March." He can trill his whistles like a flute, & plays rather fast & difficult things even the half-tones have to be produced by half covering the holes with his fingers. At the party, however, [he] used a more orthodox musical medium, the piano, upon which he played most everything you can think of, including the Concerto in B Flat Minor, played both straight & swing. He also plays drums, the pipe organ, accordion, clarinet and sax. He attended a conservatory of music for five years in New York. Screw ball that he is, he still gets better grades in radio than I. (That's not difficult, of course).

 I got the cigarettes from Ethel [aunt on his mother's side], and will drop her a note tonight.

 I'm certainly sorry to hear about Grandma's eye trouble, & surely hope that the treatment will be effective....

 Love, Bill

On Friday of that week, just days before he finished his additional training, Bill again wrote home about Szymanski, the soldier's musical antics too funny to resist telling:

This screwy Szymanski I mentioned in my last letter sent home and got a fife. Our class live[s] in one barracks, and we've been marching to & from school to the martial strains of "Spirit of '76" and "Marching Through Georgia" to the amusement of all the soldiers in the area. I've been surprised that someone hasn't jumped all over us for it, but I think the officers are so amazed to see any one marching voluntarily and marching with smartness at that, that they figure they'd better let us alone.

Elsewhere in that November 27 letter, Bill shared details decidedly less amusing – and more nose-wrinkling. He had been permitted to leave the base the previous day, and he chose to dine in a Fort Lauderdale restaurant, where he feasted on a Thanksgiving meal of prime rib. As he explained to his parents, soldiers who remained on base declared the mess-hall meal to be "really good" but "I don't care for turkey & don't think I'd like even an inch thick sirloin if I had to eat it out of the dirty mess-kit the way we eat here." More unsavory details followed:

Meals here are generally putrid. I've seen mouldy bread removed from tables twice, and have seen liver served with a mouldy spot the size of a silver dollar. Then we have to eat out of mess kits in which everything runs together & becomes hash, regardless of what it might be separately. Outside the mess hall they have a little trench with a wood fire burning in it, with a chimney at one end to provide air. Over the fire are three big garbage cans, the first 2 full of soapy water & the third full of clear water. You dip your kit in each can in turn. You can usually take it home & scrub it then as best you can, for you can imagine what the cans of water are like after two or three hundred men have gone before you. Their meals are not all bad, but too many of them are.

On Sunday of that holiday weekend, Bill took his "last and final bow as a student." If more celebratory partying or even casual beer-toasting marked the occasion, he made no mention. Instead, in his letter home a few days later, he deployed his usual self-deprecating humor to poke fun at his military accomplishments. He also rued his appearance.

Dec, 2, 1942
Dear Folks:
Eight months ago to the day I waved my right paw in the air for a brief interval and took the fateful plunge. Since that time I have made great progress. Of course I'm still a buck private and am at the moment engaged in rather disagreeable endeavors like stacking lumber and loading trucks with a miscellany of wares for the Squadron supply, but the fact cannot be overlooked that I have acquired a large number of diplomas, certificates, and other rewards for my scholastic achievements that may prove indeed useful at some future time for, say, papering a bathroom. Or, if the priorities on paper should ever make it necessary, I can think of other very useful purposes to which these documents could be put in that sanctorum....

The other night I was standing at a counter in the PX [post exchange] when someone beside me said "Isn't your name Husselman?" I looked around and admitted to a perfect stranger that it was. He said his name was Lucus & that we had gone to Law School together. The odd thing about it all is that he should recognize me in an Army PX, in fatigue clothes and a mechanic's cap, after all these years when we were apparently never closely acquainted. I hardly recognize myself so dressed when I glance at a mirror. Sometimes I scare myself, if I'm thinking of something else when I look. I look so much like a thug to me. Lucus was practicing in Kokomo [Indiana] when the Army got him. . . .

Mother, I don't know what to say to you about the Christmas question. I've no idea when or where I'll ship. Might be soon, or might not even be until after the Holidays. I guess I'll have to close. I think they are going to inspect mess-kits tomorrow, and I think mine will take some polishing up before it will get me by a "gigging."

Love, Bill

Another week passed, with Bill still marking time. In a rare break from writing to his "folks," Bill communicated directly with his father, apparently in response to a letter from Oak. Knowing his father to be a reader, Bill offered some book reviews, shared philosophical musings, and confessed to his eagerness to "move on."

December 11, 1942

Dear Dad:

I am still here and am still "on shipping." I thought I had better take advantage of the opportunity to answer your recent letter, for I don't know what my situation will be even a few hours from now. Two other men and I have been "on shipping" since Saturday but haven't yet received the final orders that will send us on our way. Meanwhile, we've been doing exactly nothing. They have a strange idea that when a soldier is under shipping orders he has to lie around continuously so that he can be located and sent off on short notice. All of this makes us very happy, but actually we kill our time by wandering from PX to PX & would be much harder to find than we would were we on work-call. The vacation has been nice, but we are beginning to feel the strain of all the uncertainty and are very anxious to go. We don't know of course whether we will at last be assigned to a squadron or will first be sent to some over-seas replacement center, like J.B. [Jefferson Barracks]. Most of the men in our group have been put on shipping and have gone since we first went on the list. We don't know what is causing the delay, which is very unusual, in our case. Perhaps some sixty-cycle clerk has lost our orders.

This unaccustomed leisure has given me the first chance to read since I've been in the Army. The PX features twenty-five cent paper-bound editions of quite a variety of books, printed in very readable type. Among others, I read James Hilton's "Lost Horizon" and am currently entertaining myself with "Wuthering Heights." I suppose you have read them both at some time. I find the Bronte book to be an extremely well done novel. The Hilton effort strikes me as being a little too much on the Jules Verne formula, although it does pose a theory interesting in the light of current events, - that civilization will likely again be destroyed by a world-wide war, even beyond the extent to which it was laid low by the wars preceding the Dark Ages. Inasmuch as we have 5000 years of recorded history behind us, with its pages filled with a succession of wars, and inasmuch as defensive technique never lags far behind the offensive, I don't take such conjectures very seriously, altho I seriously doubt if we in our lifetime ever see life as pleasant as it was in the days before the War.

For my part I will be satisfied if I can cure my itching foot and can again be satisfied to light in one spot and stay there. The Army has inculcated in me a lot of the urges that must motivate the hobo. Five or six weeks in one spot and I'm rarin' to move on. Why I'm anxious to leave here now I can explain on no other basis. While you are shivering in arctic temperatures I am basking under a tropical sun. The only complaint about the weather I could possibly make is that it is a little too hot and sultry. A mild game of ping pong or catch with a baseball will leave your clothes foul with perspiration. . . .

It is supper time, so I guess I'll conclude this and be off for the PX. (My mess-kit is packed).

Love, Bill

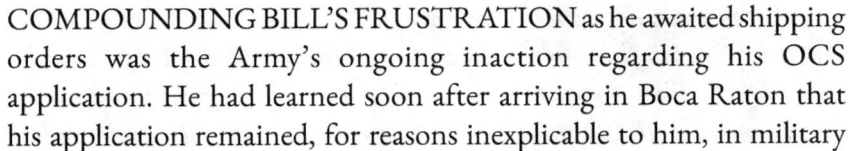

COMPOUNDING BILL'S FRUSTRATION as he awaited shipping orders was the Army's ongoing inaction regarding his OCS application. He had learned soon after arriving in Boca Raton that his application remained, for reasons inexplicable to him, in military limbo. Likewise, he had received galling news that autumn that his JAG application, completed prior to leaving Illinois, had been mishandled by his Scott Field squadron commander. Instead of forwarding it to proper authorities, the commander had belatedly sent the misplaced application to BRAAF for Bill to resubmit. Even after a BRAAF officer pledged to assist in the matter, Bill could work up little enthusiasm, telling his parents in mid-November: "I've got pretty much disgusted with the whole business."

Meanwhile, while still sidelined in Boca Raton in December, Bill received news that, if not disquieting, was at least perplexing. His commander received written notice that Bill's JAG application apparently *had* been approved, though the letter's wording was such that Bill was told to seek clarification at base headquarters. There, as Bill recounted to his parents on December 15, a secretary – "who I imagine knows as much about such matters" as her unavailable boss – told him that a JAG appointment likely would follow "in time" if he could be located. However, as Bill also explained to his parents, locating him might prove problematic. He was to leave BRAAF "under sealed secret orders," though a departure date still had not been announced.

Hours after speaking to the secretary – and after eleven days of idleness while awaiting those secret orders – Bill was "horrified" to find his name on the KP roster for that evening. Worse, the next day he and two fellow soldiers were informed, without explanation, that their shipping orders had been rescinded and that they were to report for work-call. Taking up the "impossible situation" with their commander, they were permitted to skip work-call, thus sparing them from cleaning latrines, policing the grounds for trash and cigarette butts, and being pushed around by, in Bill's words, "the lowest of all forms of brutish animal life, the K.P. pusher."

Nonetheless, Bill was sufficiently unnerved by the new developments that he decided to do what he had initially rejected doing – become an instructor. In a December 17 letter to his parents, he explained:

All of my buddies seem to think my [JAG] commission is pretty certain in time if I stay fixed where I can be found. . . . So I got half an idea last night to turn instructor, one-half because I'm burned up at always returning to K.P. & things like that at regular intervals, and one-half to protect my chances relative to the commission. At any rate, [buddies] Jansen, Holstead & I drank ourselves into a state of pleasant oblivion to our troubles on PX beer, and were presently joined by a staff sergeant with whom we had a slight acquaintance and who is the N.C.O. in charge of one of the schools. The upshot of the little party is that I'm to be a permanent "instructor" (actually I'll be doing purely office work, but have the status of instructor) while Jansen, Holstead and Pulver (we horned him in too) are "temporary instructors." They'll be allowed to play around with the equipment until they ship, thereby avoiding work-call.

We were at the school all day today. . . . I imagine I'll regret the whole business in a week or so, when I get bored. My idea is to sit down here during the cold weather & wait for the [JAG] commission. If it isn't forthcoming, come spring I'll squawk to beat the dickens for a transfer overseas. The hitch is that it isn't always possible to squawk your way into a transfer. I've got to take that chance in order to wait out the J.A.G. business. So, please resume writing me here. I'll likely be transferred to another squadron and assigned, but I'll get the mail.

I'm going to have to apologize about Christmas this year. I was restricted two weeks while on "shipping" and still can't get off the post because everybody is now restricted while new passes are made up & issued, so I've been unable to do any shopping at all. I'll have to content myself with hereby wishing you each and all as Merry a Christmas as is possible under the circumstances. . . .

With 3.9 million Americans serving in the armed forces that Christmas, up from 1.8 million a year earlier, Bill was hardly alone in sending holiday greetings under trying circumstances. By then, military duty had become unavoidable for nearly all healthy American men. Whereas the 1940 Selective Service Act had required all males ages twenty-one through thirty-five to register for military service, Congress had amended the law after Pearl Harbor to be more expansive; all males ages eighteen through sixty-four had to register, and those eighteen to forty-four were *subject* to military service. Moreover, whereas the 1940 law had authorized that conscripted men would serve only a year, the amended law required service for "the duration of the war" and up to six months after its termination.

Lewis B. Hershey (Wikimedia Commons)

Overseeing the law's implementation was a folksy but tough-minded Hoosier who, interestingly enough, grew up and attended school in Steuben County, Indiana, directly north of Auburn. Older than Bill by seventeen years and a World War I veteran, General Lewis B. Hershey would serve as head of the Selective Service System for three decades, including during the turbulent Vietnam War years when public support for the system finally collapsed – and when Hershey himself was reviled by antiwar protestors.

But Hershey was spared withering criticism during World War II as the American public generally accepted conscription and as war resisters and conscientious objectors were comparatively few in number. Of the ten million men drafted, fewer than 16,000 would be convicted for draft dodging.

Bill, meanwhile, could not dodge his confinement to base that December. While he had to put his holiday shopping on hold, family and friends were not similarly constrained, and they sent him season's greetings in the form of cards, money, cigarettes, and handkerchiefs. Even the Army gave him a present, as he announced on Christmas Eve:

The Army gave me a Christmas present in the form of a new khaki uniform. I was griping to a corporal from the 40th's supply room the other day about not having enough uniforms. He told me he'd fix me up, so I went directly over to supply with him & drew a uniform. It needs a little altering, but can be made to fit fine. That's the only thing I ever got from the Army without a lot of red tape.

Days later, with Bing Crosby's "White Christmas" still atop the music charts and with a new year about to commence, Bill learned he was to receive another Army present – a promotion. "If there is a little beer on the back of this paper, think nothing of it. I am in the midst of a little celebration," began his December 28 letter to his parents. An explanation quickly followed:

When next you write me, you can address the envelope to Sergeant Wm H. H. It will be a very substantial boost in pay. On second thought, maybe you'd better wait until a little later to address me that way: I just saw the special orders a few minutes ago and don't know whether they are effective as of today or not until Jan. 1st. The way it all happened is that all instructors were raised to Sergeant by a school order, and I am technically an instructor. I finally got a real break and got into something at exactly the right time. Well, this is just a note. I am enclosing a letter I wrote yesterday and forgot to mail.
Love, Bill
P.S. Sergeant pays $78.00 per [month].

On New Year's Day, January 1, 1943, Bill treated his parents to "behind-the-scenes" details of his promotion – and a glimpse into a sergeant's life.

Dear Folks:
I have gone into the tailoring trade. When they give you a promotion they don't like it if you don't blossom out in your stripes right away. Service at the Post Tailors is terrible, so it would probably take a week to get the work done there. You not only would not have the stripes, but you would also be out of the use of the clothes. Consequently, you sew them on yourself. I have spent the better part of 2 evenings sewing on three pairs. Surprisingly enough, I've done a pretty darn workmanlike job, altho several times I've wished my Grandmother was around to do it. It's a job that can only be well done by a machine, because the chevrons are made of very heavy material, very stiff, so that you have to really exert yourself every time you take a stitch. I will have to sew two more pairs on, then I think I'll be able to get the tailors to do the rest.

Being a sergeant is a sort of mixed blessing. It gets you off of KP & things like that of course, and out of all other physical effort except sweeping & mopping under your bed. Outside of an occasion or two when they were "gigged" for something and had to do an hour's policing up, I never knew one to do any physical work outside of his specialty line. You simply boss privates who do it. Also it is rather nice to be addressed as "Sergeant" rather than "Joe," or "Mac," or "Soldier" or "Hey You." Then of course the extra $28.00 per is not chicken feed when you are in the Army.

On the other hand, a private's life is by comparison a carefree one, for if he gets caught he can't be broken. We, on the other hand, have to be careful. As a matter of fact, we instructor-sergeants had better be darned careful. Everybody is slightly put out about our rapid rise in the world as it is, and I wouldn't be much surprised if the Squadron would enjoy ripping our stripes. A lot of the Squadron non-coms are put out because they think our promotion blocked theirs. . . .

The first day I was a Sergeant I got caught "goofing off" of calisthenics by a lieutenant. Fortunately he didn't take my name & only ordered me to go to where the calisthenics were being given. I didn't go of course, because it was dark, but it was a sort of narrow escape. I have gone a couple of times since tho, breaking a long precedent of "goofing off." The only thing I'm cutting now is Reveille. Under normal circumstances this sort of thing wouldn't be breaking grounds of course, but you can't tell about our set up. I don't know how the C.O. feels about us, & also how much the school would back us. I do know that I'm not going to let it weigh very heavily on me, for I don't intend to stay here long enough to make it really matter. . . .

Yesterday I carried a loaded gun for the first time, & I'll be in the Army nine months tomorrow. When we carry documents relating to secret material from one building to another we have to be armed. I was carrying a great big old six-shooter in a left-handed cavalry holster, so I'm sure it wasn't much protection. . . .

Well, I guess I'll say good-night & go home and sew on some more stripes.

Government stamps to buy rationed items; tokens as change. (Courtesy Sirleine Smith)

Five days later, in a letter dated January 6, Bill expanded on the life of a sergeant. He also alluded to how the redirection of food to troops impacted civilians' ability to procure items. The previous spring, the government had begun rationing sugar, with coffee added to the list in November, and with more foods – meat, cheese, fats, canned fish and canned milk – soon to be rationed.

Having few options, restaurants introduced "meatless" menus and tried to be creative with recipes. Homemakers did the same.

Dear Folks:

Judy Garland's "My Gal Sal" is playing at the Post Theatre and I want to see the second show, starting at 8:30 (2030, Army time), but I think I'll have just time enough to drop you a letter which I suspect is already overdue.

I am finding that the life of an Army sergeant is no bed of roses. I was getting along great when the darned squadron decided we'd have to earn our $78.00 per and made us Barrack Chiefs. I caught a barrack located 'way out in the wilderness, inhabited by a bunch of hoodlum students that no one had ever been able to do much with. I have to get them up in the morning and march them to reveille, & am in general in charge of the barracks, tho I don't see any of my charges from Reveille until bed time. I've got along with them fine so far but am losing sleep. They come in late at night & I have to get up at 5:20, altho they don't turn out until 6:30. I have to be all ready to go to work right after reveille, while they are free until afternoon. I just ran out of ink and had to fill up again.

I am rather lonesome, as all of my buddies have gone. I don't think it wise to get very closely associated with any of the men in my barracks, as I can handle them better by being friendly but a little aloof, so that they'll continue to be a little wary of my stripes....

I put on my khakis and went all the way to Ft. L. last night just to get a steak, & then couldn't get one, since they are awfully scarce. I went to about the largest restaurant in town too. They have just opened a new cafeteria in this area here on the post. So far few have discovered it & crowds are small, but that won't be for long. I ate there this noon. I eat mighty few meals other than breakfast at the mess-hall. It isn't that the food is too bad, it's just that I can't enjoy eating under the conditions.

... Speaking of the mess-hall, they had a terrible accident day before yesterday. A graduate was on K.P. & they set him to cutting meat with a power saw. He cut his left hand entirely off at the wrist.

I guess I'd better close now & go to the show.

SPORTING HIS SERGEANT STRIPES for barely three weeks, a jubilant Bill telephoned his parents on January 12 with long hoped-for news: He finally had been accepted into an Officer Candidate School for military police and was to report on January 30 to Fort Custer near Battle Creek, Michigan. A week later he followed up *not* with a phone call but with a bluntly worded letter: "OCS is off."

As Bill had learned in previous months, mishandled paperwork and miscommunication were a regular part of army life, and the upshot – at the time of his phone call home – was that he had been misinformed regarding his selection for officer training. "Strangely enough," he wrote home in his January 19 letter, "I felt little shock upon receiving the blow, for the element of surprise was missing. I have long ago learned that orders, especially shipping orders, are not to be taken very seriously until you are actually aboard the train." He concluded on a similarly cynical note: "I no longer think the J.A.G.D. business is going to develop either. . . . I guess you might as well resume writing to me here on your regular schedule. If I ever get similar orders, or any other good news in the Army in the future, I'm going to keep it to myself."

With his mood still sour, Bill offered his parents no rosier update five days later, on January 24:

Am having a hectic time of it. There are a few cases of measles & the entire squadron is quarantined for 14 days. We're not supposed to leave the squadron area except to go to school or the mess-hall. Aren't even supposed to go to the PX.

The O.C.S. situation is still about the same – no soap. They called me down there the other day, but all they wanted was for me to sign a new weight waiver application – a matter I thought was fully settled at Scott. Then yesterday when I got back to the barracks at 5 o'clock, from work, there was a note on my bed to report to the OCS Board that day.

It was too late, of course. The squadron has fixed me up that way twice, making no effort to notify me except leaving a note that I don't see until evening. I suppose that completely cooks any chance I might have had. They may have interviewed all of the eligibles yesterday in order to select one. I'll call them tomorrow, but I don't anticipate that it will do any good, as the reporting date is next Saturday. They must have made a selection before this. . . . I guess this will be about all. I'm not in the mood to write today.

Four days later, however, he was more than ready to put words on paper, which he did with a certain giddiness as a train bore him toward Detroit, destination Fort Custer. Convoluted as his story was, he tried to spell it all out.

1/28/43

Dear Folks:

If this letter doesn't make sense, it is because of two bottles of ale & several shots of whiskey. Am having a wonderful trip. You know where I'm going, so I won't mention it as it might conflict with some security rule of the Army.

My life for the last week has been as bizarre (spelling by Sgt. Bragdon) as any show you ever saw. Saturday the OCS office sent for me, but as usual the Squadron made no effort to locate me other than leaving a note on my bed, which I didn't see until after 5 PM. – Monday I went down to the OCS office and found that my physical exam had expired. I talked to a Miss Smith, who told me I <u>had</u> to pass a physical right away with no weight waiver, as I had at Scott. She insisted that I go to my barracks & eat a lot of bananas & drink a lot of water, to bring my weight up to 146 lb. stripped. I sent one of the instructors in to Boca Raton for bananas, but they didn't have any. So, I drank pints & pints of water. When I got to the hospital however, I just couldn't hold it until I could get weighed, so I let it go. Then they refused to examine me until Tues. morning, so I had all my suffering for nothing. They also told me weight standards had been altered so I'd have no trouble. I called the OCS office & Miss Smith told me they'd hold things up until yesterday (Wed.) noon. Tues. I got the examination, & passed it 100 %. They first told me they couldn't get the blood test out for 3 days, but by insisting I finally got it done right away. A close call, though! – Yesterday I got shipping orders.

Only two of us are going. The other is Sgt. Bragdon who I think I've mentioned as the lawyer-clerk at one of the other buildings. I've been placed in charge of the shipment, and you can rest assured that as far as he is concerned the rigid discipline of Officers Training has already started.

I think I'll pass within 20 or 30 miles of Auburn, but <u>pass</u> it will be. I think, however, we'll get a 10 day leave <u>if</u> & <u>when</u> we graduate. Incidentally, don't expect much mail from me as my time for the next three months will be fully occupied.

I guess I had Capt. Pendergrass [the new OCS board secretary at Boca Raton] figured wrong. He actually went to a lot of bother to permit me to make this class. Physicals were formerly good for six months, but just Saturday the rule was changed to three. He held off shipping orders until yesterday noon to give me my chance to qualify, then had to grab a car & carry the orders around himself to get us off in time. Miss Smith (young & personable) was also helpful. Sgt. Bragdon's story is even more bizarre than mine, but requires too much time in the telling....

Attaching a postscript to that letter days later, when his mood was less celebratory, Bill urged his parents to exercise caution: "You might be a little circumspect about whom you tell where I am. These schools in general & this in particular, I imagine, are tough. They wash out a certain percent of the classes just as a matter of course. Having been in the Air Corps I have mighty little real military background, so washing out is easily possible. It might be a little embarrassing for you if it was generally known where I was & I then didn't make it. Use your own judgment."

LOCATED JUST WEST of the cereal-manufacturing city of Battle Creek and sprawling across 16,000 wooded acres, Fort Custer teemed with activity in 1943. It was the reception center for nearly all of Michigan's inductees, the headquarters for numerous Army divisions and battalions, and a training base for tens of thousands of troops heading overseas. The previous spring, in April 1942, soldiers had begun departing the base for Iceland to protect the North Atlantic convoy routes, and eventually those soldiers, part of the 5th Infantry Division, would achieve fame fighting their way across northwest Europe. If Fort Custer commanders had hoped to catch their breath in 1943, no slowdown came. In October of that year, the base began housing German prisoners of war.

The fort's namesake was George Armstrong Custer, the calvary commander who died in an 1876 Indian Wars battle romanticized as "Custer's Last Stand." Whatever Bill thought about the long-dead

Custer, he harbored no romantic notions as he arrived on base in late January to begin his twelve-week course of study. The Military Police Officer Candidate program had recently moved to Fort Custer from Fort Oglethorpe, Georgia and was widely known to be demanding. As a new member of MP OCS Class 13, Bill had one overarching concern: He dreaded "washing out."

Sunday, Feb. 7, 1943
Dear Folks:

I suppose you are getting anxious to learn how things are going. I'm sorry I haven't written sooner, but we operate around the clock here. I think I'll have to limit my letters to one a week, as Sunday is the only day I have available for that sort of thing. You continue to write me twice a week, but only expect one from me while I'm here.

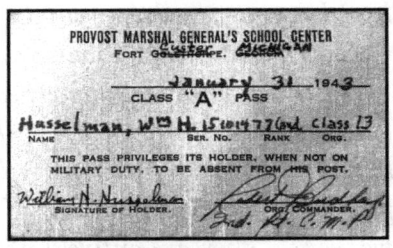

Card identifying Bill as a member of OCS Class 13

Our schedule is like this: up at 6:45, shave, clean up the barrack, breakfast etc.; to school at 8:45; school straight thru to 6 o'clock with an hour out for dinner; Supper at 6:30; & study hall from 7:00 to 8:30. Lights out at 10:30. As you can see, the whole schedule gives us only two hours of our own time, and of course it is plenty full.

Actually I usually study 30 minutes to an hour longer than required. It is the only time we can go to the PX, shine shoes, etc. etc., so there is just no time to write at all. . . .

I have no confidence at all in being able to make the grade here. "P.M.G.S" stands for Provost Marshal General's School. It is a Military Police School. We go into military law, administration and things like that, but the basic idea is to train officers to command companies and platoons etc. of M.P's, and the M.Ps are naturally a pretty tough branch of the service. Therefore the school is more concerned with whether or not you have the intangible qualities of "leadership" than with the quality of your school work.

In other words, you can flunk courses and still graduate, while on the other hand you can pass your courses with high marks and still wash out. I believe that in deciding whether you are a "leader," your voice and ability to give drill commands counts very heavily. I am greatly handicapped on this score as I've had practically no experience in drilling men and am in competition with drill masters. It is rather a difficult knack to acquire, too. Also, my voice is none too heavy for it.

The personnel of the school is rather odd. There are quite a number of lawyers, but the vast bulk are old M.Ps, mostly of high grade, i.e. 1st Sgt, M/Sgt, T/Sgt. etc. (Even two Warrant Officers). Many of these men have long military backgrounds. Mine, of course, is very poor. The Air Corps is no place to get a foundation for this sort of thing.

The things I am most concerned about aside from the drill angle are: gunnery, involving the disassembly, assembly, knowledge of function, and actual use of the Garand rifle, the machine gun, sub-machine gun, pistol etc., and judo. Many of the men have studied & used these weapons. They are entirely new to me and I have little talent for mechanical movements, marksmanship etc. Judo is an adaptation of jiu jitsu. I am neither athletic nor rugged enough to make much of a show at this.

The "leadership" business also involves another angle everyone hates and fears – a sort of popularity contest where each man on one floor of a barrack periodically rates every other man on the floor in relation to the others on personality, appearance, etc. etc.

They say [they] do not make a practice of washing out any particular number from a class, and might theoretically graduate an entire class. Actually, experience is that they drop from fifteen to twenty per cent. Most of them are not dropped until the last couple of weeks.

Discipline is not as tough as I expected. They give you "skins" for mistakes in making up your position in the barrack (making bed, displaying clothing, etc.) If you get three "skins" in a week you are restricted over the week-end. Sometimes the inspecting Officer unbuttons an inner sleeve button on your rack of clothes one day & skins you the next if you don't see it & correct it. Sometimes they give you a "Skin" for a "loose blanket" when your blanket is as tight as a drum head. I think this is to see whether you can "take it" without "blowing your top." It pays to have a philosophical nature.

On the whole, I find the school interesting and think I'll be as happy here as any place I've been in the Army, unless the physical training & judo get too painful. I'm really being introduced to the first taste of real soldiering. If I can make the grade here, I think I'd rather have a *commission in this dep't. than in the J.A.G's, because it really amounts to the difference between being a soldier and being a civilian in uniform. However, I'd feel much safer to "sell out" for that than to take my chances on this. The Air Corps is a good branch to be in, but it's not good training because of the high specialization....*

I'm standing the cold fine and feel fine. No cold.

Love, Bill

Bill's letters home in the ensuing weeks offered snapshots of his coursework and training regimen. "We spent four hours on the rifle range this afternoon, with the temperature mighty low. Somewhere around zero, I imagine," he wrote on Feb. 16. Two weeks later: "We fired on the range Friday in a regular blizzard. Pretty tough. I feel for the Russians. Tomorrow we fire again, and I certainly hope it warms up. So far I have had my hands, ears and lip frost bitten, and they are pretty sensitive to cold." If conditions outdoors were unforgiving, Bill likewise felt pressure indoors – in the classroom. He did poorly on one of his first exams, calling his performance "my map disaster." An exam in another subject, bayonet and hand grenade technique, yielded better results, with Bill writing on February 20 that "I got all of the answers right." Unfortunately, he hastened to add, that "course covers only 11 hours of work" whereas "the maps cover 30, damn it!"

Fort Custer barrack, an interior view (Willard Library, Battle Creek, MI)

Classwork recaps aside, his letters home also recounted the highs and lows of camp life. In mid-February, a measles outbreak proved especially annoying: "Our group is quarantined to the barracks area . . . I can't even go to the PX." More bad news weeks later: "The whole class was quarantined because of one case of scarlet fever. We are restricted to the company area, so I can't even phone." In a more cheerful vein, he wrote his parents soon after arrival that "two of the men on my floor of my barrack, including the man bunking next to me, are Sigma Chis. We just discovered our 'brotherhood' tonight & have been rendering Sig songs in a lusty, if not too harmonious, enthusiasm. One is from the Brown Chapter, &

the other from Bucknell. The one from Brown is also a graduate of the N.Y.U. Law School."

Fraternity connections didn't end in the barracks. Bill shared in another letter that a military policeman recognized him on a bus ride between the base and Battle Creek, leading to a friendly exchange: "He was at I.U. when I was & was a Lebanon [Indiana] lawyer until inducted 4 months ago.... We talked over the old days at I.U. all the way to B.C. He was a Sigma Nu."

Sobering, if not heartbreaking, news also made its way into Bill's letters. He reported in late February that a Scott Field friend, who later trained at a gunnery school in Texas, had been killed with eight others in a "bomber crash" in Idaho – news Bill learned from the young man's mother. After recounting the accident, Bill wrote his parents, "I think I'll close now, as I want to answer [the mother's] letter. It will be a rather difficult task. He was buried just two days after his twenty-third birthday."

Bill on a weekend trip to Auburn, early spring 1943.

With Fort Custer only ninety miles and a manageable bus ride from Auburn, Bill made four weekend trips home that winter and early spring, eliminating the need for lengthy letters between visits. "I have the time to write this afternoon, but lack news. Seems as though I covered everything when I was home, so I guess we'll call this just a note," he wrote his folks on March 10, his birthday and just days after his second visit to Auburn.

Signaling that future trips weighed on his mind, he informed his parents in that same letter that "I have decided that I won't be home this week-end, for two reasons. (1) I'll have to get a haircut (2) We have a test in Infantry Drill next week. They say that 75% of the men flunking it wash out. So, I guess I'd better study Sunday. I'll try to get home again the next available week-end afterward."

Whether wordy or succinct, Bill's letters invariably bore the same theme – his fear of not earning his commission. He passed along to his parents whatever "dope" he learned about the "weeding out" process and didn't sugarcoat his findings. "Do you remember my speaking of a Detroit Lawyer named Dick Mann in my barracks at Scott?" he wrote home in late February. "I bumped into him the other day. He is in Class 11, four weeks ahead of me.... They immediately washed 18 men out of two platoons of Class 11." In that same letter, Bill delivered other worrisome news: "As a whole, lawyers don't fare well here. They say that out of 32 men washed out of one class, 18 were lawyers."

While unloading his concerns, Bill tried to reassure his parents that he was keeping his wits and retaining his composure. Even so, they probably took little comfort in what he wrote on March 20: "At least the pressure isn't affecting me as it has some. A man in the second platoon tried to kill himself last night by stabbing himself with a nail file. He drove the blade in about two inches, between his heart and lung. [In addition] one of the boys in our barracks collapsed last night and had to be taken to the hospital."

Bill's letter the following week was anything but reassuring.

Saturday Night, March 27, 1943
Dear Folks:

... I am thoroughly convinced that I'm going to get the bounce. If I could do the manual of Arms, I think I would have made it, but it's got me stymied.

I made an ass of myself trying to do it again this afternoon. It doesn't pay to look like a rookie at anything of that sort around here, and that's just what I look like – very patently – and can't help it because I am a rookie, never having had any training in it. I can't even march with a rifle on my shoulder.

As you know, I'm pretty awkward, and lack muscular coordination to the extent that it takes me longer than it would the average fellow to get the "feel" of doing that sort of thing. My shortcomings with the gun have made me conspicuous, as they are watching me, and that is not good. You see, they'll wash about 50 men out of this class, and they're looking for most any excuse to boot that many, and I'm giving them the excuse. They called me out to drill a squad today. I don't think I did too badly at that, altho of course I can't compete with men who have had experience at it.

We might get bounced this week, but I doubt it. The following, i.e. the tenth week, is when the ax is apt to fall. Mann graduated Friday. They cut two men out of his class when they had only three more hours of school to go. Wouldn't that be heartbreaking? At least I'm fully prepared for any eventuality and am expecting the worst. I sure wish the Air Corps had had some rifles when I was taking basic. . . .

When I went before the sub-board [which he had done a week earlier and was required of all candidates] they just asked me a few questions about civilian experience in leadership, and what I had read. Unfortunately I started back too far and mentioned "Anthony Adverse" [a 1933 historical adventure novel popular during the Great Depression]. A member of the board started to question me about the book and I had to admit that I didn't have the slightest recollection about it. It's been eight or nine years since I read it, of course, and I really don't remember it at all. Then they asked me to assume that the board was a squad of recruits, & to explain "right face" to it. My explanation apparently left something to be desired. Oh yes, when I entered the room for the interview I proceeded to salute the wrong officer, which wasn't too good a start. . . .

While I believe my chances are remote, I'm going to keep plugging away, for I want to feel that I made an effort at any rate. I've been getting good grades on the tests. Tomorrow I think I'll draw a rifle if they'll let me & work on my worst weakness, although I think too much harm is already done. Maybe the J.A.G. will come along and save me the embarrassment of getting thrown out. Fat chance! . . .

Well, I guess I've given you all the bad news I can in one dose.

Bill's reference to his JAG application proved eerily prescient. On April 5, nine days after predicting he would get "the bounce," Bill wrote home with a different tale. The school's commanding officer had just informed him that, after months of delay, his JAG application had been approved in Washington, D.C., which meant that Bill – if he chose – could be "reprocessed" to enter that legal unit of the military. The commander had cautioned, however, that there would be more "red tape," with Bill required to appear before a special board of officers, get its recommendation, and take a new physical examination. With only fourteen days of class remaining, the commander had urged

Bill to finish the OCS course, assuring him – in Bill's retelling – that "there wasn't a chance in a hundred of my not graduating." Heartened by those words, Bill nonetheless expressed concern that he might yet wash out. He also worried that the JAG opportunity would be lost if he delayed accepting it. As he explained to his parents: "I told him [the commander] that if I ever got a commission in the C.M.P [Corps of Military Police] I thought I'd prefer to stay there, and this seemed to please him mightily. . . . He did allow tho, that if I got the ax he could get my J.A.G. application reinstated without any trouble, & I could then go ahead with it."

Deciding to finish what he started, Bill remained at Fort Custer and prepared for final exams. Two days later, on April 7, he wrote home that he still felt "plenty shaky" as to his chance of graduating, despite what the commander had said. On April 14, with only a week to go, he remained jittery: "Obviously they will not kick many out from here on. I doubt if more than two more. But I may be one of them, so keep your fingers crossed!" And on Sunday, April 18, as he began a long and lonesome stretch of guard duty lasting from noon until 7 a.m. Monday, he informed his parents that "this 'War of nerves' can't last much longer . . . So far as the Officers are concerned, they have pretty much relieved the pressure and you'd think everything was all set if you didn't know from past classes that someone usually gets it right down at the end of the trail."

He continued:

The story has got out in my barracks that some officer told someone that I stood number one in grades in the class. I regret it, because I know it isn't true. In fact I've worried considerably about a tactics examination I'm afraid I flunked. It covered lots of hours. It isn't that I need the points to be eligible to graduate, but about my sole recommendation for graduating has been good grades, and that might be just the thing that could eliminate me at this late stage. Well, time will tell.

The graduating party is Wednesday night [April 21]. A steak dinner and 4 ½ kegs of beer is on the program. Sounds good, doesn't it? Yesterday we had our picture taken for officer's identification cards. We've signed papers cutting off our allotments for insurance and everything. Thursday they are to pay us and Friday pay us the $250.00 clothing allowance. I didn't get a coat & don't think I will right away. I did buy a rain coat at the PX this morning. So far I have spent just about half of the clothing allowance.

There are only three days of school left. It will be all over Wednesday night at 5 PM. Well, I guess this is about all. The news in the making this week will either be awfully good or awfully bad. I'll try to let you know as soon as possible if anything disastrous happens.

Love, Bill

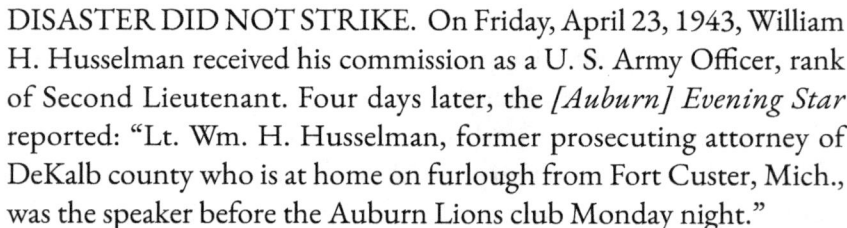

DISASTER DID NOT STRIKE. On Friday, April 23, 1943, William H. Husselman received his commission as a U. S. Army Officer, rank of Second Lieutenant. Four days later, the *[Auburn] Evening Star* reported: "Lt. Wm. H. Husselman, former prosecuting attorney of DeKalb county who is at home on furlough from Fort Custer, Mich., was the speaker before the Auburn Lions club Monday night."

Whatever nuggets or useful bits of information the former club president-turned-soldier shared with the hometown crowd, he was not pinched for material. He had worn his country's uniform for a year, experienced military life on five stateside bases, managed to move up and into the officer ranks, and was primed to ship overseas. But his shipping date?

Still unknown.

Chapter Five
MARY: 1910 - 1943

*A*UBURN, INDIANA
MARCH 12, 1943

Miss Mary Brandon,
You are hereby notified that the Auburn board of school trustees will employ you as teacher in the Auburn schools for the 1943-44 school year at a salary of $1,633.00.
Salary proposals are subject to whatever regulations may be established by state and federal governments.
Please let the board have your decision in writing on or before April 22nd. An early reply will help to reduce the year end rush of office work.
Yours truly,
H. L. McKenney
Superintendent

WHILE BILL HUSSELMAN WAS WORKING doggedly in March 1943 to earn his military commission, Mary Elizabeth Brandon – ninety miles removed from Fort Custer in her hometown of Auburn – reviewed a letter from her school superintendent and set it aside. The job offer, on its face, was fine, and Mary had ample time to reply. Her greater concern that spring was how to proceed with life. On that matter, clarity eluded her.

She was not one to deny the obvious. In a tight-knit community where many of her friends were already married, Mary, who would turn thirty-three at year's end, still lived with her aging parents, as she had since her college graduation a decade earlier. Her romance with a high school coach had failed to pan out. And with potential suitors heading off to war, she understood that her prospects for finding suitable male companions, not to mention a husband, were shrinking. In appearance and personality, she hardly fit the Victorian stereotype of an "old maid." But still, the clock was ticking.

Coupled with that reality was Mary's wavering commitment to teaching. Though she had trained for a career in education and had notched six years as an instructor, she increasingly wondered how coaxing grade-schoolers to sing on key or coaching high-schoolers to harmonize could, in a time of war, still invigorate and challenge her. Moreover, patriotic questions – namely, how *best* to serve the country – weighed heavily on her mind. Should she work for victory by staying at her home-front job, a teacher-soldier fighting for the next generation? Or should she, as many women were doing, take a higher-paying job in a factory to produce military equipment and other necessities for battle? To the latter, she said no; factory work had no appeal. But were there other options – a chance, as she would later say, to start out into the "unknown"? Intelligent and self-aware, Mary knew she had to find answers.

Her upbringing gave her confidence to confront difficult questions. Born on Dec. 29, 1910, Mary was the fourth child of Winnie and Orin "Ora" Brandon. The couple's first, Russell, was born in 1892, followed in 1897 by another son, Charles, and in 1899 by a daughter, Anne. In 1903, the family suffered a painful loss when Russell died from tetanus after stepping on a rusty nail. Mary's arrival seven years later came as Ora was about to turn forty-five and Winnie was approaching forty. No more children followed.

Adored by her parents and doted on by her siblings, Mary grew up in a large two-story home at 210 East Fifth Street, two blocks north of Auburn's courthouse square. A skilled carpenter, Ora built the home, one of many fine residences and buildings that he and a partner erected in DeKalb County in the 1890s and early 1900s. In 1903, Ora bought and managed a lumberyard a few blocks west of the family residence and, as a child, Mary often went there to play. Years later she could still recall how the stacked wood was "so fragrant, especially the cedar shingles," and how one of the sheds had a "pump with a tin cup on a string that everyone used." The cup users, in her telling, "were all pretty healthy [because] no one caught colds."

Active in civic affairs, Ora – born in 1866 and raised on a farm west of Auburn – served on the town board before city incorporation in 1900 and on the city council from 1902 to 1904. As a councilman, he supported public improvements such as Auburn's first paved streets, and his business leadership helped foster the dynamic growth the community soon experienced. His civic resume also included a three-year stint as chief of the volunteer fire company. When a history of DeKalb County was published in 1914, Ora was declared to be one of Auburn's "highly esteemed men" and lauded as a "broad-minded, upright and charitable citizen."

Mary's mother, Winnie, was also from Auburn. Born in 1871, Winnie grew up in a stately brick Italianate home on North Cedar Street, adjacent to where Ora would later erect their East Fifth Street residence. Winnie's father Frederick Raut – a harness and a bootmaker who built the brick house – died at an early age in 1875, leaving his widow, Mary Ashleman Raut, to raise Winnie and a younger brother. Helping the family through lean times was Mary Raut's sister, Barbara, whose carriage-making husband, Charles Eckhart, would eventually amass great wealth and become Auburn's leading benefactor.

Winnie, left, with her aunt, Barbara, and her uncle, Charles Eckhart, Auburn businessman and philanthropist.

Grateful for the generosity of others, young Winnie nonetheless did her part to keep the family financially afloat. She quit high school after one year to work as a seamstress, sometimes moving into people's homes to sew entire wardrobes. In April 1891, just shy of her twentieth birthday, Winnie wed Ora, who was newly established in his carpenter trade and who likely considered himself a lucky groom. As the local newspaper reported, Ora's "bride is one of the handsomest, companionable and refined of our young ladies."

(Clockwise) Mary's childhood home on East Fifth Street as it appears today. Her parents, Ora and Winnie Brandon, on their wedding day in 1891. Her brother Charles, older than Mary by thirteen years. Mary as an infant, seated on her sister Annie's lap.

Attractiveness ran in the family, and "handsome" described Charles, the brother Mary grew up knowing mostly in absentia. She was four when Charles graduated in 1915 from Auburn High School, after which he continued his education at Mercersburg Academy in Pennsylvania and then at Princeton University, where he earned his degree in 1920. Despite long absences from Auburn, Charles stayed in touch with his little sister by sending her tenderly-worded letters and charming gifts.

When "Brother," as the family referred to Charles, considered it his duty in 1917 to fight in World War I, he wrote home that spring requesting his parents' permission to join the army. Winnie and Ora urged him to wait a year, with a distraught Winnie telling him, in a letter never mailed, that "I nearly drowned in tears at the [thought] of your going to France." Sparing his mother more tears, Charles delayed enlisting until the summer of 1918. The war's end several months later meant his military service was short-lived, much to his family's relief.

While Mary knew Charles largely through letters and holiday visits, that wasn't the case with her sister, Anne, older by eleven years. The two formed a tight bond, and, as gleaned from a diary Anne kept from 1916 to 1920, big sister babysat Mary when she was sick, took her to "picture shows," and let her tag along on frequent trips to the library. When many Americans began knitting socks for overseas troops in World War I, Anne contributed to that cause and then made time for another: She knitted a scarf and a sweater for her little sister.

How much the attention and ministrations of Anne, known to the family as Annie, influenced Mary's outlook on life is not known. But two of Annie's diary entries from 1918 convey the same restlessness that Mary herself would express at the start of World War II. "I'd like to go [to war] if I had no parents and try & help do a little something. I'm sure they could find something for me," wrote Annie in March of that year. In an entry a few weeks earlier, Annie – age eighteen at the time – noted that an acquaintance had passed an exam for government war work and was employed in Washington, D.C. "That's what I want to do," Annie wrote.

In the fall of 1918, Mary's status at home shifted. Annie enrolled at Indiana University in Bloomington, her youthful yearnings about finding wartime work in the nation's capital yielding to more schooling. Mary, now the main focus of her parents' attention, went about her childhood days in predictable ways – attending Riley and later Harrison grade schools, receiving sewing and other homemaking instruction from Winnie, and enjoying the company of Ora. He continued to welcome her lumberyard visits, just as she delighted in playing cards with him at home.

As Mary readied for junior high school, her good marks earned her early promotion to the seventh grade, where she met Bill Husselman, "a shy, polite boy" with whom she became friends. Years later, Mary recalled a class outing in which the seventh-graders rode in a horse-drawn sleigh to a farm that Bill's family owned east of town. "The sky was bright with stars and the snow squeaked as the old sleigh pulled us through the wintry night," she would write in her memoir years later. That memoir singled out Bill's mother for special mention: Blanche treated everyone to hot chocolate.

By the time Mary entered Auburn High School, her outgoing personality and musical talents guaranteed her a busy social life. Her clear soprano voice earned her starring roles in the annual operettas and made her a valued member of the Glee Club, the Contest Chorus, and, in her senior year, the newly organized Pep Squad. According to the 1928 school yearbook, she rehearsed the squad every day for a week so students would know the pep songs and sing "with real spirit."

Mary's 1928 senior photo

Meanwhile, as a class officer and a club-joiner, Mary often crossed paths with Bill, who remained as she had known him since seventh-grade – serious and courtly-mannered. The two continued to be friends, though at a respectful distance. Bill dated one of Mary's closest friends, Opal Knott, while Mary – with her striking blue-gray eyes and ready smile – enjoyed the attention of numerous beaus. The yearbook caption accompanying her senior photo said as much: "Her smiles, her speech, her winning way, wiles the young men's moods away."

BENT ON STUDYING MUSIC, Mary headed in the fall of 1928 to DePauw University, a Methodist-founded liberal arts college in Greencastle, Indiana, about two hundred miles southwest of Auburn in the state's rural midsection. She arrived on DePauw's picturesque campus as the nation pulsed with "Jazz Age" exuberance and as young people everywhere reveled in new freedoms and fads.

Fully in step with her generation, Mary shortened her skirts and kept her hair bobbed. As a member of Kappa Alpha Theta sorority, she also partied with fraternity men, learned to smoke cigarettes in haze-filled "frat" basements, and enthusiastically took to the dance floor. Like many of her fellow students, she was grateful that DePauw's new churchman president, the Rev. G. Bromley Oxnam, had decreed campus dancing permissible.

Mary with her Kappa Alpha Theta sorority sisters in 1929. She is second from right, back row.

Though devoted to having fun, Mary attended to her studies and acquitted herself well in the classroom. She also honed her vocal skills by giving recitals, performing in campus opera productions, and singing classical and sacred music in the renowned University Choir, heralded in 1931 by *The New York Times* as the best in the Midwest. Recognizing Mary's busy schedule, Winnie lent "domestic" help. Whenever Mary dispatched dirty clothes to Auburn by interurban railcar, Winnie dutifully returned the garments, freshly laundered.

In June 1932, as the Great Depression tightened its grip on the nation, Mary left DePauw with her bachelor's degree in hand and with Ora breathing a sigh of relief. He would have been unable, he had informed her, to afford another year's tuition. With no offers to teach and no other options, Mary resumed living with her parents at their home on East Fifth Street. Upon the death of Mary's grandmother a year later, the three Brandons moved next door into Winnie's childhood home at the corner of Fifth and Cedar streets. That 1870s-era brick residence – the "homestead" – remains in the family today.

Cedar Street "homestead." Directly behind it is Mary's childhood home. (Willennar Genealogy Center)

The community to which Mary returned in 1932 had weathered the Depression better than many towns and cities. In 1931, the Auburn Automobile Company – the town's leading employer and maker of Auburn, Cord, and Duesenberg cars – had its best year, selling more than 33,000 stylish and well-engineered vehicles and earning a rank of thirteenth among top U.S. auto manufacturers. (Winnie's relatives, the Eckhart family, no longer owned the business, having sold it to Chicago investors more than a decade earlier.) But brisk sales in 1931 did not enable the auto company to withstand worsening economic forces. By 1937 the firm was bankrupt, and other Auburn businesses also struggled to pay bills, as did so many jobless families. The Brandons, though not wealthy, were fortunate. Ora kept the lumberyard open, Mary found work in the county clerk's office in 1934, and Winnie managed expenses well enough to preserve what she treasured – the "homestead."

To lift her spirits during that dispiriting decade, Mary indulged her love for the arts. She performed in local plays, organized a new junior literary club named the Kenwigs, established a chapter of the National Junior Shakespeare Club, and sang in area churches, among them her home church, Auburn Methodist. As she had since her girlhood, she also played cards with family and friends, eventually graduating to poker, albeit penny ante.

If conversation ever lagged at card tables during those fraught times, two stories could be counted on to enliven discussion. In 1933, a year after Mary returned to town, members of outlaw John Dillinger's gang raided the Auburn police station, locked two officers into a jail cell, and made off with the department's entire arsenal, a heist that was part of Dillinger's yearlong crime spree that terrorized the Midwest. A year later, Auburn High School track star Don Lash enrolled at Indiana University and began dominating American distance running, eventually racking up twelve national titles and setting a world's record for the two-mile run.

In 1936, Lash competed in the Summer Olympics, and though his performance in Berlin, Germany was less than spectacular, the same could not be said for his teammate Jesse Owens. The African-American track and field sensation dazzled the world by winning four gold medals and embarrassing Hitler, who had hoped his country's prized athletes would garner all the attention.

Meanwhile, the Nazi dictator was fast gaining attention himself. The world watched as he accumulated power, rearmed Germany, brutalized minorities, and moved ahead with plans – murderous plans that people in Auburn and elsewhere would have to reckon with soon.

IN THE SUMMER OF 1937, Mary's long wait for a teaching job finally ended. Hired as music supervisor in Auburn's schools, she soon was instructing students in grades one through twelve and introducing them to everything from notes on the musical scale to the works of famous composers.

In the elementary schools, her teaching method included walking up and down the classroom aisles and pausing at each child's desk. "She'd bend her head low and listen to you sing from a little music book," recalled a former student, Nancy Western [Derrow]. Another former grade-schooler remembered "Miss Brandon" less for her methods and more for her kindness. "I was fat and cross-eyed, and she liked me just as I was," said Joyce Rohm [Springer], grateful for the attention of a teacher who was "so pretty and smelled good."

At the high school, Mary's duties were predictable; she directed two choirs (one for girls, one for boys) and oversaw the annual operettas. She and the band director also organized spring festivals that attracted townsfolk en masse. For her efforts, Mary earned plaudits. The 1938 *Follies* yearbook declared: "Miss Brandon has built the [Glee Club] girls' voices into a beautiful piece of sweet harmony and deep, rich color tones." The newspaper also piled on praise. The *[Auburn] Evening Star* headlined in 1939 that Mary's direction of the operetta *The Chimes of Normandy* was "One of the Best Productions Ever Staged by High School Students." On other occasions and in subsequent years, both the newspaper and yearbook used words such as "splendid" when commenting on her work.

1939 Auburn High School yearbook photo of the social science/fine arts faculty. Mary is second from left, Berns is second from right.

During Mary's second year of teaching (1938-39), she began dating the newly hired high school history instructor and boys' basketball coach, Herman Berns. As Berns guided the Auburn Red Devils team to a regional basketball championship that winter, Mary and the coach glided into a relationship that moved from casual to serious. Berns's rugged good looks and athletic build undoubtedly factored into Mary's attraction to him. Standing six feet five inches, Berns was described in the 1939 yearbook as "tall, dark, and handsome."

At the end of that school year, Mary headed to Northwestern University in Evanston, Illinois to take classes toward her master's degree. Back home by the fall, she and Berns resumed spending time together, "making no secret of their attraction to each other," recalled a Brandon family friend, Donald Mefford. At some point in the courtship, the couple traveled to St. Louis to meet Mary's brother Charles, who by then was married and had a family. At some point as well, the couple began talking about marriage.

Berns, front row, seated with Mary's family and friends at Brandon home, date unknown. Mary is second row, left. Her mother Winnie is third from left; her father Ora is far right.

Mary confirmed years later to a family member that she and Berns had planned to wed, and close friends at the time spoke of their engagement. Yet no formal announcement ever took place. Moreover, for reasons unclear, the relationship cooled – and then ended. In late May 1940, after only two years in Auburn, Berns accepted a job coaching basketball at Wabash College in Crawfordsville, Indiana, where he had played both basketball and football. A year later, in June 1941, he left Wabash to join the Army. Assuming either Mary or Berns had hoped to revive their romance, the Japanese attack on Pearl Harbor six months later all but guaranteed no immediate revival.

Interestingly, Mary's brother had expressed relief when learning about the couple's break-up. Charles had remained protective of his little sister, and – as recalled by his daughter, Elizabeth Brandon O'Herin, who had been present when Mary and Berns visited their St. Louis home – "Brother" didn't think the match was right.

WITH PATRIOTIC FEVER running high after Pearl Harbor, Mary sought an altogether different match in 1942, one that fit the times and aligned her skills with the nation's war needs. She already had loose ties to the American Red Cross, having worked briefly for the local chapter in 1934 to compile dental survey records. After the Japanese attack and amid nationwide calls for surgical dressings, Mary reengaged with the organization and headed to community workrooms to cut cotton and roll gauze. By December 1942, she and other volunteers literally had their hands full; the need for surgical bandages had grown so great that the DeKalb County chapter was asked to prepare 47,700 dressings in a single month. As needs kept rising in lockstep with mounting war casualties, Mary did more than wield scissors; she became a workroom instructor.

Meanwhile, unlike in the First World War, when the Red Cross maintained its own nursing corps abroad, the military had decided by World War II that it would take responsibility for all medical care of troops on foreign soil. Thus, the Red Cross – still desiring to do substantive work outside the United States – reached a new agreement with the War Department. To the exclusion of the Y.M.C.A. and other civilian relief organizations, the Red Cross was granted sole authority to operate recreation clubs and rest centers in theaters of war. Moreover, its staff was similarly authorized to work directly with military personnel.

Embracing its new mission, the Red Cross moved swiftly to recruit women for overseas postings. In a carefully crafted campaign designed to attract bright and mature candidates, the organization said applicants had to be single, college graduates, and at least twenty-five years old. Along with submitting reference letters and passing a physical examination, they also had to do well in a personal interview. For every six Red Cross applicants, only one was selected – an acceptance rate that conferred cachet on those making the cut. Moreover, in the minds of many American women at the time, getting to serve in the Red Cross was superior to volunteering for military service in the WACs (Women's Army Corps) or WAVES (Women Accepted for Volunteer Emergency Service), where secretarial or clerical work was often the norm and where assignments typically were at home, not overseas.

WWII recruitment poster (National Archives)

The Red Cross's recruitment campaign was not lost on women such as Mary. Neither was it easy for her and others to miss the posters, newsreels, and magazine articles that portrayed female Red Cross volunteers working meaningfully on behalf of troops. As early as September 1942, the cover illustration for the popular *Saturday Evening Post* showed a young woman in her military-style Red Cross uniform looking askance at a store window, where elegant gloves, a bright red scarf, and a fashionable lady's hat were on display. The message was clear: Red Cross women had no time for trivial matters; the troops needed them.

It was against this backdrop that Mary began entertaining thoughts of working full time for the organization. Offering encouragement was her friend, Ruth Messenger, the county chairman for surgical dressings who had visited the Red Cross's national headquarters in Washington, D.C., and returned with information about the application process. As Mary inched closer to applying in the spring of 1943, she had more than herself to consider. Her father, Ora, then in his seventies, had suffered a stroke in the late 1930s, requiring him to walk with a crutch or a cane. Winnie, also in her seventies and a long-time headache sufferer, required frequent bedrest.

Yet the couple, their frailties aside, approved of Mary's eventual decision, no doubt aware that families everywhere were making sacrifices. Moreover, they could lean on Annie for help. After obtaining her teaching credentials, Annie had returned to Auburn and briefly taught school before resigning in 1924 to marry George Olinger, who managed the lumberyard upon Ora's retirement. Annie had given her parents the added joy of a grandchild, a school-aged boy named Buddy whom she and George had adopted.

George, Buddy, and Annie

Though Annie's immediate reaction to Mary's news isn't known, she had always been supportive of her younger sister. Annie also may have remembered her own youthful dreams of wanting to serve her country. In any case, Mary moved forward. She filled out the required Red Cross paperwork, submitted reference letters, and took – and passed – the medical exam.

In late June, with school on summer recess, Mary headed to Washington, D. C., for the final step – the personal interview. She cleared that hurdle, helped undoubtedly by her poise, and by early July the news was official: She was to be a paid staff member assigned to overseas duty, with her training to begin in Washington within weeks. In early July, too, Mary received Red Cross authorization to buy, amid war rationing, four pairs of footwear suitable for her new line of work.

Securing supplies as well as shoes, Mary spent her remaining time at home rummaging through drawers and closets, trying to decide what to pack. Should she take the brown plaid gingham dress or the seersucker? Might she need the tan suit coat? What about her black corded purse? As time grew short, relatives and neighbors stopped by to say how much they would miss her. One longtime friend, Edith Baker, dropped off a crayon-colored handmade booklet filled with whimsical advice on how, among other things, to behave around soldiers. At the booklet's conclusion, Edith wished Mary luck, sketched an American flag, and then, riffing on a familiar adage, pasted together words that read: "Red Cross Asks So Little . . . and Gives So Much."

Departure day dawned on Friday, July 30. At the appointed time, Mary traveled to the neighboring town of Garrett, said goodbye to the Mefford family who showed up to bid her one last farewell, and boarded an eastbound Baltimore & Ohio train. Three days later, she penned a lengthy letter home, reporting her train ride had been uneventful, summarizing the Red Cross instruction she was about to receive, and offering reassurances – specifically to her mother – that "I am going to be fine."

Mary's sign-off to Winnie then cut to the chase: "Would you send the Seersucker dress[?]"

Chapter Six

MARY: 1943

1 *724 WEBSTER ST. N.W.*
Washington, DC
Monday Night [August 2, 1943]

Dearest Mother & Dad & Anne and anyone else that's interested –
I'm sitting on the edge of my cot writing this to you on my knees as most of my letters will probably be written from now on. I believe I'm being fairly well initiated for I'm in a house with 10 other girls. There is an overflow at the University so the Red Cross has rented this house. It belongs to a private individual who lives downstairs and acts as a chaperon etc. I've only talked to her a few minutes so don't know much about her.

I've been pressing my dresses as well as doing an ironing and some pressing for some girls who are leaving tomorrow for their assignments. They have been here in Washington for 4 weeks before being sent out. We were told today that our school lasts for two weeks. Classes begin at 10 in the morning and finish at 5....

We have a regular schedule with hour classes. Tomorrow these are the following subjects. History of Red Cross, Organization of Red Cross, Survey of Red Cross Chapters, Services to the Armed Forces, etc. Each day is different but I won't go into that now. It all seems very much like being back in College again – what with Registration this morning and these girls here at the House....

If this whole letter sounds incoherent it's because so many people are talking and walking about in front of me....

THE WASHINGTON, D.C., IN WHICH MARY BRANDON found herself that summer of 1943 bore unmistakable signs of a city transformed by war. Antiaircraft guns sat atop government buildings to protect the White House, the Washington Monument and other symbolic targets. Within the White House, blackout curtains draped windows, gas masks lay folded in rooms, and a new underground air-raid shelter awaited occupants. Elsewhere, the Library of Congress had shipped valuable items to Fort Knox, Kentucky for safekeeping. The Capitol dome, normally lit at night, had gone dark. And the Mall had surrendered its open space to temporary office buildings, into which throngs of defense workers poured.

To say workers flooded the city was an understatement. Roughly 663,000 residents called Washington home in 1940. By March 1943, the Census Bureau estimated that number had jumped to 833,720, and more people kept coming – at a rate of 10,000 a month. Not surprisingly, the newcomers overwhelmed available housing, causing authorities to pressure homeowners to take in boarders, prompting apartment dwellers to share cramped quarters with strangers, and giving rise to makeshift trailer parks on vacant lots. Along the Potomac River, houseboat colonies multiplied. Washington's housing crisis was so pronounced that Hollywood producers mined it for humor, releasing a batch of no-place-to-live comedies such as *The More the Merrier* (1943) and *Standing Room Only* (1944). As early as January 1943, *Life* magazine had issued its own tongue-in-cheek warning: "If the war lasts much longer, Washington is going to bust right out of its pants."

Fresh off the train from Indiana, Mary set foot in the bustling capital at the very end of July. As one more newcomer squeezing into the city's metaphorically tight pants, she spent the weekend of July 31-August 1 visiting the Lincoln Memorial and other must-see landmarks, joined by vacationing friends from Auburn. On Monday, August 2, however, all sightseeing ceased. She hurried to American Red Cross National Headquarters near the White House, ready for her wartime service to begin.

Red Cross headquarters
(Photo by author)

The headquarters visit was brief. Months earlier, the Red Cross, in need of classrooms and lecture halls for its ever-expanding training program, had rented space from American University in the District of Columbia's northwest quadrant. Other government and military agencies, similarly pressed for space, also leased facilities on the wooded campus, including the U.S. Navy to operate a Bomb Disposal School. The university continued to serve civilian students, especially female undergraduates hoping to finish their degrees. But by then, most male students had left for military service, a disruption experienced by colleges nationwide. As for Mary that August morning, she registered at headquarters, then proceeded directly to the university where she located the imposing, white-marbled Hurst Hall, its corridors and classrooms flush with Red Cross trainees and staff.

Built in the 1890s, Hurst Hall as it appears today (Photo by author)

Mary would spend her daytime hours in that campus building, but the Red Cross – as her August 2 letter noted – had assigned her lodging on Webster Street, in a well-kept neighborhood three miles from the university. The large and lushly forested Rock Creek Park, where former President Theodore Roosevelt famously clambered up sheer stone walls, separated the neighborhood from campus and complicated Mary's route to class. Even so, Mary took her hourlong commute in stride, telling her parents matter-of-factly: "[I] have to take first a bus, then a streetcar, and transfer onto a bus again."

Like most everything in wartime Washington, the Webster Street home, a two-story 1920s-era brick dwelling, was congested. Filled with Red Cross trainees coming and going, the place pulsed with hustle-and-bustle, much of it reminding Mary of her college sorority days. Though cramped and noisy, the house boasted a feature that Mary found immediately appealing: a sleeping porch. She shared it with two other roommates and declared on August 3, after her first night's slumber there, that it was "very cool and comfortable." Not so comfortable that month was Washington's sweltering daytime heat and clinging humidity, prompting Mary – in that same letter and on the heels of asking for her seersucker dress – to issue a second apparel request: "A cotton dress lasts just about one day so will you please send every cotton thing I have. The brown plaid gingham will need washing – apparently it doesn't matter what one wears in Washington – one sees all kinds of clothes. So if my dresses are old it won't matter." To that wish list, Mary added, "Would you send my boots, I forgot them."

Webster Street home where Mary boarded (Photo by author)

Meanwhile, Mary's Red Cross training in the ensuing days proved demanding, due largely to accelerating wartime needs for overseas workers. Instead of putting students through a six-week "basic training" program, as earlier had been the case, the Red Cross by 1943 had compressed instruction to two weeks. Every Monday a new class entered the program; every Saturday a class graduated. The schedule left students with little free time, which Mary underscored when she wrote home at week's end.

Friday, Aug. 6, 1943
Dearest Anne, George and Bud –
This is about the third letter I've started to you but have never found the time to finish. I hope this one gets off to Auburn Ind. We, of course, are terribly busy. We leave the house quite early in the morning and don't get home until after dinner at night. Last night the stores down town were open so there was a grand rush to do the pick-up odds and ends of shopping. I thought I had finished but I found there were many things I still needed. . . . I have bought more lisle hose, an Army Musette Bag (we

must have this for on board ship), an Army knife, shower shoes, a Toilet apron, cotton gloves, jersey slips, etc. I'm going to have to send home some of the clothes I had planned to take. I've been wearing one pair of my new shoes because they are so comfortable. Washington is so hot that my feet have felt twice as big as usual. Last night was our first cool night. One feels all the time as if one is in a steam bath. Perspiration drips off my face and that's never happened to me before.

Our classes have been very interesting. Today we have had lectures and moving pictures on Military organization and Military Courtesy. We have also been very thoroughly warned on keeping our mouths tightly shut so don't expect me to be able to tell you when I am even thinking of leaving the country, however that may not be for some time. This afternoon we had a Doctor talk to us about our Health on the Job – what to expect from our immunization shots which I begin having tomorrow. Already I feel as if I had learned and saturated a great deal [of] information but next week the classes will be more intensified, I've heard we are even going to get a few lessons in Jitter Bugging which probably won't come amiss.

The two girls in the house with whom I've been palling around are very nice. One, however, shouldn't get too set in friendships here for after next week I may not see these two particular girls again. Next Saturday we are to graduate (very soon, don't you think) [and] on Monday, the 16th, we are to be cleared and sent out for our various assignments. Some of the girls are kept here in Washington in U.S.O. Clubs, some are helping out at the University while others are sent outside the city. Whatever – it will be interesting I'm sure.

Our classes are over at 1:00 P.M. tomorrow [Saturday] so I'm going out to Alexandria for the week-end. I feel already a veteran on this bus and trolley riding. I believe that I'll be able to make it across town and into Virginia alright. . . . I must write Mother so must stop – There is so much to tell you but such a little time to do it in. Will try again next week but in the mean time would like to be hearing from all of you. I'll try to tell Mother other things so if you would like to have her read this perhaps she could read yours.

As promised, Mary wrote that same day to her parents, piggybacking on news she had shared with Annie's family. In both letters, Mary referenced the immunization shots she was scheduled to receive the next day across the Potomac River in Arlington, Virginia – at the immense and newly completed Pentagon.

Aug 6, 1943
Dearest Mother and Dad,
It doesn't seem possible that it has been a week since I left. Time has gone so fast but we have been having such an intensified course that it seems as if I have been in school at least 6 weeks.

I've just written Anne and George and will try to tell you [some] different things so just consider this as a continuation of the other. I hope you can all get together on the little bits of news I'm able to write.

Speaking of news – Today was the first I had read a paper since last Saturday and I've not heard a bit of Radio news since I arrived. Here I am in the nation's capital and should try, at least to find out a little what is going on but I haven't the time. They say if we think we are busy now we don't know the half of what it will be overseas. . . .

As usual, I'm having lots of fun eating. I'll probably get as fat as I did at Northwestern – but I figure I'd better eat well here for overseas it may not be so delicious. Food is surprisingly cheap. We are allowed $2.50 a day for meals which is usually ample unless we splurge a little. We hand in a Voucher sheet, the same as I made out for my interview trip and hand it in twice a month – this is then paid to us in addition to our salary. We have been learning the many parts of Red Cross and I can sincerely say that I'm very proud to be working for such a wonderful organization. They certainly take wonderful care and consideration for all of their workers. Along with the Insurance they give us we will come under Army Regulation for Hospitalization when overseas. We will be given the same consideration as Officers in the Army if we need Medical care. They have tried to make us feel that we are working for the American people for they are the Red Cross. Everyone who has lectured to us have been so sincere and enthusiastic about their work.

Those of us who are to have our shots tomorrow morning are to be excused from the [first] test but I feel that I should read the material anyway – so I'd better stop and get busy.

Before I do stop however I've learned that they have stopped hiring Staff Assistants (which I am) so I feel lucky to have gotten in just in time. There are 182 in our class but not all of these are Staff Assistants, in fact only 45 of us. The others are Field Directors (men) and Hospital and Recreation Workers. Most of these are for Domestic hospitals.

Wednesday night after dinner we found the Club which is run by the girls getting their experience in Washington. It is for Red Cross Workers themselves and gives the others pointers in running the Clubs. It is called the Embassy Club because before the last War [it] was the Russian Embassy. Of course, it is a fascinating looking old house. The girls were very sweet and gracious to us. I simply must stop. Will write again later.

Upon getting her immunization shots on Saturday, August 7, Mary – already across the Potomac – proceeded into neighboring Alexandria, Virginia, where she enjoyed a leisurely weekend visit with a former teaching colleague, Dorothy Groscop Tuttle. Dorothy had moved to the area to be with husband, Jim, stationed at nearby Fort Belvoir. On Monday, having returned to Washington, Mary received and immediately responded to her first mail from Auburn, telling her parents: "I've just read your nice letter and I can't tell you how I've looked forward to having it. I did shed a few tears, though, because I know what nice people you both are and what a lot I had to give up to come away from you." Tender as that expression was, Mary hastened to add: "The homesickness that I was sure I would feel hasn't had a chance to hit me yet. I've been much too busy."

"Busyness" became a recurring theme in Mary's letters. She returned to it when writing Annie's family several days later, though she first expressed appreciation for homemade treats. She closed by thanking her sister for sending more wardrobe necessities.

Wednesday, August 11, 1943
Dear Annie, George and Buddy,
Since I'm not going to have time tonight for a letter to Mother and Dad, would you let them consider this letter for them, too?

First, Annie, let me tell you how much we have all enjoyed the cookies and [fudge] candy. Probably the cookies were a little more successful than the candy because that is all one big piece of syrup in the bottom of the box. Washington weather was never made for home-made candy – that, however, doesn't stop us from eating it. We all dip in with our fingers and enjoy it just as much.

We're still being very busy with our work – but a little more practical, I think. We begin at 8:30 in the morning but are finished at 3:00 P.M. This morning we did some square dancing and this afternoon we had a lecture on Recreation on the Convoy. Yesterday we had movies on clubs in Iceland and Australia, besides playing Ping Pong and Badminton. Part of the afternoon we spent, believe it or not, George, playing Black Jack and Poker. I didn't need any instruction on the two latter, so I <u>gave it</u>. You see, Mother, my Sunday afternoons and evenings of last winter will stand me in good stead. After all, they want us to know the things the soldiers will like – and I guess, Poker is one of the favorites.

It seems as if everyday there is something else we need to get to finish our shopping. I went to the dime store to buy a flat iron. They say there is really no point in taking the electric one. We're supposed to live in our slacks on the boat so if I get in a warm climate I'll be pretty uncomfortable in the flannel ones – therefore I'm going to buy some Blue Jeans – like Bud's. They'll be comfortable and cheap. . . .

The two girls here that I like particularly and with whom I eat my meals, do shopping etc. are Sally Davis, a cute little black curly headed girl from Wilkes Barre, Pa, who was a Red Cross Staff worker before she came here and Barbara Drake, from Boston, Mass. Barbara is a little older, a Vassar girl and taught at a Teachers' College in Mass. before coming here. Both are swell people and I like knowing them so much.

Thank you, too, Annie for my clothes. It surely seems good to have a change.

As Ever, Mary

The next day, August 12, Mary wrote again.
Dearest Mother & Dad –
Well, things have been going along pretty smoothly. I haven't much more to report since the letter yesterday which I sent to Anne and George but meant to include you all. Today we learned to play on some little Musical instruments called "Tonettes" – very simple and rather fun to play – rather like little flutes. The rest of the morning and all afternoon we've been learning the kind of foods that Red Cross packs in their Prisoner of War packages – also, the different army rations which are used both in the camps and while on duty in the field. These field rations are very interesting and extremely concentrated. Into a small package

smaller than a shoe box is stowed enough food to last for a week with 3000 calories a day for one man. We opened a can about the size of the small fruit cans I bought for you before I left, which contained the breakfast for one man. These rations were used at Guadalcanal, they said – it contained powdered Cocoa, fruit drops and dried biscuits – I can't say they were bad, but they weren't interesting food. There were samples, too, of all the dehydrated foods; we were given recipes on how to prepare it and recipes for feeding as many as a hundred people. You see, the men will eat at "Snack Bars" in the Clubs where I hope but rather doubt that I'll be going. Mrs. Irvin, the lady downstairs, (she has taken this course and expected to be sent overseas but couldn't pass the physical examination – her husband is a Staff worker in the Red Cross offices downtown and is leaving soon for foreign duty) told us tonight that they have so many Staff Assistants they don't know what to do with them. She doesn't think we could possibly get out of here before Christmas, if then. Maybe, we'd be sitting around Washington eating our hearts out till the war is over. It all sounds very discouraging. It may be only a rumor but I had some bright expectations. . . .

Thank You, for sending my shoes and boots – however I'm going to send the shoes back. We went out to a little suburb for lunch near the University and I found a pair of unrationed play shoes and bought them. My feet were so uncomfortable in my high heeled shoes I couldn't resist them. By-the-way, I've not had any letters – I'm beginning to feel like the "Unpopularity Miss;" only yours, Anne's and Gladys' [Duguid, an Auburn teacher] have come. It seems that all I get done during the little leisure time I have is write letters but you and Anne are all I can seem to work in. . . . I do hope you are both feeling well. I miss you a lot but maybe it won't be long.

As Ever, Mary

A mere two days later, on Saturday, August 14, Mary graduated from the Red Cross basic training course, choosing to send home a printed program rather than to describe the ceremony herself. She didn't hold back, however, in discussing her celebratory weekend, which included dining at three restaurants and seeing the newly released film, *This is the Army*, an Irving Berlin musical revue whose ensemble cast featured a future U.S. president – Ronald Reagan.

As for her dining experiences, Mary took note of "colored" employees at one establishment, her language reflecting the casual racism of the times. Left unsaid in her letter was that summer's widespread racial strife. In late June, tensions in Detroit between African Americans and migrating Southern whites – in competition for war-industry jobs and housing – had boiled into street violence so severe that President Roosevelt had to send 6,000 Army troops to restore order. Unrest followed in other communities, including in New York City's Harlem, where the shooting of a black soldier by a white police officer triggered deadly rioting in early August. Aware of those incidents or not, Mary devoted her graduation weekend letter to strictly personal matters, one of which "thrilled" her.

Red Cross graduates and trainees in front of Hurst Hall. (American University Archives and Special Collections)

Sunday [August 15]
Dearest Mother & Dad – Also Anne & George,
It's good of you all to be generous with my letters because time is limited for me....
I'm being sent to Laurel, Maryland to the U.S.O. Club there. The assignment is for two weeks so if you feel inclined to write address it Laurel U.S.O. Club, Laurel, Maryland, and mail that comes here will be forwarded but I might get it quicker and I do look forward to some letters. Most of the girls are being sent together to larger clubs but I'm being a lone wolf. This is just a new Club and only one other girl has been sent before me. I heard that she did everything from jerk sodas to clean the Johns. Whatever it will be will develop into something interesting. Rather than dreading it I'm rather looking forward to it. At least, with only one girl there they can't expect too much. I was told to bring wash dresses and low-comfortable shoes. I'm to leave Tuesday morning and the town can't be far because it only takes 20 minutes to get there by train.

I've no idea what camp is there. At any rate I'll know a great deal more about it and what is expected of me in a few days and I'll certainly let you know. It's exciting to be starting out into the "unknown" and I'm thrilled rather than scared – Already something has changed in me, perhaps.

This day, for a change, is beautiful with a brisk fresh breeze. Of course, it isn't actually cool but the humidity has dropped and we don't go around wringing wet all the time. Sally, Barbara & I (they are being sent to Camp Patrick Henry in Virginia) went down to the Statler Hotel for breakfast. We had it in a room that gave us the creeps – it looked too much like a coffin – with tufted purple stuff around the walls, gray draperies and many mirrors. The waffles were even soggy.

Last night we had dinner in an old stable called "The Iron Gate" – we entered thru an alley and into the restaurant which was more comfortable because of air conditioning than the garden outside. We like going to different places for our meals. It makes them more exciting – also it makes me fatter. Friday night we were in a place with a Southern atmosphere called the Old New Orleans. A colored man with a High hat met us at the door and there was a colored Mammy in a rocking chair sitting in the window. The food was southern cooking with a New Orleans flavor which is supposed to be the best in the country. It was good, too.

After dinner we went to see "This is the Army." It had its opening here in Washington the night before at a theatre downtown with very fancy prices but we saw it at a neighborhood theatre for popular prices. Any of you reading this who might be interested shouldn't miss seeing it. It's very good. The dinner and movie was in a little way of a celebration on our "graduating" the next day. We did have a kind of ceremony as you can tell by the program I'm sending. This was after we had received our assignments.

We've all been busy putting our clothes in order and I've been re-packing my locker putting the things in only that I will need overseas, so that when the Big Day arrives I won't have to re-arrange things again. I bought a Duffle bag and some [cellophane] packets in which I've packed underwear and blouses, also my dresses I won't be needing for awhile. My winter coat I've put in the clothes Bag and all these articles are in the Duffle bag. When we are issued our Bedding Roll at the Port of

Embarkation which is simply another big bag I can transfer these things to that. I may send home the big suit-case I bought to take with me overseas because it is much too heavy to carry. I believe I'll have plenty of room for everything I own in my locker and the Bedding roll. The suitcase can then carry just the necessities for the "Ocean Voyage." Of course, this is all a long time away – but it's better to be prepared and I may not be back here for a very long length of time again. Of course, we never know, my next assignment might be back in Washington or it could be away....

I've many things to do – so had better stop this time. Thank you, Mother for filling the Snap-Shot case – could you take some more pictures with my camera and send me more. They are awfully good to look at.

Be good.

All my Love to all of You. Mary

SITUATED MIDWAY BETWEEN Washington, D.C., and Baltimore, Maryland, the small town of Laurel had long been a popular horse-racing venue. It was there, in October 1938, that a knobby-kneed thoroughbred named Seabiscuit prepped for his upcoming match with the reigning Triple Crown winner War Admiral. Two weeks later at Pimlico Race Course in Baltimore, Seabiscuit – whose unlikely rise to fame and riches had endeared him to a Depression-weary America – defied the oddsmakers, won the match by four lengths, and secured his place as a twentieth-century sports legend.

By late summer 1943, when Mary arrived on the scene, Laurel had turned into a military town, and soldiers from nearby Fort Meade – where nearly 3.5 million men would receive their World War II training – frequented the local bars, shops, and restaurants. Laurel's hangouts included a new USO (United Service Organization) club, one of hundreds of such nonprofit centers around the country where GIs could find food, dancing, and conversation. The clubs typically were managed by women of "standing" in each community and staffed by "junior hostesses," the latter being a role Mary was to fulfill.

As it happened, Mary's first workday, August 18, coincided with encouraging war news from the Mediterranean. Allied troops, having driven Axis forces from North Africa in May, had proceeded in July to their next target – the large island of Sicily off the coast of southern Italy. After a month of intense fighting, the Allies took control of the mountainous island, with the last of the Fascist Italian and German soldiers withdrawing on August 17. In the coming days, America's attention increasingly focused on continental Europe – and the anticipated invasion of the Italian mainland.

Wednesday, Aug. 18, 1943

Dearest Mother & All

Well – I've started on my new job – Right now I'm waiting for 10 o'clock to come when we are to have a staff meeting – just what this entails I don't know but I'll surely find out soon.

Laurel is just a tiny town – population was 3,000 before the war and now is 6,000. Ft. Meade is about six miles away and apparently this is one of the few towns around where the wives of the men can live, consequently rent is very high. I have to pay $10.00 a week for a little 2x4 room which is dirty besides.

The Club here is very nice and comfortable. I learned from some of the men last night that they would rather come into this Club than stay on the post and go to the club there. I certainly got right into the whirl of things by arriving on Tuesday. Last night was a big dance – girls are brought in by the bus load from Baltimore and Washington for the boys to dance with. They are very short of help here right now – so I spent the evening making sodas, milk shakes and dishing out Cokes. I was the only one behind the counter for awhile and when my first order for a chocolate soda came up I was nearly floored. I felt like paying the soldier for drinking it instead of him paying me. But he said he liked it and would tell all of his friends which he actually did for very soon a whole crowd gathered around all ordering chocolate sodas. Two of the boys saw the state of affairs I was in and promptly offered their services so they helped the rest of the evening. Finally the ass't director of the Club, a Miss Holmes, rescued me and sent me out to dance. It was then almost too late for I had only one before the dance ended. I was a dead duck by the time I got in bed, dirt or no dirt. The B. & O. railroad runs directly in front of the house which accounts for some of the filth.

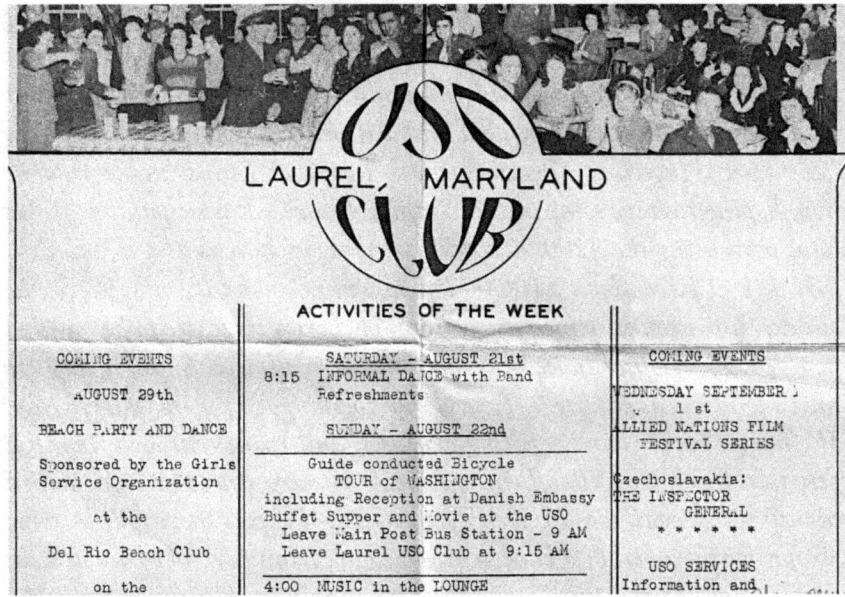

Club newsletter that Mary shared with her parents.

As you know, U.S.O. Clubs are supported by various organizations. The director here is a representative of the Y.M.C.A. There are ass't directors from both the Catholic and Jewish groups and the lady assistant is from Y.W.[C.A.]. She is a school teacher in Baltimore and is going back to her job the end of the week. The woman to take her place just came yesterday too – so we are both going to have to learn the ropes together.

The Club has a large lobby with rooms off to the sides for reading with quite an extensive library and on the other a writing & game room. There is a snack bar and at the back of the building is a large auditorium where the dances are held. I've heard there is to be another one tonight. My Gosh – I'd better stop and get on the job. I don't know exactly what my duties are. I'm just to follow Miss Holmes about and do what I can. Sometimes that's hard – she moves so fast.

I so hope you are all well. I'd like mighty well to see you – but some letters would help. I won't be having much time, I fear, to write you but I'll do my best.

The following week, on August 25, Mary wrote her folks again:
Your nice letter came this morning and I can assure you, I was more than delighted with it....

First you ask[ed] some questions which I will try to answer. I do <u>not</u> have my uniforms. We were told to go to the store in Washington that issues them the day before we left on our assignments. All I could get was a hat for a summer uniform and a Rain-hat. They didn't have my size in anything else. Therefore, when I go back I must make another trip, hoping to have some luck this time. I have not been paid yet – but have been using the $200.00 check that was given to us as a loan on the first day. I have about $100.00 left so I'm not so badly off. We make out expense accounts which are called Vouchers – these are to be handed into the main office twice monthly. We are allowed $2.50 a day for meals which is adequate in Laurel but doesn't go so far in Washington. We may Voucher our travelling expenses, and room rent and any taxi fare that has to do with official business. We are also to be paid twice a month – but that, too, I haven't seen as yet. I expect there will be some money for me when I get back to Washington Monday. They are slow, at first, I have heard – until our names are firmly established on the books. Beginning in November I'm to have $20.00 a month taken out of my check for Bonds. I put it off until then because as soon as we go overseas we do not need to pay Income tax (the 20% withholding Tax, in other words) and I thought by that time I might be gone – at least, I <u>hope</u>.

The U.S.O. and the Red Cross are not the same. U.S.O. stands for United Service Organization. It is comprised of several groups, including the Y.M.C.A., Y.W.C.A., Jewish Welfare Board, Catholic Service Organization, Salvation Army etc. These have all combined to organize Clubs for Service Men in this country. Overseas the same type of clubs are run by the Red Cross. In order to give Red Cross personnel experience the U.S.O. Clubs are using people like me. We are paid, of course, by Red Cross and are merely here to gain experience and soak up a little atmosphere. There are U.S.O. Units which are sent abroad as entertainers, like singers, Dancers or the Movie Stars. Perhaps you have read of them.

Yesterday I went out to the Post (Ft. Meade) to have a Small Pox and a [typhoid] shot. Of course, the Small Pox won't take but my right arm with the typhoid is right sore. We must have three of these shots – a week apart. We must also have 3 tetanus shots, 21 days apart. I have had one, in Washington, my next is due Saturday. There will be others depending on the place where we are to be situated permanently. Yellow Fever etc.

Mr. Freeman, the Jewish representative [to the USO] took me [to Ft. Meade], his brother-in-law, a Russian Jew who is visiting him went along with us. After my shots while we were waiting for Mr. Freeman I had a long talk with the brother-in-law, a very interesting and kindly man. He left Russia during the Revolution because he was of the Middle class and was unsympathetic toward the change. It was as good as reading a book to hear him talk.

... I had a very nice letter from a soldier yesterday who moved from Ft. Meade to Camp A.P. Hill in Virginia last week. He thanked me for being kind to him and wants to write to me. I feel very humble about the letter and not a little ashamed because I can't remember him for the life of me. There are so many to talk to, as well as dance and play with. I will try to write to him, however.

This letter has taken me all morning to write – what with interruptions concerning rooms, etc. So must stop and get busy. Please, let Anne & George consider <u>this</u> for them too.

Two days later, Mary wrote directly to Annie's family. Her "colored Band" reference reflected again the language of the times.

Dearest Annie, George & Bud –

This day, I believe, is going to be a snap. The Red Cross Blood Donor Unit has moved in and taken over the place. They come every three months for the towns-people to give a pint of blood. I volunteered, but have to weigh 110 lbs, so couldn't qualify. They have the cots set up in the Social Hall (12 of them). As soon as one cot is emptied there is someone to take their place. The blood is being collected on the stage – so far, (it's 12 o'clock) 150 pts have been donated. The lounge is filled with people either waiting to give or drinking coffee after the ordeal. The Red Cross Volunteer Canteen Unit is serving the Coffee, as well as lunch to the Doctors and Nurses. By all this activity you can see that the U.S.O. is pretty well pushed into the background which is O.K. by me.

Last night in the Club, there was little activity. I spent the evening talking to a Sergeant who confided his life and love to me. I've found that most of these boys will tell you of more intimaticies [sic] than you could get out of a civilian after knowing him for years. I [suppose] they are so starved to talk to someone neutral, someone who will listen. It's true that "Confession is good for the soul." The Sergeant came into the Club trying *to find a room for his wife. After that business was over he started talking about her and comparing her with his former wife. He must have told me <u>all</u> for after a few hours I suggested a game of Black-Jack (no money, of course) he won all the chips and left in a much better frame of mind. Sometimes when I feel that I have no great talent to contribute to this kind of work, it is a consolation to know that I can do a little something just by being a good listener and <u>that</u> nine times out of ten is what they want.*

Night before last we had a Shangri-la Lawn Party and Dance. We had Chinese lanterns and tinkling glass ornaments strung in the back yard. The punch was served out there. The only incongruous note was the colored Band. Making fifteen gallons of punch is no easy job and I had it. The juice that you and I squeezed, Annie, for the Anniversary party [Winnie and Ora's 50th wedding anniversary] was just a drop in the bucket compared to that. I had to do it with a hand squeezer and a sore arm from a typhoid shot. Speaking of shots, I'm to go out to the Fort again tomorrow for another tetanus. This one, I dread, for the last one in Washington, passed me out colder than a cucumber....

I love having your letters – so don't stop.

Mary's assignment in Maryland lasted as expected – two weeks. Returning to the nation's capital, she found a Red Cross office job awaiting her at American University. Not awaiting her was a bed on Webster Street.

Wednesday, Sept. 1, 1943
Dearest Mother & Dad –
So sorry not to have written before but I've just been too busy. I'm back in Washington again and have an office job for awhile. The work is for a Mrs. Sartoris, one of the ladies who does the interviewing of Personnel. There really isn't much to do after the work I had on Monday and Tuesday was finished. I had to make an alphabetized list of all the people who began their training on Monday. Mrs. Sartoris is in the office the mornings only – she told me I could spend my afternoons reading or writing letters, however I please. She is lovely and I'm grateful for a soft job for awhile, at least.

Laurel U.S.O. was fun but it was really work. I left there, Monday morning, and got back to the University about 11:00 o'clock. There was no room for me out at the Webster St. address so I spent the first night in a Hotel and moved out to the Residence Hall after work yesterday. All this moving about is tiresome. Part of my clothes are in one place and part in another. I'm living now with Elizabeth Shine, another girl from Indiana. She is very sweet – I knew her before I went to Laurel and was delighted to find a cot empty in her room. Barbara and Sally, my two Webster St. friends are still out on their assignments – won't be back until next week.

While in Laurel I met a Sergeant who was very interesting and attractive, he must have found me so, too, because he wants to come to Washington to see me over the week-end. I'll be glad to have him because he's fun. He's from Dayton O. – a wonderful dancer and was a Hotel Manager before the War. I'll let you know how the week-end turns out.

I called Marianna [Watson, an Auburn acquaintance living in Washington] Monday night. Myron [Marianna's husband, also from Auburn and a first lieutenant stationed in the DC area] was out of town so she met me and we had dinner together. I would like to have them meet Sergeant Sheehe but wouldn't dare to take an enlisted man to an officer's house. Wonderfully democratic, this army.

. . . Don't forget that my address has been changed again and I'll be waiting to hear how you all are feeling and what you are doing.

As Ever, Mary

[P.S.] Would you please send my Black corded purse?

Mary's relaxed work schedule and a circle of Washington friends allowed her briefly to enjoy a social life, something she didn't shy from discussing with her parents. She also didn't disguise her annoyance that she remained without summer and winter Red Cross uniforms, her petite size still apparently the source of the problem.

Tuesday, September 7, 1943

Dearest Mother and Dad:

Last night was a real field day for reading my mail. I hadn't received any since coming back to Washington because it had all piled up over at the Webster St., address. When Barbara and Sally came home yesterday from their assignment they went to Webster St. to get their luggage and brought my mail back with them. I was especially delighted to have a letter from you, Dad. I hope that you will do it again. The income tax business doesn't mean anything, I Hope, because I'm not going to do anything about it. When we are on foreign duty we are entirely tax exempt, which sounds pretty good to me.

I've just finished my work for the afternoon, so unless something turns up I'm free to get a few of those letters answered. Marianna [Watson] came out here for lunch this noon. She left about an hour ago. There isn't much out here to show her, but I thought she would like to see where we all live. I'm changing rooms at the Residence Hall this evening. Our old room was on third floor, it meant quite a bit of climbing of steps, especially when the cafeteria is in the basement. Also the new room on second floor has real beds in it (our others were cots) and there is a rug on the floor. So you can see we'll be quite luxurious.

The Watsons were nice enough to ask me out for the week-end. I had my date with the Sergeant which proved to be better than I had even anticipated. I had heard that the girls at the campus would get a lot of proposals but I didn't actually think they would get them the first week. Anyway Eddie (the Sergeant) says he wants to marry me and he's going to keep asking me until I do. It's really funny because he's so serious about it all. Myron and Marianna liked him very much, he's right smart and quite handsome. Things with the Watsons were a little stiff until Eddie quit calling Myron "Sir" and Myron [quit] calling him Sergeant....

I was caught down town last Friday in a terrible cloud burst. Of course, I have no rain-coat or umbrella and thought I would buy the latter but the cheapest was four dollars, so I decided I'd get wet and save my money. My purpose up-town was to get my uniforms but I failed again. I waited another four hours and came away with only a winter hat this time. My size is still not in. Dad, I wonder if you would be willing to sacrifice your [Number] 18 shoe coupon? I'm really needing some shoes and since you have some new ones perhaps you would let me have yours. You will have to send the whole ration book, however, because they will not accept stamps that have been torn from the books. Could you use the sugar stamps and [send] the book on to me as soon as possible, then I'll return it as soon as I can get down town again to buy the shoes. I was paid again yesterday so that brings the Red Cross up to date as far as paying me my salary....

I'd like mighty well to see you all, and especially that [neighbor girl, Marian Kaylor] next door. Give her a great big smack for me. And take several for yourselves.

AFTER SPENDING ONLY two weeks back in Washington, Mary – like clockwork – was on the move again, this time south to Richmond, Virginia, where she and other Red Cross workers settled into a private residence on the city's north side.

Postcard that Mary sent her parents showing the "Kenton Arms," a private guesthouse where she boarded.

The home, billed by its owner as a retreat for "the discriminating guest," was in a richly-foliaged neighborhood where the magnolia trees – to Mary's Midwestern eyes – appeared "huge." Urging her parents to write, Mary gave her new address as 3511 Chamberlayne Avenue.

Tuesday, Sept. 14, 1943

Dearest Mother and Dad –

I'm sorry to be so long writing to you. It isn't that I don't think of you for my thoughts are always there – but I've just now had a minute to let you know that I'm in Richmond Virginia. We came here by Bus yesterday [after] about a 4 hour ride. Such a jam at the station I've never seen. I just about didn't get on but the Bus driver knew I was a Red Cross worker so he made room for me. As it was, we sat three in a seat and stood in the aisles. There were 5 other girls sent down with me and there were about 6 already here. I had a few minutes yesterday afternoon in Washington so bought 2 two-way stretch girdles and a nylon Brassiere which all amounted to about $13.00. Yesterday wasn't my day – because I left the package in the Rest room at Fredericksburg. I called the Bus station there as soon as I arrived in Richmond but it was gone. I've just counted it up into the Profit & Loss column. However, I found this afternoon that Richmond is a wonderful place to shop – and I bought the same things over again but much cheaper.

We reported to our office this morning at 10 o'clock. They gave us a few little office jobs to do but our big duties come at night. We are at the office of Civilian Defense. They have no Club for Service men but provide dancing and entertaining by sending Hostesses and orchestras out to the Various camps around Richmond. This will be our schedule for the coming week. Tuesday night the Service Club at Camp Lee. Wednesday night – from 5 to 8 P.M. the Navy School and from 9 till 11:30 the Parking Lot Canteen. This is an outside dance hall. Thurs night will be Camp Lee again. Fri night is Camp Pickett. There is to be a dance here in Richmond at the K of C Hall on Saturday, and Sunday is a picnic at 1:30. We are more or less free during the day, although we have to report tomorrow morning again at 10:00.

I finally got two uniforms yesterday and feel very lucky because we are required to wear them here. They say they are a great protection [from unwanted advances from men]. I have a Winter uniform – they were out of summer ones but we can buy, which I did, [a different] summer one made of light grey seersucker.

The winter one will feel fine because it's right chilly. The light grey one is actually too cool for now – but they say that Washington weather keeps warm right thru October so perhaps can get some wear out of it this year yet. . . . I've more to tell you but simply haven't the time. I'm having my Uniforms altered here at a Tailors and must go down for a fitting and be at the YWCA *ready to leave for Camp Lee by 7:00. I'll try again tomorrow. This will be my address for the next two weeks.*

Love, Mary

When writing home three days later, on Friday, September 17, Mary appeared uncharacteristically cranky, taking swipes at several targets, not least toward "dopes" with whom she was expected to dance. Her unflattering – if not candid – phrase for certain servicemen usually tracked with the amount of alcohol they had consumed, as she would explain in a later letter.

Dearest Mother and Dad –

Your nice letter came this morning and I assure you it was very welcome. I've gone all week without a stick of mail. I'm sorry to hear you have been having more trouble with your eyes . . . I'll be anxious to know how you are.

This is our first all free day so far, and my room-mate and I are certainly enjoying it. We bought some oranges, milk and cookies so we wouldn't have to go down town to eat until tonight. We'll have dinner just before leaving for Camp Pickett which is about 60 miles away. Then we will dance again.

In the day we have been going to the office of Civilian Defense helping to compile information on a recreational survey which was taken last Spring of the Richmond School children. There is nothing constructive about it as far as we are concerned but they just want to keep us busy. At night [we] dance and dance some more with soldiers, sailors and the Seabees [nickname for men in Naval Construction Battalions]. Last night we went out to Sandston, an air-base, in Army transport trucks. They are really rough-riding. I don't see how the boys ride for days in them. An hour was plenty for me.

There are about 12 Red Cross girls here at this house. We are sent out in groups of twos for our various assignments at night. . . . My room mate is a girl from Atlanta[,] Georgia. I'm getting so tired hearing the Southern <u>drawl</u> both from her and the people of Richmond. She's as slow as she talks, too. We are always having to take taxis because she's never ready in time to take the Bus.

I nearly fainted when I went after my uniforms. It cost $25 to have two altered and a Raincoat shortened. You ask[ed] me if I have saved *any money – I can't with things like that and leaving $13.00 worth of girdles in Buses. I have a check yet for $66 from Red Cross and my first part of Sept. salary is due as well as 3 voucher checks. They will be ready for me when I return to Washington, I hope. We can never get personal checks cashed – so I saw no point in sending money home to the bank until I was well enough ahead and wouldn't need any money from home.*

It rained a little last night for the first in nine weeks in Richmond. Everything is very dry and brown. It was quite cool when we arrived but yesterday was very hot. The rain last night has cooled things a little.

It seemed grand to do a washing yesterday morning and hang it outside on a <u>real</u> clothesline to dry. I did my ironing this morning and have gone back to bed to write this.

Richmond is a nice town – but a little <u>horsey</u>.

It certainly is much easier to get around in than Washington. I can imagine after two weeks of dancing every night I'm going to be a little weary of that favorite indoor sport, already it's beginning to pall. They are usually such dopes I have to dance with.

I do hope you will be feeling better.

Be good, both of you. Tell Annie, George and Buddy I'll get to them some of these days.

Perhaps recognizing that she had been out-of-sorts, Mary followed up with a letter three days later, telling her parents that "believe it or not I went to church yesterday morning. It was a Presbyterian Church up the street from where we live and was convenient and handy." After church she visited a Jewish Center where she helped serve lunch, then stayed to dance and play cards with "the boys," one of whom took her to dinner and a movie later that evening. Mary's new "friend," whom she identified only as someone stationed at Camp Lee in nearby Petersburg, didn't try to disguise his interest in her. During the ensuing week he called her daily, took her to dinner on Tuesday, dropped by to see her on Thursday, and proposed that they get together again on Saturday. A mere five days after meeting him, Mary informed her parents: "He's very nice but a little intense. Talking of Philosophy, etc. was allright [sic] for one night, but a steady diet is growing a little tiresome." Still, having agreed to see him on the weekend, she added, "He's too nice to hurt."

Even as she wrote those words, Mary's mind was on more worrisome matters. A letter from home had arrived that very day, Friday, September 24, informing her that her mother – having recently consulted a doctor in Fort Wayne – might require an eye operation. Ever devoted to her family, Mary immediately penned a response and made her priorities clear: "Dearest Mother and Dad, . . . It worries me thinking about you and if you need me and want me to come home I can always resign. Just say the word and I would see what I could do about it. I only hope that it can't be that serious." Two days later, on September 26, Mary pressed her sister for details: "Dearest Annie, . . . Tell me about Mother. Does she need me to come home, I really will if it's necessary, but I do hope she will be all right."

The following Friday brought welcome news, with eye surgery not in Winnie's immediate future.

Friday, Oct. 1, 1943
Dearest Mother and Dad –
I've just finished reading your <u>nice</u> letter. It was such a good one and so newsy. I know how long it takes you to write one and I do appreciate them but you can feel that despite all your effort that I love having them.

I'm so relieved to hear that your eyes are better, you probably should have gone to a Specialist years ago, and not had all this trouble. I had the <u>swell</u> <u>letter</u> from Annie yesterday and was most surprised to hear in your letter that she wrote it when she was sick because she sounded frisky as a lamb. I think getting the hearing device is one of the best things she has ever done for herself. . . .

Last night we had our [Back to School-themed] party. We had bought popcorn and suckers for about 200 [servicemen] and since it was a rainy night there were not half that many there. Those who did attend seemed to like our Quizz program though and especially the silly consequence we had for them to do. Incidentally, I had another proposal last night at the club – of course they never mean it and one has to kid them into believing you know they, too aren't serious. He, however, was quite a sweet boy but more than cracked. He had, so he told me and which I doubt, been in New Guinea and sent back with malaria, and had just been out of the Guard House for a week for leaving camp A.W.O.L.

You ask[ed] about the Sarg, Eddie. I haven't seen him for a long time, Washington is too far from Richmond but he has been very faithful writing letters and if I return to Wash. Monday I am going to meet him Mon. night. [Mary's Richmond assignment was to end soon.] He's a right nice boy, you would like him. I'm eager to see if I still like him after three weeks. That's a long time in my life now, especially since every day is different and interesting.

We had hundreds of Jewish boys in the Club yesterday because of the Jewish New Year. They were allowed to come into Richmond to attend the Services in their churches. One man, a Sergeant, played the piano for hours, he had been a Concert pianist and had studied in Budapest. He was very charming and could play anything we asked him.

This is my day off and I'm writing this to you in bed. One of my roommates is off, too – she's reading[,] and a girl from another room is with me in my bed (I'm the only one who has a double bed) – reading, too. We are all very congenial and the admiration is mutual, I think. We are from all States. Pennsylvania, Washington, California, Iowa, Georgia, North Carolina, Mississippi, Texas, Michigan and, of course, Indiana. We all pay $2.00 a day and we've figured that Mrs. Harper, our Landlady is making $168.00 a week from Red Cross. Not a bad week's work.

Please let Annie have a squint at this because instead of writing her now I'm going to get up and find some breakfast.

All my love, Mary

Two days later, on October 3:
Dearest Annie –
I do hope this finds you feeling better. Mother wrote in her last letter that you were in bed. . . . First let me tell you how happy I am about your new hearing devise [sic]. You really should have done it a long time ago. I'm sure that any nervousness it might cause would compensate for actually hearing everything about you. You'll probably be surprised how many things you have missed.

I've just come off from taking a hitch at the switchboard. So far, I've managed to avoid it but my time finally came. I know, I cut off some conversations and hooked up wrong parties here and there. It's supposed to be done by volunteers but they don't always show up and then we have to take over whether we know how or not. I felt like the little Dutch Boy at the Dyke when the volunteer finally did come.

We had word yesterday from Washington to return tomorrow and am I glad. I don't know what my next assignment will be, but I imagine it will be there again. We feel rather left out of the excitement down here [in Richmond]. We heard from the girls that came down this week that the "Push" is beginning and about 150 cleared last Monday so we may be gone before Christmas after all. I rather look for it in a couple of weeks and I don't mind saying that I feel the Butterflies squirming a little. Always that final trip has seemed so far away and impossible and now that we actually know that people are really going I'm beginning to feel funny – <u>not scared</u>.

I'm to be on duty until 5 and then out to eat. Wouldn't you know that just yesterday we found a place where we can get really good steaks – so I'm going back and then home to pack my bags.

You'd be surprised how tough I'm getting on this Ping Pong game. I believe maybe I could take you now for one game. Really I can beat some of the boys. The other night a little Seabee (shorter than I) beat me badly[;] he was really a whizz. After the game I told him how good I thought he was. He said his wife was better, though, and when I ask[ed] about her he said that she used to be National Womens Champion.

I'll let you know next week my new address. Am going to see Eddie, "the Sarg," tomorrow night. We had this date planned for a good long time. He's cute, Annie you'd like him.

Last night was an awful night at the club. There were mostly Seabees here. They weren't tight but just on the verge and so disgusting to dance with. . . .

Do get well quickly. I'd love to see and talk with you.

THOUGH MARY'S THREE-WEEK assignment in Richmond had had its upside – giving her, most notably, a chance to visit Colonial Williamsburg – she was more than ready to head north, which she did on Monday, October 4. To Annie a few days later, Mary joked, "Well, here I am back fighting the Battle of Washington again. But it's <u>swell</u> being here. I could really love this city and you'd be surprised how well I'm beginning to know my way around in it."

The Red Cross, as expected, had taken responsibility for Mary's lodging, reserving her a room in the comfortable, if not fashionable, Hotel Benedict, a half mile west of the White House. After spending October 4 unpacking and getting resettled in the city, Mary headed the following afternoon to the Pepsi-Cola Servicemen's Center at 13th and G Streets. The center was one of three facilities (the others were in San Francisco and New York City) that the soft-drink company operated to support military personnel. As Mary explained to her parents, the new "canteen" assignment was much to her liking.

Hotel Benedict postcard that Mary sent home.

Tuesday, Oct. 5

Dearest Mother and Dad –

We've just finished our first day's work at our new assignment and it's a grand place to be. The Pepsi-Cola company sponsors the Club which is right down town. The actual floor space is quite small but there are four floors. On the first is a long bar where Pepsi Cola (as much as they can drink) is given free. They can also buy for 5 cents, Hamburgers, Hot Dogs, Coffee, Doughnuts, Egg sandwiches, and Milk. We worked part of the day behind the counter giving out the sandwiches and mixing the Pepsi-Colas. They have hired colored help to actually fry the Hot Dogs & Hamburgers, also to keep the glasses filled with the Pepsi-Cola syrup, we just put in the charged water. The men, also Waves, Wacs and Marines, are lined up three deep at the bar all the time. They carry their orders to tables and the colored girls clean the tables. We, too, by the way, can eat anything at any time, all free of charge. On the second floor is a check-room and reading & writing room, the third floor is a game room with a piano and 4th floor is a shower room for the men. Pepsi-Cola of course, is not making any money but it is a marvelous place and certainly is good advertising. Everything is so attractive and colorful also very clean and efficiently run. The building is on a corner and on the two street sides, it is entirely of glass with huge red columns. It makes one feel as if they were sitting in an open air cafe.

We work 8 hours a day. Today I started at 1:30 and worked till 9:30 tonight. Tomorrow I'll begin at 9:30 in the morning and quit at 5:30.

I called Marianna [Watson] this morning and she met me downtown for lunch before I started to work. I called Dorothy [Tuttle] too but she couldn't make it. We three are going to meet for dinner tomorrow night because both their husbands have to work.

Eddie, the Sarg, came in last night. In one of the Hotels we just happened to see Myron and Marianna [Watson] and with them David Sellew [a prominent Auburn businessman]. It seemed grand seeing someone from home. I wish we could have sat with them but besides a Captain (Myron) – there was a Colonel, and Sergeants and officers can't mix. So we sat in lowly splendor.

This is a nice quiet little hotel. I have sort of a dopey room-mate but I don't see her very much. She's slow as Christmas. She's been trying for an hour to get her bath taken – but can't seem to make it. It's now 1:15 and I'd like to go to sleep. . . .

Do write when you can. I think of you both so much and even if I am busy, miss you like sixty. Maybe you'll think I'm queer but do you know I've not been homesick yet. Not that I haven't thought of home and wanted to be there to see you, I have, but to actually be homesick like I was in college, <u>that</u> hasn't happened and I'm so grateful. Maybe it's because we're so busy all the time.

I was so relieved that you feel your eyes are better, but don't forget if you do want me, all you need to do is say the word.

All my Love, Mary

At the end of that week, the Pepsi Center celebrated its one-year anniversary, marking the occasion with an eighty-pound birthday cake and attracting "thousands of Service people," which for Mary meant "a mighty busy day." She offered no complaints, however, and indeed was disappointed when two weeks later she was reassigned to American University, where she manned the information desk in the Women's Residence Hall. She initially resisted moving to campus, because she was tired of continually packing up and because the Hotel Benedict suited her. But before long, the demands of her job – "Keeping about 250 women satisfied is no picnic" – convinced her to move back into the dormitory.

Throughout much of October, Mary expressed optimism that she'd soon be sent overseas, optimism fueled by departures of fellow workers. "I had dinner last night with two other of my friends that left today for the West Coast to leave from there. They were told to leave all their warm clothes at home. It sounds like India to me," Mary wrote on October 21, addressing her parents as well as Annie's family. She added, "I know it will be hard for you but please, don't worry. If there was any danger at all Red Cross wouldn't risk sending so many of their people across."

Days earlier, in a clear indication of her eagerness to depart, she had communicated a "secret" plan to help her family decipher her overseas location.

Tuesday, Oct. 19, 1943

Dearest Mother and Dad –

. . . I'm getting anxious to get going. You must not be worried if you don't hear from me for a month or two. I will keep writing you but no letters can be mailed until we have reached our destination. . . . I've decided that I better code to let you know where I finally land [so the code] would be to begin each paragraph of one of my letters with the letters that spell the name of the place. I rather think I'll be going to the Pacific so it will take longer to get there – but above all don't worry. No Red Cross people have ever been lost.

Be good and write when you can.

Mary's "code plan" notwithstanding, the news for which she waited – assignment to India, the Pacific, anywhere overseas – did not come, causing her mood to sour and her anxiety to heighten. "If I'm going, I'd like to be on my way. There is such an emotional tension about feeling either your turn is next or else you may not be going at all," she wrote her parents on October 26. A letter to Annie soon followed, with Mary continuing to vent: "Rumors are always rife around a place like this so I don't know just what to expect. It's really an emotional strain not knowing from day to day just what is going to happen."

By month's end, homesickness also began surfacing in her letters, as when she wrote on October 31, "This is a beautiful Sunday and I wish I were home taking a ride in the country with you and Dad. Maybe we would be gathering hickory nuts and hunting for apples and bitter-sweet." Likewise, her correspondence revealed feelings of loneliness and self-doubt.

November 3

Dearest Mother and Dad –

… Did I tell you I have two new room-mates again? They are both older women just beginning their training. Most all of the girls I have known are either gone or are out on assignment and I really feel lonely. Every call for a new shipment seems to miss me. I don't know what the trouble is but I'm trying to console myself with the idea that they are saving a <u>special</u> spot for me. That wouldn't be true, of course but I must be patient. Everyone assures me there is nothing wrong with me.

Tell everyone "Hello" for me. I would write Annie but I haven't anything to say. Some of these days I'll be full of news and write her a long letter.

Do write as often as you can. Letters help so much.

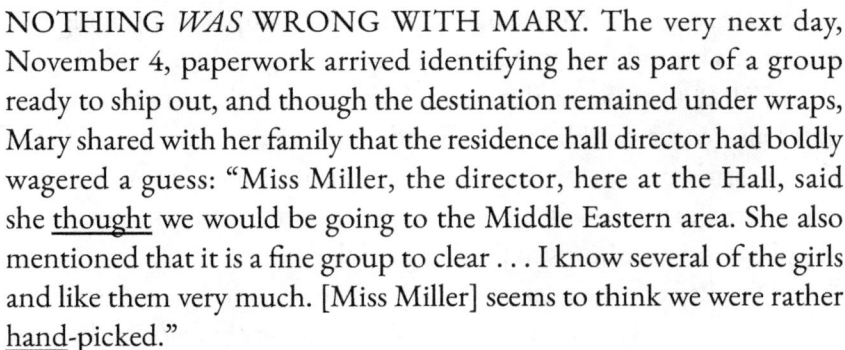

NOTHING *WAS* WRONG WITH MARY. The very next day, November 4, paperwork arrived identifying her as part of a group ready to ship out, and though the destination remained under wraps, Mary shared with her family that the residence hall director had boldly wagered a guess: "Miss Miller, the director, here at the Hall, said she <u>thought</u> we would be going to the Middle Eastern area. She also mentioned that it is a fine group to clear . . . I know several of the girls and like them very much. [Miss Miller] seems to think we were rather <u>hand</u>-picked."

During the next several days, Mary prepared "for clearance" by attending numerous meetings, one of which was off-campus and which – to Mary's dismay – took place as First Lady Eleanor Roosevelt visited American University. "I would have liked to have heard her – she talked on her recent trip to [visit troops in] the South Pacific and then came over to the Residence Hall and looked through some of the rooms in the Dormitory. Everyone says she was most gracious and very charming," Mary wrote her parents on November 6. That same evening, Mary informed Annie that she still did not know her destination but had been informed of the port from which she would depart and the nature of her next assignment: "I'm awfully thrilled with it – because it is not the usual kind – more than this I dare not tell you but may be able to later on."

Working hurriedly through her "to-do" list, Mary squeezed in farewell visits with her friend Dorothy Tuttle and enjoyed an evening having dinner and attending an opera performance of *Faust* with her friend Marianna Watson. Mary also finished packing, even as efforts to load her footlocker proved especially vexing. "If I've packed that thing once – it's been a half dozen times. We had to take all the glass out of it – so I decided to start from scratch," she wrote home November 10. Upon learning she would not need to pack soap, she told her parents she was sending the excess home. Ditto for another seemingly important item: "Do whatever you want to with the T. paper."

With her bathroom items jettisoned and her locker locked, Mary was ready when ordered to report the weekend of November 13-14 to a "camp" on the Atlantic seaboard. Though not permitted to name the place, she was sent to Camp Patrick Henry, then a newly built military installation stretching across 1,700 acres of boggy pine forest in the far southeast corner of Virginia. The camp was a staging area for troops bound for overseas duty, and during 1943 and 1944 more than 750,000 uniformed men and women would pass through its gates and enter the Hampton Roads Port of Embarkation. One of the nation's busiest wartime ports, Hampton Roads was home to transports, cargo vessels, and warships, all waiting to take personnel, supplies, and munitions to far-flung combat zones.

On Sunday of that weekend, Mary wrote her folks the following:

You may assume that we are already gone from the post-mark on this letter, but we are still in the States, although I dare not tell you where, except to say we are not in Washington or New York and are on the Atlantic coast.

Our camp is a [censored], where most of the men are [censored], to leave the country. So far, we've not had much time to see the camp, we've been too busy with meetings, etc. Yesterday morning, we were finger printed and our pictures taken for State Dept. passports, in the afternoon we had a lecture on safeguarding military information and censorship, [and] were issued gas masks. We learned how to wear them. It was all very funny seeing these queer faces glaring at one – much better than Halloween. We were even given little nose protection masks, to guard against dust.

We are living in regular army barracks – like the men and Waves that are here, too – thirty to a barrack, all complete with two stoves[,] army cots etc. The beds are comfortable but no sheets and the blankets are strictly G.I. They are warm, however – quilted and wool filled but definitely not satin [or] taffeta, the color is the usual G.I. too.

Headquarters, Camp Patrick Henry (U.S. Army Signal Corps)

Just now, we've come back from dinner, which is served in the Mess Hall. The food isn't too bad and we actually have butter. The coffee is served in large cereal bowls – no handles and almost too heavy to carry to one's mouth.

Several of the girls that were in Richmond with me are in the group. I think we are going to have some good fun. There isn't so much I can say concerning the physical set-up of the camp and otherwise there isn't much to tell you. I'm feeling very well, the air is invigorating and [I] have a wonderful feeling of anticipation. We're very well taken care of, and will be I'm sure. There's not a thing in the world to worry about, Mother, dear, so don't please.

You might have to ask the bank to transfer that Christmas check I sent you to my checking account. I can't remember if I left my money in a savings or a checking account. They will transfer it if you ask them to.

Please, please don't forget to write me and tell my friends, too. The address of A.R.C. 930 H St. Washington will reach me here.

I Do hope you are all well and I love you both so much.

Later that Sunday, Mary wrote Annie, sharing much of what she already had told her parents, with one fresh bit of news. She had met at evening chapel a young lieutenant from Washington, Indiana, and he had invited her to join him afterward at the Officers' Club. Mary took a "rain check," with the rescheduled outing to take place two days later, as her parents were to learn.

Tuesday, Nov. 16, 1943
Dearest Mother & Dad –
We've been busy as beavers these last few days. I really meant to write you yesterday but didn't have a minute to get anything sent off to you. Yours & Anne's letter[s] came this morning and I can't tell you how glad I was to get them. As I've said before you are not to worry a minute – the first realization of having me gone is far gone by now. I <u>do</u> want you to miss me but not grieve, Mother, dear, please, don't. It's all going to be so exciting and thrilling – not always fun, I know, but plenty of pleasure, too. It won't be too long before I'll be coming back.

I can't remember sleeping so well as I have since being here. It's much like camping out or being at a cottage at the lake. Lights are out at 11:30 P.M. and so, of course, we all get a long nights sleep. It really isn't so bad sleeping without sheets – they're not actually necessary.

We've had beautiful weather until this evening. The sky is puckering and looks as if it might rain any minute. But yesterday was like a spring day, with the bluest sky tucked in among the tall green pine trees.

Right now the Chapel bells are ringing – there is church every night in the little white chapel in the woods.

I was to have gone out with a little Lt. I met Sunday night . . . . He took a rain-check and I'm to see him tonight.

All my very best Love, Mary

Mary's date with the lieutenant, assuming it took place, faded into irrelevancy as more pressing matters quickly grabbed her attention. Within days she and fellow Red Cross workers were marching in full gear toward a Hampton Roads pier. There, as a port band played patriotic songs, she and her colleagues joined a contingent of nurses and more than five thousand GIs in streaming up gangplanks onto the *Empress of Scotland* for a scheduled November 21 departure.

Boarding the ship, as Mary would later write her family, was "quite an experience." Swelling up in her were emotions that she could not ignore.

We had to be in our full army regalia for many hours and it was quite a weight on the shoulder muscles. We had our own musette bags over our right shoulder, gas mask on the left, our pistol belts with canteen and first aid kit around our waists, and heavy helmets on our heads.

MARY: 1943

We wore our warm underwear, sweaters, suits, top-coats and raincoats. With my height, I looked as broad as high – my pockets were filled with little things that couldn't be pushed into any corners of my luggage.

We marched for what seemed like miles – several girls fell and had quite severe bruises from so much added weight.

As we approached the dock an army band was playing to keep up our morale. It did help – but I had a pretty big lump in my throat.

Red Cross workers in full gear at Camp Patrick Henry, ready to ship overseas from Hampton Roads Port of Embarkation. These women departed in late February 1944, three months after Mary and her similarly suited-up coworkers shipped out. (National Archives)

THE *EMPRESS OF SCOTLAND* – Mary's assigned ship – was built in 1929 as a British-Canadian luxury liner that operated initially under the name *Empress of Japan*. Throughout the 1930s, the liner had transported the rich and famous, including baseball great Babe Ruth, to ports in the Far East. But with the outbreak of war in 1939, it soon was converted to a troopship and purged of any name reflecting an "enemy state."

Aboard her new floating home, Mary quickly discovered how a ship designed to carry fewer than 1,200 passengers accommodated nearly five times that number. In her small stateroom were two sets of quadruple bunks, with Mary claiming one bunk and her seven roommates the others; their collective gear was crammed into any remaining space. Once at sea, as Mary would later write, she slept fully clothed with her life jacket by her side.

Empress of Japan before being renamed and converted to a troopship. (City of Vancouver, Canada Archives)

By day, strapped in that jacket, she roamed the chairless sundecks and watched waves break from the bow of the ship, the resulting foam "the most beautiful heavenly blue."

Assigned to dine with officers in their mess, she – like everyone else on board – ate two meals daily, breakfast and dinner, with the former "mighty important" and consisting of fruit, cereal, kippered herring, and cod poached in milk. Preferring to steer clear of the crowded and smoke-filled officers' lounge, she returned to the decks between meals, where her stomach and legs withstood rough-and-tumble waves. To Winnie, she would later write: "Mother, you would have loved it, as much as you used to like to swing – for there were several days when there was a great deal of pitching. You should be very proud to know that I didn't have a sea-sick moment. Most of the girls and nearly all of the men were really sick for a few days."

While most ships crossing the Atlantic Ocean traveled in convoys due to threatening German U-boats, the *Empress*, known for its speed, went alone, steaming south near the coast of Brazil, then eastward along the Equator. "We had," in Mary's retelling, "an escort of planes for awhile on leaving and then on arriving we had some protection." But in between, nothing – "we just ran like hell."

Exactly where Mary "ran" in those final days of November her parents did not know. They had heard not a word since her letter dated November 16. On December 1, however, a Western Union telegram, courtesy of the Red Cross, arrived at the Brandon home. It read in its entirety: *GLAD TO ANNOUNCE SAFE ARRIVAL MARY BRANDON IN NORTH AFRICA*

No country, no port, no other scrap of information.

No hint of Mary – in Casablanca.

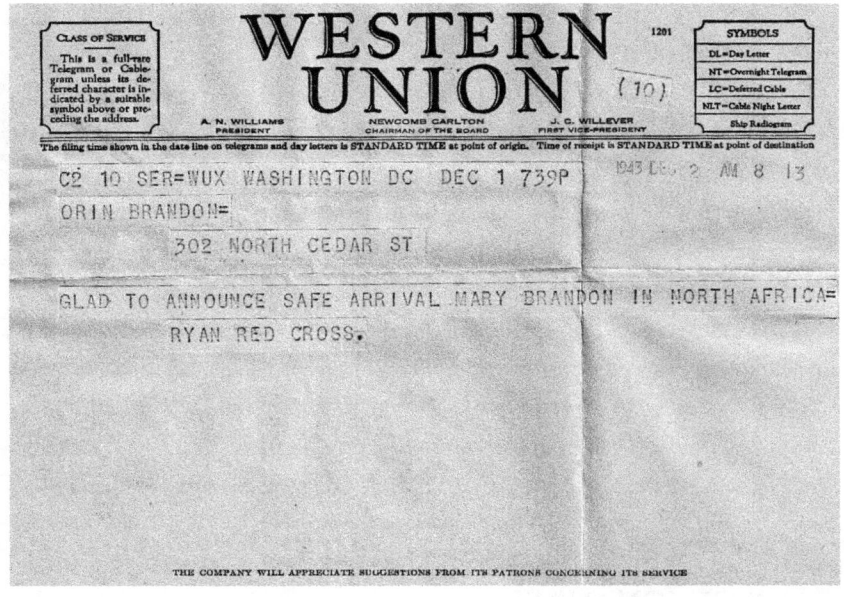

Chapter Seven

BILL: 1943 - 1944

Camp Shelby, Miss.
May 7, 1943

Dear Folks:
Sorry I haven't been able to write sooner. Suppose you've been wondering what has happened to me.
Seven of us came down together . . . There were two trains out of [Chicago] Tuesday. One left at 9:50 AM and one (solid Pullman) at 3 P.M. The late train got to Hattiesburg first, but we couldn't get a reservation so had to ride the slow one. Couldn't get a Pullman reservation on it either, so we were in pretty bad shape when we got here Wednesday noon. . . .
It is hot. I had to buy cotton uniforms right away. I'm sort of messed up on clothes. My foot locker isn't here yet.
We are living in "hutments" – sort of frame tents if you know what I mean. They're covered with roll roofing instead of tenting. The camp really isn't so bad. . . . This is just a note to let you know I'm alive. I'll write more fully later.

THREE MONTHS BEFORE before Mary Brandon began her Red Cross training in Washington, D.C., Second Lieutenant William H. Husselman headed south again – not to Boca Raton, Florida but to a military base in the Deep South: Camp Shelby, Mississippi. Fresh out of Officer Candidate School at Fort Custer and refreshed after spending a week in Auburn, he arrived at camp on May 5 as a member of the 512th Military Police Battalion. The newly activated unit was part of the U.S. Third Army, then under the command of Lieutenant General Courtney H. Hodges, a World War I veteran. Though Bill was unclear as to what his assignment would fully entail, he knew the new gold bar on his uniform accorded him access to Officers' Clubs, and he immediately availed himself of that privilege.

"I am now a full fledged gentleman (by Act of Congress) and can eat and drink with even Colonels (haven't seen any Generals around) and could even consort with Army Nurses & [WAC] Officers if I (& they) so desired," he playfully wrote his parents just days after his arrival.

Camp Shelby, as Bill's "slow" train ride had confirmed, was located in Mississippi's southeast corner, just outside Hattiesburg, a moderately sized city and bustling railroad hub seventy miles from the Gulf of Mexico. The camp sprawled across miles of pine-forested countryside, its acreage growing to meet fast-paced wartime demands. Numerous army divisions and infantry battalions had already begun training there in 1943, including the Japanese-American 442nd Regimental Combat Team, soon to become one of the most decorated units in American military history.

The rapid influx of troops had led the Army to hurriedly assemble row upon row of "hutments," the temporary structures that Bill's letter referenced and that collectively created a tent city. As the camp's population swelled, Army and civilian engineers rushed to construct hundreds of buildings and to improve 250 miles of roads. By 1944, more than 100,000 soldiers – far exceeding the camp capacity of 85,000 – would

A typical camp hutment (Mississippi Armed Forces Museum, Camp Shelby)

be stationed there, making Camp Shelby the army's second largest training site, behind only Fort Benning, Georgia. Within Mississippi, Camp Shelby's population was second only to that of Jackson, the state capital.

During his first week on base, "Second Louie" Bill jumped from job to job, none of which he found interesting, though one included a perk: "Yesterday I drove a 'jeep' for a little way. They're right cute toys," he wrote home on May 9. He had expected to be given a communications assignment, for which he believed he was well-suited given his training at Scott Field and Boca Raton. But that job "in the typically army way" failed to materialize, leading him to explain to his parents on May 22: "If you remember, I always said I did not feel I was qualified to be a line officer in actual command of troops in a combat area, and never figured that I would get that job, whatever else I might get out of the army. Well, that is just the kind of job I have landed in. I am to be a platoon leader in this company."

Bill's unease about his new assignment sprang from his limited training a year earlier at Jefferson Barracks. "I am supposed to teach basic training, which I never even had myself," he lamented in that same May 22 letter. He also questioned his physical fitness. In his first week at Camp Shelby, he had been ordered to run an obstacle course that included a twenty-foot-high log ladder that leaned forward by fifteen degrees: "You have to climb up, over the top, & down the other side. I can just barely make it. The course leaves me utterly winded."

The platoon (about forty soldiers) that Bill oversaw was part of Company A, one of five companies in the 512th. He and other platoon leaders immediately were tasked with explaining army rules and procedures to recruits, most of whom hailed from southern states. As he explained in his May 22 letter, "Our recruits are mostly from the hills of Tennessee and places like that. A goodly percentage of them sign their names with an 'X'. . . . The Colonel figures fifty percent of them are not capable of doing Military Police work overseas, and is moving Heaven and earth to get some replacements."

Bill's reference to illiteracy was no exaggeration. An article that very summer in *Liberty* magazine stated that the Army had thus far rejected more than 750,000 able-bodied men because they were unable to read or write. Alarmed by those figures and hoping to salvage manpower, the Army had begun calling men up on a trial basis and offering them thirteen weeks of literacy instruction. If they could pass fourth-grade tests, they would be inducted, with the Army estimating that 200,000 would learn to read in 1943.

Much to Bill's surprise, he liked his new assignment and showed signs of being a competent instructor. "It is really fun to train men," he wrote home on June 6. "The progress they make is amazing. Most of ours [recruits] have been here about three weeks now, and you can hardly believe that they are the same boys we received from the Reception Centers. Their shoulders are rolling back, they are learning to wear their uniforms, and they are marching instead of 'walking behind the plow.'" Despite having little experience in "handling soldiers," Bill also shared in his letter:

. . . nearly every day I give instruction in close-order drill and other basic subjects and frequently handle the whole company in marching. Yesterday all the company officers just up and took off at noon and left me stuck with two hours and a half of instruction in rifle marksmanship for the entire company and a portion of Headquarters Company without more than ten minutes for preparation.

All I know about a gun and its use is the little I learned in OCS, but I was able to make good enough use of the non-coms [non-commissioned officers] as demonstrators and assistants that I got by the scrutiny of the Executive officer [a major] and the supervising officer who listened to my instruction for some time.

Even as Bill's confidence in his leadership skills grew, insecurities still dogged him. In that same June 6 letter, he informed his parents that the battalion soon would run the obstacle course, and, in anticipation of it, he mocked himself for being unable to set a good example: "Of course I am about as apt as someone's maiden aunt at that sort of thing. I usually finish last regardless of the size or caliber of the field."

Several days later, he again referenced his fitness, noting that his feet were extremely sore following an eleven-mile hike: "The arches stood up well enough, but the bottoms need plenty of toughening before I can undertake to march 20 to 25 miles a day."

A week later, Bill appeared to be making an effort to tame his insecurities. Following a twelve-mile hike that included an overnight bivouac, he refrained from scolding himself and instead gently poked fun at his sheltered childhood. He likewise lauded a fellow Hoosier.

June 17, 1943
Dear Folks:
At last I have achieved a life-long ambition – an ambition that you thwarted many years ago. I slept on the ground under a tent. To be more accurate, I should say that I <u>laid</u> on the ground and battled mosquitoes all night, and came off definitely second best. We marched out six miles Tuesday afternoon, set up camp, broke it next morning and marched back. My feet held up well.
You know I've never done any field soldiering before, so I have a difficult time pitching tents, selecting sites etc. Fortunately I have an Irish platoon sergeant (from Indianapolis) who mothers me like a hen with one chick, seeing that I get my pack on right, pitching my tent, etc. Trouble is, they've just made him 1st Sgt, so I may have to shift for myself now.

Meanwhile, as summer progressed, the recruits in Bill's platoon continued to show improvement, especially in the realm of discipline. At month's end, Bill shared an anecdote that obviously pleased him.

Sunday, June 27, 1943
Dear Folks:
… We marched out five miles for an overnight bivouac the other night & got caught in so heavy a rain that the major decided to return to the camp rather than to pitch tents in the wet ground. My platoon was in high spirits all the way back. They called themselves the 'rough & rugged third' [Army] and me that 'rough & rugged Lt. Husselman.'
Discipline was good however. As we marched thru a little town 3 girls were standing alongside the road. When I noticed them I turned & told the men 'You can <u>look</u> all you want to, but no comments – no yoo hooing or anything.' So they looked in utter silence.
We make left turns at road intersections by flanking movements. We had to flank across the road just opposite to the girls, so I called them to attention, counted cadence to get them in step & then flanked them over. A platoon in a column of threes is no easy thing to control from the front, but I guess I was showing off a little too, for I threw my voice away & got off the command loud enough that the men executed the movement with precision from end to end.

Anyway, the girls were so startled to see a whole platoon advance on them suddenly in a platoon front that two of them dropped their jaws & the third took to her heels. This tickled the men no end.

When we got back I inspected the feet of the platoon. I went into one barracks and enquired whether there were any sore feet they wanted to complain about. One soldier drew himself up proudly and said 'Of course not. Sir, this is the rough and rugged third!'

Love, Bill

THE "ROUGH AND RUGGED" CHANT might just as easily have applied to Bill's workload, with the army assigning him one administrative duty after another. In May, Bill was named the battalion's insurance officer, charged with preparing and consolidating a steady stream of reports. In July, he was assigned, with little advance warning and little familiarity with military law, to prosecute court-martial cases, many involving soldiers who had gone AWOL (absent without official leave). By August, he was serving on Third Army's Section Eight Board which, as he explained to his parents, "passes on the discharge of men who are mentally unfit to be soldiers. Maybe it would be more fitting if I were put on the other side of the table." That same month, he also was appointed to Third Army's General Courts-martial, where he served as assistant defense counsel for those accused of murder, rape and other serious offenses.

As was customary for officers who were attorneys, Bill also volunteered his legal services to the rank and file. On one occasion, he even enlisted the help of his father – this in the case of a soldier, previously from Fort Wayne, Indiana, who wanted to know the status of a divorce filing by his wife. "I'll not deny that his [legal] position has a slightly odorous twang," Bill wrote to Oak Husselman in early July, "but it is of course manifestly to the public interest to keep one of the better Company "A" cooks happy and contented and out of the toils of the law. You could therefore make a substantial contribution to the war effort if you would check the record the next time you are in Ft. Wayne and advise as to the status of the case."

Company A, 512th MP Battalion, Camp Shelby, July 1943. Bill, arms at his side, is fifth from left, front row.

Oak reported back that the divorce had been granted, with the soldier/cook ordered to pay support and attorney fees. Meanwhile, court-martial cases kept coming Bill's way, prompting him in late August to tell to his parents that "I really have more law business than I would have at home. And it's all in addition to regular [military] duties too."

Oak Husselman in his Auburn office, assisting Bill from afar.

Though many days were a "grind," camp life was not entirely devoid of pleasures. "Last Sunday night I went dancing for the first time in a long long time," he wrote home on July 10. "They opened [yet another] new Officers' Club for the entire camp, and quite a delegation of our outfit, headed by the Colonel, attended and had dinner. There were about five of us present who had no ladies, so one of the boys called up the hospital and got five nurses to come out. I ended up with one of the nurses and got sufficiently dazed on beer before the evening was over to dance nearly every dance. We had fine steak dinners. They really reminded me of peace-time steaks."

Lydia Cattell

To satisfy his parents' curiosity, as well as that of his still spry grandmother, Lydia Cattell, Bill sent home thumbnail sketches of his associates from time to time, as had been his habit since first enlisting. He described the battalion's commanding officer, Lieutenant Colonel Thomas F. Flynn, as a widowed, alcohol-abstaining disciplinarian who had "a love for a uniform. Regular Esquire type of Officer – swagger stick (imported English) and all." Much of the time, Bill considered Flynn, a World War I veteran who in civilian life had been a newspaper sports editor, as a "nice guy." But Bill also described the colonel as someone who "is always provoked" and who likes to "rant & rave & raise hell." Trying his best to stay out of the colonel's crosshairs, Bill told his parents in late July that "there are about a half dozen [officers] he'd like to get rid of if he could. Fortunately, I'm not one of them, at least at the moment."

Bill attached the same phrase – "nice guy" – to his company commander, a Lieutenant Johnson, with whom he twice caught a ride to New Orleans for weekend outings. Johnson became scarce when they arrived in the city, preferring to find female companionship. Even so, Bill enjoyed roaming the famed French Quarter with other officers, of whom there were many. "There are more Army & Navy Officers in N.O. than you can imagine. The war must be good for the town," he wrote home following his first visit in late May. During a second visit in late June, Bill treated himself to a boat cruise, during which he observed numerous freighters tied up at the wharves and noted that most of the foreign ships were from Argentina, with a few of Spanish registry: "You could easily tell what nations were at war. The Allied ships were all equipped with heavy deck guns and were either painted blue-gray, or were camouflaged. The neutrals were covered with painted flags."

Meanwhile, as much as Bill liked visiting New Orleans, he swore off any more auto trips with Lieutenant Johnson, telling his folks after the June outing: "He is . . . a little too wild with a car for me. He drives a Ford and on one stretch of a not too good road had it hitting an even hundred miles an hour. Eighty-five is nothing to him."

As for other battalion officers, Bill opted to give his parents a rapid-fire summary rather than delve into details. That was especially the case in his July 18 letter:

There is Carroll, the young scion of a society Kentucky family, educated at Harvard and girl crazy; Riley, the Los Angeles cop; Pratt, a red headed New Englander with several years as a Tennessee State Police Lieutenant; Miller, a huge Jewish Philadelphia Cop; Simmons, the little sawed-off Miami Beach copper; Winsberg, the cultured Jewish personnel man for Macy's; [Robert] Remley and Peterson, old Army men; Lovick, a big Fond du Lac, Wis. Policeman; Keller, a youngster with whose background I'm unacquainted but who hails from Huntington, Indiana; Sudbury, the traffic man from Texas and so-on. You will notice the predominance of policemen.

Bill's commentary on camp inhabitants was not limited to the officer ranks. When describing one particular soldier, he pointed out an irony: "We have one man in the company who was making two hundred dollars a week [good money for the times] before he was drafted. He was half owner of a bottling company. Yesterday the Colonel complimented him on the good job he had done as latrine orderly, so you can see money doesn't mean a thing any more."

Bill also did not skimp – on descriptive details or candor – when writing his parents in late June about his closest friends, especially Second Lieutenant Robert G. Wilkens, a New Yorker with whom he shared a hutment.

I think I'd go stark raving mad around here if it wasn't for my friend Wilkens. He and I can lay in the hutment and chew the fat for hours on end about this and that. He is a highly educated screw ball from a wealthy Long Island family. He spends half his time imitating an English aristocrat with an improvised [monocle] and the other half talking in pretty fair burlesque German. . . . He was a New York maritime lawyer, and is now Adjutant [administrative assistant] of the battalion. Our hutment mate is the Battalion S-4 (Supply) who also speaks considerable German. We're going to have the F.B.I. down on us if we're not careful.

In mid-summer, as the camp's population continued to grow and as officers were reassigned, Bill got a new roommate – one that he was not altogether prepared for given America's sworn enemies at the time. "He is, of all things, a Jap!" Bill wrote home in late July, undoubtedly certain his parents would be jolted by the news. A native Californian, the roommate was a dentist who, along with another first lieutenant of Japanese descent, had been assigned temporarily to Camp Shelby. In mid-August, after getting to know both men better, Bill spelled out his thoughts about the newcomers: "The Jap dentists have sort of become buddies of mine, especially the one living in my hutment. They are swell fellows, and are essentially no different than other young American professional men except in appearance. They talk, act and think just like the rest of us. Neither has ever been in Japan."

Referencing the soon-to-be-famous Japanese-American 442nd Regimental Combat Team (RCT), Bill further informed his parents that "there is a regiment of [volunteer] Japs in training here, and I would feel safe in saying that they are far and away the best troops on the post."

What Bill undoubtedly knew, given how closely he followed the news, was that eighteen months earlier – in February 1942 – President Roosevelt had ordered the forced relocation of tens of thousands of Japanese-Americans to barbed-wire camps in the country's interior, out of fear that they would remain loyal to their ancestral home and pose a national security risk. Decades later, the government would apologize for that shameful episode in the nation's history, acknowledging that there was little evidence of disloyalty and that fundamental civil liberties had been disregarded due to "racial prejudice, wartime hysteria, and a lack of political leadership." To remedy the injustice, Congress passed legislation, signed by President Reagan in 1988, that authorized payments of $20,000 to each camp survivor, with the government issuing the first of the redress checks in 1990.

442nd Regimental Combat Team, Camp Shelby, June 1943. (Library of Congress)

AS MISSISSIPPI TEMPERATURES and humidity climbed throughout the summer, so did Camp Shelby's misery index. Bill's complaints about the heat ("terrible," "awful," "hotter than blazes here") began soon after he arrived in May. By June he was grousing about "tropical rain" and endlessly muggy days that, among other things, gummed up the inner workings of his watch and left his knife "a rusty hunk of junk."

Bugs added to his misery. "You are completely covered with insect bites, chiggers, etc. in no time. I have never seen so many horse flies in my life," he wrote home on June 6. Four days later, another rant: "Don't wish me to stay here until Mardi Gras time. A man would go stark mad living here that long. The weather is terrible & the insects! Ants are so bad now."

Lest his parents deem his complaints overblown, he began attaching numbers to the discomfort he experienced, writing in late June: "The temperature seems to hit between 115 and 120 about every afternoon. On the drill fields in the sun it will be between 125 and 130. You start sweating first thing in the morning and within half an hour your clothes are almost unbearable." The heat eventually claimed victims, as Bill reported on July 25:

Dear Folks:

The 512th has suffered its first casualty of the war. Friday was a stifling hot day – about 100 degrees – and we went on a 7 1/2 mile road march. Probably 30 men in the battalion were forced to fall out & were picked up in jeeps following the line of march. Shortly after we got back two men in "A" Company became violently ill of sunstroke & were packed off to the hospital. One [Elmer W. Dunham] died during the night. The other six men hospitalized by the march are doing O.K. This man [Dunham] was 31 yrs old & was from Flora, Indiana. Sunstroke is very dangerous. It causes the body temperature to rise until the brain cells are destroyed. The medics say this boy probably had a temperature of about 112 degrees just before he died. Last week we did a forced march (nearly 5 miles in an hour and five minutes) in extreme heat and "A" Company alone must have had 30 men drop out. However, there was no serious injury.

This climate is brutal to train in. Deaths on the post from sunstroke are not rare. I, now, am tough as an old pine knot. I let my platoon, strung out in a tactical formation, march entirely past me so I can check over my men and instruct them, and then double time back to the head of the platoon again. I never have trouble from heat. One thing, I sweat profusely. The Colonel says the only man in the whole battalion who even rivals me in this respect is a fat boy from "C" Company sometimes used as a K.P. at the officer's mess.

Naturally everyone is a little upset, but that sort of thing can't be helped. The men have to be brought into condition before they are taken overseas, or they'll really get into trouble then. We may be pushing them a bit hard for their present state of training at that, but it will probably prove to be a good thing in the long run. . . . Oh well, the war seems to be progressing nicely. Maybe it will be all over in a few years.

Good bye now. Love, Bill

Bill's remark about the war "progressing nicely" was likely based on developments in the Mediterranean, where Allied troops had recently invaded the Italian island of Sicily. On August 8, just days before Axis forces began withdrawing from the island, Bill offered his folks more war commentary and laced it with confidence:

Last week was certainly a banner one for the Allies, wasn't it? It appears to me that the Germans are definitely going down hill. For the first time the Russians have been able to put on a sustained Summer offensive [on the Eastern front]. I wouldn't be too surprised if the European end of the war were over in six months. You know the Germans are not much inclined to carry on a losing war. I surely hope that this battalion goes east and not west [to the Pacific].

As for Bill getting leave any time soon, he advised his parents – in that same letter – not to count on it: "The Col. thinks this outfit is red hot and is likely to get orders to go over most any time after basic training is finished the latter part of this month."

Red-hot or not, the 512th MP Battalion was still a work in progress. On the firing range, soldiers put in long days shooting round after round with the "damn" Springfield '03, the Army's standard issue bolt-action rifle that – as Bill explained to his parents – caused men to suffer "black eyes, battered shoulders, and banged-up noses and mouths." When not practicing his own marksmanship, Bill strategically roamed the range, communicating with the firing line by field telephone and trying to keep his wits amid all the din. "Yesterday I spent all day in a fox hole with rifle bullets whizzing over my head. A few struck in the hole itself, not much over a foot above my head. They would crack like a cannon," he wrote home on August 10. "Tomorrow we go out on the range again, this time to fire the .22 cal. rifle against moving targets."

Marches also remained part of the training regimen, including "motor marches" with heavy trucks and jeeps, during which soldiers practiced traffic control. Officers received specialized "motor" training, prompting Bill to inform his parents mid-summer that "this will probably be a shock, but I am now a motorcyclist! All of our officers have to learn to ride. Even the Colonel." That aside, foot marches continued to define camp life, and enlisted men and officers – alike in their grime and sweat and blistered feet – racked up miles. "Wednesday night we went on a sixteen mile hike, starting at seven and getting back a little after three A.M. . . . Shortly we are supposed to have a twenty-five mile march," Bill wrote on August 19. Lest his parents wonder about the late-hour start, he offered clarity: "There have been so many deaths from sun stroke here that there is a directive against marches in the daytime."

Meanwhile, despite sometimes questioning why he ever wanted to be an officer, Bill considered himself fortunate to have received his commission when he did. Word had begun filtering through the ranks that summer that the Army no longer needed officers and actually had a surplus. Such talk soon was confirmed, notably when *Newsweek* reported in its November 15, 1943 issue that "many Officer Candidate Schools are being closed and the pool from which candidates are drawn has been cut drastically. From a peak annual capacity of 66,000, OCS output will drop to approximately 12,000" in 1944. Though not personally privy to those numbers, Bill – when writing his parents in early August – had accurately sized up the "surplus" situation: "[I] just about made the last boat. I think OCS is already pretty much a thing of the past. In a way [I was] lucky to hit this outfit."

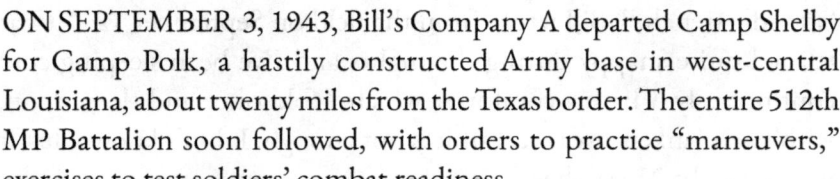

ON SEPTEMBER 3, 1943, Bill's Company A departed Camp Shelby for Camp Polk, a hastily constructed Army base in west-central Louisiana, about twenty miles from the Texas border. The entire 512th MP Battalion soon followed, with orders to practice "maneuvers," exercises to test soldiers' combat readiness.

Three years earlier, in the spring of 1940, the army had begun training troops for the possibility of war by staging mock battles in Louisiana's sparsely populated backcountry, a vast expanse of rivers, marshes, uncharted swamps, and tracts of pinewood hills. Two small "Louisiana Maneuvers" had taken place in 1940, followed by larger corps-versus-corps contests in August 1941 and again in September of that year, just months before Pearl Harbor. Ordered by Army Chief of Staff George Marshall, these peacetime exercises were designed to do more than test troop fitness for combat. The mock contests of 1940-1941 also allowed military brass to evaluate whether mobile armored units could replace horse cavalry, whether newly formed paratrooper units could be dropped en masse, and whether the Army's professional officer corps possessed the initiative, resourcefulness, and leadership skills to conduct modern warfare.

The answer to the last question was encouraging. A number of "Louisiana Maneuvers" officers acquitted themselves extremely well, among them Omar Bradley, Mark W. Clark, George S. Patton, Joseph Stilwell, Leslie J. McNair, Walter Krueger, and Eisenhower, all of whom would rise to senior roles in the coming war. Indeed, soon after the September 1941 maneuvers, Eisenhower was promoted from colonel to brigadier general, and in December – eight days after the Pearl Harbor attack – Marshall tapped "Ike" to join his staff in Washington, D.C. By late June 1942, Eisenhower was in London, planning that autumn's Allied invasion of North Africa, after which he commanded the July 1943 invasion of Sicily. In early September 1943, following the Allies' success in Sicily, Eisenhower was overseeing the newly launched campaign to take control of the Italian mainland – this as Bill and Company A were "invading" Louisiana.

By design, maneuvers were anything but cushy affairs. "We are living a pretty rugged life. Sleeping in little shelter tents, no facilities for bathing except sponge baths, & not much water for them, no toilet facilities except that unique army instrument of torture known as a 'straddle trench,'" Bill wrote from the field on September 12. "It has turned quite snappy during the nights and I've been sleeping cold continuously. I have a comforter which I fold once and sleep upon, with two blankets over me, but it is not enough. I don't know what it will be like by November."

During the day, Company A carried out traditional military police duties – establishing traffic control for units entering and leaving the maneuver area and enforcing traffic regulations. At night, the company furnished "patrol" for the nearby town of Leesville, where pigs roamed quiet streets just a few years earlier but where, since 1941, village life had been redefined.

"Leesville is probably the toughest town in the U.S. for Military Police," Bill wrote home soon after his first patrol there. "Physically it reminds you of a movie set for a Western bad[lands] town. Some of the streets are not paved. Nearly all are lined with saloons. The men on maneuvers are restricted during the tactical phases, but there are breaks every three or four days when they may have passes. They usually then go to town, get drunk, puke all over each other, have fights, riots etc. ... Can you imagine me of all people swaggering around a gold-rush town as a sort of marshal, with that peculiar swing of the hips a heavy gun on a belt gives you?"

Bill did not overstate the "roughness" of Leesville. *Look* magazine featured the small community in a September 7, 1943 photo essay titled "Don't Visit Your Husband in an Army Town" – a well-documented account of the congestion, lack of amenities, and substandard living conditions that wives encountered when visiting military spouses. A photo of Leesville's "main drag" carried a caption that doubled as a summary: "Besides the 37 bars in and near Leesville the town offers little more than some trinket shops, half a dozen restaurants, a shooting gallery, a few grocers, makeshift stores, a courthouse and jail. Rooming houses dot the side streets. There are no parks, playgrounds or libraries. Streets are cleaned irregularly."

Had *Look's* editors known about Bill's reportorial skills, they might have employed him to elaborate on Leesville life, something he did freely in a letter to his father the following month. Instead of merely describing sights and sounds, Bill cut to the chase – sketching the "action" on Saturday nights. His letter also underscored a reality: The U.S. military, like much of America at the time, was racially segregated, and Bill, like so many of his generation, mindlessly accepted ugly racial stereotypes and tropes.

10 Oct 1943

Dear Dad:

Leesville is unbelievable, fantastic, incredible, and indescribable. Basically it was a sleepy little Southern Parrish [sic] seat town of about three thousand. ... A court house rather attractive on the outside but a little dingy in the interior stands in the center.

Now it has twelve or fifteen thousand inhabitants. Most of the overflow population live in habitations that make those of the Tennessee hills look like comfortable middle class homes. Every manner of shack and piano box has been utilized for housing. Hundreds, of course, live in trailers. A good sized carnival is stranded there for the duration because of the tire shortage, and runs full blast every night. Saloons, penny arcades, cheap photo shops, and all other enterprises that are common to army towns line the main street.

One edge of the town, called Leesville Crossing, is solid Negro and possibly the most dangerous spot in the U.S. I don't believe a white man going down there alone and unarmed would last five minutes. Every shack is a juke joint. Negro troops flock there by the hundreds, getting drunk on bad whiskey and crazy on jive music. They knife each other, hurl bricks, and otherwise demonstrate the violent tendencies of their race. I have gone through the area in a jeep, armed with my .45. It is, of course, off limits to white troops and is policed by colored MPs.

To get the full flavor of the town, you must see it on a Saturday Night during a "break" in the maneuvers. That was the state of affairs last night. Thousands of Camp Polk troops and thousands of maneuver troops massed into the town.

The Maneuver troops were really raring to go after being isolated in the woods for quite a spell, and almost without an exception came to town to get plastered. The bars and sidewalks fill up until you can hardly get through. The overflow gets into the street and makes it difficult to drive. Soldiers pass out everywhere; they get sick and puke all over the streets and over each other; fights break out with startling suddenness. Soon the streets are littered with broken bottles.

I was O.D. [Officer on Duty] last night, but had lots of help as seven other officers of the battalion were sent in to help control the situation. The Battalion had perhaps sixty MPs on duty, and various other units had enough additional men on duty to bring the total of MPs to perhaps 115.

Two "meat wagons" were busy all of the time hauling arrestees into the stockade. The MP Substation was in a continual uproar as the men were brought in for booking faster than they could be handled. The stockade was soon full and overflowing.

Due to the unusually rough night anticipated each of us officers took a high ranking non-com with us in addition to our driver. I drew Master Sergeant Sandham, the Battalion Sergeant Major, and boy was he a comfort. Six feet two and well over 200 pounds. He and I didn't use the jeep much, but wandered around afoot. We kept working through *the back alleys and streets where the soldiers crawled to quietly pass out, or where they went to fight. We arrested only those we felt couldn't get back to their organizations, except for a couple of characters who chose the center of the street as the proper place to urinate. All in all, a Saturday Night in Leesville is quite an experience.*

Officers cause considerable trouble too. Friday night our Lieutenant Snodell picked up a drunken Major for transporting liquor in a government vehicle. He politely asked the Major to accompany him to the Substation, and the Major agreed readily enough. The Major got in the front seat of the jeep with the driver & Snodell in the back. Snodell thought everything was all OK until he saw the Major fairly tearing him to pieces with his eyes (thru the rear view mirror) and grasping his whiskey bottle by the neck, obviously weighing the desirability of wrapping it around the lieutenant's head.

After some time he gave up the idea, which was very good judgment on his part. For what he didn't know is that our Mr. Snodell, an old hand at this MP business, carries a shell in the chamber of his .45 and all of the time had it leveled at the small of the Major's back. Now Snodell is the lousiest shot in the battalion—he being the only one who is entitled to carry a pistol who couldn't qualify—but even he couldn't miss at a range of about six inches so I think that a move with the bottle would have put a hole about the size of your fist right through the Major's middle.

Incidentally I think I'll start carrying my gun with a shell in the chamber. I usually have only the magazine loaded and would have to pull the operating slide back and release it to load the gun. This would require a second's time and an obvious move, and might be disastrous some time. . . .

This has turned out to be a long letter, and has occupied me until bed time.

Love, Bill

While Company A was responsible for patrolling Leesville, Bill "worked" the streets only one night out of every five. His other duties included assisting in the office of Provost Marshal, which oversaw all military police operations in the maneuver area. To give his parents a flavor of his administrative responsibilities, Bill shared the following in a mid-September letter:

There were about forty generals here this morning for a meeting. The Hq. commandant forgot to make arrangements with this office handling their traffic and parking and I had to take care of it with only about thirty minutes notice. The job entailed getting extra M.Ps here, properly dressed, posted and instructed, and the generals started to arrive before I could even get the men here from the 215 MP Co, so you can imagine that I was pretty busy and sort of on the spot.

However, the men finally arrived and I quickly got them posted and instructed and things went along O.K. after that. Col. Kurr, the Hq. Commandant, can't squawk because he obviously should have given us at least several hours notice.

That same day another unfortunate matter occupied Bill's time: "There was an auto accident last night in which two Headquarters Officers were killed, and I've been running around on that a good part of the day."

Still, aside from the occasional bustle at the Provost Marshal's office and the wild nights serving as Leesville "sheriff," Bill found life "pretty dull" that autumn. He resumed practicing law by preparing a "power of attorney" document for a soldier. He headed to the pistol range to practice his marksmanship. And with time on his hands, he closely monitored news from overseas, especially as U.S. troops struggled to secure beaches at Salerno, the coastal city south of Naples where Allies – as part of *Operation Avalanche* – had invaded the Italian mainland. "According to this morning's paper the situation at Salerno looks much better," he wrote his parents on September 19. "I didn't like the looks of things there for two or three days. Reinforcements seem to have arrived in the nick of time."

Not surprisingly, Bill also allowed his thoughts that autumn to drift to the calendar, as noted in his September 22 letter: "In ten days it will have been a year and half since I quit the law and started to make my living 'with the sword.' I hope it's all over before another year and a half passes, but I haven't much faith in it. The German phase will be over, of course, but the Japs – ."

A week and a half later, with his mind still focused on calendar milestones, Bill penned yet another "anniversary" letter, this one rich with musings on his transformation from citizen to soldier.

Leesville, 2nd Oct 1943
Dear Folks:
Exactly one and one-half years ago today a raw, spindly, thirty-one year old recruit marched rather self-consciously into a low rough board building at Fort Harrison, and with his right hand raised mumbled the words that made him a member of the Army of the United States.

As I recall, he was a little bewildered, he having spent the last three days stalking up and down the long corridors of an army hospital stark naked, with a lot of other men in the same fix, periodically stopping to be looked over, prodded, and questioned by a lot of M.D.s masquerading as Army Officers.

He had yet to be introduced to the technique of making a bed, army style; to know the discomfort of countless "shots" for this and that; to learn to march to the "Hup, two, three four" of a drill sergeant; to learn to make sense out of the dits and dahs of Morse International Code; to know the emotional torture of a candidate school; to experience the exquisite thrill of passing from chevrons to shoulder strops; and to see a batch of raw recruits gradually transform into a trained battalion with a high priority rating.

In short, a hell of a lot of water has gone under the bridge in the last eighteen months, hasn't [it]? I got to thinking about it today and couldn't help remarking on it in this letter.

Besides the experiences mentioned, there have been many new acquaintances, a few of whom have been real friends. They come and go, and are nearly forgotten, as could only happen in War.

I suppose you find philosophy of [this] sort a poor substitute for news, but of news there is little to relate. Most news revolves around people and is only of interest if you know the people. The most important piece of information regarding someone you know, is that I am suffering from one of my old time stitches between the shoulder blades. It is probably due to trying to sleep (and trying is used advisedly) with nothing between me and a hard board floor but a thin comforter. Fortunately, the cots arrived today so I anticipate a decent night's sleep for a change, abbreviated cruelly by an early morning traffic detail....

I have to get up very early in the morning, so I think I'll say Good Night.

Love, Bill

Interestingly, Bill referenced Mary Brandon in a letter that autumn. His parents apparently had mentioned her in their correspondence, likely sharing the news that Mary had joined the Red Cross and was preparing to go overseas. Bill's parents also apparently invoked the name of Mary's former beau, Herman Berns, perhaps informing their son that the relationship – however tenuous it had become – was fully broken. "Yes, you were right about Mary's affair with Hermie. I guess the war just lasted too long," Bill wrote back to them.

Meanwhile, military maneuvers lasted too long for Bill, with boredom increasingly gnawing at him and depriving him of major news to send home. He succumbed to repetition when describing Leesville's "hoodlum" drunks. He asked about IU football, then reported game results he had read. He requested winter underwear – "I've got to find some way to stay warm enough to sleep at night" – but insisted his parents not send a comforter. For want of livelier topics, he even highlighted his "horse trade with the Colonel," confident he came out ahead when the two exchanged cigarette lighters.

Regardless of subject matter, Bill's dry humor remained intact. "Was on duty at the Provost Marshal's office today & saw a lot of generals. They had a conference. I wasn't invited," he wrote home on October 8. That same letter mentioned a bombing and strafing exhibition where, as Bill put it, "I was so busy running a parking lot for about 1000 vehicles in a stump field that I didn't see too much of it." Even so, the day wasn't a total loss: He managed to witness "a whole battalion of medium tanks cut loose with 75 m.m. cannon."

As October drew to a close, Bill began hearing rumors that the 512th Battalion would be moving again, likely to Fort Sam Houston in San Antonio, Texas, which alternated with Atlanta, Georgia as headquarters for the Third Army. Of more pressing concern to him, however, was the matter of his leave. He had not been home since graduating from Officer Candidate School the previous spring, and he was due for a break from the military grind. He was equally concerned about getting promoted, a concern fueled by War Department rule changes and Army snafus that kept delaying his upgrade in rank. As luck would have it, and to his surprise and great delight, both matters resolved themselves neatly on November 15. That's when he officially became a First Lieutenant, allowing him to exchange the gold bar on his uniform for a silver one. That's also when he headed to Auburn for a two-week leave.

While on break, he indulged in familiar pleasures – basking in the attention of his parents and grandmother, catching up on the law business with his father, savoring a home-cooked Thanksgiving meal, and soaking up football talk as his alma mater IU suffered a narrow 7-0 defeat to arch-rival Purdue University in the season-ending "Old Oaken Bucket" game. At his leave's end, he boarded a train in Fort Wayne and, after a day's travel, returned to Camp Shelby on December 1. His full battalion was back at camp, too, the Louisiana maneuvers having finished and the rumored move to Fort Sam Houston still just a rumor.

Certificate of Bill's appointment to First Lieutenant

Returning to military life wasn't easy. "I just don't feel like getting down to work at all. Maybe next time I come home, it will be for good," he wrote his parents upon reaching camp. Five days later, on December 5, Bill repeated that sentiment: "The worst thing about a leave is the readjustment when you return to duty. It is awfully hard to get into harness again. I guess I'm getting a little tired of the war." That day, as he often did on Sundays, he listened to classical music programs on the radio, allowing New York Philharmonic concerts to mentally transport him away from camp life.

Hard as the readjustment was, Bill was soon working at top-speed. He had been reassigned, several weeks prior to his leave, to the 512th Headquarters Company, where he supervised four clerks and oversaw all battalion records. Staff depletions around the time of his return had left the office short-handed, forcing him to put in longer hours and to suffer "nervous tension, just like practicing law." Still, his office job spared him from spending rainy nights in the field with the rest of the 512th. It also made him privy to the latest news, which he shared with his parents on December 18: "Big things are in the making. The 512th is going to war. <u>Confidentially</u> we are alerted and have a readiness date." Offering no particulars, he informed his parents a few days later that "due to the great press of work resulting from the alert orders," he would remain with Headquarters Company a few more weeks before transferring back to Company A.

Christmas 1943, his second away from home, came and went for Bill. So did New Year's Day 1944. But hours earlier, just before the new year rang in, Third Army – which still encompassed the 512th Battalion – officially changed its designation from "training" to "combat." By then, more than 9.1 million Americans were serving in the armed forces, more than double the number from a year earlier. Moreover, roughly 3.7 million servicemen and women were already overseas. Knowing his own unit was about to join the fight, knowing he was likely to ship soon, Bill sat in his hutment on a quiet Sunday afternoon, January 2, and collected his thoughts. To his parents, he confided: "I am rather looking forward to 1944 as the most eventful year of my life. I have a hunch it will be one of those periods the living of which is painful, but for the memory of which you wouldn't take a million dollars when it is over."

WITH HIS DEPARTURE IMMINENT and much to do, Bill worked around the clock to get ready. Along with attending to all the office paperwork, he had to put his own financial affairs in order, carve out time for a rigorous troop inspection, and grab his pack and carbine for a twenty-five-mile hike led by none other than Colonel Flynn. While the middle-aged Flynn fared well, Bill found the seven-hour trek to be torturous and faulted himself for lapsing "back into poor condition" due to his office job.

"I finished [the march], or perhaps it would be nearer the truth to say it finished me. I can't walk tonight – I can only hobble in pain if movement is essential," he wrote home on January 15. Even so, he asked for no sympathy, knowing he deserved no coddling: "I think I'll crawl out to the latrine and try to sooth my aching body with a little hot water. Somewhere, troops are not so fortunate. They make their 25 (or 30) mile marches and sleep in a fox hole, half filled with water, under shell fire." A week later, his "old carcass" was still feeling the effects of the hike, and he had to have a foot blister re-opened, drained, and dressed. But the medical procedure had an upside: He got a date with a nurse and went to a dance – a celebratory rounding out of his days at Camp Shelby.

Not long after that, Bill boarded a train for New York and reported to Fort Hamilton, which sat at the entrance to New York Harbor, from which nearly 3.2 million American troops would depart during the war. Bill arrived there on January 27, having been sent north as part of an advanced detachment. He had orders to ship out a month ahead of his full battalion on a vessel headed *east*.

Making the most of his leisure time in the Big Apple, Bill reconnected with a woman he had met a few months earlier. "Do you remember my writing about a girl I met on the train when I returned from my [November] leave?" he wrote his parents on January 29. "Well, I ran into her again and had her out to dinner and a show a couple of times. Quite a gal. She is an actress, [playwright], and radio script writer. A Southern Belle, too."

As enjoyable as that reunion may have been, it was short-lived. Bill soon received word to gather his belongings, including the requisite steel helmet and life belt, and report dockside to board the *Queen Elizabeth*. Like her sister ship, the *Queen Mary*, the *Elizabeth* was a British-owned luxury liner that had been repainted battleship gray, outfitted with anti-aircraft guns, and repurposed to carry up to 15,000 soldiers, an entire division, to war. Since 1943 both vessels, having earlier carried troops to battlefronts in Asia and Africa, had been permanently assigned to shuttle American and Canadian GIs to Great Britain for what was long-rumored and highly anticipated: the Allied invasion of Nazi-controlled western Europe.

On a chilly February 2, with no rain or snow in the forecast, the high-speed *Queen Elizabeth* set sail on yet another shuttle-run. As had become customary, soldiers jammed the decks and leaned over rails, straining to catch a final glimpse of the Statue of Liberty as the *Queen* cleared the harbor. Three days later, long enough for Bill to acclimate himself to the ship's layout and daily schedule, he penned his parents a brief letter, though he knew they would not receive it until the ship made her return voyage.

Dear Folks:

I am somewhere out on the ocean – headed for I dare not say where. The sea has been quite calm, but I do not believe you would like the trip, Mother, as the ship has much more motion than the Lake Erie passenger boats.... I cannot tell you where we embarked nor to where we are bound, nor can I describe the ship. About all I can say is that I am in good health and am deeply interested in what is going on around me.... Until then, this sort of letter will have to do. – Love, Bill

---

The three largest ships in the world, together in New York in 1940. Left to right are the Normandie, Queen Mary, and Queen Elizabeth. The two "Queens" were soon converted to troopships. The Normandie was destroyed by fire at a Manhattan pier in 1942. (Mitchell Library, State Library of New South Wales via Wikimedia Commons)

Chapter Eight
MARY: 1943 - 1944

CENSORED
NORTH AFRICA

Dearest Mother & Dad –
Sunday morning [November 28, 1943] and I returned from Church where, I assure you we all gave thanks to be safely ashore. There wasn't a day on the [Empress of Scotland] that I didn't wish you, too, could feel the assurance that all was well. Our voyage was without any mishap except to lose one of the propellers. It's most awfully hard to collect all the thoughts and impressions I have had to give you a clear picture of the whole thing. Many things will have to wait until I see you again.

Right now I'm sitting outside our barracks in the warm African sunshine and it certainly feels good. Last night was mighty cold – we had plenty army blankets but the night air is really chilly. We were taken from the boat in trucks yesterday afternoon to a camp where we are to be held in quarantine for a few days. The ride was beautiful, along a palm tree highway – we could see orange trees and the flower hedges were all in bloom, pink, purple and white. The air is wonderful – it feels like a sunny bright day in early May. There are some Italian prisoners in front of me now. They are talking very fast in their native tongue and suddenly add an American O.K. They have been most helpful, bringing us cots and mattresses. The Red Cross wasn't expecting us last night and had prepared for 30 men and to have 70 women descend on them made a few complications....

All my love, Mary

AFTER A WEEKLONG VOYAGE across the Atlantic in late November 1943, Mary Brandon was indeed lucky to be safely ashore. Her ship, the *Empress of Scotland,* had steamed into port at the French Moroccan city of Casablanca on November 27, little worse for the wear. But just a day earlier, an Allied troopship, the HMT *Rohna,* had been attacked by German bombers twelve miles off the coast of Algeria and left to sink in the Mediterranean Sea. Rescue boats managed to save hundreds of *Rohna* crew members, but more than a thousand American GIs, dozens of British and Indian troops, and three Red Cross workers died in the disaster. It was the greatest loss of troops at sea in U.S. history – and a calamity about which the public knew little at the time due to wartime secrecy.

Military secrecy was still new to Mary. When she wrote her first letter from overseas – the one penned on Sunday morning after church – she divulged her North African location, prompting military censors to literally cut the word "Casablanca" from her heading. In the coming days and weeks, Mary would better understand what she could freely communicate and what phrasing would escape the censors' scissors. But at the time, and given the headlines linked to Casablanca, she could hardly be blamed for wanting to identify her spotlight-grabbing locale.

U.S. troops had come ashore near there one year earlier as part of the massive Anglo-American invasion known as *Operation Torch.* Two months later, in January 1943, President Roosevelt and British Prime Minister Winston Churchill had met at Casablanca to chart the war's course and announce that the Allies would stop fighting only when the Axis powers – Germany, Italy, and Japan – unconditionally surrendered. Around that same time, Hollywood released to a national audience the Oscar-winning and now classic wartime melodrama *Casablanca*. That Mary would find herself in a place so vital to Allied military interests – and so celebrated on the silver screen – no doubt left her head spinning.

Roosevelt and Churchill in Casablanca (National Archives)

But if Mary was awed by her new surroundings, she also found living conditions to be "rugged." Within days of her arrival, she underscored that point in a letter to Annie's family, one that also bore signs of the censors' scissors.

Dearest Annie, George and Bud –
Right now, I'm warm for the first time since hitting North Africa and it feels divine. I'm sitting in front of a huge fire in the Recreation Hall with just about every article of clothing I own draped in some manner or means about my form. This is the coldest spot I've ever been in and no chance of actually thawing out unless we come here because it has the only fire in the whole camp. Our barracks are like ice boxes. They are white-washed cement with open screened windows which do not keep out the mosquitoes. We took "atabrine" which is a substitute for quinine on the boat every night so I suppose it wouldn't really matter how much they bite, besides, we've been told this isn't the malaria season. I have some kind of bites (tiny red spots) all over my face from some manner of bug, consequently I slept last night in my mosquito net – a gadget which fits over the face and proved quite helpful. I'm sleeping on an army cot with 8 army blankets and one rolled up for a pillow over which I have placed my best white silk scarf to make me remember there were such things as downy white pillow slips once. I'm sure that after we get assigned things aren't going to be quite so rugged but right now this is some life. I'm not really complaining because it is actually fun but gosh it's cold.

We had breakfast this morning at 7:00 and were all ready to go on a tour into the city but the trucks didn't come. It was most disappointing but perhaps tomorrow we can make it. The army has that reputation for "Hurry Up & Wait" and we are beginning to find that out. They say the city is most interesting and I'm terribly eager to see it. What little of it

Film poster (Warner Bros, Inc., artwork by Bill Gold via Wikimedia Commons)

we saw on our way here from the boat was fascinating – I'm itching to go. We passed some beautiful houses and gardens, palm trees and orange groves, dirty Arabs with donkeys and, Annie, real live camels, sauntering down the road like cows on some lane at home.

I'm beginning this again after lunch, gee it was good and the first time I've felt satisfied. We had a Red Cross Club man talk to us yesterday afternoon and he said we will be continually hungry in Africa. The people aren't starving but there just isn't enough to quite satisfy our American appetites. We eat from tin mess kits – (army issued) which were quite a problem at first but we're learning to manipulate them. They are in two parts with a knife, fork & spoon – the parts may be assembled into one complete piece held with a handle and are then washed by ourselves in hot soapy vats over a camp-fire. There are three of these vats; one to wash, one for rinsing and the other for scalding. They dry by themselves. Our own body washing is a little more complicated since the water is either too scalding hot in the showers or completely cold. I gathered my courage last night and had a cold shower. It was mighty cold but certainly worth it for I hadn't a complete bath since leaving the States. Our latrines are the good old fashioned four-holers and we're all getting quite chummy over our bath-room troubles.

This morning was a big event because a P.X. was opened out here. We are given ration cards which must last us until Jan. 28. We may purchase each week a box of cookies, one box of hard candy, 2 packages of gum and one candy bar. I took up a lot of precious room in my suitcase to bring over a whole box of Clark Bars – but I'm really hoarding those [because] there may be no post exchange where we are going....

We are told we won't be here much longer than a few days – and will move on to another country for assignment. Washington headquarters told us before leaving that we were to be in Rest homes for pilots but they seem to think over here that we won't get them. The Rest Home would be the most wonderful assignment possible but I'm afraid my luck wouldn't hold for that.

We are guarded continually by M.P.s and are protected by a barb-wire (so well, in fact, that one of my special friends ran into one the other night and cut her face quite badly. Someone made her a service ribbon with the Purple Heart, the American Theatre and the North African Theatre. The M.P.s are really funny, they start talking to us the minute we stick our heads out in the morning. I think, though, our washings hanging under their very noses had them really confused. They just stood and looked at our <u>dainty</u> lingerie for awhile. Everyone had a lot of dirty clothes accumulated from the boat. I was lucky enough to wash four of my blouses on the boat and by greasing the palm of one of the stewards was able to iron them. Here, we do our laundry in the top of our helmets.

Do tell Mother & Dad "Hello" and everyone else who might be interested. Don't for heavens sake forget to keep on writing me. We won't get any mail for awhile but eventually it will catch up and will that be a Happy Day.

All my Very Best Love, Mary

At the end of her first week ashore, Mary had so much news – good and bad – to share that she opted to inform the entire family in a single posting.

North Africa, Dec. 3, 1943 – Friday
Dearest Mother, Dad & Everyone –
This letter was started yesterday but the heading was as far as I progressed – will try again tonight.

I might as well begin with the unpleasant news and get that off my chest for I have so many wonderful things to tell you. Last night we had our first rain of the season and have been actually swimming all day. When I awakened this morning my clothes were really drenched. Since the cot next to mine was empty I had my things laid out there. In my uniform hat there was a pint of water. My open suitcase was filled. It practically ruined a lemon yellow native leather portfolio I bought Wednesday in town. You may surmise that our roof leaks – <u>it does</u>. There are huge knot holes all down the barracks – some were not quite so unfortunate as I, for which I was extremely grateful. I've been wearing borrowed clothes all day. We have sort of a meager fire in one corner. The place was a mess kitchen so we are making use of the old fashioned oven. It isn't too good for drying but eventually things will be all right for wearing again.

Day before yesterday we received our assignments and although I can't tell you where I'm going I can tell you how pleased about it I am. Our group leader said some very nice things to me and I feel that I am really receiving one of the best assignments. Out of 73 people 30 of us are getting, I think, the choice spots. We will be working in groups of three and the two *girls with me are very <u>swell</u> people.* Dorothy Dennis is the widow of Dean Dennis who was the head of the speech department at Northwestern, the other is Anne Pendleton, the daughter of the late General Pendleton. She has lived all over the world and is a good friend of General [Douglas] MacArthur. They both, of course, are older than I; and are to be my superiors, of course, but I know we will all work together in fine shape.

There are two Red Cross Clubs in the city and when I visited one the other night I met two boys from Indiana that are going home. One asked me if there was anything I would like to have him write my mother when he returned so I gave him your name and address. I do hope he writes you. The Clubs are wonderful places for the men – the larger one is in a huge hotel. We visited the Snack Bar, of course – one may have three articles of food for ten cents. There is a garden in the rear with beautiful native trees and flowers and a small fountain. The bananas on the trees are just beginning to ripen, bougainvillea spreads a riot of purple blossoms all along the wall. There is another strange tree that has yellow flowers that look like huge lilies that drip down. The verbenas grow in huge shrubs instead of tiny plants like at home. There are all kinds of palms and a strange kind of pine.

The city itself is perfectly wonderful but very dirty and Mother, you were right about the smells. The native women are arrayed in all colors, black & white, pure white, striped, saffron yellow, violet, but always with their faces covered. There are many children on the streets and they have picked up many American phrases from the soldiers. It seems most queer to have an Arabian child come up to one and say "Want a shine, lady." Of course, they are always begging and if you give them a few francs they will follow you for the rest of the afternoon.

The buildings are quite modernistic in design but they are all mixed up with the native architecture [so] that it's hard to tell where one century ends and another begins. The traffic problem would drive an American policeman crazy. The French Gendarme stands in what is supposed to be the center of the streets, he gives fancy flourishing gestures but the traffic moves just as it pleases anyway. Most of the taxis are the horse-drawn variety, there are a few foreign made cars, many donkeys & burros (the riders legs sticking far out to the side) and although I haven't seen any camels in the city itself we pass them on the road on our way into town. This may seem very rambling, but there is so much to tell you I can't *seem to assemble my thoughts into anything consistent. On the way into town, too, there is a great field of Yucca (like you have at the kitchen door, Mother) but the blossom grows as high as a tree.*

The Army has certainly been wonderful to us. They have sent a mess detail to feed us and we've been having good food. The only trouble is in eating fast enough to still have it warm. The breezes blow thru the building and the tin kits from which we eat aren't exactly the right facilities for keeping food hot. Last night we had marvelous fried chicken. Most of the food comes from home, canned vegetables, & fruits – but we have no fresh or green vegetables. There is only one kind of fruit from here that we eat, Tangerines, but are called Clementines. To go back to the Army – they send trucks for our transportation several times a day. We usually go into town in the afternoons to look around and shop. I had my filthy hair washed in a French shop – I didn't feel it was too clean and it definitely didn't get dry – (they only allow ten minutes under the dryer) but it was much better than before. The trucks will take us into town in the evening too for the movies. The theatre is run by Red Cross and is a very beautiful one. It is entirely free for both officers and men, in fact the native populace is not allowed. They run four shows a day and a different movie each night. Most of them are the newer pictures.

One of the Transportation Lieutenants has been squiring me around to some of the spots, we went the first time in a 3/4 ton truck, the next time in an ambulance and I had a note from him last night which said he would pick me up this afternoon at 2:00 in some kind of conveyance. I have my doubts what it will be – I hope a Jeep. We went Thursday night to an officers club which was very nice. It is constructed so that there is a kind of balcony around the floor and over the floor itself is a large tent, so that in the warmer weather it can be removed and dancing is under the African skies. Now they have trapeze bars and swings hanging from it to give the circus effect. The Army, too, is sending out a doctor each day to see those that have colds. Many do have rotten colds and we all have coughs. I still have mine left over from Washington but am feeling fine and believe that I really have built up a wonderful resistance against this African weather. It's very rugged.

I'm about to get out of bed and wash my face in my good old helmet. That, actually, is the only use I think we will ever find for the heavy ungainly things. I have some water heating over the stove in my canteen cup. *The needs of life, I have found, can certainly be simmered down to only the essentials. We, at home, actually lived in the greatest luxury.*

I do hope you are all well – please, don't worry about me – we're all having such fun. Give my love to everyone – keep most of it for yourselves.

As Ever & Always, Mary

ON DECEMBER 7, 1943, TWO FULL YEARS after Pearl Harbor and after Mary had been in North Africa less than two weeks, she scribbled a quick note instructing her parents to use a new Army Post Office mailing address. She was about to be transferred to her new assignment, and though not permitted to say where, she was headed for the Isle of Capri, nine miles west of Sorrento, Italy, in the Gulf of Naples. Fascist forces there had surrendered to the Allies in mid-September, and soon afterward the U.S. military had designated the island a rest center for Army Air Force personnel, many exhausted from having participated in anywhere from two to four dozen combat missions. Capri was the latest in a string of places in the Mediterranean Theater where servicemen were sent to relax, their stays typically lasting for seven to ten days in hotels requisitioned by the Army and staffed by the Red Cross. Notably, such centers were but one component of Red Cross operations. Throughout the war's course and in all military theaters, the Red Cross managed recreational clubs in rear-staging areas and mobile coffee units closer to the front.

With her Capri orders in hand, Mary embarked on a multi-leg journey, the details of which are sketchy. She traveled east, likely by train, to the Tunisian capital of Tunis, where seven months earlier German and Italian forces had surrendered to Allied troops, thus completing the Axis collapse in North Africa. From Tunis, Mary continued by plane to the Italian port city of Naples, which Allied forces had entered on October 1 following their successful but costly beach landings at nearby Salerno. In a published interview years later, Mary recalled that her Mediterranean flight was memorable for reasons beyond scenic window views. Onboard the aircraft were Hollywood film star Humphrey Bogart, of *Casablanca* fame, and his wife, Mayo

Methot. The celebrity couple was on a USO tour of North Africa and Italy, and Bogart – according to Mary – spent time in the cockpit where he reportedly was permitted to pilot the plane.

Mary spent only four days in Naples, which was long enough. The Allies had repeatedly bombed the city, and German troops, upon finally departing that autumn, inflicted even more damage – booby-trapping infrastructure, destroying cultural treasures, and leaving starving residents traumatized. When cleared to resume her journey, Mary traveled to Capri by boat.

Dockyard wreckage in Naples, 1943 (National Archives)

It was not until December 21, after a two-week lapse in corresponding with her family, that she finally penned a lengthy letter home. She combined it with a follow-up letter on Christmas day. In the latter, she also surreptitiously disclosed her location by encouraging her parents to read an article in the November 15, 1943 issue of *Newsweek* magazine. The article, a copy of which her family presumably tracked down, described life on the small mountainous island, as seen through the eyes of a correspondent.

> Two hours due south of the Italian war by slow boat lies paradise. It is a place where battle-weary fliers sleep between clean white sheets on 'Beautyrest' mattresses, have breakfast tea served in bed by immaculate white-coated waiters, bathe in tiled bathrooms, and then eat ham and egg breakfasts in a dining room glistening with polished glass and silver. It is a place where they can spend the rest of the day sipping wine, eating minestrone, ravioli, and steaks – hiking, swimming, or just sitting in the piazza watching the day go by and missing the next boat to the mainland. It's easy to miss the next boat because the plaza clock runs about an hour slow and strikes 11 when the hands point to 12:30.

Even without reading the article, Mary's parents undoubtedly were pleased to learn that their daughter's new location was, in her words, "divine." They likely also enjoyed reading about how Mary celebrated the Christmas holiday.

Dec. 21, 1943

Dearest Mother & Dad –

. . . So much has happened since I last wrote you that I hardly know where to begin. I haven't written because I simply didn't have the time. Now that we are settled and with our jobs half way started I may be having a few minutes now and then.

We are in a perfectly divine spot – so beautiful it is actually breath taking. Although it seems cold because there is no heat indoors, the flowers are all in bloom. We've been trimming our Christmas trees with geraniums and roses because we have no Christmas tree decorations. We are at a Rest Camp for the Air Force and I have been assigned to an enlisted men's Hotel. All the management is taken care of by the army and we are only to lend the feminine touch, as it were. All day we [Mary and her coworker, Elizabeth Richardson of Providence, Rhode Island] have been decorating the hotel. This morning we took the Gardener and one of the soldiers who speaks Italian way up into the hills to an abandoned Villa to gather greens and berries for the decorations. We have cotton on our Christmas tree as well as little red ribbon bows – there are no others.

Life is extremely gay here since the boys come for a rest and diversion [and] the Air Corp tries to give them the things they want. There are conducted tours and dances nearly every night. All the boys live in Hotels while we are staying in a small Villa. Since the space we are occupying is limited as well as rugged and mountainous every little bit of ground is utilized. The streets are no wider than a good sized side walk with walls about everything. . . .

Dec. 25, Christmas Day and

<u>*Merry Christmas*</u>

I'm still in bed Christmas morning and have decided that early morning is about the only time I have for my personal things. I hope, so much, you are all well and having a happy Christmas.

Yesterday was a full and busy day for us. After a presentation of a gift to a visiting general, the orphan children were parceled out to the various hotels for a treat.[1] *We had expected at our hotel 75 and when twice that many came we scurried the men around to make more paper sacks for candy, find chairs and the kitchen help to make more hot chocolate. We had all little six-year old boys who were beautifully behaved. It was very colorful too. The little boys were dressed in black dresses with white collars, the two nuns who brought them were in black & white, too, of course. The dining room as well as most every room here at this spot is white washed and then with our Christmas decorations of bright green with touches of red ribbon. A few of the men took pictures. I do hope they are good. Outside of a letter from home I had the best Christmas present possible. Yesterday my Footlocker and Bed Roll arrived. Now I'll be able to get a change of clothes. Living out of a suitcase for six weeks has been a problem. I still have had <u>no mail</u> and feel like a poor orphan myself.*

Last night before dinner we had a Christmas punch bowl which the boys seemed to enjoy. There is no whiskey here, practically nothing but wine – we had Champagne with our dinner. I ate with three of the boys who are leaving today and they wanted a little celebration. At 11:30 last night we went to a church Service held in a little gem of a German church with the chaplain of the group in attendance. It was [an] Episcopalian service of Communion but on Christmas we [of] all faiths are mingled. Five of us Red Cross gals had a little choir and I sang my usual Christmas solo. It seemed awfully good to be singing again. The leader of our group here sent us all a green orchid to wear. They are quite common here. And Mother, the oranges are beginning to blossom – such fragrance. However they (the oranges) haven't all been picked yet – so we have all the fresh fruit we want. English walnuts grow here too so we have had plenty of Christmas nuts.

I am so behind of news of this place to tell you – I hardly know where to stop. I do, however, want you to find a copy of the magazine "Newsweek" Nov. [15], 1943. It has an article about this place in it. They may have a copy in the library but have Annie try to find someone who takes it.

---

1. The general might possibly have been Allied commander Eisenhower, who toured Capri on December 24 before returning to his headquarters in Tunisia to share a Christmas meal with Churchill, who was recovering from pneumonia.

Last Saturday night I was invited with three others to have dinner with a visiting General – we are not allowed to give names of men beyond the rank of Colonel. He was a very nice man and we all had a game & pleasant party. At the dance, however, I saw a boy I knew in school, Jo [Joanna Rhoads, an Auburn friend] will remember Johnny Biggerstaff, a Sigma Nu at DePauw who is a Lt. Colonel. I saw him quite by accident on the dance floor and he picked me up and whirled me around like a long lost chicken. He is about to become a father on the 28th. I asked him to hold off one more day for my birthday. Of course he won't be able to hear for several weeks. He is extremely popular with his men. I have been hearing from the men in our Hotel how much they like him. Our boys are all mainly Staff & Master Sergeants who form part of the crew of a plane. There are usually three officers and two enlisted men to be the crew. Our boys (I sound possessive all ready, don't I, but they are such swell kids and are so appreciative of the little things we can do for them) are either Crew chiefs, radio operators, or supply Sergeants etc. Honestly it's almost pathetic the way they feel about us. Most of them haven't talked to a girl (besides an American one) since they left home – some for over a year – but they are very respectful and gallant. They like to hold my hand, smell my perfume (and boy am I glad I've got lots of it) and occasionally catch me under the Mistletoe.

I must stop now and get to them. It doesn't feel much like Christmas morning but next to being home with you – it's the best feeling I can have because I know how much we are appreciated.

With all my Very Best Love. Forever, Mary

Four days after Christmas, on December 29, Mary marked her thirty-third birthday. Coworkers and servicemen treated her to a party, which she recounted in a letter the next day. She also confirmed that she was in Italy, leaving her precise location undisclosed.

Dearest Mother & Dad –

I know I am neglecting you fearfully but there just aren't hours enough in the day and the few moments we have to be alone are very rare.

First I must tell you about my wonderful Birthday party. The boys who are stationed at the Hotel as permanent personnel really threw themselves [out] for me and it was so sweet and touching. This sounds trite, I realize as I write it, but they were so terribly sincere in wanting it to be a grand party and it really was, I assure you. The dining room was decorated beautifully with flowers. At every place there were small bouquets of roses, mimosa and iris and in the center poinsettias and mimosa which I have on my table in front of me as I am writing. The boys gave me a coral necklace and a scarf which they shopped for themselves. There are hundreds of shops here to choose from and I can just see them going around making their selections.

The Italians are wonderful pastry makers, you know, so the two cakes were perfect, flavored with wine and beautifully decorated. The first was a huge white one with "Happy Birthday, Mary" and I nearly fainted when they brought in a second one of chocolate. The food is really very good here. Of course, the chefs have regular army rations to work with but they are so disguised by the art of Italian cooking that the meals are very good. We usually have one Italian dish at each meal. The water is very scarce so we rarely drink it but have wine with our meals and endless cups of coffee.

Quite a few of the girls gave me gifts, nice little things that I hope I can find room to bring home with me someday. After dinner we went to an entertainment given by some of the native people. They sang their folk songs and did their folk dances, most interesting and beautifully colorful. The costumes are many colors, chiefly, greens, yellows and reds. The men wore little red caps with tassels on them – like little night caps. The band which consisted of a drum, two clarinets, a mandolin, an accordion and castanets & cymbals sat in a semi-circle about the stage while the singers and dancers stood in the middle. There is hardly a moment of the day when I don't wish for a camera and some film to record forever a little of this paradise to bring home to you. The land is very mountainous and when the sun shines as it has been these last few days the reflection of the sun on the rocks and the white houses is simply breath-taking.

As I said before we have very little time for ourselves – so I haven't even unpacked my trunk. I just drag out clean clothes as I need them and hope to goodness a day will come when I can find time to put some things away. My laundry is done for me at the Hotel entirely free and such wonderful ironing as they do. Mother, I don't even wash out my stockings. Besides that luxury we have our breakfast brought to us in bed each morning. I'm going to be rotten spoiled when I get home....

I do hope you are writing – I've still not had any mail.

Much of what Mary saw on the Isle of Capri can be seen today - the clock tower in the town of Capri's main square, the lush foliage on steps leading to villa entryways, the narrow walled streets, and the breathtaking views of shimmering blue-and-green water and craggy limestone cliffs. (Photos by author)

AS THE NEW YEAR BEGAN and as Mary waited for word from home, she penned letters to her brother Charles's family and to Annie, adding fresh details to what she earlier had shared with her parents. To Charles, she zeroed in on the basics, telling him in a January 2, 1944 letter that her job was to entertain both officers and enlisted men – no small task given that the Army was prepared to house as many as one thousand pilots and their crews on the island. Mindful of her hostess duties, Mary dined and watched movies with the men, sat in on their bridge and poker games, and twirled with them on the dance floor. "Of course," she explained to Charles, "there are never enough girls to go around so we switch dancing some days with the officers and then back to our own [sergeants]." Knowing her brother remained protective of her, Mary added:

I have never been treated in all my life with such loving respect and admiration. Of course I realize there is no competition but it almost hurts to realize how well behaved our American men are away from home. A man is simply removed by his hair by his buddies if he even thinks of making the slightest break. They tell me that it's because it's been so long since they have seen an American woman they have forgotten how one looked. The first few days the boys come in they are tired, shy and are doing a great amount of drinking but after that they want to talk about home and look at the sights which are many and terribly beautiful & interesting.

In that same letter, Mary also informed Charles that she had begun taking Italian lessons taught by an old baron: "He is very tall & straight with thinning hair and no teeth. He wears a moth eaten black cape which he swirls about his shoulders. He's a perfect example of the old nobility with impeccable manners." Mary also elaborated on the small choir she and coworkers organized in a local church: "The boys have said that it's grand hearing girls sing again. The Church itself is a little jewel, tiny but perfect. We have a little pump organ with a lovely tone and a violinist (a Native) that looks like Paganini. He has a bar called the Maestro's Bar where he wanders around playing tunes and occasionally Jitter bugging for the boys. But on Sunday morning he is as pious as the occasion demands."

Mary returned to the theme of dancing when writing Annie on January 4. She also highlighted the improvisational sandwich-making that typically preceded Red Cross dances:

Mac [a young serviceman] was grand about helping me yesterday making sandwiches for the dance. We made 300 from Corned beef which had to be disguised greatly for the boys have it so much that they wouldn't eat it unless they didn't know what was in it. To one huge can of beef we added one onion, a bowl of Walnut meats (there are bushels & bushels of walnuts as well as Filberts here), two cans of Tomato puree, 2 cans of pickles and mustard. The boys seemed to love them and the Italian girls ate them with gusto. They said if they had such good food every time they would come to every dance.

That is one of our biggest problems getting enough girls for the boys to dance with. The village maidens must be very well chaperoned and are not always allowed to come. We Red Cross gals really take a beating as far as dancing is concerned. Our legs are nearly danced off us. We get about two steps in with one partner before he is tagged and that continually changing partners goes on all evening. I'm learning to be the best little follower you ever saw, and am doing everything from a polka, the Peabody down to Jitter-bugging – yes – I've reached that stage.

Mary likewise reported, for Annie's benefit, that servicemen were treating her respectfully. She also emphasized how they savored reminders of home.

This morning Mopsie (my workin' partner) and I had a letter from 3 of the men who left. It was such a touching thing – telling us of their appreciation. I had lunch with them the other day and listened to them telling of their experiences (you get the most amazing stories) and then they asked me to talk to them for exactly 15 minutes just about home. Always when they find we have just arrived their first question is 'How is it at Home' 'What are people doing and saying.' Gosh – these soldiers of ours are swell, Annie. They like to hold my hand, touch my hair and smell my perfume (I'm afraid I haven't got enough) because they say there is nothing in the world like an American girl. I know it isn't me but only that I can remind them of someone back home. And I'm sure trying to give them the best time they can have on their little vacation.

Mail from Mary's parents finally arrived on January 7, prompting her to dash off a note thanking them for the Christmas and birthday cards and informing her dad, who would turn seventy-eight on January 11, that she had just cabled him a birthday greeting. Soon more mail began arriving with greater regularly, and Mary – as had become her habit – resumed asking Annie to send additional clothing items. In a January 20 letter, Mary reminded Annie of postal service regulations for overseas mailings, rules imposed to insure military cargo received shipping priority.

Dearest Annie –

Your letters are coming so faithfully. I'm always so terribly happy to have them. I thoroughly enjoyed the joint letter from the Poker gang – it was wonderful having a note from everyone – almost like a visit.

The longer we are here the more I'm amazed about the possibilities and personalities around here. Right now we're seeking for a villa which will do us a library – when it's found the army simply takes over. Yesterday some of the girls had some wardrobes moved in from one of the vacant hotels. Then – there are the most extraordinary people.

Yesterday I heard a lecture at the men's villa given by a world famous Historian and Art critic on the history of this particular spot. He is a White Russian [A term for those who opposed the Bolshevik Revolution] but has lived here many years. His wife, a world famous concert pianist, is to give a concert for us Sunday night. They both are most hospitable and have done much for us. In return they ask no money but <u>food</u>.

Today, after lunch we had a funny little artist come to our hotel to suggest something to paint over the bar. He, too, is to be paid in food. He's very small and delicate, was once a dancer. He wears a beret (as do most of the men, here) a red scarf, a bright coat and smokes a huge carved wooden pipe. The negotiation for the painting was so funny but typical of the way business is carried on – I had to go away and laugh. Mopsey, my partner, and I were trying to talk to him thru an interpreter with the assistance of all the Italian waiters and coffee girls as well as the boys themselves. The little artist stood very benign and calm in the midst of all the mess and let us go about our business of engaging him.

Our house-keeper, Stella, is a beautiful woman who speaks perfect English. She was born in America and her father was an Italian doctor. She is married to an artist and has three small children. Her baby, 4 months old, is wrapped in swaddling clothes to keep him warm these cold months.

We are having fleas these days and in our beds, too. So I've been very busy keeping myself scratched at all times. The itching has been waking me in the early morning so I've been trying to make use of my time by writing some impressions of the things I have seen but dare not write home about. Time is such a stealer that I want to set it all down before it fades – not that I could forget it – but first impressions are best. When I get home I can read them to you.

Annie, I understand that if you show my request to the Postmaster for the contents of a package under five pounds it will be sent. But he must see the request. If it is over 5 pounds permission must be sent from my commanding officer. Either you or Mother could send these things for me if you would. Please use my money.

4 pairs white pants

1 pr. black high heeled pumps (for dancing) 5 1/2 A from Talberts in Ft. Wayne.

1 Sweater set (maybe Chums) from Wolf & Dessauer any color but something to go well with our uniforms.

My Beige summer dress with the green bunnys.

These may weigh more than 5 pounds so send just the ones you can get together.

All my Very Best Love, Mary

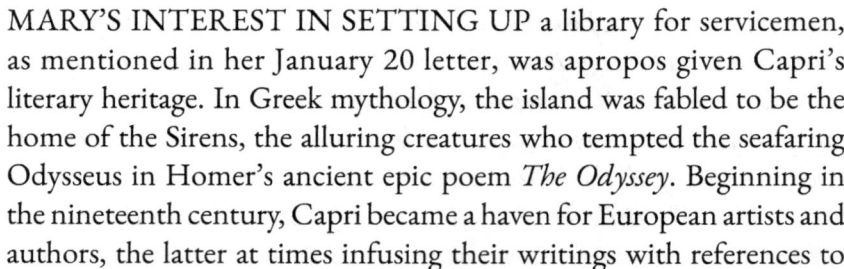

MARY'S INTEREST IN SETTING UP a library for servicemen, as mentioned in her January 20 letter, was apropos given Capri's literary heritage. In Greek mythology, the island was fabled to be the home of the Sirens, the alluring creatures who tempted the seafaring Odysseus in Homer's ancient epic poem *The Odyssey*. Beginning in the nineteenth century, Capri became a haven for European artists and authors, the latter at times infusing their writings with references to the island. When Allied forces took control of Capri in the weeks prior to Mary's arrival, the commanding officer – apparently sensing what was appropriate – is said to have asked a New York *Herald Tribune* war correspondent to help draft the terms of surrender, saying "I am giving Capri back to the writers." The correspondent was John Steinbeck, who only a few years earlier had published his celebrated novel, *The Grapes of Wrath*.

Mary had every reason to believe, as she and colleagues hunted for library space, that a suitable villa could be found. A popular resort spot since Roman times, Capri had an abundance of pastel-colored dwellings, many having been the homes of not just artists but also of Europe's monied elite. Even so, not all of Capri's villas were habitable. A number had fallen into ruin, the most famous being the Villa Jovis, the sumptuous palace completed in AD 27 for the emperor Tiberius, its archeological remains visible to Mary when she hiked the island's trails.

While pressing forward on the library project, Mary and coworkers could not ignore the war. In mid-January, the Allies launched an attack sixty miles north of Naples on a vigorously defended German stronghold – the mountain town of Cassino and the sixth-century Benedictine monastery that overlooked it. Soon afterward, on January 22, Allied forces swarmed ashore on Italy's west coast near Anzio, a town notable for having been the birthplace of two notorious Roman emperors, Nero and Caligula. Preparations for both battles, especially for the Anzio attack, had required aerial assaults to destroy enemy communications and airfields, meaning few U.S. airmen could be spared for rest and recuperation on Capri. For Mary, the absence of military personnel meant leisure time, not all of it welcomed.

Mary's first mention of her "vacation" came in a letter the day after the Anzio landings. While giving no reason for her free time – her reticence undoubtedly due to censorship – she appeared to make an extra effort to assure her family she was well.

January 23, 1944

Dearest Winnie & Ora –

Sunday morning – and I like to imagine what you are doing – Dad is reading the papers, the Radio is on, and Mother, are you in the kitchen making it smell good for dinner or have you gone to Sunday school and left the roast for Dad? Are you having Annie, George and Bud for dinner? I'm there too, you know, even if you can't see me – you feel me, don't you? Do I sound homesick? I'm not – truly, but sometimes I'd like to be with you mighty well.

We had a beautiful day yesterday. We're still having our vacation – so our time is pretty much our own. Five of us rented carriages in the Square and rode down the mountain to a little village beside the sea for lunch. We ate outside on a terrace in the bright sunlight, steak, potatoes, wonderful apple pie and wine. Directly below us on the beach was an old woman mending fishing nets. She sat patiently for hours on the stones, holding the nets with her bare toes as she used her hands to sew with the big wooden needle. There were fishermen, too, who had just come in with their catch. I took a picture of them. . . .

Thursday night we had a square dance – and such fun. There are always a few Italians at our parties and it was something to see them do our American folk dances. They seemed to enjoy it and danced very well. The funniest part, though, was getting an Italian orchestra to feel the rhythm of Turkey in the Straw. A few trials and they were off as well as any mountain hill-billy. Worse luck – I turned my ankle (in my flat heeled shoes) and had to quit. It's taped and will be well in another day.

When we returned yesterday from our little trip I found Conchita, our little maid, scrubbing our beds & floors to rid us of the fleas – so I hurriedly made some changes in furniture. There is a little corner fire place in our room that had been lost from view by one of the beds. We put both the beds on the other side of the room – and then in front of the fire place our chairs & table.

Ceramic Madonna made it home safely and remains in the family today.

Secure in a niche over the mantle there is an Italian Madonna that I bought. So help me, I'm going to get her home if I have to carry her in my arms. She is made of glazed pottery glazed with beautiful colors. She has brown curly hair, a gray purple robe, a baby in pink in her arms and a little brown fawn at her knees. I've also bought a jam jar with cherries over it that I want to go in your kitchen some day.

Mopsey, the woman I've been working with, has had orders to return to Naples for re-assignment – We're all afraid our turns will be next. I hate to leave here – it's been so perfect – but I'm crossing bridges – it may not come.

Do be good – and remember I miss and Love You, Mary

The following Sunday, Mary wrote again:
Dearest Mother & Dad –
Time passes so quickly. I can hardly think that a whole week has gone since I wrote you. We have had plenty of leisure but too much free time makes one lazy so I will have to use that for my excuse. We still have no guests to entertain and are just wandering around soaking in as much as we can. Last Sunday night we heard a Piano Recital given by a woman who has had a great career in Europe. She is quite old but still plays beautifully. Her husband is a historian and Art Critic and lectures to us on the history of this place. They will give their recitals and lectures to our guests when they return in payment of which the Red Cross will furnish them with food.

This morning, Fritzie Haugland, a girl from California who was in Richmond the same time as I, [2] *went with me for a walk up one of the mountains.... The whole side of the mountain is a garden with terraced walks where once the Romans built their Villas – some of the columns are still standing. On the very top is the ruin of a Roman castle [Tiberius's Villa Jovis]. There is a long walk lined with Cypress trees which leads to a Greek shrine of white marble – all about are wild narcissus filling the air*

---

2. Fritzie's brother was Vern Haugland, an Associated Press war correspondent who became the first civilian to be awarded the Silver Star medal. In 1942, when a bomber in which he was a passenger ran out of fuel, he parachuted into the jungles of New Guinea and managed to survive forty-three days before being rescued by missionaries. Honored by General MacArthur for his heroism, Haugland, who was near death when rescued, recovered and resumed his war reporting in the Pacific Theater.

with their heavy fragrance. In a few more weeks the whole mountain will be covered with all kinds of flowers we have been told. We did, however, this morning gather a lovely bouquet of purple heather, roses, narcissus, and other flowers I've never seen so have no idea of the names. We left them at my Hotel to brighten the living room.

Yesterday after lunch, Hank, the boy who runs our Hotel, and I went out to sit in the garden. There is a terrace there – under the trees are tables where we will be eating as soon as the weather is a wee bit warmer. We wandered about until we found ourselves in the Monastery gardens – one of the fathers showed us about. The Monastery is very old and has partly been restored but [is] all terribly interesting.

Hank is quite a nice person from Atlanta Ga. He says he is very much in love with me but that is just another of those things. I can usually kid them out of it. He is a little more persistent than the others but we do have good fun. He and the Mess Sergeant manage the hotel so anything I want I usually get. Two days this week I spent in bed – not very sick, just a little. He flooded me with dainties from the kitchen. Too much attention, Mother, I'll never be the same. All I have to do [is] <u>hint</u>, not ask, and I receive. Such a hard way to fight the war. We have had some indications of the recent <u>push</u> which I daren't mention otherwise we are so isolated we might as well be in another world. . . .

Please keep well and let me hear from you. I've had no mail now for 2 weeks and am getting mighty hungry.

All my Love, Mary

Several days later, on February 3, Mary wrote her Auburn friend, Joanna Rhoads, and mentioned that she was in her "third week of enforced vacation" and "getting fat as two horses." Mary also told Joanna that she had spent the previous morning doing an inventory of books for the "boys" – signaling that a suitable villa had been found. In a same-day letter to Annie's family, Mary confirmed the securing of a villa, then included vignettes about islanders, some in uniform, some not.

Dearest Annie, George & Bud –

. . . Yesterday morning I helped make an inventory of some books in the Library of an Englishwoman whose villa the R.C. has taken over as a source of recreation for the men. It is in a fascinating and beautiful *old villa. There are many South African hunting trophies all about the walls and the library is one of the most complete private ones I've ever seen. These people here have certainly had a wonderful and gracious way of living. But in all the luxury and beauty of the place there are no bathrooms and we were eaten alive by fleas.*

In the afternoon I attended a rather strange ceremony. One of our gals, "Liz" Elliott, was baptized by the chaplain. She has fallen head over heels in love with him and I'm not sure whether it's her love of him or whether she did feel the need of the Holy Water that prompted her act. It was touching, though, just me, another girl, and one of the Captains were the only witnesses in the little German Chapel. The love affair is a rather hopeless but plutonic [sic] affair. The man is married, has children and has been transferred to another post. He's a swell person and we'll be missing him.

This is quite an artists' colony and one of the Artists, an anti-Nazi German, has been doing portraits of some of the girls. I went with one of them for a sitting the other day and watched the old boy work. He is very good but very much on the modern flashy side – bringing out characteristics rather than making a true likeness of his subjects. Another day, my room-mate, Blenda Larson, and I went for tea at the villa of the woman who helps us in the R.C. office. Her husband, too, is a painter, but does landscapes – not too good, I'm afraid. They have three small boys – one is 3 yrs – another 24 mos and the baby 5 mos. The baby, Carlo, is still wrapped in swaddling clothes but is a darling. He lies in a little boat cradle all day and never cries – the other is in a crib all day and never cries – probably because they haven't the energy to cry. Their little hands were blue with cold.

I think I mentioned to Mother how much I'm going to be needing stockings. Sometime if you think of it stick a pair in a letter – a large Airmail envelope – I would appreciate it so very much. Size 8 1/2, <u>short length</u> and I'll love you the rest of my life. I made a great mistake when I first came here by sending all my stockings with my laundry. They were ironed with a hot iron and came back filled with tiny holes so I'm getting very low – and Gosh I've just started. . . .

Do be good, all you kids, write whenever you can. Letters are <u>sure</u> swell to get.

All my Best Love, Mary

While the fighting at Cassino and Anzio continued, and as the Allies attempted – but failed – to advance toward Rome, Mary tried to win her own battles against boredom. She read, cloud-gazed, and even typed a play, the performance to take place when airmen returned. Mary also enjoyed the company of a four-legged friend, news she shared with her parents in a February 6 letter:

Marble bust, circa AD 30, of the Roman emperor Tiberius, who spent the final decade of his reign (AD 14 - 37) on Capri. The portrait bust is housed in the Archaeological Museum in Naples. (Photo by author)

We have a new addition to our midst – a black kitten that we are calling Tiberius, for the old Roman Emperor who has a castle near here. He came night before last. Yesterday he had a bath and last night insisted on sleeping with me. Since we all have fleas we can't be afraid of him and only hope he will absorb our supply. He's really very cute and as black as night.

We are still groping about for something to keep us busy. Yesterday morning I typed a play (about women) that we intend to start rehearsals for this afternoon. When our guests come back we will have a few tricks up our sleeves to present them.

I did my work in the other Villa where the other gals are staying. It is a perfectly beautiful home. All the bedrooms have roomy terraces, the living room is all book lined with a wonderful fireplace – at one end is a huge window that brings the outside right in. I spent the afternoon there on a divan under the window watching the clouds and the mountains, reading a little and even some snoozing. Many of us have been taken away for new assignments and perhaps I'll be next – but those of us who do stay are going to find a more comfortable villa. Ours is not bad but there are many more which are more comfortable. Our room, for instance, hasn't a single chest of drawers and it's hard to make it look neat with clothes piled about. . . .

We've had a few rainy cold days lately but today is bright with sunshine but still chilly. I'm sitting now in the sunshine to try to keep warm – we have no heat and these are cold tile floors. Spring will soon come though – the trees are budding – the peach and almond trees are both out. The almond blossoms are lovely – they look much like apple.

I wish it could be spring for you, too. I do hope you are all well. Be good and remember I love you all very much.

It seems hard to be so far away from you but I wouldn't trade this wonderful experience for a great deal. I've never regretted my decision in coming. Just now I feel as if I weren't earning my salt but there will come a day, soon, when we'll begin to get busy again.

As Ever & Always, Mary

Barely twenty-four hours later, Mary shook off her boredom, welcomed news about her next assignment, and hastily informed her mother – in a note that bypassed censors – that she was leaving Capri. She had orders to return by boat to the Italian mainland, around the very time, coincidentally, that her friend and fellow Auburnite, Bill Husselman, was disembarking from a troopship anchored off the Scottish coast. While Bill and his mates were readying for the invasion of northern Europe, Mary was about to plant herself – to use Churchill's phrase – in Europe's "soft underbelly."

She surmised her new assignment would *not* be soft. She fervently hoped she would earn her "salt."

Monday Feb. [7], 1944

Dearest Mother –

This is only a note to tell you that a Major who is leaving tomorrow for the States offered to take some of our mail back home with him and mail it from there. Consequently I can tell you where I have been for the past two months – On the Isle of Capri.

We were in Naples four days in Dec. before coming here. The irony of the whole thing is that I have had orders to go back to Naples for re-assignment and will be leaving this Thursday. We go by boat which takes several hours.

I am then to go to Casserta [sic] which is about 12 miles from Naples to be in a Rest Home for Infantry of the 5th Army. They are boys just back from the front and I feel that I will really be doing a job there. We are to live in a Palace which is very beautiful but very cold – I've heard. My room-mate whom I like very much is going with me.

When you write – don't mention this – only that you received my letter of Feb. the 6th.

Will write again when things are more settled.

All my Love, Mary

P.S. Mother – this is only for yours & the family's information.

Italy

Upon departing Capri, Mary would see other parts of Italy - on assignment and on leave. The cities noted above are but a few of the places she visited during the war, as recorded in her letters.

Chapter Nine

MARY: 1944

*I*TALY
FEB. 13, 1944

Dearest Mother & Dad –
I am now started on my new job and if ever there is a contrast this is it. I grew fat, lazy and spoiled in the lap of luxury – this is completely reversed, however, I think there will be a great satisfaction in this work. The men are combat troops fresh back from the front. They come in so tired and exhausted that they are perfectly dull. The camp is anything but attractive but is the first bit of civilization they have seen for some time. They can at least, have hot showers and sit in front of the fire places. There are movies and shows for them to see and shops to buy presents to send home. . . .

MARY BRANDON'S REASSIGNMENT, as she had confided to her mother before departing Capri, took her north of Naples toward the town of Caserta. While her new workplace was militarily significant, it was also distinctive. The "camp" was actually an eighteenth-century palace from which Lieutenant General Mark W. Clark of the U.S. Fifth Army and British General Sir Harold Alexander of 15th Army Group were directing troops up the Italian peninsula. Stiff German resistance – at the rain-swollen Volturno River north of Caserta, on the beaches at Anzio, near the mountain town of Cassino – had slowed the Allies' march to Rome, leading to heavy casualties and leaving soldiers in desperate need of rest. The Red Cross, in keeping with its mission, operated a recreational club at the palace complex. Mary, as before, was to cheer and comfort the battle-weary.

Describing her surroundings as "anything but attractive," Mary might have spoken differently had she visited Caserta a century or more earlier. In 1752, Charles VII of Naples – the Bourbon monarch who later became Charles III of Spain – laid the cornerstone for the Reggia (Royal Palace) of Caserta, intending for it to rival Versailles near Paris and the Royal Palace at Madrid. Workers toiled for decades, and the result was a massive twelve-hundred-room mansion, the largest palace erected in Europe at that time. The interior featured a ramped marble staircase, a theater with forty boxes, baroque frescoes and furnishings, and other eye-popping displays of opulence, including a gold-lined bathtub for the queen. The palace grounds were equally stunning, with gardens, fountains, cascades, reflecting pools, and ornate sculptures gracing a vast park. Woodlands, interspersed with hunting lodges, stretched beyond.

But years of neglect and war had taken a toll on the property. By autumn 1943, when Allied forces arrived, the cavernous palace was associated more with fleas, banging shutters, inadequate heat, and a confusing maze of rooms reached only by fatigue-inducing flights of stairs. For the fifteen thousand soldiers who would eventually live and work there, Allied commanders hurriedly converted rooms into dormitories, dining halls, bakeries, and laundries. They likewise set up makeshift offices, complete with plywood-and-sawhorse desks, maps pinned to walls, and cable and phone lines running in and out of windows, due to the walls being too thick to thread wire through. For servicemen needing a haircut and shave, an in-house barbershop was made ready; officers needing cognac slaked their thirst in an improvised bar. As the author Rick Atkinson noted in the second of his World War II trilogy, *The Day of Battle,* the palace soon became "a baroque parody of the Pentagon."

Meanwhile, troops sent there for R&R found plenty to like. Palace rooms and outbuildings were outfitted with game tables, musical instruments, and letter-writing supplies; a spacious salon doubled as an indoor basketball court. Outdoors, where many soldiers bivouacked, parkland gave way to shower huts and, in good weather, to softball diamonds and volleyball courts. North of the palace, near an elaborate fountain depicting the Roman goddess Diana, generals escaped to summer houses built by army engineers.

Within this largely all-male colony, Mary was assigned lodging on the fifth floor of the palace proper. She slept on a cot, using her bathrobe as a pillow. Her sleeping quarters were decidedly unusual, as her February 13 letter to her parents – her first from Caserta – noted:

We are living in a Palace which may sound elegant but is far from that. There are flights & flights of stairs to climb.

We live on the top floor – no heat in the apartment and Blenda [Larson] & I are living in the Bathroom. (At least it's very handy – besides I'll be knowing the state of health of all my co-workers.) It really isn't quite that bad because the Bathroom itself is a huge affair and the business end is glassed off to one side – but the sounds still carry through.

Mary on the palace grounds. (Courtesy Gloria Fink)

A week later, on February 21, Mary shared more camp details, remarking to her friend, Joanna Rhoads, that the palace reminded her of a movie set. Interestingly, in 1942 an Italian motion picture, *The Three Pilots (I tre aquilotti)*, had been filmed there. Decades later, Hollywood would discover the palace and incorporate it into several films, including *Star Wars Episode I, The Phantom Menace* (1999), *Star Wars Episode II, Attack of the Clones* (2002), *Mission Impossible III* (2006), and *Angels & Demons* (2009). Knowing that Jo, a teacher, would be interested in her "classroom," Mary offered the following:

Dearest Jo –

… This place is really something out of this world – it actually looks like a movie set but not the beautiful variety. The [Red Cross] Center

itself where we spend our days is in an old stable – a huge place that can hold hundreds of men. They have partitioned off a few rooms – so beginning tomorrow it is my task to decorate the Music room – sounds pretentious but actually very meager – I'm going to do the walls in red and on the upper draw some lines and staffs complete with notes, clef signs etc. It's the old music teacher in me, I guess.

I went into the city [Naples] Saturday for my day off and had a wonderful time having a bath and simply being there. Here I talk all day long until I'm really speechless at the end of the day. I'm so glad to know that Barney [Jo's cousin] is near me somewhere. I'll look him up some of these days. I had a long talk with Sterling Ward [a mutual soldier friend from their home county] over the phone, about a week ago. He promised to come here to see me and bring Phil Berg with him if they weren't transferred. They haven't appeared so perhaps they are on their way again.

Do keep pouring in the letters, Jo. I enjoy them so very much. . . .

As Ever, Mary

At month's end, in a lengthy letter to her parents, Mary began with a bit of news that likely pleased them: She had had a dinner-and-dancing date with a "very nice young" captain, and they were to go out again. Mary then switched to describing soldiers on leave at the club, and her parents, simply by following war developments, likely deduced the battlefronts from which men came and to which they would return. Despite having launched a beach assault at Anzio in late January, Allied forces remained pinned down there. Likewise, the Allies had yet to oust Germans from Cassino, even though twelve days earlier – on February 15 – American bombers had dropped nearly six hundred tons of explosives, reducing the historic abbey overlooking the town to smoking rubble.

Hampering Allied efforts to secure Cassino was a foe separate from the Germans. Sleeting rain on steep, muddy terrain continually slowed foot soldiers' progress. Years later, John McNeel, whose anti-aircraft unit saw action with the U.S. Fifth Army at Cassino, wrote an article for *Virginia Quarterly Review* stating: "I don't think it is an exaggeration to say that the battle of Cassino was fought out in some of the worst weather and terrain conditions that confronted any troops in either world war. German troops who had served on the Russian front have been quoted as saying that they would crawl back to Russia on their hands and knees to get away from Cassino." As McNeel also explained, "It seemed to us that the sleeting rain never once stopped; it fell steadily day and night. Once drenched it was almost impossible to get dry. What was worse was the icy morass that we lived in and which sucked the shoes right off your feet."

Those wretched conditions are what Mary alluded to when referencing the "boys" and frostbitten hands.

Sunday, February 27

Dearest Mother & Dad –

So sorry not to be able to get more letters in to you but there just doesn't seem to be enough time. Yesterday on my day off I spent it in front of a fire in the Officers' quarters just sitting doing nothing and it felt mighty good. I've been having some pretty good attention from one of the Captains who is the Medical officer for the permanent party. A very nice young man who took me into the City Friday night to a fancy Officers' Club for dinner and dancing afterwards. It almost felt like being home and driving to Ft. Wayne for dinner – but instead of having a closed car with heat we were in a Command Car with a G.I. driver. I felt, too, like a Country bumpkin eating in a beautiful dining room with real China and regular silver. It's strange how a few weeks in the sticks can put the hayseed in one's hair. The Captain ("Doc" we call him) insists on going back next Friday night and I'll certainly take him up on it.

Today we are having what we call "Change Day." The boys who have been here for five days are leaving and the new group is coming in. The building is cleared for a few hours and the Italians working here have a chance to get the place cleaned out with no boys to step over during the process. We moved some of the furniture around and made some other changes. But now, the boys have checked in, found their billets, have been assigned and are now here looking the place over. We have a music room in the back where there is a piano, several guitars, an accordion, and a bass fiddle. All day long and evenings too those instruments are in use. It's most interesting to go back and watch the expression on the faces of both the boys who casually pick up the instruments to play and those who gather around when the Hill Billys really get started. Not a flicker of expression crosses their faces, they will both perform and listen with such solemn faces. I like to go in and show a little enthusiasm for their playing and watch the smiles creep into their mugs. A few of them are pretty good too and have been in Radio back home. We have another Music room too where there is a phonograph with some really good records, also the popular variety which disappear so rapidly that we can scarcely keep it supplied. Last week I noticed a boy who sat in the little room all day just playing the good records. When I went in to talk to him I found that he had graduated from Oberlin School of Music with a Bachelor Degree in Piano. He had taught Theory for awhile before joining the army and hopes to go back home to get his Master's at Yale. The poor guy hadn't touched a piano for six months and with a little coaxing he came out to the piano and played Brahms and Bach so beautifully even with his still black hands. Gosh it hurts to see boys like that. We both had a wonderful time – he playing and me drinking in his lovely music. There are always a lot of drunks around who feel that's the best way to relax and forget the things they have just come from and will have to go back to – but there are a few like the other boy I mentioned. There was another, too, Charlie, who spent all his time at the piano playing popular music and very well too. He had had his hands frozen and they wouldn't work too well – but he had a wonderful time. We found out that we had come over on the same boat. He said that he was one of the few of his group left. It seems so strange to think that I feel I've only just arrived but to him and boys like him it has been a whole hellish life-time.

Once during the time each group is here we serve them Coffee and Doughnuts and do they ever gobble them up. We have between 5,000 and 6,000 doughnuts but every one is lapped up with the greatest gusto. Mother, I'm so proud of these boys – they are the bravest in the world and are having a mighty tough time of it. All they can think about is getting home – some have been away for two years and have been in the front lines for long periods and they are tired and homesick – poor, poor guys.

... Must stop now and go for evening "chow." Do write when you can.
All My Love, Mary

Just days earlier, Mary had sent home a V-Mail, a letter copied onto microfilm then reprinted at about sixty percent of its original size – a form of communication the military encouraged to free up needed cargo space on ships and planes. Knowing V-Mail could be hard to read, Mary apologized for resorting to it. She also regretted the brevity of her message, telling her parents that "this is about as much time as I will have. We have certainly been busy, some days working from 8 in the morning until 10 at night." Referencing Annie Becker, a Red Cross group leader who recently had visited Caserta, Mary added:

Annie admits we have a hard rugged job but she insists we can take it. In a way I feel very humble, all the boys are so appreciative of any little thing we can do for them. I've been singing all afternoon with a group around the piano. I promise to get another of these [V-Mail] off to you this week. I do hope you are all well.

Mary turned to V-Mail again that month when writing her thirteen-year-old-nephew, Buddy, to whom she described a boy orphaned by the war. The Italian campaign, already so deadly to combatants, was taking – and would continue to take – a heavy toll on Italian civilians. At least one young victim of the violence, as Mary noted, benefited from the kindness of U.S. soldiers.

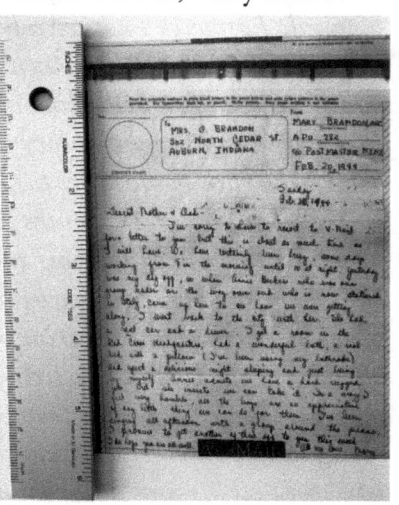

V-Mail, short for "Victory Mail"

Feb. 29, 1944

Dearest Bud –

... Last night in the Center there was an Italian boy who reminded me very much of you. He is about your age and has been adopted by some of the boys as a mascot. His father was killed by the Germans and his home was gone – he wears regular G.I. clothes like all the soldiers and is very proud to be one of them. He is looking forward to going to America after the war. The boys call him "Charlie" and he sat at my [knee] and sang some beautiful Italian songs for all of us. He stays up at the front with the soldiers and came down here along with some of his pals for a rest.

We are all working very hard and keeping mighty busy. The mud is perfectly terrible – it has rained for a solid week. Tonight is my night off –

so I'm going to the opera. One of the Captains is our camp is taking me. I would love to hear what you've been doing both with school and your social life. It should be pretty good. Say Hello to everyone for me.

IN EARLY MARCH, soon after telling her parents and Buddy about dating a "captain," Mary expanded on the subject in a letter to Annie. Given that Mary had written home about other soldiers, most notably the sergeant in Washington, D.C., Annie likely found the news interesting but, for the time being, not particularly consequential. Even so, Mary made clear to her sister that she enjoyed the captain's company. She did not give his name, leaving her family to know him only as "Doc."

March 3, 1944
Dearest Annie –
... Besides being very busy here at the Center, a Capt., the Surgeon of the Area[,] is keeping me pretty busy after working hours and on my day off. He is very attentive and a little more than interested. He's really a swell person and wonderful company. He's been away from home for so long that even I look good to him. We are going into the City tonight again for dinner and some dancing.

In that same letter, Mary relayed news about her roommate, Blenda Larson, a Massachusetts native who had taught health education at the University of Georgia before joining the Red Cross. The two had a "history" together, as Mary explained:

I've just had the news that Blenda, the gal that came with me from Capri[,] is going to have to go to the hospital for an operation and I'm to take over her duties. She is a Program director so I can see how much busier I'm going to be. God help me. We've really been having some good talent appear and all we have to [do is] pick it out and it performs beautifully – incidentally they like to hear me sing too. Gosh – I'm going to miss Blenda – she felt like my last link both with home because we came over together and lived together before. The gals here are old timers and are pretty clicky – some how I'll have to worm in.

A week later, Mary informed Annie that her work life remained unchanged: "We have the same mobs of men but with new faces, the same horror stories, the same hill-billy music with occasionally a good musician thrown in. Right now our phonograph is broken so there isn't quite as much music in our ears all the time." Mary also shared good news about Blenda and again mentioned Doc: "Blenda is back with us. She didn't need her operation after all. Last night we collected in Doc's Dispensary for a game of Bridge. It wasn't like the usual session at home – but we did play on his desk and the drinks were medicinal alcohol and fruit juice. I believe we had just as good a time."

Not long afterwards, Mary enjoyed the company of another army captain – Richard (Dick) Fink, the son of a prominent Auburn family and heir to one of the city's major businesses, Auburn Foundry. Younger than Mary by nearly eight years, Fink had received his military training in ordnance inspection and recently been reassigned to Italy from North Africa.

[Monday] March 13

Dearest Mother & Dad –

This is one of the few beautiful days I have seen since coming to this spot. Perhaps the rains are over, I hope, for more than one reason. I have lost my rain-coat and attempted to buy one in the city the other day only to find that the exceptional one that fit me cost $70.00. I can be wet for that price. I am saving some money... there seems to be nothing to spend it on and one of these days I'll send it home in the form of a money order.

I hitched myself a ride into the city [Naples] Saturday morning, had lunch, my hair washed and hitched back again. There is never any trouble getting a ride. All the traffic (and there is a great amount) is military and any soldier is more than happy to pick up an American girl.

Yesterday afternoon Dick Fink came to see me. He learned where I was from [Red Cross] headquarters in the city. We had a grand visit and I'm going to meet him next Saturday night for dinner in the city. He hasn't been in Italy very long. He looks well but a little older. When he said he had a slight sore throat I took him to the dispensary to have it swabbed by my "Doc" – the Captain.

I don't have a lot of news to tell you. Life goes on just about the same. We do about the same things in the Club every day. Last night I played the piano for the boys who gathered around to sing for about three hours. We quit only after we had exhausted three books of songs. On the first night the boys are here we have two Italian accordionists come in. I always sing with them – They seem to like it. We have set up a Snack Bar in a bombed out building near by where sandwiches and coffee are served every night. One of us on the staff have to be there to dish out the chow. Great vats of sandwich spread we whip up out of C Ration Corn Beef disappear like magic. One night during the five we have Red Cross doughnuts. Would you believe that 5000 doughnuts last just two hours. That seems like a lot of doughnuts but we have a lot of boys.

I do hope the stockings will be coming soon. My reserve is fast dwindling to nothing. It's terribly hard to write a very clear letter with so much confusion around all the time – so if my notes sound screwy you will have to pardon them. I've not have [sic] any mail from anyone for a long time. I do hope it doesn't mean that you are not well. Do be good.

All my Love, Mary

Knowing her parents would enjoy hearing more about Fink, Mary wrote home the following Sunday and summarized their weekend outing. The two had dined together Saturday evening in Naples, then spent the next morning driving through the countryside before returning to Caserta. Mary's cultural biases seeped into her letter when she mentioned both Italian villagers and North African Arabs.

Sunday March 19, 1944
Dearest Mother & Dad –
Yesterday Doc took me into the city [Naples] in his ambulance so that I could keep my date with Dick Fink. I don't think he was too happy about doing it because he had ask[ed] me to a dinner dance in the city too – but he was just too late. Dick and I had a fine time. He called for me this morning at R.C. headquarters where we always stay while in the city. It was our intention to go to the famous mountain near the city but we got off on the wrong road and by the time we found our way back to the city it was time for us to start back here.

There are some beautiful cascades & fountains back of the palace where I live so we drove up there and took some pictures. I do hope they turn out well. This was such a beautiful day to drive – perfectly clear and bright. The road back here from the city is quite interesting. It is lined on both sides with vineyards. The vines hang on the trunks of great sycamore trees. Of course the trees are always trimmed so that the vines will have light – but now that there are no leaves on the vines – it gives one the impression of a great forest with its hair all cut short. There are a few villages on the way too – such dirty ugly gray looking buildings and the people are actually dirtier than the Arabs. Dick came over here [to the palace] with me for lunch. We eat with the officers so, of course, he was welcome to be my guest. He is such a handsome boy.

Mary and Auburn friend Dick Fink in front of an ornate fountain at Caserta. (Courtesy Gloria Fink)

I had looked forward to having a hot bath at the Headquarters but they had a few hot spots [shelling] close to them the other night and there wasn't a window left in the place. Our dear good friend of the boat, Annie Becker is there now as head personnel of all women in this theatre. By the way, while Doc and I were having lunch at the R.C. Mess Saturday noon, Madeleine Carroll, the movie actress came in and ate lunch at the table next to ours. She is a R.C. Hospital worker and looks and dresses just like all the rest of us. Annie Becker says she is very charming and an extremely nice person. Annie has been wonderful to me – she realizes that we have one of the toughest club assignments they have to give out – but oh Mother, it's so satisfying. I don't see how I could ever be happy in a purely conventional club after this. We work hard and put up with a lot of troublesome things but it's all worth every bit of it.

We may be trying to find some new living quarters. Living in a palace is not all it's cracked up to be. – However, I'm getting so used to my little bathroom-bedroom that I hardly notice the bowel movements of my associates anymore. Doc had some sheets made for me by the taylor [sic] here out of some unbleached muslin they had in the dispensary – which I thought was very thoughtful of him. Everyone is so nice to us – bless them.

I do hope you are all well – Spring will soon be coming and I know how you both perk up in the warmer weather.

Speaking of warmer weather – I wish you could send me my white dress – the one with the blue embroidery in it – that and some perfume if you can find any. I thought I had a large supply but I use so much of it. It is so popular with the boys – sometimes as I walk by them they stop me – just to smell my hair – and if they like it I'm going to keep on wearing it as long as I can....

Thank you so much for "The [Auburn Evening] Star" – It almost felt like sitting down at home and looking thru the paper. It has come twice and I'm looking forward to its continuance....

Do be good darlings.
All my Love, Mary

AS IF WAR WEREN'T ENOUGH, the Italian people and Allied forces faced another menace in early 1944. Mount Vesuvius, the volcano overlooking Naples and its famous bay, began to wake up after having been relatively quiet for more than a decade. The Associated Press reported on January 9, 1944 that "a huge and spectacular 'V' sign has appeared on the slopes of Mt. Vesuvius facing toward the 5th Army front. It was formed by two long streams of fiery lava that spilled from the crater and slanted down the side of the volcano, finally converging some 400 feet below."

While some Italians viewed the "V" as an omen of an early Allied victory, many others grew worried, and rightfully so. On March 18, the volcano erupted, spewing thick oily smoke, rocks the size of basketballs, and fountains of boiling lava that soon swept down the cone and incinerated nearby villages. Nearly twelve thousand civilians were displaced and twenty-six people died, most of the deaths occurring when roofs collapsed under heavy accumulations of ash. The U.S. military responded to the crisis by pulling troops away from the war effort to oversee public safety and evacuations.

Mount Vesuvius erupting in March 1944 (National Archives)

Though no servicemen died as a result of the eruption, the military suffered considerable property damage. Ash and debris ruined the braking drums in vehicles and the bearings in ship engines, leading to a slowdown in troop traffic and a reduction of supplies in the Mediterranean Theater. Raining ash and lava rock also destroyed eighty-eight Army Air Force B-25 bombers parked at an airfield near Pompeii, the Roman city destroyed in AD 79 during Vesuvius' most storied explosion.

Mary and her colleagues were never in harm's way; the palace at Caserta was more than twenty miles from the volcano. But the eruption was definitely a novelty, as Mary's next letter home noted.

March 22, 1944

Dearest Mother & Dad –

The packages arrived this afternoon and were they ever a welcome sight. Thank you so very much for them. I wonder whose shoe ration coupon I used. They fit beautifully and I put on one and paraded down the center aisle of the club with one dirty galosh on one foot and the beautiful new shoe on the other. The boys got a terrific bang out of seeing a new pair of real American shoes. The Italian women wear mostly wooden shoes that clump at every step. They have very high heels and are the wedgie variety. Very ugly and look most uncomfortable.

The white sweater is a [beaut]. I can hear the whistles I'll get when I wear it all ready. Along with the packages came five Evening Stars. It's wonderful to read the old paper.

Tomorrow on my day off Doc is going to try to get a Jeep and we're going to see how Vesuvius is coming along. Everyone who has seen it says it's really something and an experience that one shouldn't miss. Even as far away as we are the flame and smoke of it can be seen at night.

Yesterday I drove to a little town near here with one of the gals that I knew at Capri. She was trying to find Charcoal and what a time [of it we had] while we waited for the sacks to be filled; we were absolutely surrounded by I'm sure, every child in the town – such dirty, quaint but appealing and surprisingly pretty children. They are all dirty as the old rags they wear and are covered with skin sores. Their bare little legs were blue with cold but they didn't seem to mind it. They were full of laughter and good humour.

We are working out a new schedule and since the men are here for a five day period we get one of those five off. Instead of having a certain day of the week free the second day of each five will be mine for leisure. We'll be working harder and longer while we do work but actually there will be more time all together for a little playing....

You both be good and you know of course, how much I love you.

Meanwhile, as Vesuvius was unleashing its fury in mid-March, the Allies launched another major offensive at Cassino, dropping more than one thousand tons of bombs and firing nearly 200,000 artillery rounds to try to dislodge the defending Germans. Hitler's troops, aided by the Nazi 1st Parachute Division, still refused to cede ground and clung grimly to mountaintop ruins, forcing the Allies – confronted with their own mounting casualties – to call off the attack on March 23. In letters to family and friends during this period, Mary shared snippets of her daily life. And while she never specifically mentioned the fighting at Cassino, she acknowledged that war helped focus her mind on what was really important.

The ruined abbey at Monte Cassino. St. Benedict established his first monastery atop that promontory in the sixth century. (Imperial War Museum via Wikimedia Commons)

March 17, 1944

Dearest [brother-in-law] George:

... There isn't a great amount of excitement for us on our free hours. Tuesday night 'The Doc' and some of the other officers took me for a stroll

down into the town to attend a movie, my first since being here. We had all heard that it was a good new one from home, but Gosh we had to leave after the second reel. Such silly trash coming from home almost made me ashamed. Maybe we have lived too close to people that have seen enough of life and death that their sense of values have had some influence in changing our attitude too.

I had my first Coke yesterday, and it certainly tasted swell. They have them now at the PX but we are rationed to one a week. It wouldn't go very far on a large evening, would it. We get seven packages of cigarettes a week, one candy bar and one bar of soap. Once a month, if we are lucky we can get a box of Kleenx [sic] and a bottle of shampoo. Our needs are actually so simple that everything we get is adequate. . . .

March 20, 1944
Dearest [friend] Katie [Manon] –
. . . This is a much different situation than the one I was in when writing my last letter to you. It certainly lacks the comforts and beauties of the other job [on Capri] – but the compensation comes from the great satisfaction there is in working with these men. They are all tired both physically and mentally from the front lines which isn't too far away. I get a great kick out of thinking that we are as close to the front lines as Club workers go. There is, of course, no danger, but plenty of excitement. The traffic is a continuous line of vehicles at all times carrying things to the lines. . . .

March 25, 1944
Dearest Annie –
. . . It's so darn cold tonight – an inch away from the stove and your breath pours out like smoke. It was spitting snow when I walked over here [to the club] tonight. What do they mean "Sunny Italy" –

If you haven't had a chance to find a dress (print) yet, skip it because there is certainly no place here to wear it. . . .

March 31, 1944
Dearest [friend] Jessie [Baxter] –
. . . You probably know from Mother what kind of a job I have now. The comforts of life are much less than they were on Capri but the work is

better. These men, just off the front, seem to appreciate us so very much. I'm going to have a terrible time getting my head turned around again when we come home. We have so many men that there is actually so little we can do for them except provide them a Club of sorts. It is in an old stable – the roof leaks on rainy days and it's cold except for around the two big fireplaces and a few stoves we have scattered about. We provide a package wrapping service which is constantly busy, writing desks where hundreds of thousands of letters are always being written – this is their first & last chance sometimes, two pianos that are always being played, a phonograph and radio and a special music room where a jam session (usually Hill Billy) is going every minute.

We live in a most pretentious Palace but don't let that throw you. It's cold as forty hells and has 185 steps to climb. We live in the Wicked Fairy chamber away at the top. I lived in the Bathroom for about six weeks but have now graduated to the first room which has a fire place (ironically enough we have no fuel to burn). The rooms all progress backward railroad fashion so that to get to one's little cot all the rooms must be travelled through. Living in the first room I now get all the traffic – the bathroom was the last – so I got it all there too besides knowing the exact bathroom troubles of all my co-workers....

DAYS AFTER WRITING her friend Jessie, Mary returned to the subject of her palace apartment and her move to the front room. In a chatty letter to her parents, she detailed a "little surprise" – namely, her discovery of a small door that overlooked a "wonderful golden room." The door most likely allowed workmen to access the upper reaches of the palace's throne room.

April 3, 1944

Dearest Mother & Dad –

Let's have a little visit, shall we? How I wish it could be really in person. There are so many things I could say but haven't the talent to write. What almost scares me sometimes is that there are so many little things that seemed important and interesting at first that are now commonplace and I will forget them.

Blenda and I have moved from our Bathroom Bedroom into the first of the series of rooms. We even have a fireplace but have no fuel to burn in it unless we or our "beaux" bring it laboriously up the stairs. I still haven't seen much of the enormous place in which we live but I did have a little surprise this morning. Since I had to be at work by eight I was the first to leave and as I went thru the dark living room I noticed a wee crack of light coming from a little door I'd never seen before. When I opened it, there to my surprise I found I was away high almost to the ceiling of a wonderful golden room – it must have been a small throne room.

The "little door" Mary opened likely led to this ledge that overlooks the throne room.

Restored throne room today (Photos by author)

It is entirely frescoed in gold leaf and on the ceiling was a beautiful painting. I was almost too close to it to get the detail. My little niche was so far away from the floor and I couldn't get to the edge close enough to see any doors [below] but just the wonderful effect of the walls and beautiful ceiling.

There are only four girls here now at this Center – two are still in the hospital, so it keeps the rest of us pretty busy. From eight in the morning till ten at night is a long day. Last night was one of the nightmare variety. Our Italian help (we have 5 of them) in the Snack Bar made sandwiches all yesterday afternoon but we ran out in one hour after we started serving at 7:30. From then until 10, I and two of the boys spread Bread and Jam until we were blue in the face. I'm not going to be able to look a sandwich in the face. We have to do it all over again today starting at 1:00. Tomorrow's my day off, whoops.

I'm going into the city to get paid since I haven't drawn my salary for quite a while. The 'Doc' is going to take me in and while I'm getting my hair washed he's going to get us some tickets for 'This Is the Army' – I hope – they may be hard to get, everyone will be wanting to see it.

After work last night Doc, Blenda, a news correspondent who has been here for a few days gathering material for an article in the "New Yorker" and myself had a little party in the dispensary. Doc whipped up some Coffee on a little oil stove and had sandwiches from the kitchen (all of which I couldn't look at after dishing out 4 30-gallon cans of coffee and millions of sandwiches – but we all had a good time.

My <u>duty</u> calls. Will write again as soon as possible.

The following Sunday, April 9, was both Easter and her parents' fifty-third wedding anniversary. When writing home later that day, Mary briefly reminisced about Winnie and Ora's fiftieth – the "Golden Anniversary" the couple had celebrated in 1941 with an "open house" at their Cedar Street home. Organized by Mary and Annie, the daylong party was attended by more than 150 friends and relatives who delivered gifts and good wishes. Attired in her mother's wedding dress, Mary had served as greeter.

I can imagine you have had a good Easter dinner with Baked Ham, I hope. Besides being Easter, this is your 53rd Wedding Anniversary, isn't it. Do you remember our party? I still look back at it with a great amount of pleasure. I hope by next year I will be home to help you celebrate it again.

Ora and Winnie's party in 1941 with Mary, seated left, in her mother's wedding dress.

Our Club is filled with flowers today. The Italians who help us here gave the [Red Cross] gals two beautiful baskets – one of white camellias and another of pink & white camellias with beautifully fragrant Freesias and heather. We're very grateful for their thought of us. This morning I went to a Church service with 'Doc' but it was anything but Eastery. The Chaplain was the good old fashioned revival kind. There were no flowers or sun shining thru stained glass windows. It was held in the dark Post Theatre.

We all worked very hard for the Jewish Pass-Over Feast which was held here Friday and they ask[ed] RC to decorate the Mess Hall. We got truck loads of greens from the Palace gardens and bought 800 daffodils; also we had a few young apple [blossoms] as well. The Mess Hall is so enormous that it took loads & loads of greens & flowers to even make a dent.

Yesterday afternoon late Doc & I took a little picnic out into the mountains. We drove about an hour and a half before we could find a suitable place – but we wound around little country roads and into little villages entirely untouched by the war. There weren't many places to choose for our lunch since one is either in the valley where every inch of ground is cultivated or directly in the mountains. The fruit trees are all in blossom. I've never seen such deep pink as on the peach blossoms. The vineyards are interesting – the vines grow on huge trees that have their tops cut out to let in the sunlight. I imagine they will be a beautiful sight when the leaves & then the grapes come on. We found a little grassy knoll that was just perfect. The wild flowers in among the rocks looked like a real rock garden – There were narcissus, green iris with black tips – grape hyacinths and a little purple starry flower much like our anemones.

For physical food we had a can of Vienna sausages which we roasted like Hot dogs, a loaf of bread, a half pound of butter, a can of salmon, can of pineapple and some cake as well as coffee and a bottle of Champagne. The Sergeant who works for 'Doc' collected our food for us – so today I took him over a box of Red Cross doughnuts. The little spot we found was truly peaceful & beautiful. We could look over the valley in front of us with the high mountains at our back and then gradually the moon began creeping over the country-side lighting and whitening all the rocks and flowers. It was wonderful and we're [planning] on going back again.

Friday night I went to another little town for a dance but first went out to one of the camps for dinner if one could call it that. We ate cold C rations in a tent but I got to see how the boys really live.

Mother, don't be afraid for me as you indicated in your letter. In the number of miles we are not far from the front but I might just as well be at home as far as any danger area here is concerned. It is all very peaceful *except for the great amount of traffic and the number of combat troops we are seeing continuously. <u>Don't</u>, <u>don't</u> worry – there's nothing at all to be frightened about....*

All my Love to All of You, Mary

Despite her assurances, Mary was never entirely out of danger. Even drives through the countryside, with Doc and others, carried risks. Asked years later if she ever had been afraid during the war, Mary told an interviewer, "Yes, one time, especially. I was with a captain, and we were on the road near Caserta, and planes were flying in and there was a lot of shooting going on. I was afraid that time."

Meanwhile, Mary's relationship with Doc continued to flourish, and by spring she was referring to him in letters as her "beau." She did so in a late March letter to Auburn friend Katie Manon and again in an April 17 letter to her sister. As to why she was so fond of the military surgeon, Mary told Annie the following:

It doesn't seem right ever to have a beau that I can't bring out to your house for you to approve. You'd like "Doc", how much I wish you could know him. He's all kindness, goodness, fun, intelligent and extremely thoughtful. The 29th of this month will be my 6th month anniversary overseas and will end two years overseas duty for Doc. He was in England & Ireland and all three [of] the African Campaigns. He has really seen this war. Being in this spot is like having a vacation for him.... We plan to have a celebration [for our anniversaries]. I imagine it will be a pretty good one. He has a bottle of Kummel price $17.50 saved back with the greatest care.

IN LATE APRIL, after more visits from Dick Fink and a planned visit with another hometown acquaintance, Mary – expressing amazement – wrote her parents: "Honestly, I never dreamed that I would see so many people from Auburn Indiana. It's a small world, isn't it." By then, Mary already had been amazed by something entirely different, namely, opportunities to attend opera performances in a country beset by war. The highbrow entertainment came courtesy of the San

Carlo Opera Company of Naples, which under an arrangement with the Army, visited Caserta twice weekly and performed in the palace theater. The Army liked the arrangement because it offered troops a needed distraction; the financially pinched performers liked how they were paid – with Army food rations. By mid-March, Mary had managed to see four operas at the palace, and to a friend she declared, "they're better than the movies."

Better still for Mary was what she was treated to on April 21. American songwriter Irving Berlin had taken his stage show *This Is the Army* – the film version of which Mary had seen in Washington, D.C. – overseas in late 1943 to boost the morale of U.S. troops massing in Britain. At the recommendation of General Eisenhower, who saw the show in London in February 1944, Berlin and his musical troupe began traveling to other fronts, first to North Africa, then to Italy. Arriving in Naples in late March 1944, Berlin's company – 150 members strong – rehearsed in that city's war-damaged, but recently reopened, San Carlo Opera House, Europe's oldest opera venue. By April, the wildly popular revue was playing to sold-out audiences, with soldiers coming by truckloads to enjoy a few hours of rousing entertainment.

And rousing it was, as Mary would report. She attended a Friday evening performance with Doc, who had managed to snag tickets. Together, they watched Berlin – age fifty-five and still energetic – captivate the audience with his show-stopping rendition of "Oh! How I Hate to Get Up in the Morning." Days later, on April 24, Mary described the evening for her parents, emphasizing a surprising turn of events:

Irving Berlin performs for a packed audience of troops at San Carlo Opera House, April 1944 (National Archives)

> *Doc and one of the lieutenants and myself went to a nearby town Friday night to see "This is the Army." It is a wonderful show. Irving Berlin is still with it – perhaps you have been reading about it in the paper. We were a little late in arriving and the only vacant seats that*

were left were in the General's box – so we sat with him as big as you please. The boys insisted it was because I was along but I think it was because they were so dressed up in their blouses – no one ever dresses much out in these parts.

In that same letter, Mary – always eager to help her "boys" – mentioned how she escorted a soldier that very morning to an interview with the Special Services, the army's entertainment unit. The soldier, as Mary explained, "was a professional tap-dancer before the war and would like to get into 'This is the Army.' He is to be interviewed by them this afternoon and I sincerely hope he makes it. He has been overseas for two years in an Engineers outfit." Mary never reported whether the soldier made the cut, but he may have been needed at some point. After entertaining thousands of troops in North Africa and Europe, Berlin's hard-working theatrical company was sent at year's end to the South Pacific for a new round of rigorous touring.

Besides all the theater talk, Mary's newsy April 24 letter also included an update on Doc, who – along with two colleagues – had secured an apartment in Naples:

Saturday night we had dinner there – it was so restful and the quietness could almost be heard. One of the Italians working here at the Center was an orderly to an Admiral in the Italian navy – he both cooked and served the dinner. It was such a treat to have good china, table linen and crystal on the table – besides the dinner was excellent. The best steak I've had since I left the states. We're all looking forward to many more such dinners. They have made it [the apartment] very comfortable and attractive.

Perhaps feeling a little guilty for enjoying herself so much and to quiet her mother's ongoing fears about her safety, Mary ended the letter by saying, "Remember not to be frightened for me. We are all having a wonderful time. You see – it's almost our duty to forget about the war and to try to give only pleasure to the men who are trying to forget it for a few short days. In fact, I feel actually farther from the war than I did at home."

If Mary deliberately wanted to steer her parents' thoughts away from Doc and his off-base apartment, her letter a week later, on May 1, may have done so. A colonel inspecting military bases for the U.S. War Department had observed Mary the previous day as she worked in the snack bar kitchen. As Mary recounted for her parents:

I ask[ed] him if he had seen the Club and when he said 'No' we made a little tour. He is going to come next Friday afternoon to take me to one of the most beautiful resort towns near the ocean. It's only a little way from the place I was before [Capri] and he said he would arrange for us to go over there. It's going to prove most interesting, he may not even show up. He seemed to be very satisfied with the work we are trying to do and felt that the men were benefited by it.

Making good on his promise, albeit at a later date, the colonel escorted Mary to Sorrento on Tuesday, May 16. From a hotel terrace in that clifftop town overlooking the Bay of Naples, Mary claimed she could glimpse the craggy coast of Capri jutting from the sea. As for her overnight lodging in Sorrento, Mary found the situation to be humorous. Her May 19 letter explained:

Sorrento was beautiful. . . . I drove down with my Colonel friend on Tuesday night. There was no room at the Officers' Rest Camp Hotel so the Bell Boy led us to a private home where we could stay. We walked into a very laughable situation. It was a very nice Italian house. Everyone in this country lives in apartments which are built directly on the streets. There are always courtyards with trees and gardens inside and off the street.

Scenic Sorrento, a tourist destination celebrated for its beauty. (Photo by author)

When we had climbed the steep steps we were greeted by four Women, two children and two old men all bowing and scraping to show us the way in. They said 'of course they had three beds, one for the driver, one for the Colonel and one for me' but led us to their living room set up with all three beds in there.

It struck me so funny that I sat down in a chair and giggled, they, of course thought I was fully in approval of their arrangement. Needless to say we made a few changes. We started back after lunch the next day. It was a beautiful ride and I was happy to get away for awhile....

In that same May 19 letter, Mary unloaded news that surely caught her parents off-guard – and in all likelihood disappointed them. Why she made the revelation at that particular time isn't clear. It's possible that she had just learned the truth and thought it important to share. It's also possible that she had been withholding information from her family and could no longer bear to do so. Whatever the reason, she continued to withhold Doc's formal name.

You keep asking about Doc. He certainly isn't an easy person to describe because he has nothing that makes him very much out of the ordinary. Don't get too excited about him – we are only good friends and enjoy each other's company. He is married and apparently very happy but even married men want some feminine company especially when they haven't seen their wives for over two years. I've never seen such a married army – there seems to be very few single men, especially in my age bracket.

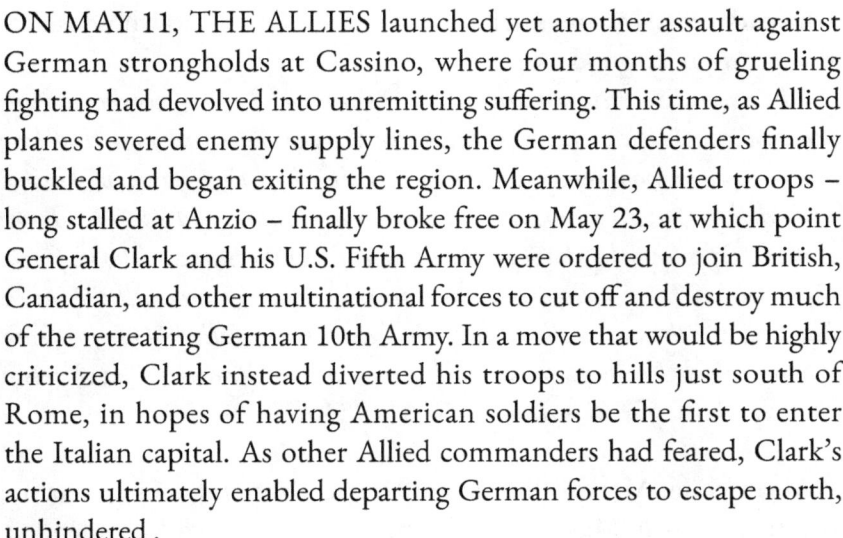

ON MAY 11, THE ALLIES launched yet another assault against German strongholds at Cassino, where four months of grueling fighting had devolved into unremitting suffering. This time, as Allied planes severed enemy supply lines, the German defenders finally buckled and began exiting the region. Meanwhile, Allied troops – long stalled at Anzio – finally broke free on May 23, at which point General Clark and his U.S. Fifth Army were ordered to join British, Canadian, and other multinational forces to cut off and destroy much of the retreating German 10th Army. In a move that would be highly criticized, Clark instead diverted his troops to hills just south of Rome, in hopes of having American soldiers be the first to enter the Italian capital. As other Allied commanders had feared, Clark's actions ultimately enabled departing German forces to escape north, unhindered.

Mary tried to follow all these rapidly unfolding events as best she could. But as she told her parents in her May 15 letter, "We all realize that there are big things happening around here but you at home probably know more about it than we do. We must listen to the radio from home to hear about the progress." Four days later she wrote again, telling her folks her stay at Caserta appeared to be coming to an end: "Yesterday we received some news that made us very happy concerning our future. We are to be kept together as a unit when the time comes to move on again. We were afraid our group might be broken up and all sent to different clubs."

Not surprisingly, Mary's workload lightened considerably amid all the troop movement. "Right this minute we have scarcely anyone in the Club," Mary wrote her brother-in-law George on May 25. While waiting for troops to return, Mary informed George that she had had a constant companion for several days – a "red-headed freckled face" boy who purportedly was a "Prisoner of War escort at the front" and who claimed to have played the part of 'Alfalfa' in the popular "Our Gang" comedies of the 1930s. On that latter claim, the boy was definitely pulling the wool over Mary's eyes. Carl Switzer played the role of Alfalfa in the 1930s comedies and, in 1944 at the time of Mary's writing, Switzer was in Hollywood making movies. That aside, entertainers apparently were on Mary's mind. In that same letter to George, she invoked the name of songwriter and vocalist Tony Sacco, who had several hit songs to his credit in the 1930s – and whose talents the Army put to good use:

The Special Service company here [at Caserta] which gives shows, runs the movie, athletic equipment etc. have been working very hard of late getting a new show ready and yesterday they had their preview which I attended. It's really a wonderful show – almost as good as "This Is the Army." Of course they have the best talent from the States to choose from. One man, a Tony Sacco, is a song-writer, he not only wrote all the music but is in the show as well. One of the best tunes is called "G.I. Joe from Anzio" which I'm sure, will be a hit tune on the Radio if it ever gets a chance. Watch for it. – Another is "Mail Call."

Meanwhile, Mary and Doc continued to spend their free time together. Early in May, weeks after the Vesuvius fireworks had ended, the two visited Pompeii, where first-century inhabitants had been entombed under scalding rock and ash spewn from the volcano. In a

May 7 letter to her parents, Mary described the ancient city as "most interesting but I was surprised to find how small the houses were. Some of [Pompeii], of course, has been reconstructed and is pretty highly commercialized. We saw a few of the skeletons & mummys of people just as they had been buried [in AD 79] under the ashes of Vesuvius."

Sightseeing aside, Mary and Doc also seized opportunities to relax at a beach, presumably one near Naples, though the location was never specified. In a May 20 letter to Annie's family, Mary described driving past "green fields blanketed with red poppies and some other strange blue and yellow posies" before arriving at a beach "so peaceful it was hard to realize that only a few miles [away] a war was going on. We could hear the artillery fire and planes were constantly droning overhead." A week later, Mary wrote about a second visit: "Saturday Doc and I had another day at the Beach. The water was so warm and comfortable but so darned salty. It's actually warmer than [Indiana's] Lake Gage. We took a little lunch with us. Doc had some sandwiches made in the Mess kitchen and I brought some fruit (wonderful cherries – like Michigan ones and oranges, juicy and sweet) that I bought down town in the native market Saturday morning."

The final days of May saw Mary focusing, ever more intently, on her next assignment. She was reasonably sure where she would be sent, but had received no confirmation and was not at liberty to speak freely. To her parents on May 30: "We are not at all busy these days. The boys are too occupied to be sent here but we have great plans for the future. I only wish I could tell them to you. Make a good guess and you will probably hit it." To Annie on May 31: "I haven't much news to write you. We are still not busy and feel as if we are more or less marking time. . . . We have been told where we might be going and it sounds thrilling."

As Mary wrote those letters, Fifth Army's drive toward Rome, which had been slowed by German resistance on the city's outskirts, accelerated. On June 3, German forces retreated without a fight, and on the evening of June 4, Clark's long-awaited moment came. His troops marched into the city, making it the first of the three Axis capitals (Rome-Berlin-Tokyo) to be liberated. The following day, as more Allied soldiers arrived, jubilant Italians flooded the streets, tossing flowers, offering kisses and wine, and wildly cheering their thanks. In a radio broadcast in the United States that same day, President Roosevelt rejoiced at the news of Rome's fall but warned that the struggle in Italy and across Europe was not yet over.

The next day, Tuesday, June 6, Mary – like most of the world – began processing even more news. Early that morning Allied troops landed on beaches in Normandy, France, signaling that the invasion of northwest Europe had begun. "How do you like that?" Clark is said to have uttered when he awoke. "They didn't even let us have the newspaper headlines for the fall of Rome for one day."

Headlines or no headlines, Mary's days at the drafty, dirty, down-at-the-heels Caserta palace were over. Her next assignment: The Eternal City.

Opposite: The palace today, restored to much of its earlier splendor.

Reggia of Caserta

Mary never returned to the royal palace, which after the war underwent major restoration and today is a UNESCO World Heritage site. It remains famous for its ramped staircase, massive inner courtyards, neoclassic-styled chapel, and ornate park statuary. (Photos by author)

Chapter Ten

BILL: 1944

Feb. [14] 1944
Dear Folks:
At this time I cannot tell you where I am. In a little while I shall be be able to give you my general location....

Feb. [20] 1944
Dear Folks:
I still am not in a position to tell you anything about my location, so there is nothing I can tell you except that I am well....

Feb. [27] 1944 'Somewhere'
Dear Folks:
Another Sunday, and time to drop you another note. I still can't tell you anything about where I am....

REQUIRED TO KEEP his whereabouts under wraps, First Lieutenant Bill Husselman left it to his parents in February 1944 to logically deduce where he was. In all likelihood, they did.

The planned Allied invasion of Nazi-occupied France, its start date still a matter of public speculation, appeared to be drawing near as the war in Europe bore deeper into a fifth year. Great Britain – the "Somewhere" in Bill's letter – was widely known to be where U.S. troops were assembling in preparation for the massive attack. Bill already had tipped off his parents in mid-December 1943 that his battalion was "going to war," signaling he expected to see action soon. Likewise, before shipping overseas, he had revealed that his next assignment was "in the right direction," shorthand for Europe rather than the Japanese-controlled islands of the Pacific, where on beaches and in jungles the fighting remained savage.

Bill had made his way to Britain aboard the *Queen Elizabeth*, the one-time luxury liner that in wartime more closely resembled a cattle boat. Sailing from New York City, the crowded troopship had zigzagged its way across the North Atlantic to evade menacing German U-boats and then steamed into the Firth of Clyde off Scotland's western coast. There, near Greenock, twenty-five miles northwest of Glasgow, the *Queen* had dropped anchor on February 8. The weeklong journey had taken place without incident. Greenock, in contrast, still bore scars of "incident." In May 1941, Germany's Luftwaffe had targeted the town and nearby shipyards as part of its monthslong bombing blitz over Britain. Two nights of intensive aerial attacks had reduced much of Greenock to rubble and left nearly fifteen hundred people dead or injured.

Whatever might have caught Bill's eye upon his arrival, the sight of thousands of GIs coming ashore was nothing new for the locals. American troops had been dispatched to the United Kingdom (Great Britain and Northern Ireland) a full two years earlier, in January 1942, and they had continued coming in intermittent waves – airmen to help the Royal Air Force carry out retaliatory bombing raids on German cities, soldiers to resupply Allied forces in North Africa and the Mediterranean. In autumn 1943, as plans to invade Europe across the English Channel advanced, U.S. troop shipments to Britain accelerated, especially shipments of combat divisions. When Bill arrived in early February 1944, U.S. ground forces in the United Kingdom totaled nearly 344,000 troops. By month's end, combat troop strength would jump by another 100,000. Combined with air force, supply services, and headquarters personnel, America's military presence at the end of February 1944 would exceed one million uniformed men and women – or, put another way, a lot of Yanks in an island nation about the size of Oregon.

Where to put all the newcomers was no small problem. The first waves of American troops were housed in barracks vacated by British forces. Field camps also were established, with servicemen living in

Nissen huts, semi-cylindrical steel structures notorious for being cold and drafty in chilly Britain but nonetheless widely used because they were portable and could be easily erected. By early 1944, however, the huge influx of American soldiers had created an "accommodation" crisis. As a result, servicemen increasingly were billeted in private homes, an option previously available only to American officers above the rank of major.

For Bill, still attached to the U.S. Third Army's 512th Military Police Battalion, the new housing policy suited him splendidly. Indeed, when military censorship was somewhat loosened, he confirmed that he was in England and living rather grandly.

England, March 12, 1944

Dear Folks:

... [Louisiana native and fellow officer Bill] Winsberg and I are billeted upon a family named Ditchfield, and are we lucky! What a place to land.

The household consists of Mr [John] and Mrs [Catherine] Ditchfield, a couple about sixty, I imagine, one of their sons who is about my age, and the maid, Bessie. They had three sons in the Army. One of them was killed in action, one [Tony] is a Major, and the one at home [Dave] was an artillery officer in the 8th Army, serving through the African campaign. He [Dave] was badly wounded and has lost the use of one arm, so he has been discharged. He is an Oxford man. This is a typical upper class English family, except that they aren't nearly so reserved as the average. As I am writing I am sitting with them in their parlor listening to the "wireless."

Our day starts when Bessie knocks on the door. In a few minutes she is back again with our tea. Today, Sunday, I was a little slow getting up so I actually had my tea in bed. Tea is beginning to run out of my ears – all day long they are handing us cups.

Mrs Ditchfield wouldn't let them bring army cots into her house, so we are sleeping in twin beds, just as soft as my bed at home. Boy, will it be tough when the time comes to go back to the field. We have a swell room, nice rug on the floor, one overstuffed chair and two other chairs. (You know when I first went into the Army the things I most missed were rugs and chairs.) Bessie makes our beds and cleans the room. Fuel is closely rationed so we don't have a fire in the fireplace in our room. That is why

I am writing downstairs. However, fortunately these people are not at all fussy about the use of hot water, and have it all the time. Many people are quite tight with hot water. Almost no houses in Britain have central heating.

These are really lovely people. I think they are a little lonely and rather like to have us around. They certainly have made us feel at home.

The English are very fond of "sweets" and can get mighty few of them. I wish you would send me a box of assorted candy – I don't know whether fudge would get here in good condition or not. Whatever you send would have to be very securely packed. I really don't need cigarettes now, as Winsberg is now here and I will take half of his ration....

Well, this is the long letter I promised. I'll write another in a few days and try to describe some of the things I've seen over here.

Love, Bill

While permitted to describe how and with whom he lived, Bill was not allowed to disclose the Ditchfield's address. Much later, when that prohibition was lifted, he informed his parents that the Ditchfields lived on Osbert Road near the coastal town of Crosby, not far from Liverpool. That slice of northwest England, especially the counties of Staffordshire, Cheshire, and Lancashire, soon teemed with GIs assigned to the U.S. Third Army, newly under the command of Lieutenant General George S. Patton, Jr. The hard-driving and charismatic Patton, well-known for having played a leading role in the invasion of North Africa and Sicily, had been summoned to Britain in late January 1944, just two weeks ahead of Bill's arrival, and informed of his new assignment by General Eisenhower. Barely a month earlier, Eisenhower had been named by President Roosevelt, with British Prime Minister Churchill's assent, to be supreme commander of all Allied forces in Europe and to direct *Operation Overlord*, code name for the upcoming invasion.

Though the Germans fully anticipated an attack, they remained ignorant of details, namely, the time and the place. With the Allied high command making sure those details remained shrouded in secrecy – and with military censorship still in place – Bill steered clear of any war talk in his letters home that spring. Indeed, he rarely mentioned his battalion work, though in one early letter, dated March 15, he shared with his parents that "I have so far spent my time as liaison officer between our outfit and the British. I am enjoying it very much, as it gives me lots of opportunity for making contacts."

Making contacts – friendly contacts – with British troops and civilians was exactly what top U.S. military officials wanted and what Eisenhower, in particular, deemed a strategic necessity. The British people, having stood up bravely to Hitler since 1939 and having suffered through bombings, blackouts, and persistent hardships, had been relieved when America finally entered the war; initial shiploads of Yanks had been greeted with enthusiasm and curiosity. But as the so-called American "occupation" of Britain continued, tensions increased, partly due to low morale among bored GIs and partly because many Brits disliked the brash and pushy ways of many servicemen. Tensions were particularly strained between GIs and "Tommys," as British soldiers were known. Tommys resented that American troops received higher pay and had better-looking uniforms, advantages GIs used – with considerable success – to attract women in pubs and dance halls.

Anticipating Anglo-American complications, the U.S. War Department in August 1942 had begun issuing pamphlets to arriving servicemen, instructing them on British life and customs and offering pointed advice, as in "Don't be a show off," "Don't make fun of British speech and accents," and "NEVER criticize the king or queen." That advice notwithstanding, Americans still managed to rub their hosts the wrong way. TIME magazine reported in December 1943 that "it has become increasingly obvious that the people of Britain are annoyed by the free-spending, free-loving, free-speaking U.S. troops" and that many had "now come to think of the U.S. soldier as sloppy, conceited, insensitive, undiscriminating, noisy." Having reached the same conclusion much earlier, British soldiers derisively described the Yanks as "oversexed, overpaid, overfed, and over here." Parrying with an equally biting quip, GIs claimed the Brits were "undersexed, underpaid, underfed, and under Eisenhower."

If Bill had unpleasant encounters with the British people, his letters made no such mention. To the contrary, he stressed to his parents how much he liked the Ditchfields and how he sensed they were fond of him. Mr. Ditchfield, in Bill's telling, looked forward to the two of them playing billiards in the evenings, with the older gentleman always hoping to knock the "pants off" off his American houseguest, even as Bill wielded a competitive cue stick. Likewise, Mrs. Ditchfield appeared to enjoy mothering Bill, arranging to have his linens washed and ironed (without him having to ask) and inviting him to attend a new theatrical production starring the well-known British actress Beatrice Lillie. Not to be outdone, even the maid Bessie strived to make him comfortable. When she learned that Bill had begun departing the house earlier than usual per new orders from his commander, she adjusted her schedule. "The first day I slipped out without my tea and mortified Bessie almost to death. She said 'Mr. Bill' couldn't go out in the cold morning without his nice cup of hot tea. Ever since she has been getting up a half hour earlier herself so that it won't happen again. What a family!" he informed his parents in an early April letter.

The Ditchfield's hospitality included sharing their pantry contents, an especially generous act given the shortages, and unavailability, of food within the country. The British government had imposed rationing in January 1940, two years before the United States did, and from the outset the British people found it difficult to obtain dietary basics such as meat, fresh vegetables, and fruits. Fresh eggs were especially rare, with many Brits grateful to eat one a month. U.S. troops, in contrast, ate much better largely because the War Department, at the American public's insistence, made sure soldiers were well-fed. GI meat rations, for instance, were three times that of British civilians. Moreover, as Bill told his parents, the meat was of a sufficiently high quality: "We get choice beef, chicken, pork chops etc."

Bill ate his meals in unit messes, as did other officers billeted in homes, a policy designed to maintain troop cohesion and eliminate undue friction between host families and servicemen. Still, the Ditchfields refused to be stingy, and as Bill noted in a March 26 letter, "In spite of rationing they are always insisting on our eating their biscuits, cake, pie etc. and are handing us a cup of tea all day long." Desiring to repay the hospitality, Bill asked his parents on repeated occasions to send treats for him to share. "I wonder," he queried in that same March 26 letter, "if you would be allowed to send a pound or two of tea in your next package? If not, candy is about the best thing to send."

While openly discussing his chummy interactions with the Ditchfields, Bill said nothing to his parents about any socializing he may have done with English women – in pubs, dance halls, or elsewhere. Such an omission fit a pattern. Other than referencing a few dances he attended while stationed at Camp Shelby and his dates with the "Southern Belle" while marking time in New York, Bill kept his "private" life private – likely out of a sense of propriety and possibly because he had little to report. He had fewer reservations, however, about mentioning his friends' romantic interests, as when he informed his parents in an April 23 letter: "Winsberg has a lunch engagement with a beautiful (his description) blonde." In an earlier letter: "Dave Ditchfield [the family's injured son] became engaged this afternoon to the nurse who has taken care of him when he was in the hospital. She has been visiting the Ditchfields this week-end, and is an awfully nice girl."

If Bill was disinclined to discuss the sexual side of military life, the U.S. War Department did not have that luxury. By autumn 1942, venereal disease rates among GIs in Britain had soared, and by 1943 a full-blown VD epidemic was underway. Forced to take action, the U.S. Army heightened its "safe-sex" education campaign, arranged for condoms to be freely distributed, and partnered with the American Red Cross to open prophylactic stations in its recreation clubs throughout Britain. By spring 1944, the epidemic showed signs of abating, helped in part by the cancellation of leave as invasion day neared. By then, however, military officials had other headaches, specifically the surge in Anglo-American marriages as jittery GIs took "war brides." Meanwhile, top Allied commanders in Britain were not immune from the need for female companionship, not least among them Eisenhower. When first sent to London in 1942, Eisenhower was assigned as his driver the Irish-born Kay Summersby, who eventually would become his secretary and remain a close friend until the war's end – a friendship that generated gossip among staff and was the source of long-simmering irritation for Ike's wife, Mamie, who had remained in the United States.

Against this background and mindful of censorship, Bill looked for safe subjects to address when writing home. Knowing his parents had never traveled abroad, he did his best to sketch the English countryside, to offer mini-lessons on British history and architecture, and to shed light on topics certain to interest his Midwestern family. A sampling – from over the course of one month:

14 March 1944

Dear Folks:

... I took quite a long ride in a jeep this afternoon and became chilled to the very bone. I took a hot bath as soon as I returned and have been toasting my shins in front of the fireplace all evening. The [Ditchfield] family went out for dinner tonight, so I have had the parlor to myself. Bessie was just in with tea and cakes. I am getting so I have to have my tea every evening. I am regarded as an ideal "guest" because I don't use sugar in my tea....

England, in spite of the generally foul weather, is very pretty. It has a wide variety of scenery. Some of it is flat, some very hilly. The roads are universally paved, and very good, but curve and wriggle like a snake. The whole country is so closely built up that it is difficult to tell whether you are in town or the country. There are practically no frame buildings. Brick is the predominant building material, with stone running second. Most of the houses are very large by our standards and, of course, very old – altho there are a surprising number of fairly new ones – due I suppose to an expanding population. Many of the towns and villages consist of very narrow twisting streets, lined with quaint old houses.

Their railroads differ from ours considerably. The locomotives are tiny by our standards, and the freight cars (called "goods-wagons") are little four wheeled affairs not over sixteen feet long. The passenger coaches are usually built in compartments which you reach directly by an outside door. There are quite a few canals in use. Most of them are for horse drawn barges, and they operate just like ours did 100 years ago. One horse, trudging down the tow-path, can haul an amazingly large barge of freight ("goods"). In the cities the street cars (trams) and buses are universally double deckers. One odd thing about the roads is the fact that there is always a sidewalk ("pavement") down at least one side – even out in the country.

England is a land of many hedges – always well trimmed. I don't know what sort of plant it is, but some are green all winter....

Well, this is already overlong and it is bedtime, so good night.

Love, Bill

26 March 1944
Dear Folks:

Bill Winsberg and Dave Ditchfield went to a concert this afternoon and were then going to a neighboring town for dinner and a picture. I was going too, but found myself on duty for the day and couldn't. Darn it!...

I had occasion to be gone for several days. When I returned Mr. Ditchfield was not feeling well and they hustled him off to bed about 9 PM. He protested that he shouldn't be going to bed like that, "with Bill just coming home." They really missed me.

I had an opportunity to visit Chester, the seat of Cheshire, while on pass. It is one of the most interesting cities in England, as its history has extended over many centuries. It was an important town during the days of the Roman occupation.

It still has the ancient town wall, the only town in England with the complete circuit intact. The wall, about two miles around, was originally built by the Romans but was subsequently largely destroyed. In its present form it was built in the 10th Century. The town has grown so much that the wall now runs through the heart of the business district. The towers along it are all covered with historical lore. From one, Charles II watched the defeat of his armies.

The Rows, Chester, circa 1895 (Library of Congress)

There is also a large, old and beautiful cathedral. Many of the town's buildings are fine examples of 17th century timber work – they being built of timber frames with brick filled in between the timbers. Several streets contain what are called "rows." There are balconies supporting a second floor level sidewalk which permits having one row of shops above another.

When you are driving about the country[,] getting directions is quite difficult, as the English are very vague with them. They have an expression that has become famous with the yanks. You ask them the way to some point and they'll say "Just go straight ahead; you cawnt miss it." We not only "cawn" – we generally do!

Love, Bill

17 April 1944
Dear Folks:
English Aprils are much like those of Indiana – clear one moment, raining the next; warm in the morning – cold in the afternoon. However, the soft balm of Spring is definitely in the air and it [has] brought out the English gardeners everywhere. It is hard to imagine English gardens without having seen them. Every house has its garden, some large, some very small. All are of the conventional, or formal type, with every blade of grass on the lawn trimmed to an exact length, and without even a suggestion of a weed in the cultivated squares set aside for vegetables or flowers. These people really love their gardens, and spend much of their leisure time working in them. Grandma would feel right at home.

English farming technique seems to consist of crop rotation, plus yearly applications of manure and lime. The former is generally spread by hand with the aid of a fork. Lime is used in great quantity, apparently to counteract a natural tendency of the soil toward acidity. Horses are used much more extensively here in farming than in the States, although it is not particularly unusual to see an International 10-20 at work with the usual tools. Much hay is made. It is stored in great barns, usually built of brick or stone, and occasionally attached to the house.

One of these days I'm going to visit a Solicitors office and see what an English law office is like. Maybe I can pick up some innovations to drop into Hoosier jurisprudence.
Love, Bill

IN EARLY MAY 1944 – as America's troop strength swelled to 1.5 million and as an estimated five million tons of trucks, tanks, artillery, planes, and other equipment jammed England's depots and blanketed the countryside – Bill bid farewell to the Ditchfields, his days of billeting in their home over. By then, invasion speculation was rampant, with the majority of Britons expecting the assault to take place any day, even as a growing minority, according to a government report, doubted it would ever occur. Like virtually everyone outside Eisenhower's inner circle, Bill remained in the dark about the operation. Still, his letters hinted that something was afoot, and he itched to share more. Writing his parents on May 13, he noted: "It is getting difficult to find anything to write about. There is so much that would be of interest if it were not for censorship."

By then, Bill could speak with some authority about censorship. He had been tasked with reading the outgoing mail of his company's soldiers, careful to excise any words or phrasing that might compromise military security. Whether he liked the job or not, he nonetheless gained insights into the men under his command. In a May 11 letter to his parents, he shared a poignant observation about soldiers separated from wives and children:

I am sorry to hear that Max [a cousin] is about to be inducted. It is really tough on men with families. I never realized just how tough it was until lately, since I started to censor quite a bit of the company's mail. You can tell from their letters that the family men are really hurting. Most of our men have only been in a year. Think how it must be for some of the British troops who have already been in for nearly five years.

Days earlier, in another letter to his parents, Bill had again referenced the British, though in an entirely different context. He disliked how his fellow Yanks disparaged the islanders.

Some of our fellows suffer from acute anglophobia. Personally, I have found the English to be like people elsewhere – some you like and some you don't. Generally speaking, I like them. There just aren't finer people in the world than the Ditchfields – they couldn't have treated me better had I been one of the family. I miss them a lot.

Along with missing the Ditchfields on a personal level, Bill also missed the physical comforts of their home. Pre-invasion preparations required him to live with fellow soldiers "in the field," specifically in a pyramidal tent "somewhere in England." To bathe, he drove several miles to Army mobile showers, which – as he told his folks – consisted of a "big truck equipped with a pump and heater big enough to afford a continuous supply of hot water to about a dozen shower heads." Not all was misery, however. Bill counted himself lucky to have "three families living adjacent to our camp who take in laundry and do a beautiful job of it." He also was fortunate to have rank. Assigned to his tent was an orderly – "a little scared looking Southern boy with a charming smile who makes our beds, keeps our shoes shined, cleans our weapons, etc." Even the meals passed muster, with Bill writing home in mid-May that "eating has been good lately. We had a chicken dinner yesterday and Saturday we had steaks. The other day we had french fries – unusual in an Army mess. They seem to give you more and better rations when you are in the field."

If any of Bill's mates worried that they were being fattened up for slaughter, such worrying was premature. Third Army was not slated to participate in D-Day, as the June 6 attack would famously become known. Eisenhower had made the decision months earlier that Third Army would cross the English Channel only after the U.S. First Army, commanded by Lieutenant General Omar Bradley, had firmly established itself in France. Disappointed in Eisenhower's decision, Patton had been in no position to argue. When given command of Third Army in January, Patton – having disgraced himself the previous August for slapping two hospitalized soldiers in Sicily – had been glad to get a chance to restore his reputation. He had willingly accepted Eisenhower's offer to be part of *Operation Overlord*, though it meant, at the time, settling for a less than starring role.

Even so, Patton was the central figure that spring in an elaborate deception operation involving an imaginary army. The Allies had designed a plan to trick the Germans into thinking they would invade the continent where the channel was narrowest – at the Pas de Calais sector of northwest France, opposite the English town of Dover. The ploy entailed stationing dummy airplanes and landing craft near Dover, setting up decoy tent cities and fake military equipment in the neighboring countryside, and creating bogus radio traffic. Continuing the deception, the Allies also leaked word that Patton would lead the cross-channel invasion, information the Germans deemed credible because they considered the fiery general to be the Allies' best battlefield commander and the candidate most likely to be given the assignment.

To keep German attention focused on Calais – and away from beaches one hundred miles farther south, where the Allies actually planned to invade – Patton allowed himself to be photographed in and around Dover. But most of the time, he kept a low profile, crisscrossing the UK to tour camps and installations housing soldiers of his "real" army. Moreover, everywhere he went, he admonished troops to keep his presence a secret. "I am not here!" became his refrain, whereupon – dressed resplendently in his tailored battle jacket, gleaming riding boots, and polished helmet – he would deliver profanity-laced remarks designed to stir morale and inspire his men to fight.

Not surprisingly, Bill's letters from this period never referenced "Old Blood and Guts," as Patton was nicknamed. In all likelihood, however, Bill heard a version of what came to be known as "Patton's Speech to the Third Army" – an address that acquired iconic status in 1970 following the release of the movie *Patton*. The actor George C. Scott, portraying Patton standing before an enormous American flag, recites a sanitized version of the speech in the film's opening scene. Patton always spoke without notes and was renowned for improvising. Hence, soldiers from camp to camp did not always hear identical remarks delivered in the same order. Nonetheless, the substance of his message – fight to win – never changed, and troops, most of them awestruck at seeing their commander in person, invariably showed their appreciation by listening intently, slapping their thighs with approval, and laughing raucously when Patton gave it to them "double dirty," his phrase for his vivid profanity.

General Patton reviewing his Third Army troops, April 1944 (U.S. Army Signal Corps via Wikimedia Commons)

Before leaving the speaking platform, Patton always urged his men to focus on the future and assured them they would feel proud at war's end – as noted in this reconstruction of his famous speech, pieced together by the British military historian Terry Brighton:

Then there's one thing you men will be able to say when this war is over and you get back home. Thirty years from now when you're sitting by your fireside with your grandson on your knee and he asks, 'What did you do in the great World War Two?' you won't have to cough and say, 'Well, your granddaddy shoveled shit in Louisiana.' No, sir, you can look him straight in the eye and say, 'Son, your granddaddy rode with the great Third Army and a son-of-a-Goddamned bitch named George Patton!'

AS MAY INCHED TOWARD JUNE amid intensifying D-Day preparations, Bill reported being "quite busy," though he did not give his parents any particulars and continued to assure them he was well. "I really haven't any news so I'll just drop a few lines to let you know I'm O.K.," began his letter of May 18. On May 23, much the same: "I have just time enough to drop you a few lines before dark, to let you know I am O.K." Ditto on May 30, when Bill repeated almost word-for-word what he had penned days earlier: "I have just time enough before dark to drop you a few lines to let know you I am O.K."

Those assurances delivered, Bill filled his late-May letters with bits of innocuous news and pleasantries, the sort of chit-chat his parents undoubtedly welcomed. He reported that their package of tea had arrived safely and that he would forward it to the Ditchfields. He mentioned that he weighed 153 pounds ("dressed, of course") and that his appearance otherwise remained unchanged, except for needing a haircut. He rued that the Chicago White Sox, per usual, had started the season poorly.

Into this mix, he also commented on the lengthening of days ("daylight around 4:30 and [it] isn't dark until 11"), chided himself for having broken his watch ("I stripped the gears on the stem . . . it won't wind"), and disclosed that his duty assignment had required him to spend "both of the last two nights in a jeep, and boy is it cold!" He furthermore issued a formal request: "If . . . you ever get the chance to send packages again, try to buy me some vitamin capsules called Unicaps. The diet is sadly lacking in calcium & vitamins B & D, which all tends to cause dental trouble, and the medical officer recommends Unicaps. He has been unable to get them here."

The light banter aside, Bill closed his May 30 letter on a serious note. Having begun by saying he was "O.K," he concluded by apologizing in advance for his future correspondence, which he anticipated being bland.

I am afraid my letters from now on will be pretty brief and limited to letting you know I'm O.K. I have described the country and people about as fully as I can, and there really isn't much to talk about. Obviously I cannot describe our daily activities in any detail without compromising security. I certainly enjoy reading your letters which keep me pretty well posted on the daily doings of the Husselmans, and wish I could respond with the same type of letter, but of course I can't.

Less than a week later, on the evening of June 5, Bill again picked up his pen to write home. Seated in the cook tent, a mug of lukewarm coffee at his side, a kerosene lantern offering light, he began: "I should be going to bed as it is about 2300 hours and I have to get up by about 0545 tomorrow. But I'm not sleepy." A few hundred miles away, on England's southern coast, tens of thousands of men also could not – and would not – sleep. Eisenhower had decreed hours earlier that the invasion, already delayed due to bad weather, would commence the next day.

And so it did. Soon after midnight, paratroops and glider troops began dropping into Normandy, France – well to the south of Pas de Calais – and a few hours later underwater demolition engineers began clearing obstacles in the channel to allow landing craft to reach shore. By 6:30 a.m. June 6, assault troops aboard an armada of 6,000 ships stormed Normandy's beaches in the largest amphibious invasion in history, and by nightfall 156,000 American, British, and Canadian troops occupied a fifty-mile stretch of France's northwest coast. Allied casualties that day were high, upward to 10,000. But Hitler's "Atlantic Wall" had been breached.

General Eisenhower addresses paratroopers before they board planes for the D-Day invasion. (National Archives)

News of the invasion flashed around the globe, with Radio Berlin announcing the Allied landings as soon as they began, thus informing listeners across all of occupied Europe. The BBC followed with its own broadcast, American radio stations issued updates, and newspapers everywhere rushed effusively headlined dispatches into print – this as church bells rang out in Britain, the United States and Canada, as Philadelphia's mayor sounded the Liberty Bell for the first time in a century, and as hope spread, not least among POWs and those in concentration camps. Even fifteen-year-old Anne Frank, hiding from the Nazis in a cramped attic in Amsterdam, heard the news and, as she so often did, turned to her diary: "'The invasion has begun!' – that means the 'real' invasion. English broadcast in German at eleven o'clock, speech by the Supreme Commander Dwight Eisenhower.... I have the feeling that friends are approaching."

Bill's thoughts went unrecorded, and days passed before he wrote home again. Like the rest of Patton's Third Army, he was still "somewhere in England," still waiting to join the fight.

June 10. 1944

Dear Folks:

I am late for dinner now, but am overdue with a letter, so I'll drop you a line to let you know I'm O.K. before the mail goes out.

I suppose you keep your ears glued to the radio since the invasion started. You are in a much better position to keep track of it than we are. We haven't a radio in the entire company, and seldom see a newspaper until it is nearly a day old.

I haven't been out of camp except on duty since we've been here, so there is really nothing to write about.

Love, Bill

Chapter Eleven
BILL: 1944

*E*NGLAND
12 JUNE, 1944

Dear Folks:
Your mail is coming through somewhat irregularly now, so I suppose mine is too. I really haven't any news anyway.
The other night I took a motorcycle ride for the first time since leaving Louisiana. This time I was on a highway, put her in high gear, and went spinning merrily at 40 or 45 per. Lots of fun. Guess I'll get one when I get home. (You needn't ever worry about that. After all the travel I've had in army vehicles I'm going to buy the biggest sedan with the softest cushions I can find.)...
I believe the mess in the army is now better here than I've ever known it to be anywhere. For instance, today for dinner we had good roast beef, mashed potatoes with gravy, fruit (canned) and some second vegetable I can't now recall. Tonight for supper we had steaks, boiled potatoes and gravy, green beans, coffee, fruit salad, and bread and butter. Since men are going out or coming in from duty at all hours, the kitchen operates 24 hours a day so you can drop in anytime of day or night for a sandwich of some kind and coffee....
I hear that the PX supplies are in so I think I'd better close and go over to draw my ration.

DAYS AFTER THE LAUNCH of *Operation Overlord*, Bill Husselman and his fellow U.S. Third Army soldiers – 250,000 men strong – awaited the green light to join the fight in France. No one itched to get Third Army moving more than its commander, Lieutenant General Patton. But the elaborate Allied plan to mislead Hitler had not only worked but was *still* working. Many seasoned German tank and infantry units remained in the Pas de Calais, with the Führer believing that the D-Day landings on Normandy's beaches were only a feint and that the main Allied invasion was still to come. Moreover, Hitler still believed that Patton would lead the all-important assault across the English Channel, meaning the American general had to stay out of sight so the Allies could keep transmitting disinformation. For Bill and his mates, the ongoing ruse boiled down to this: They were to lay low, keep training, and wait.

Improved "chow" helped make the wait bearable, as Bill's June 12 letter suggested. So did news from home. But the invasion, not surprisingly, had hampered mail delivery, and it wasn't until nearly two weeks after D-Day that Bill finally received a packet of letters from family and friends. Seemingly energized by his postal windfall, he treated his parents to a lengthy letter, assuring them he was not in danger and confirming he had remained diligent in writing them.

18 June, 1944

Dear Folks:

I don't really owe a letter yet – I wrote only a day or two ago – but this is a rainy Sunday night and seems like a good opportunity to write. So, here goes.

There was a Red Cross Clubmobile out here at our camp this afternoon. They make doughnuts and coffee on them. One of the three girls with it had been raised in New Haven [Indiana], and knew some of the people in Fort Wayne whom I know.

Yesterday I received your long letters of June 7th. We all knew that our mail wasn't getting through and knew that the folks at home would imagine that whomever they were interested in was in the first waves of the invasion, but there was nothing we could do to relieve their worry. We are still "somewhere in England," and as long as we remain here we are in just about as much danger as we would be in Union Township [the Husselmans' Indiana township]. Whenever you don't get my letters just when you think you should, please don't worry, as there are a million and one things that might be the cause.

Captain Remley [Bill's company commander at Camp Shelby and a member of his OCS class at Fort Custer] and I visited a pub last night and had quite an interesting evening. It was a typical country pub, so far off the beaten track that we were the only Americans there. It is in an old building that must be a hundred fifty years old and has solid masonry walls about four feet thick. Its patronage was practically all English farmers. They get fairly tight as the evening progresses and a little noisy, but it is all very orderly. They never get ugly or pugnacious and seldom even tell off-color stories.

It gave me a chance to satisfy my curiosity about English agriculture. Land, in this area at least, seems to have an average value of about £60 per acre, for the free hold. It rents for anything up to £8 or £9 per acre. The practice of renting on crop shares is unknown. It's all cash rent. Farms are usually small. They even consider a four acre patch a farm, altho some may have two or three hundred acres. Potatoes, cauliflower (Sp?), beets, and other vegetables, together with hay, wheat, oats, barley and a little rye are their crops.

These pubs have to close at 10 o'clock by law, so at that time the proprietors, a man and wife of about forty, cleared it of their British customers but Bob and I stayed on for an hour or so to drink with them. It was very interesting to get their reaction to things in general, and compare it to that of the Ditchfields, who are of course from an entirely different social stratum. For instance, the Ditchfields contend that the throne is essential to keep the empire cemented together, as it is the only thing in common that the various colonies and Commonwealths have. Too, some of the native populations look upon the throne in much the same awestruck manner with which American Indian tribes once looked upon the "Great White Father" in Washington. The couple of the pub, however, are not so sure and are just a little suspicious of the value of the Crown. Ditchfields condemned [King] Edw. VIII not for marrying an American Commoner, but for choosing one who was twice divorced. These people, however, admired him greatly for having guts enough to do what he did.[1] They claim he was the common man's man and they

---

1. Edward VIII abdicated the throne in December 1936 to marry American socialite and divorcee Wallis Simpson.

were 100% for him. They despise Baldwin, for the stand he took and speak with sympathy about Chamberlain.[2] *Both these people and the Ditchfields had one political reaction in common – a hearty dislike for Princess Elizabeth, which they seem to share with about sixty million other British. I get the impression that she has been a swell-headed little brat.*[3] *I think the King [George VI, the brother who succeeded Edward] and Queen are popular in a sort of insipid way.*

The British have gone in for the war much more "all out" than have we. Practically all civilian men you see are in some sort of service – home guard, air raid wardens etc. The women have been drafted into the various services like the WRNS, ATS, WAAF and Land Army, just as ruthlessly as the men. The Land Army takes the beating, as I see it. They are drafted – some from the cities – to do farm work. They are issued a sort of fatigue uniform and don't even get clothing ration coupons. The

---

2. Stanley Baldwin served three times as UK prime minister before stepping aside in 1937. During and after World War II, he was sharply criticized for his complacency toward Hitler and for not sufficiently rearming Britain. Baldwin's successor was Neville Chamberlain, best remembered today for having signed the 1938 Munich Agreement that ceded the Sudetenland region of Czechoslovakia to Nazi Germany. Chamberlain, who presided over Britain's entry into war in September 1939, was replaced in May 1940 by Winston Churchill.

3. In February 1945, Princess Elizabeth - nine months after her name surfaced in Bill's letter - joined the Auxiliary Territorial Service (ATS), the women's branch of the British Army. She trained as a mechanic and truck driver, though the war ended before she could be assigned to active duty. If teenaged Elizabeth was disliked by some Britons, the public warmed to her when she ascended to the throne upon her father's death in 1952. As Queen Elizabeth II, she reigned for seventy years until her death in 2022 at age ninety-six. Her reign was not without controversy but her personal popularity remained consistently high.

WRNS and WAFF are the popular services and the ones the girls all try to get in.

Well, I imagine you have had about enough British Economics, politics, and sociology for one sitting, so I think I'd better sign off and go to bed.

I just happened to think that this is Fathers Day, so please accept my sincere Fathers' Day greetings.

Love, Bill

Along with mail from Auburn, Bill's mid-June postal packet had included a note from Mrs. Ditchfield. Though he didn't disclose the contents, he told his parents that "she had had a letter from you, and had written to you again" – suggesting the military had cleared him to share the Ditchfield's address. That same packet also contained correspondence from Mary Brandon, and while he did not fully share the contents, Bill let his parents know that he was peeved: "I wrote her before I left [Camp] Shelby, in fact I believe it was in December. She certainly took plenty of time in answering, didn't she? However it was a very interesting letter when it finally came. She apparently has been very close to the war in Italy and has had some very interesting experiences."

Not long after Fathers' Day, Bill wrote his parents again, hinting that he had relocated and inserting a clue as to his new whereabouts. Knowing Oak to be well-read, Bill shared just enough information to assist his father in any sleuthing: "I have just been reading a historical novel covering part of the period of the Napoleonic Wars, some of the scene of which is laid right where we are. Towns lying within four miles of us are mentioned and figure in the plot. I wouldn't dare mention the name of the book." The novel, identified in later correspondence, was C.S. Forester's *A Ship of the Line,* which featured the fictional British naval genius Horatio Hornblower.

Assuming Oak picked up on Bill's clue, he may have correctly identified his son's location as Cornwall, a region in southern England known for its rolling moorland, extensive coastline of windswept cliffs and secluded coves, and quaint fishing villages. Bill's battalion, along with the rest of Patton's Third Army, had been ordered to the coast to prepare for eventual transport to France. As soldiers waited for a transport date, they assembled in tent camps vacated by the recently departed D-Day troops. Bill's camp was between the towns of Truro and Redruth, less than a dozen miles from Falmouth, a major D-Day port of embarkation.

Bill loved the Cornish countryside. Months later, when censorship was relaxed and when he had seen more of Europe, he informed his parents that "Cornwall is far & away the most beautiful country I've seen. . . . It would be a swell place if the climate were more moderate. Forester in 'Ship of the Line' mentions Truro, Redruth, Camborne, Bodmin & others, all of which I have seen, and which have changed very little since the period covered by the book." In another letter written months later – this one to the Auburn Lions Club and reprinted in the local newspaper in late December 1944 – Bill expanded on his affection for that slice of England: "Cornwall is a very beautiful county. It is rough and hilly and has many magnificent views of the sea. It is sprinkled with dozens of picturesque old towns, many of them famous in history. Penzance, which figured in one of Gilbert and Sullivan's operas [*The Pirates of Penzance*], is in this section and picturesque beyond description."

Charm and beauty aside, Bill enjoyed his time in Cornwell for another reason. "All I'm doing these days is reading historical novels, and sleeping," he wrote home on June 26, then added:

By the time an outfit has been trained enough to be sent overseas it just sort of runs itself, with very little direction from the officers. When we are not actually engaged in some sort of operation, the officers really take it easy.

It's utterly amazing how much differently an outfit functions with a period of training. You can hardly believe the men are the same as the ones you got from the Reception Centers.

To underscore how comfortable life was, Bill shared in that same letter that "four or five of us go for breakfast every Sunday, at about 0930" to a private home across the road from camp. His meal there the previous day had included "a bowl of dry cereal, toast, tea, two fried eggs on a sort of fritter, ham, two fish cakes, jelly rolls, etc., all for about forty cents. The same people bootleg Scotch for £5 a quart." The Scotch, he attested, was "not worth it."

As June slid into July, the leisurely pace of Bill's life continued, causing him to strain to find news to report home. He began his July 1 letter on a sour note:: "I might as well spend this very rainy Saturday afternoon writing letters. [Captain] Remley is away on pass for about three days, which leaves me as acting company commander. In as much as the Old Man [Colonel Flynn] is in a terrifically bad temper this week-end, it isn't a very pleasant assignment." Bill shifted next to family matters, expressing relief that his grandmother's blood pressure was under control and inquiring about the telescope his father had built ("How is the astronomical observatory doing now?"). Upon exhausting all small talk, Bill surrendered: "Well, I guess I'll close – not for want of time but for want of news. I just can't seem to find anything to write about this time. Maybe I'll be better inspired the next."

Inspiration soon came, though not as he had wished. Bill received word in early July that the Ditchfield's son, Tony, the twin brother of David, had been killed in France during a protracted battle to take Caen, an ancient city near the channel that the Allies had hoped to seize on D-Day. Tony, a major in the British Royal Artillery, had died on June 17, when the invasion was not yet two weeks' old. As Bill would explain in a July 12 letter to his parents, he and fellow officer Bill Winsberg had only recently learned of Tony's death from a Mrs. Irvine, the Ditchfield's neighbor.

They [the Ditchfields] asked her to write us immediately when they got the telegram from the War Office, and she wrote us the day following the evening upon which the news was received. I recite the details because it shows the way the Ditchfields regard us – practically as members of the immediate family. While Bill [Winsberg] and I never met Tony, we were both greatly shocked. The family had talked of him so much that we both felt that we did know him. I understand from Mrs. Irvine that the news hit the family very hard, as none of them are in too good health. It left me with a very difficult letter to write, which I composed last night.

In expressing his condolences to the Ditchfields – a family forced to bear the loss of two sons killed in battle, with a third son wounded so severely as to render one of his arms useless – Bill no doubt reflected again on the steeliness of the British people, who had been standing firm against Nazi aggression since 1939. He likely also reflected on the war's heavy toll on UK troops, a fact not lost on Prime Minister Churchill. By 1944 the British military faced a severe manpower shortage, and if the Allies were to sustain their advance into Nazi-occupied territory and liberate western Europe, they would need steady and hefty infusions of American personnel and armaments. Infusions were coming; Bill had every reason to believe they would include him.

ON JULY 18, six days after Bill informed his parents of Tony's death, he and his 512th Battalion arrived in France. Though not yet cleared for battle, the U.S. Third Army by then had begun the weekslong process of mobilizing, with ship after ship transporting men, vehicles, and supplies across choppy channel waters. Third Army's destination was Utah Beach, the westernmost of the five beaches the Allies had invaded the previous month. The bloodletting at Utah had not been as severe on D-Day as it had been at neighboring Omaha Beach. Even so, as Patton's forces filed ashore, they bore witness to the wreckage strewn across Utah's white sands – smashed landing craft, charred jeeps, crippled trucks, broken rifles. Making their way inland, GIs saw more ugly evidence of battle: minefields marked with skull-and-crossbones warnings, entanglements of barbed wire, grey stone homes damaged by artillery shells, and fields dotted with crosses where the dead had been hastily buried. Farther inland on the Cotentin Peninsula, in towns such as Sainte-Mère-Église, the ugliness gave way to uplifting sights and sounds: civilians cheering the soldiers' arrival, men and women rushing to shake their hands, children flashing the victory sign.

Patton had arrived in Normandy on July 6, exactly one month to the day after the invasion. He had established his headquarters in an apple orchard near the town of Nehou, twenty-eight miles inland from Utah Beach and twenty-one miles south of Cherbourg, the coveted port city on the Cotentin Peninsula's upper tip that the Allies had recently seized.

Though still under strict orders to keep quiet, Patton wasted no time inspecting his troops as they set up inland camps. He also met with various commanders, including General Omar Bradley, whose U.S. First Army forces had been fighting since D-Day. To Bradley, a restless Patton pleaded: "For God's sake, Brad, you've got to get me into this fight before the war is over."

General Bradley visits liberated Cherbourg, summer 1944. (National Archives)

With military secrecy blanketing all aspects of Third Army life, Bill breathed not a word of his new location to his parents. Writing them on July 21, three days after transferring to the continent, he acknowledged that "this letter is several days overdue, but it couldn't be helped, as I have been awfully busy for the past several days. I really only have time now to drop a few lines just to let you know that I am safe and well." He passed along one notable tidbit – his receipt of a second letter from Mary Brandon. "There doesn't seem to be much chance of my ever running into her. Other people seem to always be running into former acquaintances, but I never seem to. Must get busy now, so good bye."

During the coming days, Bill continued to keep mum as to his whereabouts. "Don't worry about me. I wouldn't be much safer right at home [than] I am here," he wrote his parents on July 24. Four days later: "Since the rules of censorship don't at present permit me to disclose my location, there is absolutely nothing I can say except that I'm O.K." Several more days later, on August 1, he wrote a longer letter, revealing nothing about his location but offering reassurances about his well-being.

This morning I have finished censoring the mail a little early, so I think this is a good time to drop you a note to let you know that I am still hale and hearty. I was reminded this morning that a year ago today I was on the rifle range at [Camp] Shelby, for the first time in bivouac for more than one night at a time. What a whale of a difference a year can make! Now I'm so used to living outdoors that it almost seems to be the natural and sensible thing to do.

I guess the human being is capable of adjustment to almost any condition. The odd thing is that most conveniences of civilization are apparently constitutionally bad for you. I was never in better health and in spite of exposure to rain, cold and everything else, I can't remember my last cold.

Incidentally, the weather at the moment is beautiful – cloudless skies, the temperature just comfortably warm with a field jacket on.

I am gradually coming around to agreement with those who think the war won't last much longer. I have been pessimistic for a long time, but either due to the current news or to the optimistic attitude of most people around me, which I have heretofore regarded as 'wishful thinking,' I have come to think that perhaps the European phase may end in 1944.

I surely hope so – even though 1944 has been the most interesting year of my life. Maybe it's too interesting. Anyway I sure would like to come home....

Bill's upbeat assessment about the war coming to a quick end likely sprang from several factors. Nearly two weeks earlier, on July 20, a group of German army officers had attempted to assassinate Hitler and, though the effort failed, it signaled trouble for the already paranoid Führer. Moreover, the gloom that had settled over Allied forces, weary and bloodied from weeks of combat, had begun to lift. The U.S. First Army had recently broken through Normandy's dense hedgerow terrain and advanced into the neck of the Cotentin Peninsula, setting the stage for Patton and his army to at last enter the fight. Indeed, at noon on August 1, the very day Bill shared his newfound optimism with his parents, U.S. Third Army became fully operational and began speeding in three directions across the French countryside – west, south, and east. As Bill would soon tell his parents: "I wouldn't miss this show for anything."

AND WHAT A SHOW it proved to be. Thrilled to be unleashed to fulfill what he saw as his destiny – namely, "to do something spectacular!" – Patton launched his troops on a drive that August that saw them liberating one French town after another and advancing virtually unchecked toward the German border faster than Allied planners had ever imagined. Ordering one corps to race west to seize Atlantic ports in the historic province of Brittany, Patton sent three other corps roaring eastward and southeastward to the Seine and Loire rivers. His army's lightning march helped pave the way for a Free French armored division and an American infantry division to free Paris on August 25. By month's end, Third Army had swept northeast into the province of Lorraine and was closing in on the so-called Siegfried Line, concrete pillbox defenses protecting the western entry into Germany. Bill eventually would be permitted to tell his parents the names of French cities and towns through which his battalion traveled – places such as Granville, Avranches, Rennes, Le Mans, Saint-Dizier. But with censorship still in place, his letters in August 1944 focused on the people and his adventures as a liberator.

France, 12 Aug. 1944
Dear Folks:
At last we have the go sign and can admit that we are in France. I suppose you've suspected it for some time but my being unable to say so has made it very difficult to write anything at all. I have seen many of the towns that have been made historic by American Arms. As you can well imagine, many of them are now only heaps of rubble.

Inability to speak French is quite a handicap. You rarely run into English speaking French in this area. Conversation with the people consists mostly of gestures. Contrary to the impression you may have gathered from the press, I should say that 98% of the French are glad to see us here, and look on us as liberators rather than as an invading Army. This, of course, is just my opinion based on personal observation.

Two sisters, aged 11 and 5, and a brother of 6 hang around our camp most of the time – cute as the dickens. The older girl, Jacqueline, had a year of English in school and carries a little French-English dictionary around with her. She is sharp as a tack and always manages to get her idea across in some way, usually with a combination of French, English, and gestures.

"A" Company seems to have adopted a little Frenchman, age 12, who is a refugee from Paris. He has been with one of our detachments for some time and I guess he'll go with us as long as we are over here. The mess sergeant, who is the smallest man in the company, fixed him up with a complete G.I. uniform. He speaks only the English he has picked up from the boys (some of it not of a parlor variety), and answers to the name of Junior.

I had a letter from Mrs. Ditchfield yesterday. She said she was writing you too. She wanted me to look up Tony's grave if I ever get the chance. I don't suppose I'll ever get close to it, though. She said Dave's engagement is off, but didn't give any details.

I got the box of vitamin pills the other day. I think I have enough for the duration now. You can see from this letter what I now need most – stationery. I wish you'd send me some. I can't get anything like that here. Our food is getting better as time goes on – I even had steak and fresh eggs for breakfast yesterday. The eggs weren't issue, of course.

Don't worry about me. I'm not engaged in very dangerous work, so my chances are extremely good. I wouldn't miss this show for anything.

France, 18 Aug. 1944
Dear Folks:
Time to let you know again that everything is O.K. I've been pretty busy lately – I think I have put 1000 miles on my jeep in the last eight days.

Speaking of my jeep, it is named "Taxi Honey" – why, I don't know. The drivers name them. My driver is a 20 year old Mississippian named Allen, who fortunately possesses the virtue of only having to take a trip once to be thoroughly familiar with the road. Boy, do I need that kind of driver. We took one of the front seats out of a wrecked Boche [German] sedan the other day and I had it put in the jeep in place of its regular hard seat. It makes a long trip at least 50% less tiring.

You ought to see our camp area. It is in a large apple orchard that slopes gently down to a little rock-bottomed river about 70 feet wide and quite deep in places. The water is clear enough to permit swimming and bathing, and how the boys love it! There are several boats on it so there is rowing as well as fishing and swimming. The fishing isn't so good, possibly because some of the officers went fishing with demolition hand grenades!

Captain Remley with his "catch" after fishing with explosives. Bill mailed this photo home months later.

Before we moved here we were in an area at the edge of a little town where Americans had never been before. [Captain] Remley let the civilians in the camp and they simply swarmed all over the place. It reminded me very much of the DeKalb County Free Fall Fair, and also gave me an idea of how a monkey in a cage at the zoo must feel. While at that place some of us officers went to a beach on a little stream for a dip. When we drove in the people just flocked around our jeep and made us feel about like Caesar must have when he entered Rome victoriously.

We stopped at wine shops ("bestros") in several towns where no American troops had yet been, and created quite a sensation with the populace.

France is a land of wavers and hand shakers. Every Frenchman wants to shake hands with you, and if you drive by waves, salutes, or doffs his hat. The French Tri-color and the Stars & Stripes are displayed from almost every house and building. The American flags are home made and some are strange indeed. Their conception of the proper number of stripes and of stars differs widely.

Horses are extensively used here. All horse drawn vehicles – wagons, buggies, etc. – are two wheeled. Teams or spans are always harnessed in tandem, so that the rear horse does all the work and the rest of the animals droop along with the tug chains hanging slack. There are many herds of beautiful beef and dairy cattle. Why the Boche left them, I don't know. I guess they didn't have time to do anything else. I've had quite a little French wine – including champaign [sic] that would be priceless in the States. You can get it, and all the fresh eggs you want for a couple of packs of cigarettes or bars of soap.

I think, in fact I'm sure, that it has been announced in the papers that a Free French outfit is over here, so I guess I won't be violating security to mention that when it went through the people lined the roads shouting "viva-la France" "viva-DeGaule" etc. According to Stars & Stripes [the army newspaper] an American jeep went by with the legend *"Prestone 1943"* stenciled under the windshield – Immediately the shout went up *"Viva la Prestone!"*

As you drive along they are continuously waving wine and cider bottles at you, offering a drink. They are good moochers, too. The kids here don't say "any gum chum," they say "cigalette for Papa." (They sound r as l and ieu as r for some strange reason). . . .

French farming methods are ours of fifty years ago. [They] use horses and oxen. Thrashing is done by steam engines which are not self propelled, but animal drawn. Houses and barns are usually built together, of stone or brick, and a typical set of buildings frequently consists of a sort of court yard with buildings on three sides, all joined. All buildings are very old. The Catholic Church is very strong. The center of every town is a church, often very magnificent. All over France you see many crosses or crucifixes erected as monuments. The cemeteries all have, as a sort of salad dressing for the headstones, ornate wrought iron work, giving them a rather weird appearance.

It is getting [almost] too dark to write, so I'll just say good night.

> France, 23 Aug. 1944
> Dear Folks:

. . . I have long heard of the merits of French Cusine Cuisine (KWe-ZEN') (is the spelling right?) and finally, last night I sampled it & found it up to its reputation. An upper-middle class (one servant) family consisting of an old gentleman, his wife, her sister, two daughters – one about 40 and the other about 30 – and an assortment of small children have a summer home a short distance up the river from our camp. They invited Capt. Remley and me to dinner last night. The two daughters both speak English.

I shall set out the menu in detail, as you are always interested in them. The first course was a thick soup, of about the consistency of a milk gravy. The Entree (?) was roast duck (very good – they prepare it so the meat is dry and mild, like chicken) hash browned potatoes, new garden peas, small green beans, & brown bread. All during this course & the salad they keep your glass filled with port wine, very good. The third course is the salad, consisting of fresh leaf lettuce with a tart dressing and some finely chopped meat, looking a little like caviar. The fourth course, dessert, consisted of cake, and here the wine changed from port to a lighter type. After dessert, we retired to the terrace garden where we had coffee and cognac.

This was the first really well cooked dinner I had had since leaving America. Everything was excellent except that there was no butter, & the coffee was errsatz [sic]. The French in the country have plenty to eat. They have been sending packages of food to relatives in the cities all thru the occupation in defiance of German orders.

It has just been announced over the radio that the F.F.I. [military arm of the French Resistance] have driven the Boche out of Paris. Great news. [The city's complete liberation came two days later.]

One of our boys picked up a couple of 19 year old Boche this morning & brought them to camp before taking them to the Prisoner of War enclosure. I got a chance to try out my college German. I can manage to converse with them a little. We have picked up quite a few Boche from time to time & one of our officers, Capt. Weis, can talk with them quite fluently.

One of our men, a private, was directing traffic one night near an abandoned German tank that mounted a pair of .50 cal. anti-aircraft guns, when Boche aircraft raided. He jumped on the tank and opened up with the machine guns, which he had put in order that afternoon. The plane came down and the commander of a nearby anti-aircraft battery gave him credit, claiming his cannon were not in action when the plane came down. Well, the idea of an MP shooting a Jerry down with a Boche gun was rather intriguing, so the reporters interviewed our man & took his picture etc. Actually he didn't shoot the plane down, as Capt. Remley captured the pilot & said his leg had been cut off cleanly by flack, & that doesn't come out of a machine gun. However, why spoil a good story. I suspect the story & picture may be turning up in Life or somewhere shortly.

I went out and made a reconnaissance for a bivouac area for us to move into when we move forward again. I found some beautiful wooded pastures around an old chateau. I talked to the people who lived there & told them I'd probably move a company into their fields. They thought the "off-i-cer's" ought to take rooms in the chateau, so possibly I'll get to see what a bed is like again.

France, 30 Aug. 1944
Dear Folks:
Did you ever see "Peter Pan"? I did while in England. There was a little spirit, called "Tink" I believe, which showed up only as a spot of light and a tinkle of tiny bells. I have a tink with me in the tent now, who answers to the name of Ziggy.

He is a little bit of brown fluff that you can carry in the palm of one hand, and as he plays about friskily along the floor he is accompanied by the tinkle of tiny bells attached to his little collar. The bells are not altogether a useless affectation – they serve to warn of his presence under your heels and probably save him from many a sore paw. He has had a lot of fun lately cavorting about with a big tame rabbit one of the boys has. He'll tease the rabbit until it gets fed up, then it will leap clear over him, rolling him over & over with a good belt from its hind legs as it goes by. Ziggy is very cute. Lt. [Phillip J.] Fowler takes him along when he visits his nurse and the nurses polish his nails a violent red and daub him with perfume.[4]

I suppose that as our armies approach nearer and nearer the German [border] you speculate more and more on my chances of getting out of the army after the European brawl is ended. The chances don't look too good to me. But there is one hope. When they reorganize they may not be too keen on Junior officers 33 years old. Actually I am having quite an interesting experience, and am moderately enjoying myself. The chief difficulty, and the thing that makes me [want] to get out, is that it comes in too long a dose. You know the pleasure of a trip comes in its recollection, not during the making of it.

The other day I saw a church part of which was finished in 1214. Age here is even more impressive than in England.

G.Is like France 100% better than England and like the French better than the English. I believe this to be due to the fact that France is much more nearly like the U.S., & the French are temperamentally much nearer Americans. Much of the country we now see looks like our Middle

---

4. Lieutenant Fowler acquired Ziggy that summer in exchange for three bars of soap. Fowler and his "nurse," who worked at a nearby military evacuation hospital, were engaged.

West. I've often thought as I drove along that if I were set down over here in a place where French buildings & two wheeled carts weren't in sight, I wouldn't realize that I was out of America. This is only true when you get out of the hedge country, of course.

Compared to the British, whose stuffed shirt-reputation is not unmerited, the French are a lusty, happy-go-lucky people, with many characteristics that we Americans have. Their [cuisine] is probably the finest in the world, while the British is definitely the worst. Every town and village seems to be made up mostly of restaurants, cafes, and hôtels. Their cars are large and their roads straight & wide, to permit rapid traffic as we are used to. Generally speaking they have more modern up to date features than the British in their cities.

Oddly, the war hasn't hit the French so hard except in heavily shelled areas. They seem to have much more to eat than the English, and their shops are infinitely better stocked with consumer commodities than are those in [Britain]. I suppose they must have hid large stocks from the Germans. Or perhaps the German occupation wasn't nearly so burdensome as we believed. Nevertheless, they welcome allied troops with genuine enthusiasm and are merciless in handling the relatively few who trafficked with the Boche. In almost every liberated town they have rounded up the harlots who were German mistresses and have shaved their heads, which is a sort of poetic justice, don't you think?

I have received the package with the fudge, dried corn & nabiscos. The corn & nabiscos were O.K. The fudge as usual was moldy & had to be thrown out, so don't try to send any more. I wrote weeks ago about receiving the sugared popcorn, which came thru O.K. You mention in your letter of Aug. 13th that I hadn't mentioned it, so perhaps one of my letters didn't get through.

Well, I don't know when you'll get this as I am out of airmail envelopes and haven't any stamps. I'll try to get some stamps as soon as possible, but it is not easy. I don't like V-mail. . . .

Ziggy is pestering me, so I guess I'll have to close & entertain him.

Months after posting his August letters, Bill sent home photos referencing what he observed that summer. Along with the picture of Captain Remley holding two dead fish, which – according to Bill – the captain caught by "tying a demolition hand grenade to the detonator of a land mine & throwing the whole business" into a river, Bill included a photo taken at Troyes, France. He had already informed his parents, in his August 30 account, that French citizens "in almost every liberated town ... have rounded up the harlots who were German mistresses and have shaved their heads." When Bill sent a collection of photos home in December 1944, he described the picture from Troyes as "one of considerable historic interest, so I don't believe it violates postal regulations. It was taken several months ago ... when the F.F.I. clipped, stripped, and tarred several women who had 'slept with the Germans.' You can see the remains of their 'crowning glory' lying on the ground. That is the Nazi salute they are giving, of course."

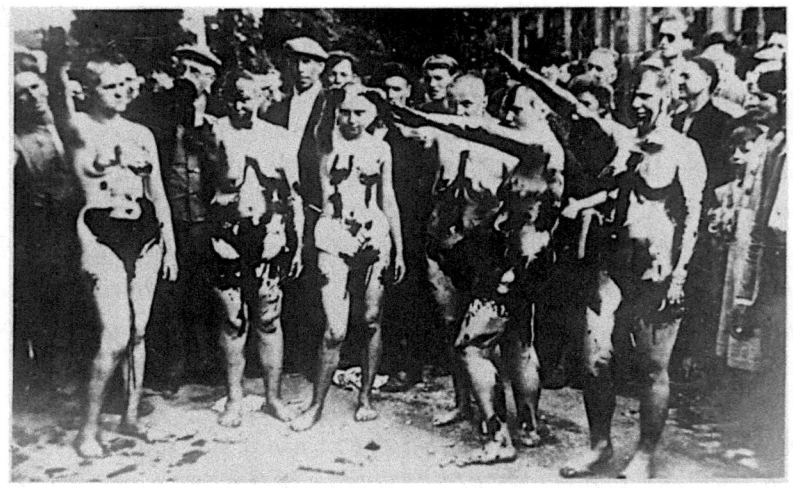

Photo that Bill enclosed in his December 18, 1944 letter to his parents. (Photographer unknown)

THIRD ARMY'S AUGUST TRIUMPHS – cheered and applauded by freedom-lovers everywhere – predictably infuriated the Führer. As of August 26, in less than a month of combat, Patton's forces had killed 16,000 Germans, wounded 55,000 enemy soldiers, and taken 65,000 prisoners. In addition, Patton's juggernaut – a blend of infantry, armor, and artillery, with air support from the XIX Tactical

Air Command – had captured or destroyed more than 4,300 German tanks, artillery, and vehicles across hundreds of miles of territory stretching from the Atlantic to the Meuse River in eastern France, not far from the German frontier.

During that same period, Third Army losses were relatively low, helped by Patton's insistence on speed and aggressive offensive action. Third Army suffered an estimated 1,930 deaths, with the number of wounded pegged at 9,000, non-battle casualties at 5,400, and missing at 1,800. Patton's forces also retained more of their equipment, losing 3,000 fewer tanks, guns, and vehicles than the Germans did. The lopsided numbers suggest why Bill could admit to his parents, as he did in his August 30 letter, that despite being in a war zone "I am having quite an interesting experience, and am moderately enjoying myself."

As Bill surely knew, however, "enjoyable" was a subjective term. The first waves of Allied troops on the continent – those who witnessed the carnage of D-Day, battled for weeks in Normandy's claustrophobic hedgerows, saw their pals' limbs blown off in cities such as Caen and Saint-Lô – would define that summer's soldiering experience in darker and grimmer terms. Indeed, the famed war correspondent Ernie Pyle, known for his ability to identify with rank-and-file soldiers, was so revolted by all the suffering he observed during his June-August assignment in France that – as he would later tell a reporter – "I damn near had a war neurosis. About two weeks more and I'd have been in a hospital." By early September, the Hoosier born-and-reared Pyle would tell his readers that he was signing off for a while: "I've been immersed in it too long. My spirit is wobbly and my mind is confused. The hurt has finally become too great."

For Bill and his Third Army mates, the coming of September also would spell hurt, though of an entirely different kind. Patton's fast-moving army literally ran out of gas at the end of August, its vehicles hurting for fuel at the very moment that the general's forces had hoped to charge into Germany. No fuel meant delay.

Delay meant trouble.

Chapter Twelve

BILL: 1944

*F*RANCE
11 SEPT 1944

Dear Folks:
...I am in command of a small detachment of men in a French town. It is all torn to Hell by the combined effort of German and American bombers.

We are living in a bombed out building, in a wing that is intact except that all the windows are missing. We have a kitchen set up, draw our own rations, and in general lead a pretty independent existence.

There is a cathedral in the town, built in 1645, still in quite good condition except that all of the stained glass has been blown out. I went thru it the other day; it is really beautiful.

Cpl. Nadler and I went thru the cellars of an old building – possibly a convent – that had been completely demolished. We questioned a nun regarding its age – the cpl. using very expressive sign language supplemented by a touch of Latin contributed by me, and found that it too was built in the 17th century. The workmanship shown in the hand-cut stone foundations is wonderful.

We eat fairly well. We draw canned rations supplemented by fresh meat & bread. We buy or trade for eggs, vegetables & fruit from the French. How well you live depends mostly on the initiative of your non-coms.

Laundry has never been a problem in France. You can always get it done cheaply & well if you furnish a little soap. Love, Bill

HAD LIEUTENANT GENERAL PATTON HAD HIS WAY in late August 1944, the U.S. Third Army would have continued its sweep across eastern France, overrun the lightly defended Siegfried Line inside the German border, and pushed toward the Rhine River with the goal of crossing it at Mannheim and Mainz. By Patton's reckoning, such swift and aggressive action would have hastened Nazi Germany's collapse and ended war in Europe by Christmas.

But Patton's army was a motorized force. Its tanks, trucks, and jeeps were all dependent on gasoline and diesel fuel, as were by extension the soldiers who drove the vehicles, piled inside them, and rode atop them. In the waning days of August, Third Army – which had been consuming 350,000 gallons of fuel a day as it dashed across France – received smaller-than-requested gasoline shipments and, by August 31, its reserve was nearly dry. Though fuel was plentiful in supply dumps on Normandy's beaches, the famed truck ferrying service – the Red Ball Express – could not transport gasoline fast enough to match Third Army's speed.

Complicating matters, General Eisenhower had recently granted fuel priority to British and American troops planning to invade northern Germany via Belgium and the Netherlands. Thus as September began, a virtually immobilized Third Army remained in eastern France waiting for gasoline and, as days and weeks went by, scores of other crucial supplies. Seizing opportunity, the German army brought in reinforcements, shored up disorganized battle lines, and dug in to defend the homeland. For Patton's soldiers, Bill Husselman among them, the heady days of continuous movement were over, and a protracted military campaign near the German border began.

A corporal with the 783rd MP Battalion signals to a "Red Ball Express" convoy to keep moving. (National Archives)

Before the slowdown, Bill and his 512th Military Police Battalion had played a pivotal role in Third Army's eastward thrust. MPs had kept troop traffic flowing by removing knocked-out vehicles from

French roads and highways, by directing convoys at vital intersections, and by finding alternate routes. They likewise had maintained law and order, especially as growing numbers of captured Germans were herded into prisoner caging areas. In addition, MPs had helped distribute goods that the routed Germans left behind. Tons of grain, sugar, and rice, as well as carloads of coal, were turned over to the French civilian population while frozen and canned beef – and less nutritious items – went to the troops. "We have lots of cognac," Bill wrote his parents on September 5. "We captured a lot of it from the Germans, so [commanders] decided to issue it. The stuff is just like liquid dynamite, only not so weak."

The region where Bill found himself that autumn was known as Lorraine, a French province that was no stranger to armies. In 1916, the Battle of Verdun – the longest and more ferocious contest of World War I – had been waged on Lorraine's soil. Bordered on the north by Belgium and Luxembourg and on the south by the Vosges Mountains, the province stretched westward to the Moselle River, a major French waterway. To the east lay Germany, which had annexed Lorraine in the 1870s, only to have the territory returned to France at the end of the Great War in 1918 and then be reclaimed by Hitler in 1940.

What Patton's forces quickly discovered, when some troops resumed moving that September, was that Lorraine's terrain was a soldier's nightmare. Water was a major battlefield impediment, with soldiers required to cross many fast-moving rivers and streams. Likewise, GIs had to attack uphill across rolling farmland and through forests, becoming easy targets for German defenders. Worse, the province's many ancient towns and cities were heavily fortified. Patton's XII Corps managed to liberate Nancy, the province's historic capital, on September 15 after a ten-day battle. But the city of Metz, thirty miles north of Nancy and protected by a chain of several dozen forts, proved to be a more formidable obstacle. In early October, the Germans repulsed an assault on Fort Driant, the anchor of Fortress Metz, forcing an angry Patton to admit that Hitler's forces had given "me my first bloody nose."

Roughed-up noses aside, U.S. infantrymen would spill plenty of blood that autumn in a disjointed and piecemeal Lorraine campaign. Third Army battle and non-battle casualties throughout the fall would reach nearly one hundred thousand, in sharp contrast to the relatively low casualty count Patton's forces suffered in August. But heavy losses did not erase what would be the campaign's most defining feature. Without adequate supplies, Patton had to keep Third Army in a defensive posture – something he despised and deemed to be warfare folly. "When I am not attacking, I get bilious," he would write his wife Beatrice in October, urging her to send him bottles of "pink medecin." Bill's response to the slowdown was less visceral, but hardly favorable, evidenced by remarks to his family on September 16: "Just had a long discussion. The topic: is this Saturday or Sunday. Decision: Saturday. It is very difficult to keep track of the time. Every day is the same."

To break the monotony, and perhaps to assure his parents he was out of harm's way, Bill penned a lengthy letter home on September 18. He indulged in his forte: describing the sights around him. He also expressed a weariness he attributed to his age.

France

Dear Folks:

I'm writing this without having much idea when it will go out. This is one of those periods when the mail service is a little spotty. I have a bad headache tonight – very unusual for me. Just took two [aspirin] tablets and they haven't taken effect yet. I guess I'm just getting too old for this sort of life. The other day I happened to think that it was sixteen years ago this month that I started to college! Sixteen years is a long time. You needn't worry about my staying in the Army any longer than I have to. I'll get out at the first opportunity, but I don't look for that opportunity to arise for about two years. I might get a break of course, but I'm not counting on it.

Today was some sort of church day – first communion, I think, and all the children in town were all dressed up – the girls in white robes and with a headgear like a bride wears, and the boys in sort of Etonian suits with a white cape-like affair. Not a very artful description, I fear, but I am not familiar with such things.

French funerals are quite a sight. The procession lines up something like this: First comes a guy in a black robe and a black cockade (three-cornered) hat. Then comes the black hearse, drawn by two black horses. After that comes the priest, decked out like a cardinal, and other church dignitaries, followed by nuns and the mourners, all marching in a sort of loose column of four formation. They proceed on foot from the church to the cemetery.

You get the impression in the States that the French, from the sexual standpoint, have very low morals. Actually, they are about as high as those in America & are incomparably higher than those of the British. Morals in wartime Britain just about don't exist. The French give an impression of loose morals by peculiar standards – such as that which only slightly arches an eyebrow at relieving yourself in public.

The French are having their day now. German prisoners seem pretty shy around them – particularly in the presence of the F.F.I. [French resistance fighters]. Every dog has its day. The Daschhund (I hope that's close enough to the spelling that you can make it out) had his for four years, & now it's the poodle's turn. The Master Race is looking pretty badly washed out.

This morning we sent one of the drivers to a ration dump for rations for the detachment. He came back with a quarter of beef that taxed two men to carry and I didn't know what in the world to do with it. It was frozen stiff of course, & we have no suitable butcher knife, no block, no saw and no cleaver. Finally we solved the problem by sending it around to a Restaurant and giving them a chunk off it in exchange for their cutting it up. Improvisation is the watchword of the Army in the field.

Sept. 19th.

Well, my [aspirin] took effect last night & relieved the headache. This morning I feel O.K. You mentioned [nationally syndicated political columnist] Drew Pearson's prediction that the war in Europe would be over by Sept. 15th. He proved a little over optimistic. However, the news in yesterday's paper was very encouraging. At least I wish that the Jap situation was as near the end as this one.

Love, Bill

However encouraging European war developments may have seemed in mid-September, news a week later was anything but good. Plans to invade northern Germany – the operation to which Eisenhower had given fuel priority – collapsed after Allied troops failed to secure bridges in the Netherlands. For Bill and his Third Army mates, that failure to their north was accompanied by foul weather in their midst. Cold sheets of rain had begun pummeling the ground in Lorraine, with precipitation heavy throughout the autumn. Writing his parents on September 28, Bill noted:

I can well understand the reputation France got in the last war for mud. It has been raining for days and the portion of the country I'm in is a sea of mud. It is not as bad as it must have been in '17, of course, for now the roads are paved. We are camped on a rather steep wooded slope. The air is damp and chill, and I can feel age creeping into my old bones. I hope we move into billets when we move again. The only advantage of this area is that there is a public shower room within seven or eight miles. Until we came here I had gone seven or eight weeks without a bath other than a couple of dips in a river, and what I could do out of a wash basin.

Bill, as required, omitted the location of his encampment. Days earlier, however, he had written openly about towns and cities through which he had traveled in France, as well as in England and Scotland, telling his parents: "Censorship has been somewhat relaxed, so that I can mention the names of towns so long as they are more than 25 miles from where I am now located." By checking a map of France, his parents may have deduced that he recently had moved from Vitry-le-Francois (the "torn-to-Hell" town referenced in his September 11 letter) to an encampment well beyond Saint-Dizier, home to an airfield from which the German Luftwaffe had been driven. Bill skipped any mention of the airfield but highlighted Saint-Dizier's many balconies of "wrought iron fancywork" – the kind he had seen in New Orleans' French Quarter. In Saint-Dizier, too, he enjoyed some ice cream: "It wasn't the best I'd ever had, but it was the first in eight months."

With his current whereabouts under wraps and limited in what he could reveal about his duties, Bill peppered his September and early October letters with a range of musings. He speculated his Army tour might stretch into another four years, fretted his legal skills were slipping from lack of use, and claimed the $150 a month he was saving from his Army paycheck was "more than I'd ever save as a civilian." He also informed his parents, in response to their query, that he likely would not accept a promotion to captain – should it be offered – because "company commanders and such have an awful lot of grief."

When not writing home, Bill bided his time by pitching horseshoes, even becoming a recognized company expert: "A couple of days ago I pitched ten ringers in two games . . . Quite an accomplishment, don't you think? Our officers' orderly, however, can humiliate me terribly. He pitches practically nothing but ringers." Bill also passed the hours by playing cards, though he deemed his skills mediocre and frequently rued his losses: "My poker isn't up to Army standards, and I'll play it in spite of the fact that it is just pouring dough into someone else's pocket when I have money because I get so infernally bored."

The antics of Ziggy – the furry brown mascot that Bill's tentmate, Lieutenant Fowler, had acquired – also helped ease daily boredom. Bill grew especially attached to the dog, calling him "my little pal" and tolerating Ziggy's habit of sleeping at the foot of his cot. When Ziggy's sleep pattern changed, Bill admitted to his parents that the pooch "is getting to be an awful pest." But Bill also blamed hospital evacuation nurses, in whose care Fowler sometimes left the dog, for contributing to nocturnal unrest: "Lt. Fowler left [Ziggy] . . . for two or three days, & the nurses spoiled him. Now he insists on scooting, head first, into my sleeping bag and wrapping himself around my knees. I've ejected him a dozen times a night but it doesn't do any good. The next time I wake up he's back again. I am afraid of rolling on him & hurting him because he is so tiny."

For reasons unrelated to Ziggy, Fowler's name had surfaced in a letter Bill penned a week earlier, on September 24. The celebrated American crooner Bing Crosby had been singing his way across France, entertaining GIs in mess halls, in fields, even on the back of trucks in liberated towns. Before and after his USO shows, Crosby typically mingled with servicemen. As luck would have it – and as Bill's parents were informed – Fowler happened to be at the right place at the right time during one of the entertainer's tour stops: "Lt. Fowler of A Company married his [evacuation hospital] nurse the other day and who do you suppose sang 'I love you truly' at his wedding? None other than Bing Crosby, himself, in person!"

BILL'S DAYS OF CAMPING in the Lorraine countryside, in a tent on a steep wooded slope, ended in early October. So, too, ended his need for a cot. "I am now a hotel soldier, and not a field soldier. A bed really feels good for a change," he announced to his parents on October 7. Days later, he detailed additional comforts: "I am writing this with a crackling wood fire in the fireplace in my room & it really feels good. A Lt. Norris, who is attached to us, and I are sharing a room which has two beds, two easy chairs, a desk & desk chair, a clothes closet, a lavatory, etc. besides the fireplace. Some war, huh? It certainly beats our last bivouac area, which was damp and chilly."

Bill's hotel, which he left unnamed, was likely in or near the city of Nancy, where Third Army had recently set up its headquarters. Known as the "Paris of the East" and famous for its architecturally stunning public square, Nancy had been spared destruction in mid-September when American bombers called off a scheduled aerial assault – the last-minute cancellation coming as beleaguered German forces abruptly evacuated the area. With Third Army soldiers taking up defensive positions around city, Patton settled into one of Nancy's villas, a coal baron's mansion replete with statuary and tapestries. When given "leaves," GIs swarmed into Nancy to take a hot shower, eat a cooked meal, or simply soak up what they needed – a break from shelling at the front.

Occasionally, 600-pound shells from German rail guns, situated twenty-five miles away, struck the city; notably, one night's shelling shattered windows in the villa occupied by Patton. Even so, Nancy remained firmly in Allied hands, and if artillery incidents rattled Bill, he studiously avoided alarming his parents. "Don't worry about my personal safety," he wrote home that October, repeating earlier assurances of his well-being. "I have never been closer than ten miles to the actual front, and am subjected only to possible enemy air action & sniper fire, neither of which is as dangerous as spending a week-end in Chicago."

Bill took pains, however, to avoid another enemy. Lorraine's incessant rain and soaked ground wreaked havoc on footgear, making soldiers vulnerable to trench foot, a blood-vessel and tissue injury caused by prolonged exposure to cold, wet conditions. Aware that the injury could make walking impossible and even require the amputation of toes, Patton ordered his troops to change into dry socks daily. Those instructions notwithstanding, trench foot soon became a serious problem, especially for infantrymen having to ford waist-deep rivers. By early November, in just one Third Army division alone, three thousand cases of the crippling malady had swept through the ranks. By winter, thousands more of Patton's men would be pulled from the front lines due to trench foot, making it an enemy almost greater than the Germans.

Just as dry socks were important to soldiers' well-being, so too were proper-fitting boots, especially combat boots big enough to accommodate layers of woolen footwear. To Bill's relief, he secured a pair in early October after waiting in line more than two hours at an Officers' Quartermaster store. He soon had to repeat that wait, as he explained to his parents: "Capt. Remley wanted some too & was too busy to get them, so I stood in line three hours the following day to get a pair for him."

While the strain of inaction continued to take its toll on Patton, necessitating "pink medecin," Bill appeared to be in good spirits when the calendar flipped to November. His October letters, noticeably short and bland, gave way in the new month to lengthier and chattier missives. His first letter opened with a grabber.

2 Nov. 1944, France

Dear Folks:

I had quite an experience today – for the first time I was kissed by a Frenchman. He caught me unawares! He was a lawyer at that, the first French brother at the bar I have been in contact with. I went to see him, with an interpreter, about a billet we were interested in. From his house (which also contained his office) I should say that law business in France must pay, as his establishment is almost magnificent.

I had my hair cut in a French shop the other day. Their barber shops are about like ours, except they don't use such a great variety of tonics. Their chairs are not adjustable as to height, and they use the old hand operated rather than electric clippers. Otherwise I should say their establishments are neater & more modern in decorations and fittings than ours. There is one great advantage of having a French barber – he can't bore you with his small talk while he snips because neither of you compré what the other is saying.

About the French lawyer, I think the reason he greeted me with such enthusiasm was because he is an ex-French officer and was a prisoner of the Germans for 14 months. I therefore appear to him in the role of a fellow barrister on a crusade of liberation.

The French are an excitable people anyway. Their conversations are quite animated – with the hands used about as much as the mouth. The other day I saw a man & woman arguing on the street. She was really giving him fits and he finally got as much as he could take, so he hauled off and socked her in the face.

Indiana (University football team) must really have a power house this year. It's too bad Illinois nosed them out. I'm interested to see how they'll fare against Ohio State this week.

Well, I can't think of anything else I dare write that you'd be interested in, so I'll say good night.

Love, Bill

Five days later, Bill again wrote at length, telling his parents, among other things, that he recently had seen a USO show featuring the singer and film star Marlene Dietrich, a symbol of glamour on both sides of the Atlantic. "She must be over forty, and would probably look it if all the paint and varnish were scraped off. Her show was pretty fair, but she could contribute very little besides her name and her figure, as vaudeville definitely is not her medium. I will say for her, however, that she has given a lot of her time and gone through much discomfort for the U.S.O. without any return in either money or publicity."

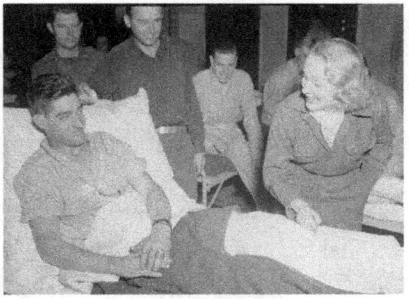

Marlene Dietrich autographs a U.S. soldier's cast at a hospital in Belgium, a few weeks after Bill saw her performance in France. The U.S. and France later honored Dietrich for her efforts to improve the morale of front-line troops. (National Archives)

Dietrich's visit also prompted Patton to take up his pen, though he confined his remarks to his diary in an entry dated November 5. Unlike Bill, Patton passed on being generous: "Had Marlene Dietrich and her troupe for lunch. Later they gave us a show. Very low comedy, almost an insult to human intelligence."

Meanwhile, each passing day brought colder weather, a topic Bill pounced on in his next letter. A more pleasing topic followed – his new souvenir.

France, 12 Nov. 1944
Dear Folks:

Winter is fast coming to France. Snow is falling almost every night. I hate to see it, for even under the best conditions possible, Winter and the Army do not combine for comfort. Allen, my driver, has acquired plex-i-glass from a crashed plane and made huge wings for my jeep. He has also acquired tin and hinges and made doors for it which help considerably, but it is still a long ways from being a Sedan....

I acquired my first real souvenir of the war today. One of the enlisted men attached to us had obtained a pair of German binoculars from a Frenchman at a cost of two cigarettes. He decided he didn't want to bother with them and just gave them to me.

They are the finest pair of glasses I ever saw – huge ten power affairs with two-inch object glasses. They are worn, but still optically and mechanically sound and worth, I would guess, considerably more than a hundred dollars.

The Germans make the finest optical instruments in the world. These have Mill scales etched in the lens, and were undoubtedly the property of some German artillery officer. They should make a mighty good gadget for football games sometime in the future.

This boy was very foolish to give them away, but nearly all the men want only pistols as souvenirs, and I wouldn't give a franc for a gross of them. I have known soldiers to pay as high as $175.00 for a German pistol called a "P-38" and it isn't so good a gun as our own .45, which I'll bet you could buy for $5.00 after the War.

I see that once again Indiana has demonstrated her political contrariness. I suppose that as usual the DeKalb County Democrats took a lacing in the county election. There just aren't enough Democrats in some places, I guess. According to Stars & Stripes, the vote of G.I.s overseas is running about 67% for Roosevelt.

The French celebrated Armistice Day yesterday with parades and all the usual frills. Not in very good taste at a time like this, I should say.

I owe letters to [friends] Paul, Lois, and Mrs. Ditchfield, so I think I'll say Good Night now and write to some of them.
Love, Bill

AFTER WEEKS OF STOCKPILING AMMUNITION and after finally receiving Eisenhower's blessing, Patton on November 8 ordered an all-out assault on Metz, the German stronghold north of Nancy that had remained impregnable in the face of Third Army's earlier and limited attacks. Patton also ordered his troops to advance toward the German border, with top commanders by then having cleared him to get his army moving. Though frightful weather would make advancement difficult and though supplies remained low, Patton was thrilled to be back on the offensive. He was especially eager to bid goodbye and good riddance to that mud-and-blood corner of France where his men had been locked in a monthslong war of attrition. "I hope that in the final settlement of the war you insist that the Germans retain Lorraine," a frustrated Patton had cabled Secretary of War Henry L. Stimson in October, "because I can imagine no greater burden than to be the owner of this nasty country where it rains every day and where the whole wealth of the people consists in assorted manure piles."

Predictably, Bill's November letters made no mention of Third Army's movements. Neither did Bill comment on Patton's entry into Metz on November 25, just days after the grueling siege had ended and after GIs, though successful, had paid dearly to flush Germans from the garrison's tunnels. Patton arrived on the scene as a hero, welcomed with screaming sirens, salutes, and honor guard music, after which he awarded medals to the valiant and presided over the return of Metz to French custody. In a letter Bill wrote home that very day, he stated that he had just returned from an "official business trip" but the "business didn't take long," raising questions – but not answering – if he had helped arrange the triumphal visit.

Bill's November 25 letter also included bittersweet news: "Ziggy is no more." Throughout the autumn, Bill had shared lighthearted stories about the friendly canine – everything from Ziggy being a constant companion ("He just came up on my lap where he is 'helping' me write.") to the mascot's occasional misdeeds ("Ziggy just sprinkled the carpet in front of the fireplace. He always seeks out my room for that.") Bill's letters also had raised concerns about the dog's health, as when he wrote home in early October that "I think [Ziggy] has worms. They gave him a good dose of castor oil at one of the Evacuation Hospitals but it didn't seem to do much good. He is an awful baby – requires constant attention or he isn't happy."

Weeks later, no better news: "Ziggy is still sick. In fact, he has distemper now. He has been to a vet twice for shots. The second time he began to yell as soon as he saw the needle. I think he'll make it O.K." A few days later, no improvement: "Ziggy just crawled out of my sleeping bag – I don't know how he got in. He used to be fat as a butter-ball, but now he's skinny and frail. Poor little fellow is having an awful battle with distemper. He should have been vaccinated against it."

By the third week of November, Ziggy's condition remained poor, with the shivering pooch unable to ward off the cold. His plight prompted one of Bill's fellow officers to cut holes in a wool sock and make Ziggy a pull-over sweater. But the effort was for naught. A week later, in the letter reporting Ziggy's death, Bill offered this eulogy: "He and his bells were about the cutest things you ever saw."

With little else in the way of "cute" to record in a war zone, Bill filled his letters in early December with ho-hum bits of this and that – of finding his lost knife, receiving a damaged Christmas present, breaking his resolution not to play poker (and then winning $30). On December 15, however, he dashed off a letter that may well have left his parents unsettled, if only because the news seemed "too good" and because the address line omitted any reference to France, raising questions as to where Bill might have relocated.

With 3rd US Army
15 December, 1944
Dear Folks:
Every once in awhile in the Army you hit a "cushy" spot that reminds you of the song "You're in the Army now, Mr. Jones" and the cartoon "This ain't the Army." We've hit one of them now.

France

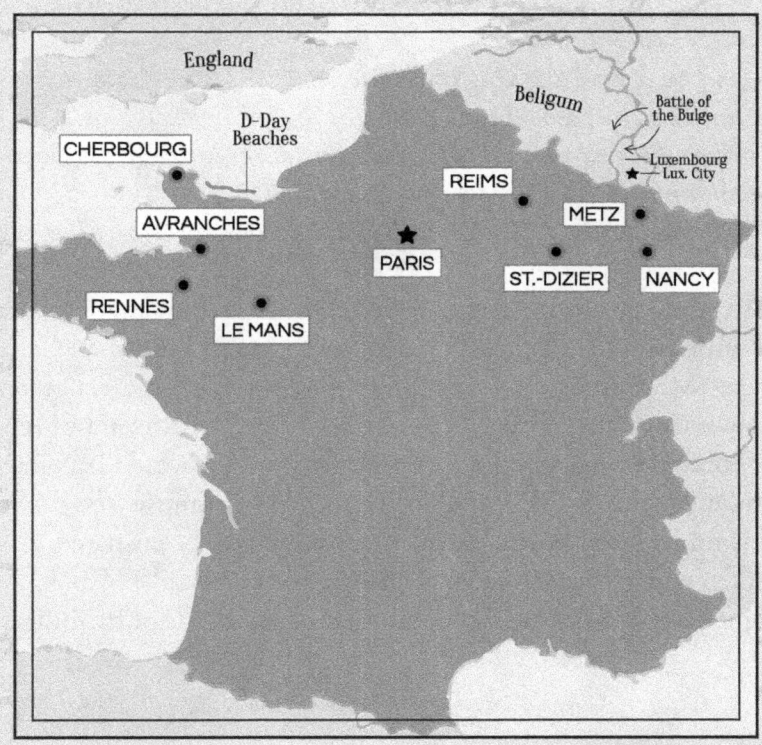

In letters he sent home during the war, Bill reported passing through or staying in various French cities, including those listed above. He identified the cities and towns only when army censors permitted.

The company has taken over an apartment hotel that is still in first class condition – automatic elevator still working, etc. The four officers have an apartment on the 3rd floor consisting of three bedrooms: a lounge with overstuffed furniture, a built in divan (upon which I'm writing this), a swell radio; a kitchen; and a blue tile bath with hot water! Steam heat throughout, of course.

The only trouble is, I know from experience it is too good to last. This definitely "ain't the Army."

It will be a very pleasant interlude while it lasts. Right now we're listening to Benny Goodman "send" (as the bobby soxers would say) on the radio. This all reminds me of my first weeks in the Army when my greatest ambition was to have some place to sit down....

Well, the "makin's" [for cocktails] have arrived, so think I'll sign off.

Early the next morning, with Allied high command caught unawares and unprepared, the "makin's" for disaster emerged along the German border. More than a quarter million Wehrmacht soldiers attacked at dawn through the rugged Ardennes forests of Luxembourg and Belgium, smashing westward in an offensive that would become the bloodiest of the war. Bill, awaking from a night of music and cocktails in his undisclosed hotel apartment, would soon be ensnared in that conflict, which the Germans called *Wacht am Rhine*.

Americans would know it by another name: Battle of the Bulge.

Chapter Thirteen
MARY: 1944

ITALY
JUNE 15, 1944

Dearest Family –
I'm sorry to be so long writing you and now to only offer you V-Mail but thought this would be the quicker way to let you know how busy we have been and a better letter will follow at my first chance when I will have more time to tell you in detail of the new things we are doing and our new set-up.

Joyce, Eleanor and I had a five day vacation on the Island of Ischia [in the Bay of Naples, not far from Capri] which was very restful. We avoided all Americans and simply spent our time lying on the Beach. The rest we had stood in well for when we returned we found the Club all packed and ready to move out [from Caserta]. The last few days have been hectic getting an entirely new Club set up in two days – but the pressure is off now and we are in the most amazingly beautiful place now imaginable. It is exactly the opposite of our last place both in comfort & beauty.

WHEN MARY BRANDON RESUMED writing her family in mid-June 1944 following Rome's liberation and the D-Day invasion, censorship rules still dictated that she identify her new location only as "Italy." Her letters soon made clear, however, that she had been reassigned to Rome, specifically to a military rest center north of the city's historic core. As had been the case at Caserta, the U.S. Fifth Army operated the facility, its troops by then having moved halfway up the Italian peninsula, though efforts to drive Hitler's forces from the entire country were far from over.

Mary had had an inkling, in the weeks prior to her move, that she might be headed to Rome. Allied forces in late May had battled their way to the city's outskirts, leaving Mary and her Red Cross colleagues with little work to do at the palace in Caserta, 125 miles to the south. Sometime after June 5, when the Allies took control of Rome, Mary and two coworkers were permitted to vacation briefly on the scenic island of Ischia, after which they were sent immediately to the Italian capital. There, in a matter of days, they set up a Red Cross club for American servicemen.

Mary's journey north had been memorable. The route from Caserta to Rome passed "through some of the most bombed towns in Italy. We passed through Cassino which I dare not describe but will never forget it so some day I will tell you," she wrote her parents on June 18, referencing the famed mountain stronghold where months of fighting had obliterated the ancient abbey and where skeleton trees, charred stumps, and granulated rubble covered hillsides. Two weeks later, in a letter to her brother Charles, Mary offered a more personal "take" on her travel north:

Our trip here was both uncomfortable and extremely interesting for we passed through some of the most devastated towns imaginable. There were eleven of us along with our Field Director and our dog as well as eleven bed-rolls, eleven foot lockers, eleven duffle bags, eleven musette bags and eleven suit cases jammed, stuffed and crammed into a Command Car, a Weapons Carrier and a [Jeep]. We were in an English convoy whose drivers [you might think] could[n't] ever handle a bicycle let [alone] a vehicle.

Convoy travelling is a little precarious at its best but in the best [convoy] Etiquette every car stops each two hours for the usual calls of nature. We being ladies didn't dare to stick our noses outside and since there are no filling stations on the road to Rome or anywhere for that matter we made the ten hour trip in stoic silence.

Trip discomforts aside, Mary was further inconvenienced upon her arrival. In that same letter to Charles, she explained:

> *The [German] soldiers and officers who had occupied the building before left in a mighty great hurry. I made the mistake of picking up a mattress for my bed and only added to mosquito and flea bites some bed bugs. I had bombed the room with a gas bomb (to kill insects, etc.) but I guess there were too many. Needless to say, I threw the mattress away and am now sleeping on three G.I. blankets....*

Her complaints began and ended there, however. She had landed, as she also told Charles, in a "spot simply out of this world. The boys come in completely oogle-eyed – they can't believe that this place could be for them." To her parents that June, she reported the same:

> *I cannot begin to describe this place even if I dared. The facilities for the boys are endless and they are certainly enjoying them. Our Club is in a building with the most enormous swimming pool I've ever seen. It took the Engineers three days to get enough water in it for swimming. Our club is beside the pool but shut from it by immense glass doors. The doors extend to the second floor where we have our writing and music rooms. We are just now getting a Snack Bar set up in the basement. On another floor is a pool for the officers which is a little gem. The top opens to let in the sun and with its white marble pillars and clear blue water it looks like an ancient Roman watering place.*

That Fifth Army soldiers were "oogle-eyed" wasn't surprising. The U.S. Army had chosen to occupy a former military school and sports complex that Italian dictator Benito Mussolini had ordered built beginning in the 1920s. The complex's grandiose design was inspired by imperial-age Roman forums, giving rise to its name Foro Mussolini, today known as Foro Italico.

Intended as a place to instill Fascist ideals in Italy's youth, the complex included an Academy of Physical Education, an Academy of Political Education, a Fencing Academy, a fifty-meter-long indoor swimming pool (which Mary's letter referenced), and a 20,000-seat stadium. Mosaics celebrating Fascism were prominently displayed throughout the campus, as were marble statues that borrowed heavily from antiquity. The stadium alone featured sixty statues depicting different sports and symbolizing masculine strength and virility. The complex's showpiece was the fifty-five-foot-high Carrara marble obelisk at the entrance, engraved with the words "MVSSOLINI DVX" or "Mussolini, the Leader."

Because Il Duce, as Mussolini was known, had hoped to host Olympic games in Rome, construction at the site had continued well into the 1930s, with plans to build an even larger stadium and an outdoor swimming pool. Mussolini's dream of serving as Olympic host went unfulfilled when the games were cancelled in 1940 and again in 1944 due to war. Even so, the would-be Caesar was proud of his eponymous forum and, when visiting there, he enjoyed his private marble-walled gymnasium and the indoor swimming pool with the retractable roof (the "gem" that Mary's letter referenced).

By late July 1943, however, Mussolini's days at his forum were over. His Fascist government, which had made a war pact with Hitler in May 1939, fell to forces loyal to King Victor Emmanuel III, and the king – who two decades earlier had acquiesced to Mussolini's power-grabbing – ordered the ousted leader arrested and imprisoned. In early September 1943, as Il Duce was slated to be

Benito Mussolini and Adolf Hitler in Munich, Germany, June 1940. (National Archives)

turned over to the Allies (with whom the new Italian government had signed an armistice), German commandos freed him from a makeshift jail in the mountains east of Rome. Later that month – and on Hitler's orders – Mussolini set up a Fascist regime in German-occupied northern Italy. By then worn-out and politically crippled, he was little more than Hitler's puppet, with his communications and travel restricted by his Nazi "liberators." As for the newly arrived American liberators of Rome, they moved into the imposing buildings that Mussolini had left behind.

For Mary, those buildings became both her home and workplace. Having labored feverishly in early June 1944 to set up the new Red Cross facility, she and her colleagues soon settled into their daily routine of managing the club's snack bar and spending hours on the dance floor. They likewise wrote letters for soldiers, joined in their games of cribbage and checkers, and listened to them talk about wives and sweethearts. The entire complex, renamed the United States Army Rest Center, could accommodate up to 2,500 soldiers at a time. With new truckloads of GIs arriving regularly, faces at the club changed constantly. Mary's workload did not.

Soldiers arriving at Rest Center, June 1944 (National Archives)

Despite her busy schedule, Mary was determined to see Rome's famous sights, particularly attractions that she had learned about in her high school history classes or had seen pictured in Latin schoolbooks. Writing her parents on June 21, soon after her arrival, she noted:

We went into the city this morning – I with my pockets [bulging] with money to buy all kinds of treasures but the prices have soared so just in the little bit of time we have been here that I came home empty handed with only a gardenia in my button-hole to show for the morning's effort. We did some walking however in the ruins and I spotted some places that I want to go back to and spend some time. Rome is a strange beautiful conglomeration of a city – with ancient ruins, medieval and modern buildings all thrown in together.

A small medical procedure – the removal of a corn on her toe – forced her to abruptly, though temporarily, put her sightseeing on hold. The attending surgeon was none other than Doc, who had been assigned to the Rest Center and who, with other military officers, had traveled with Mary and Red Cross staff from Caserta. Having already informed her family about Doc's presence in Rome, Mary invoked his name again in her June 27 letter. She also highlighted a personal anniversary, one that surely resonated with her parents:

Dearest Mother & Dad –

... I've had a bad corn on my little toe for some time and have run out of corn pads so the "Doc" cut it out yesterday afternoon. I had no idea it would be such an operation, for after the novacaine [sic] ran out it has

been most painful. I can't get a shoe on nor will for several days, he says. But I'll never have another so that is some consolation. . . .

Things are going pretty smoothly at the Club. We have a dance band to play every afternoon and so, of course, have been doing a lot of dancing. Well, I won't be dancing for a few days now, at least.

We are really in a very beautiful spot not far from the city. From our windows just across the [Tiber] river we can see very modern and beautiful apartment buildings that remind of the buildings along Michigan Ave. in Chicago. One of the boys stationed here with the Cadre is helping me with Italian and since he speaks it fluently is going to take me sight-seeing some of these days.

It doesn't seem possible that just about a year ago this time I was getting ready to go to Washington for my [Red Cross] interview. And in another month I will be gone a year. It can't possibly be that long.

I do hope you are all well. Our mail isn't coming through so well lately so I'll be waiting patiently to hear from you.

Knowing her family expected a medical update, Mary obliged within days:

I have my shoe on today for the first since my "corn operation." I hope it will heal soon for I'm missing a lot of good sight-seeing days. I've been wearing a soft bed room slipper and the bottom of my foot is more sore from walking on the marble floors than the corn itself. One of the boys who came to the center gave me a nice looking pair of oxfords which fortunately fit me. He had taken them from a German who had in turn taken them from an Italian – now I have them – a vicious circle.

By early July, with her toe on the mend and having found suitable shoes, Mary resumed sightseeing. A chance meeting with an acquaintance resulted in her first visit to Vatican City and a brush with Pope Pius XII, who just weeks earlier – on the evening of Rome's liberation – had addressed the rejoicing throngs in St. Peter's Square and given thanks that both the retreating Germans and advancing Allies had spared the city from destruction. The pontiff was popular among Italians, in stark contrast to the despised Mussolini and the fascist-tainted King Victor Emmanuel. After the war, Pius's reputation would suffer, with critics arguing that he had been sympathetic to Hitler and had failed to vigorously denounce Nazi persecution of Jews. Mary's initial impression of him, however, was favorable, as her July 7 letter attested:

Dearest Family –

... While I was down in town the other morning doing a little shopping I chanced to see Major Carman, the Chaplain we had with us on Capri. He was on his way to see the Pope so I went with him. I hurriedly bought some Rosaries and had them blessed. ... We stood for a long time in a very crowded and hot room only to be changed to a larger audience room. During the change the Major and I were lucky enough to get directly on the aisle and in front. I could have reached out and touched [Pius] as he was being carried by me.

A souvenir Mary collected in Rome.

He is a very plain and simple man and talked to us very kindly – first in English and then in French. He was carried on a throne on the shoulders of the Swiss Guard in their brilliant medieval costumes. He was accompanied by several Cardinals in their red robes and he was [wearing a] dazzling white gown with an enormous jeweled cross. As we entered the audience room we were given the Medal and pictures which I've enclosed. Perhaps you would like to give it to one of your Catholic friends – It would mean so much more to them. After he finished his speech the Major went directly up to him, kissed his ring and ask[ed] him to especially bless my [new] rosaries. We didn't have time to look about St. Peters much for I had to be back at work at two o'clock – so the Major brought me home and we had lunch in our Snack Bar. ...

Do write whenever you can. The mail hasn't been coming through too well and I'm getting lonesome for some letters.

All my Love, Mary

In a letter a day later, Mary reported another celebrity sighting. She had listened the previous evening to a concert at the Rest Center by the eminent Russian-American violinist Jascha Heifetz. "It was truly lovely," she shared with Annie's family. "Hearing such beautiful music and so superbly played was like having food after being hungry for a long time."

Her reference to food was apt. Mussolini's government – with its graft, wasteful spending on expensive monuments, and questionable outlays for military arms – had set the stage for Italy's impoverishment, which in Rome grew more dire during the Nazi occupation. Hitler's henchmen had stripped the city of goods and materials, even removing Rome's streetcars for reuse in Germany. Rome's residents, meanwhile, had resorted to selling their possessions to buy, at exorbitant prices, dwindling supplies of food and charcoal, the latter needed for cooking in homes without electricity and heat. When the Allies finally arrived, food supplies were so low that the bread-rationing the Nazis had instituted – one hundred grams of bread daily per person – remained in effect. By summer's end, the Allies would double the daily bread portion to two hundred grams and begin stabilizing the prices of fruits and vegetables. But as Mary noted in her July 8 letter to Annie, food – more than Heifetz's music – was what she really needed:

Your package arrived this morning and indeed thank you but Gosh I could have used more than two cookies. I ate one and gave Doc the other – maybe sometime you'd make us some more. While speaking of food we are all growing thin – our rations have been considerably cut. We have fresh meat very rarely and dehydrated vegetables which are far from tasty. Even P.X. rations have dwindled, consequently we are being very conservative on our cigarettes. The only thing I did have is a box of Hershey bars – and always we are able to get Tootsie Rolls in the P.X. That's just a tip if you ever want to send another package....

The description of your vegetable garden makes my mouth fairly drip. I do wish I could taste some of it.

Mary returned to the subject of food in a V-Mail four days later, telling her parents "our rations since moving have been very meager and sometimes actually poor. Vienna sausages and Spam get mighty monotonous." She and Doc, nonetheless, had had the good fortune the previous evening of being invited to a "real Italian dinner" hosted by friends of a military friend. Along with fried chicken, the meal included "real Spaghetti" and "a very tasty vegetable, a sort of Squash called Zucchini," all of which Mary deemed "simply delicious."

While encouraging her family to send whatever edible items they could spare, Mary gained insight that summer into the volume of letters and packages sent and received by troops. Writing Annie in July, Mary noted: "We really have a big business in this Mail Censoring room. I have charge of it every other day. Today there were seven officers censoring letters with another [officer] for packages. The Post Office is in the same room . . . Thousands of letters are sent out each day." Whether censors opened packages or not, Mary knew from firsthand experience that vermin and weather often damaged contents. When weeks later she opened a much-welcomed package from home containing two cans of shrimp and a can of cookies, she discovered that "the can of cookies had been opened and several bites taken out – consequently they were very stale." But Mary saw a bright side: The cookies "smelled like home and that was good."

IN ROME, AS HAD BEEN THE CASE since she arrived overseas, Mary encountered soldiers with ties to Auburn or neighboring towns. They included family acquaintances, relatives of her friends, and "boys" from her days as a student and a teacher. "I sang at church this morning and after the service met a Lt. Getts from Butler. He is Jo Holsinger's brother. You will remember that she is married to Lynn Holsinger," Mary wrote her folks in early July, connecting the who's-related-to-whom dots. In that same letter, she mentioned meeting a lieutenant who recently had seen Jack Berns, younger brother of Herman, her former fiancé. From that lieutenant, Mary learned that Jack Berns was a captain stationed near Rome and that Herman, with whom Mary appears to have had little or no communication in years, was still at an Army Air Corps base in Illinois. Later that fall, Mary would encounter Jack when he visited Rome and, over the course of several days, he would join her social circle at a dinner-dance and at other gatherings. "We've had a perfectly swell time since he's been here," Mary would write her parents, adding that Jack said little about his brother. She, in turn, chose not to probe: "I inquired about his Father & Mother and Herman, of course, but all he said was the big so-&-so had only written him three times since he'd been in Italy, so we both dropped the subject."

Foro Italico in Rome

Foro Italico, operating today as Rome's major sports complex, looks much as it did when Mary worked there. Still present are the red-brick buildings, marble obelisk, glass-enclosed swimming pool, statues of athletes encircling the stadium, and pavement covered with mosaics spelling "Duce," Mussolini's title. (Photos by author)

Pleased as she was to see old acquaintances, Mary also found that they served as a reality check. In late July, she received a visit from Sterling Ward, who had graduated from high school a year ahead of her in the neighboring town of Garrett. A technical sergeant in the army's railway operating service, Ward had served in North Africa and Sicily before being reassigned to Italy. "Had a visit from Sterling Ward this morning – honestly I didn't know him, at first. He looks so much older – but then it must be ten years at least since I last saw him," Mary wrote her friend Joanna Rhoads. Days later, following a dinner with Ward, Mary shared the same thoughts with her parents: "It was nice seeing him again but I wondered whether I looked as old to him as he did to me. Sometimes, unless I'm reminded, I forget the years are creeping up on me too." During Mary's evening outing with the sergeant, the two bumped into another Auburn acquaintance, Phil Berg, who served in the same railway unit and who – eager for hometown news – accompanied them back to the Red Cross club. Both soldiers promised to treat her soon to "a real Italian dinner" and "some American whiskey."

When not encountering fellow Hoosiers, Mary loved hearing from them by mail. Among her most faithful correspondents was the aforementioned Joanna, whose letters made their way to Mary wherever she relocated. In appreciation for her friend's unwavering dedication, Mary sent a gift from Italy and was happy to learn, in late July, that it had been safely delivered. "It was swell having your letter . . . and knowing that at last you had received the comb. It just about hit your birthday, didn't it?" Mary wrote back to Joanna. Mary added that she recently had met a lieutenant who served with Joanna's cousin, Barney Seeman. "I told [the lieutenant] to tell Barney to get down here to play with me for a day, but I suppose he's too busy. Our staff has been decreased so we are all being busy too these days."

As for other dependable letter writers, Mary appreciated hearing from members of Tri Kappa, a philanthropic organization to which she belonged and which periodically supplied her with much-needed items, especially stockings (size 8 ½ short). So, too, did Mary hear from Auburn's older residents. "I had a nice letter from Mrs. Husselman [Bill's mother] this morning," Mary informed her parents soon after arriving in Rome. "[I] shall try to answer her soon."

Former Red Cross colleagues also stayed in touch with Mary, and she welcomed their occasional visits. Elizabeth (Mopsey) Richardson, Mary's partner on the Isle of Capri, stopped by the Army Rest Center one night in July for a brief reunion. Soon afterward, Blenda Larson, Mary's roommate at Caserta, arrived and stayed for several days. Mary accompanied the vacationing Blenda on a tour of the Vatican, where she had her second encounter with Pope Pius. The pontiff, who enjoyed granting audiences to Rome's liberators, allowed Mary to shake his hand and – as her July 29 letter noted – "he asked me in his very gentle voice if I was British or American."

In that same letter, Mary shifted to another topic – one her family may have found a bit startling and even a tad amusing:

Yesterday morning I really had a treat in the form of a hot shower. It is the first hot water I've felt since June 9th. It was in a tent in an outdoor shower unit but it couldn't have felt better even in a marble bath. The unit is stationed here in our area so that the boys when they come in can have a hot bath and exchange their dirty clothes for clean ones. Yesterday morning, then, they roped off the area and handed it over to Red Cross gals. Bathing in cold water in a wash bowl doesn't leave one exactly clean so I imagine I washed off about a peck of dirt.

Shower updates aside, Mary kept her family informed throughout the summer as to new friends she was making. Among the first of her Rome-based pals was Gertrude Dyer, a Chicagoan who Mary met while setting up the Red Cross club and who shared her interests in music and drama. A day after the club's opening, Army Signal Corps personnel took photographs of soldiers enjoying themselves around the premises, and Mary, Gertrude, and other colleagues – all wearing colorful new pinafore aprons – appeared in several staged shots. Some of the photos have been preserved at the National Archives, including one of Mary – misidentified by the photographer as Gertrude – seated atop a piano with soldiers gathered around.

Weeks after that photo session, Mary referred to it again in a July 17 letter to her parents. She enclosed a photo and mentioned that Gertrude was the "swell girl" in the swimming pool seen playfully pulling Mary's arm. While that letter survives, the "arm-pulling" picture does not. Regardless, Gertrude already had left for home, for reasons that remain unclear, and two other colleagues recently had transferred from the club, causing Mary to feel "a little pressed." Her July 17 letter continued, "I came on at eight this morning and am supposed to stay until 10 tonight – however I believe I'll take off about 8 instead. A twelve hour day is long enough especially when there are no completely free days." That particular day was to feature a Scottish Highlanders band playing bagpipes, prompting Mary, perhaps with some relief, to remark: "I'm afraid no one will know how to do a Highland Fling so no dancing this afternoon."

A pinafore-clad Mary, misidentified by the photographer as Gertrude Dyer, enjoys some music with soldiers during an Army Signal Corps photo "shoot" at the Rest Center in June 1944. (National Archives)

As demanding and erratic as her work schedule was, Mary still made time for Doc. Through him, she forged friendships with other military officers, including two who lived in a nearby British encampment.

Italy, Aug 1, 1944
Dearest Mother & Dad –
Well – tomorrow marks one year with me in the Red Cross – It certainly doesn't seem possible that I've been gone that long. Surely, one more year will find me home again.

The party with our British friends the other night was most enjoyable. Last night Doc and I returned the compliment and they were our guests for dinner. Capt. Egerton is a fat jolly Londoner, while lean, blond handsome Major Forgan is a Scotsman. It is much easier for me to understand the latter with his burry R's than the Capt. But all four of us are firm friends. The two of them live in half truck affairs which resemble our trailers at home. Their men have made them truly beautiful with pieces of old wood they picked up at Anzio – cut it with all its beautiful grain showing and made an interior as charming as an old cabinet.

After dinner we took a look around their camp, visited their canteen where the men were drinking hot tea on a hot night and then watched a cricket game. We had nothing so [diverting] to offer them except to sit out on our terrace after dinner and watch the moon get yellow over the Tiber.

Shifting to other topics, Mary continued:

This morning I went with Ardith (one of our gals) and her beau (our Red Cross Field Director) – Bert – to the Vatican Art Museum to see all of the old Roman and Greek sculpture. Coming upon pieces like the Apollo Belvedere was like seeing an old friend after viewing pictures of the statues in books and never thinking that one would actually have the opportunity of realization. The statues are all beautiful beyond description – what these early people could do to marble is amazing. We also had a look in the picture gallery to see some of the most famous religious pictures ever painted. After centuries their colors are still bright and beautiful.

I'm so sorry to find that my Italian camera is no good (or as we all say now in Italian "non buono"). I'm afraid that all the film I've taken so far is ruined. The camera lets in light and of course spoils the film.

Do write when you have time. I hope so much you are well and that the summer is not being too hot for you. I was thinking before I went for my dinner tonight what I would like to have. Would you like to know? Fried chicken, a baked potato, Roasting ears and apple dumplings. Maybe it won't be long.

We have had a swimming meet in our pool over the week-end with the Hawaiian boys from a certain Division carrying off all the honors. They are truly wonderful swimmers and play around like seals in the water. Today the pools have had to be closed because of lack of purifying materials. I hope they find some soon else how can I soak off the dirt?

Goodbye, my darlings. Mary

THROUGHOUT THE SUMMER OF 1944, the Allies kept pursuing Hitler's forces north of Rome, driving them from towns in central Italy and from strategic ports on both coasts. By early August, the beloved Renaissance city of Florence was liberated, though not before retreating Germans blew up the city's bridges – an exception being the centuries-old Ponte Vecchio, which Hitler was said to have admired. Encouraged by their successes, the Allies kept thrusting forward. But their progress soon was slowed by heavy German fortifications stretching across Italy's upper leg. The barriers included bunkers, barbed wire, anti-tank ditches, and more than 2,300 machine-gun nests. Known as the Gothic Line, these fearsome fortifications – combined with the rugged crests of the Apennine Mountains – were intended to block Allied passage into Austria, thus making them Germany's last major line of defense in its Italian campaign.

Formidable as the Gothic Line was, Allied forces that summer faced a problem of their own high command's making, namely, the withdrawal of troops. Months earlier, U.S. and British units had been pulled from the region to prepare for the D-Day invasion of northwest France. Following that June attack, even more U.S. troops and French units departed Italy for a second invasion of France – this time along the Mediterranean coast. Known as *Operation Dragoon*, that assault began on August 15, with Allied troops landing on the French Riviera, seizing much-needed ports, driving rapidly up the Rhone Valley, and eventually offering flank support to Lieutenant General Patton's Third Army, which was racing toward the German border. By summer's end the Italian campaign, already relegated to the back pages of American newspapers, appeared destined to take a backseat in the overall war effort. Soldiers who remained there increasingly saw themselves as fighting a "forgotten war."

With military talk off-limits in her correspondence, Mary penned a letter in early August that shed light on how disruptive the war had been – and continued to be – for civilians. Her thumbnail sketches of club workers revealed that many were refugees from Nazi aggression.

Aug 10, 1944

Dearest Mother & Dad –

I had your letter yesterday telling of Dad's illness – I so much hope he is improved by now – if not – all well. I remember how hard it was to keep him from doing too much after he got up and around the last time; so you just take a rope and tie him securely in a comfortable chair on the porch – don't let him cut the grass, or rake the lawn, or wash out the basement or polish the car, or haul the ashes or stoke the furnace.

Speaking of Dad's ailments, I have acquired one of his pets with a rheumatic ache in my knees. They are stiff and sore – but in a way I'm rather glad for now I'll have an excuse not to do so much dancing.

I really don't have much news to give you for I haven't done anything since I wrote you last but you might be interested in hearing about a few of the people who work for us here at the club. We have a tall very thin & gaunt man [Vladimir Wolkonsky] who is our artist – he makes signs and illustrations when we need them. He is a perfect and gracious man who speaks excellent English. He is Russian and went to art school in Paris. He has told me many tales about when the Germans were here and he had to hide. One of the handy man's name is Pompeo but I call him "Atlas" for he carries the most enormous loads on his head. He is very ugly with red hair and only scattered teeth – he never wears a shirt but always one of the soldier's hats. He brings great loads of boxes (on his head) into the package wrapping room. Sometimes his load is so high that he has to crawl on his knees to get through the high door sills. I'm sure he is the strongest man in Italy and he is quite a "show-off" about it.

He holds up his strong arms and ripples bicep muscles for me to admire. One day he carried on his back a Ping pong table up several flights of stairs when it had taken six other men to do the same thing. Lily, our housekeeper, left us this morning to have her baby. She is Yugoslavian. When the Germans invaded her country she came on a refugee boat to Northern Italy with her parents. As the Germans came into Italy she walked with her husband (another Slav) to Naples, hiding in the woods until they reached the city. Both she & her husband have been with this same Red Cross since Naples, then our previous place [at Caserta] and now here. She is very intelligent and a beautiful blond.

Vera and Magda help us at the Information desk. They have both lived here in the City but are not native Italians. Vera is a Hungarian married to an Italian and Magda is Polish. Her native city is Lvov which recently fell to the Russians again. She escaped from the Germans in Poland and was held in a concentration camp later to come to Italy where her sister lived. She is a charming girl and very helpful for she speaks six languages. This morning some people from the Polish Red Cross came in – she was so happy to see them.

I'll try to get in a note to you tomorrow and will appreciate hearing how you both are progressing.

Mary, as promised, wrote a day later and shared what her family likely had been waiting for – a photo of Doc. Given that her Italian camera wasn't working properly, she used his to snap the photo, and in forwarding it asked her parents a favor: "Will you please keep this for me – I think it is a good one of him. He usually doesn't smile when he is having a picture taken but I made him laugh."

Mary's letter also mentioned ongoing swim meets at the Rest Center, with winning athletes permitted to stay for upcoming

Mary's photo of a smiling Doc

competitions. "Many of the boys are Hawaiians and wonderful swimmers. We have had a chance to know them better than most of the boys who are here for just a few days and have grown very fond of them, [as] they are of us." The swimmers may have been attached to the Japanese-American 442nd Regimental Combat Team, a unit Bill Husselman was familiar with from his Camp Shelby days and whose ranks included many islanders. Of them, Mary added:

Yesterday they made us real Hawaiian leis out of real flowers that we wore all yesterday afternoon. I still have mine on the center of my coffee tale. It makes a beautiful decoration – all of lovely marigolds. Some were of dark red clover blossoms and some of carnations.

With seemingly little objection from censors, Mary also filled her letters that summer with matrimonial news involving coworkers and military personnel. She sent home her first such dispatch in early August, referencing her colleague Joyce Gregory. Joyce, in Mary's telling, had "fallen in love" with a Special Services soldier who performed in "one of the G.I. shows." In deference to the soldier's wishes for a Catholic wedding, Joyce had begun taking instruction in the faith from an Army chaplain and had asked Mary to serve as a witness at her confirmation. In a follow-up letter to her family in late August, Mary explained that she had obliged her friend. She also offered revealing details about Red Cross discipline.

Aug. 22, 1944

Joyce is leaving us tomorrow to start back to the States. She had planned to go in September but her trip was hurried up a bit because of a little rule infraction. Her beau has been changed from our area up into the combat zone. She wanted to see him very badly so she got a ride up that way and since she went without travel orders from Red Cross she is being reprimanded by being sent home. She really doesn't mind in the least because in this way she is getting off a little earlier than she expected. We are going to miss her – she has been a lot of fun. I'll have her write you when she gets home so she can tell you exactly where we are. Bill (her beau) was here Sunday to see her confirmed and baptized in St. Peters. I went along as a witness and she chose my name for one of her new names. So she is now Joyce Rosamund Mary Gregory. The ceremony was very interesting although I didn't know very much about what was going on.

In another August letter, Mary shared news about Miriam "Mim" Martin, a coworker whose September wedding plans appeared at one point to be in jeopardy. Mim's fiancé was a paratrooper, and shortly after midnight on August 15, nearly 400 aircraft – carrying more than 5,000 paratroopers with the 1st Airborne Task Force – roared off from airfields around Rome, signaling the launch of *Operation Dragoon* into southern France. In a letter three days later to her family, Mary referenced the invasion, though not by name.

We had a couple of hard days last week "Sweating out" the fact that "Charlie" the prospective bride-groom might not be around for the wedding. He is a Paratrooper and has jumped on every invasion to date. He, of course, was alerted on the last one and wasn't able to tell Mim whether he would jump or not. When, on the night after the invasion he walked into the Club we were very relieved. He had gone along with the troopers but just for the ride. He has many interesting stories to tell as you could imagine. Now that he is back, plans for the affair are getting into full swing. It will be in Mrs. [Mary] Munford's (our Director) very beautiful apartment – the very good Italian orchestra that we have here at the Club will play. They are frantically searching for the music to "Because" (a favorite of Charlie's) for me to sing. . . .

Determined to do right by the soon-to-be-wed couple, Mary didn't give up when the needed sheet music could not be found. She instead hummed the tune to the orchestra's piano player, who wrote it down, and later – when rehearsing with the musicians – she was pleased to discover that "it sounded as if they had played it for a dozen weddings." Other pre-wedding headaches surfaced, however. The maid-of-honor's dress was ruined during a cleaning, and the bride's dress, which Mim's mother was shipping to Rome, had not yet arrived as the big day approached. Even so, when Mary wrote her parents on September 6, several days after the wedding, her account suggested that all went well.

The wedding was held in Mrs. Munford's apartment which is very beautiful. The service proper [was] on her roof porch. One whole side was made into a bank of greens and flowers. The vows were read by a Methodist Chaplain. I played my usual role at weddings and sang Charlie's (the groom) favorite tune "Because" . . . There was a beautiful wedding cake and we had little sandwiches and salted nuts. Mim had invited just the officers and enlisted men who have been with the Rest Center for a long time – so everyone knew everybody else and it was a gay and happy party. Doc and one of the Lieutenants were the Bar-tenders. We had Gin and Lemonade and Rum with Coke – almost like a party at home. Mim and Charlie have taken an apartment across from the [Tiber] river....

Meanwhile, another of Mary's coworkers, Utah native Ardith Spalding, remained tight-knit with Bert Arnberg, the Swedish-born Red Cross field director who previously had worked in North Africa and whose duties would later take him to Germany. Bert's work entitled him to an agency car, which proved advantageous when he and Ardith invited Mary and Doc to join them on social outings. One such outing was to Rome's zoo, which Mary described in an August 8 letter to her parents:

The Zoo itself is a fair one – but not to compare with the St. Louis one. They did have, however, the most lovable Giraffe that ate bread right out of our hands. All the animals seem very hungry, food is hard enough to get for civilians let alone the animals in the Zoo. The wild dogs were a pitiful sight – so thin and scrawny. The monkies [sic] were so funny as they always are – for candy and chewing gum there was one little Joe that would quickly turn a somersault and jump to attention with the Fascist salute – then he would stick his arm through the cage for his reward. It seemed a shame to be giving it to the animals when there were children standing around drooling with their tongues hanging out.

Other outings for the foursome included dinner at Mim and Charlie's apartment and picnics at a nearby black-sand beach, most likely the popular Lido di Ostia. As Mary told her family following a group excursion in late August, "the Beach is one of the most famous in Italy but has been pretty well shot up by the war. In fact there are no dressing rooms still standing – so we undressed before God and everybody but all the time being very decent and well covered." When Doc was unavailable, either due to work or other obligations, Mary assumed the role of "third wheel" and tagged along with Ardith and Bert, as was the case one Sunday in early September.

Sept 10, 1944
Dearest Mother & Dad –
... This morning Bert, Ardith and I went to St. Peters. One could go there every day and find something new and interesting [as] well as beautiful to see. It is simply immense; one can't describe the vastness of the place. It was filled with the aroma of incense from the many masses going on in all parts of the church. There were processions of priests in their colorful costly robes. A sister had a group of little orphan boys in black dresses and white collars. Their little wooden shoes click-clacked on the marble floors like a whole drove of little delicate donkeys. We saw a wedding and a baby in a long elaborate christening robe waiting to be baptized. Then we saw the treasures of the popes – great jeweled crosses, rings heavy with diamonds and other precious stones, cups and chalices studded with pearls and diamonds. In one little room there must have been millions of dollars in gold and jewels. All that wealth and with people always starving in this country. Does the Lord approve, I wonder?

Hotel Campo Imperatore, 1943 (German Federal Archives via Wikimedia Commons)

Mary did not ask her parents whether *they* approved of a trip she took later in September. Along with Doc, Ardith, and Bert, she and another acquaintance – a Captain Clancey – traveled by car and by jeep to a mountain resort seventy miles east of Rome. Though Mary did not identify the place by name, she wrote her sister Annie on September 17 that she was headed to a "famous skiing resort" and a "swanky Hotel."

The group's destination may well have been the Hotel Campo Imperatore, an art deco-styled resort high in the Apennine Mountains where, a year earlier, Mussolini had spent twelve days under arrest in a hotel bedroom. Italian authorities had transported him to the remote location by way of a funicular (cable car) railway. On September 12, 1943, German paratroopers aboard gliders landed on a plateau near the hotel, overwhelmed Italian guards inside the building, and within minutes whisked Mussolini away to a waiting aircraft, after which he was transferred to a larger plane for a meeting with Hitler in Germany.

The commando operation, one of the most daring of World War II, was led by an equally daring Nazi officer, Otto Skorzeny of Germany's elite Waffen-SS forces.

When writing home at her trip's conclusion, Mary made no mention of Mussolini, and it remains unclear whether the now-storied Campo Imperatore was the resort she visited. That aside, Mary's letter did invoke the name of Auburn resident Gene Browand, a major with the 113th Quartermaster Regiment who had visited her several times in Rome and who had access to transportation. When Browand said he could provide a jeep for the outing, Mary gratefully had accepted the offer, glad to have an extra vehicle in which to haul the group's food and gear. As for the trip itself, Mary gave it high marks and looked forward to visiting the resort again.

Sept. 21, 1944

Dearest Mother & Dad –

Well, we certainly had a wonderful vacation. We arrived home yesterday afternoon in the pouring rain which put an end to the whole affair in a typical vacation manner. The weather, however, was perfect until just about 20 miles from home. Gene Browand sent us a Jeep which Doc and I plus the rations and baggage rode in. Ardith, Bert, their friend Clancey and Bert's dog, Joe Red Cross, went in Clancey's car. We made quite a convoy travelling through the little out-of-the-way Italian villages in the mountains for we were lost.

There are many bridges out causing detours – so on one of them we missed the Highway and wandered around for hours in an entirely different range of mountains. Doc's Italian is pretty good and finally through talking to the natives found our way to our destination. If it had taken us weeks to get there it would have been worth any of the effort for it was simply lovely. We went straight up the mountain which was a mile high although it took 12 miles zig-zagging back and forth to get there.

The view was simply superb – one could see for hundreds of miles. It reminded me very much of our trip to Denver – the scenery was about the same.

The Hotel was very comfortable with excellent cooking. They gave an Italian flavor to our American rations and added a few of their dishes besides. One night for dinner we had fresh mushrooms of a variety I had never seen. They looked like sea-weed but with that wonderful mushroom flavor.

The whole area on the mountain is a winter skiing resort. One morning we took a guide to show us where to climb. We walked through green pastures where sheep were grazing on the greenest velvet grass I've ever seen – all dotted with crocus blossoms, butter-cups were blooming too. The air is very fresh and like early spring. There are great shady forests of beech and pine – the other trees are just beginning to change color. It will be still lovelier there a little later. The guide showed us the Finicular [sic] railway that takes the Skiers to the top of the mountain. It takes an hour and a half to walk to the top but only <u>40</u> seconds to come down on skis. I believe I'd prefer to walk <u>down</u> too. We were very reluctant to leave but hope to go back again sometime. . . .

All my Love, Mary

A FEW WEEKS BEFORE HER TRIP, Mary had expressed work fatigue borne from never having an *entire* day off. "I'm afraid my cheerfulness is a little forced at times," she had confessed to Annie. Bone-weary or not, Mary was not nostalgic for her former line of work, as she made clear to her parents in an early September letter: "It's hard to believe that at home school has started. I'm really glad I'm not back to start it too." In a letter the next day, September 7, she asked her nephew, "Are you really in High School, Buddy, and how does it seem? I must say I'm not sorry to be back starting with you."

Around that same time, Mary's duties at the club changed. The Red Cross director, Mrs. Munford, left for home and was replaced by Lucile Brown, who Mary described as "a much younger woman, very attractive and, I believe, quite efficient." The club's program director also departed, with Mary – a staff assistant – named as the replacement. Though Mary had not actively sought the job and "didn't much want" it, she nevertheless tackled it with confidence and with fresh ideas, as she informed her parents in mid-September:

I think I told you that I have been put in charge of Program. It takes a little more of my time but I'm pretty used to the idea and know just about the sort of thing the boys want. Yesterday we did something a little different though. We had six babies and very small children in. It was really very touching. The boys (many of them with similar children of their own at home) would carry the babies around, stick candy in their pockets and cookies in their mouths. One boy with a 2 1/2 yr old baby girl at home that he has never seen played first with one child and then another all morning long.

"Mac" in Rome

More staff changes were afoot, especially one to Mary's liking. Newly assigned to the Rome club that September was Eileen "Mac" McEown, a North Dakota native whom Mary had met in Washington, D.C., and with whom she had traveled overseas and worked alongside on the Isle of Capri. The two women quickly resumed their friendship, and Eileen, a former high school physical education teacher, even limbered up Mary's tennis arm. As Mary told her parents not long after Eileen's arrival, "We have some wonderful Tennis Courts here but I hadn't played on them until the other night when Mac gave me a workout. It has been such a long time since I've played that I certainly wasn't much good – but it was fun."

Meanwhile, Red Cross workers were treated to some dress-up fun when Army officers hosted a big "affair" at the Rest Center in late September. The evening festivities, which Doc helped organize, included a cocktail reception, dinner and dancing, and a floor show. "We all wore our fancy dresses – I bought a harem veil in Casablanca and it looked very nice with my dress. The orchid from Doc helped too," Mary wrote home in early October.

By then, Mary had learned that another staff departure was imminent. Eleanor Sawtelle, with whom Mary had vacationed on the island of Ischia in June, was preparing to leave, and her departure presented an opportunity. The U.S. Army had requisitioned living quarters throughout the city, and Eleanor – for reasons unclear – had been allowed to live rent-free in an apartment across the Tiber River, opposite the Army Rest Center. Soon after Eleanor vacated the apartment, Mary was granted permission to move in, and she described the place as thus in an October 10 letter to her parents:

It's very attractive and comfortable and I think it will be lots of fun to have a 'home' again. I don't plan to move all my clothes over [from the Rest Center] but will just stay there on my nights off. The gas is turned on from 10 in the morning till 2:00 P.M. so I may be able to cook a lunch now and then. There is a small kitchen, a dining room, bedroom, bath and living room and furnished very nicely. I think I'll have a house-warming in the form of a Halloween party. I wish you could be here to help me scare my guests when they arrive.

Several days later, Mary shared more details, acknowledging the apartment's limitations but happy to embrace the place as her retreat.

Yesterday I had to go to town for the keys to my apartment and last night went over to take an inventory of the things (furniture). I must make several copies to be sent back to the Real Estate office and others. It will take several pages for I listed every little article including light bulbs. There is a living room with a studio couch, 2 overstuffed chairs, some straight chairs. I plan to take over the radio that Joyce gave me when she left. The dining room is the same size as the living room with heavy carved furniture. The stove in the kitchen is Gas but doesn't work so if I do any cooking it will have to be on an electric plate. The bedroom is very nice with a great wide bed that I know would[n't] be too comfortable to sleep in, besides I don't have sheets to divide between my quarters here and there. The bathroom is good as most Italian bathrooms are, a nice big tub, but, of course, no hot water.

Hot running water continued to be a luxury, and bodily grime continued to frustrate Mary. In early October, a week prior to getting the keys to her apartment, she hit upon a solution:

This morning, being our A.M. off, Mim, Ardith and I went to town at one of the fancy hotels to have a Turkish Bath. My impression had always been that only Sportsmen and old sots frequent Turkish Baths but we were getting desperate for any kind of a hot bath, Turkish, Egyptian, or what have you. It had been 8 weeks since I'd had a hot shower and boy, what came out in that steam bath would have surfaced the road from Auburn to [northern Indiana's] Lake Gage. But in all seriousness it was wonderful, we had the works, from the steam room, a hot shower with someone to scrub our backs, a dip in a cold pool and a massage. I nearly forgot a shampoo and wave and all for the sum of two bucks. We were all so clean and pleased we plan to make it a weekly mission.

ON OCTOBER 23, MARY HEADED north through hilly and bucolic Tuscany, grateful to have a four-day leave. Her destination was Florence, long celebrated for its beauty and art and once peopled by the likes of Leonardo DaVinci, Michelangelo, Botticelli, and the Medicis.

Whatever charm Florence exuded that autumn, the Tuscan capital also showcased battle scars. Occupying German forces had done more than blow up five of the city's historic bridges when they retreated in early August. As a final act of vengeance, they also demolished all houses on both sides of the Ponte Vecchio, the lone span that was spared. Altogether, one-third of Florence's medieval structures were destroyed, leaving the streets awash in rubble. Weeks earlier, German soldiers had trucked away much of Florence's prized artwork, including more than two hundred paintings from the renowned Uffizi Gallery. Hitler's troops also contributed to the disfigurement of the city's centuries-old botanical gardens. Florentines, short on wood for coffins and unable to access German-controlled cemeteries to the north, had little choice but to dig trenches in the gardens and line them with the city's dead.

If Mary had been inclined to report such details, she thought better of it. Instead, upon returning from her trip, she chose to write about the graciousness of the city's residents – and her shopping experience.

Oct. 28, 1944

Dearest Annie –

Have you broken your good old right arm. I haven't heard from you for so long – not since summer and Gosh that's too long for me to be without news of the Poker playing Olingers.

I'm sending you some things today I bought in Florence. Florence, you know, is called the City of Flowers and one can really believe that it is correctly called when one sees the flowers in the shops and stalls.

The dahlias are so perfect they look artificial – the chrysanthemums are gorgeous. But it seems strange to have Narcissus at the same time. When we admired the gardenias a man in the shop buying flowers presented us with one. The Italians are very gracious and polite people. They are even the hand kissing kind. But to get back to Florence – since it is called the City of Flowers everything that is made there is stamped with the Florentine Lilly. You will see it inside the velour hat I'm sending you. Have it blocked any way it suits you. I thought it looked yummy and would love to have one, too. The tiny box which I thought you could put in your purse for saccharine [Annie was diabetic] has the lily motif around the outside and is stamped again on the back. You will see the same design on the paper knife for George which he might like to use at the office. Both the box and the knife I purchased in a little shop on the Ponte Vecchio which means Old Bridge. There are tiny little stores all the way across on the Bridge. The bell from Capri maybe Bud would like to wear on his jacket.

Florence is truly beautiful – it is so very old and medieval. It seems incongruous to see people in modern dress walking through the streets. They should be wearing long velvet gowns and soft shoes. The trip there and back was very beautiful but it rained all the time. There are many mountains to cross and it must be beautiful on a sunny day. Several of my friends are there, Joyce and Eleanor, so I had a fine time seeing them again but was glad to get home again.

Do write when you can. I miss you like sixty.

All my love, Mary

The letter's closing reference to Joyce Gregory likely surprised Annie. Mary earlier had informed her family that Joyce was to have been sent home for a Red Cross infraction, stemming from an unauthorized trip to see her fiancé. Joyce apparently had been granted a reprieve and reassigned to a new club near Florence, closer to the Gothic Line – and to where Bill, her betrothed, was stationed. Eleanor, whose apartment Mary had just inherited, had likewise been reassigned closer to the combat zone.

Having scolded Annie in that October letter for her lax correspondence, Mary dashed off a note of apology the next day: "Today I must write taking it all back for a letter from you and

Mother arrived this morning dated Sept 19. Our mail has been held up somewhere along the line and is only beginning to come through again." The delay was tied to absentee balloting in the November 7 presidential election, which pitted New York Governor Thomas E. Dewey against Roosevelt, who was seeking an unprecedented fourth term. As many as twelve million Americans were away from home that autumn, and Congress recently had passed legislation hoping to increase voting among those serving overseas. The law did not succeed as much as was hoped, with only about twenty-five percent of uniformed personnel participating. Even so, in an Election Day letter to her nephew Buddy, Mary reported "our mail has been so mixed up lately ... They say that the heavy soldiers' voting has delayed the mails."

As she was writing Buddy, Mary informed him that the electricity had just shut off. "The lights have just gone out (a usual occurrence about this time of evening) so I'll have to stop and put out the candles." While Buddy's letter was not the first in which Mary mentioned utility shutoffs, her frustration at being inconvenienced became more pronounced as the weather turned colder and daylight hours grew shorter. Days earlier she had reported buying some steak that she planned to cook in her apartment. To Annie, she had quipped: "Hope the electricity stays on long enough to make at least a rare one."

The cause of Rome's utility woes was no mystery. Departing German troops had dynamited power plants to the city's northeast, and the Allies had reserved all shipping for military purposes, thus denying Romans access to surplus coal on the neighboring Mediterranean island of Sardinia – coal they were accustomed to getting in peacetime. In a November 14 letter to her parents, Mary reported that the Red Cross club was not heated "but the pool is – so we have opened the great doors all along the side [between the club room and the pool] to keep us a little warm, consequently we have a very steamy & chlorine smelling place." As for her apartment across the Tiber, Mary had no such door-opening options: "There is no heat ... so I haven't stayed there but a few times." Even so, she was just days away from hosting a November 18 gathering at her retreat, writing "Saturday night I'm going to have a Birthday party for the Doc and an Anniversary party for Eileen [Mac] and me – one year overseas. I'll have to tell everybody to keep their coats on to keep warm."

In arranging that merrymaking, Mary was not ignoring her regular duties. By November, fewer soldiers were arriving at the club, the result of troops having moved closer to front lines in the mountainous north. In addition, even though Fifth Army had begun receiving reinforcements, the number of new troops did not compensate for the units diverted to France. "Time hangs heavy when we haven't much to do," Mary had written her parents at the start of the month. A week later, she reported she soon might get more time off, though "sometimes I wonder what I'll do with it."

As for the birthday party that doubled as an anniversary celebration, Mary recapped the "peculiar" gathering in a November 20 letter to Annie. Mary began by referencing soldiers fighting on the Gothic Line and closed on a note of wistfulness, suggesting she wished to be closer to the action. When summarizing the party, Mary omitted giving Doc's age; he turned twenty-nine that weekend, making him Mary's junior by nearly five years.

Dearest Annie –

. . . Gene Browand [the major who procured the jeep for Mary's mountain trip] dropped in on me again the other night. I was working but he stayed around until I had finished. We went over to our Bar and had rum and Coke. Just like home. At eleven when the Bar closes we tapped a bottle of Shenleys of Doc's. The officers are allowed a bottle a month. We, in the rear areas, probably now have more than people at home. Never feel sorry for us – just the boys up there who are pitching.

The other night a Sergeant came up to the Desk to bat the breeze with me and we discovered we had been in DePauw the same time, a Deke [Delta Kappa Epsilon fraternity], from Indianapolis. He came back to my room [at the Center] and we had a long school day discussion. He came fresh out of his fox-hole to the Rest Center and he tells me that our <u>advanced</u> age is pretty difficult to serve front line duty along with the younger boys. He was a very nice person – hope he can get back again.

Saturday night I had a birthday party for Doc. It was a rather peculiar army party because I'd invited the enlisted men from the Dispensary along with the Lt. Col. who is our Commanding Officer. Mrs. Brown [Red Cross director] dropped in with a full colonel. They all did have a good time though. Ranks were forgotten, perhaps the Rum helped. The Poker game lasted till three in the morning. The

Mess Sergeant whipped up a delicious Birthday cake and wonderful sandwiches.

This place is getting so far away from the front that I'm getting itchy to move on. Of course, it's very comfortable and lots of fun but comfort wasn't exactly the thing I came over for.

Do be good, don't work too hard.

Less than a week later, Mary described several days of being extra busy, though not for the usual reasons. Along with decorating the Rest Center's mess halls for Thanksgiving feasts, she attended a dinner-dance and a movie premiere hosted by the area's commanding officer, and she met Alexander C. Kirk, the soon-to-be U.S. Ambassador to Italy. A longtime foreign service officer known for his charm and taste for fine living, Kirk was preparing to officially reopen the U.S. embassy in Rome, closed since December 1941 when the two nations severed diplomatic relations.

Umberto II in 1944 (Wikimedia Commons)

As if those social engagements weren't enough, Mary capped off the Thanksgiving weekend by having lunch with royalty – Umberto II, the only son of King Victor Emmanuel III. Granted governing powers by his father when the Allies liberated Rome, the Crown Prince visited the Army Rest Center on November 25 for an inspection tour and stayed to eat in a mess hall. Writing her parents at weekend's end, Mary declared, "So between sitting beside a General at a movie, meeting Ambassador Kirk and lunching with the Crown Prince of Italy you can see how it's a little hard to get out of the Clouds. But Mother, I'm sure something is wrong with my social graces for I'd much rather talk to the boys in our Club than these big people."

MARY: 1944

HAVING TOLD HER FAMILY little about her snack bar work, Mary set aside time in early December to rectify that omission. She also updated them on friends and coworkers, current and departed.

Dec. 3, 1944

Dearest Mother & Dad –

I'm writing this Sunday night letter on a big table in the Supply Room of the Snack Bar waiting for the closing hour of nine. Each night I work it is my job to check at intervals how things are progressing, to count the tickets and cash at the close and to lock the doors. We are able to give the boys cookies, rolls and cake, ice-cream which isn't much good (made with water) and free coffee. The Snack Bar itself is in the basement of the building and was once a laundry. When we first started operating the boys were having to eat their snacks amid the machinery and boilers of a laundry. Now it is more attractive with a gay painted counter, an Ice Cream Bar, a piano, and many plants that the gardener takes loving and tender care [of]. The Prince on his inspection said about the place, 'This is cute.' Netty, one of our civilian helpers came in and when I told her I was writing my Mother she wanted me to give you her regards. Netty is a fine worker, a Scottish woman who married an Italian. Even after speaking Italian for many years she still retains a thick Scottish brogue. Her husband is a school master and receives in the equivalent of our money $20.00 a month. I'm glad I wasn't a school teacher here.

There hasn't been much on the unusual side happen for the past few days so I haven't much news to give you.

Ardith and [Field Director] Bert left for Florence this morning, Ardith for a visit to the city and Bert to be assigned from there for another place to work. We have become fast friends – it is hard to see them go. Ardith will be back but I'm afraid she will be so unhappy without him that she will ask to leave. Then only me left of the whole old gang that came here in June. We have had word from [former club director] Mrs. Munford since she went home. She is now on her way to Honolulu to work in Red Cross there.

Time to stop, my darlings – I do hope you are both well.

In the preceding weeks, Mary had been giving other updates, not about friends, but gifts. The calendar had barely turned to November when she announced to her folks, "O happy day – the Christmas packages are beginning to come. Yesterday was the first – one from Annie. I had to take off the outer wrapping so I could feel it better, and shake it and smell it." When another package arrived days later, Mary confessed to the same urge: "I was tempted to open it but I just squeezed, poked and rattled. I hope I hold out six weeks – but Dad's printing 'Open Christmas Morn' will keep me straight, I think."

The gifts kept coming, first in trickles, then a wave.

Dec. 5, 1944

Dearest Mother & Dad –

Yesterday morning Red Cross headquarters Mail Room called me at the Club and said they wished I could come and get my packages. They were cluttering up the place so I sent our Taxi down to get them. Imagine ten packages in a huge mail sack. The driver looked like Santa Claus bringing them in.

Everyone was so jealous of me and I was so excited looking them all over but I only opened one – <u>From You</u>. The box had broken so I could see in and know that it was the Pop-Corn and things for my house. It was a lovely box, thank you for everything.

Not surprisingly, Mary's bounty made her increasingly self-conscious. "It's practically getting to be a joke the number of packages I'm receiving – seventeen to date. I'm having a terrible guilty feeling how can I repay all these people," Mary wrote Annie on December 9. Two days later to her parents: "Now I have nineteen packages. I'm getting teased shamefully about bribing my friends to send me Christmas packages."

Having temporarily abandoned her apartment in town, Mary stored the gifts in her room at the Rest Center. She soon would hang a wreath in her quarters, but first she joined colleagues in decorating the entire army complex, a task that included making ornaments for ten trees. "Decorations for trees here are simply sky high and it would be impossible to trim even a table tree," Mary had explained to Annie in the December 9 letter. "So we and our civilian help have made everything. Paper chains, angels, stars and garlands of bells. We have covered paper balls with tin foil and made grape clusters of foil too. Then from tin cans we have cut stars and birds. It seems as if we have made enough stuff to do a hundred [trees], but it's all been fun."

With the fun came funny business. In a December 11 letter to her parents, Mary highlighted some playfully naughty decorations, compliments of the Russian artist:

Our artist [the English-speaking Vladimir Wolkonsky] has made Merry Christmas letters to put above the Information Desk. He is so very clever, each individual letter has a dwarf on it somewhere doing various things. The last little man on the S. has a candle in one hand and a little "potty" in the other while on the letter itself is hanging an enema bag. The two dwarfs that join the M. and the A. before him are pointing to him and laughing. I want to have a picture made of it.

Nine days passed before Mary wrote home again. She apologized for the communication lapse and offered an explanation:

Dec. 20, 1944
Dearest Mother & Dad –
Perhaps you are thinking I've forgotten how to write – it isn't true – only the usual pre-Christmas business that has kept us all very busy. But now every last ornament has been made and the ten trees are all decorated so we can sit down to admire our handiwork. I will say the trees look as well as those at home and everything we have made, even to the twisted icicles made from tin cans. I've just mailed a package to you which has . . . some little doll angels for you. Too late for this year but next year will do. They were so attractive I couldn't resist them. They are made by a woman who is a war refugee.
Yesterday Ardith and I were down town for a bath and the first person I saw when we stepped into the Hotel was Dick Fink [the friend from Auburn who had visited her at Caserta]. He is here for a few days leave. He is coming out to dinner tonight. I've had a package from his Mother. My packages keep mounting – the total now is 25. Everyone agrees we will have to have the party in my room to save me the effort of carrying them around. One of the last ones to arrive was one from you and another from Annie. Oh, happy day – how can I repay everybody for being so kind and thoughtful.
Yesterday afternoon the Red Cross staff (we are seven) got together and pooled everything we want to give away (old clothes and our PX rations) to our 53 Civilian employees. We really had quite a lot of stuff all together – then last evening we made three hundred sacks of candy, cookies, gum

etc. for the children's party [on Christmas Day]. They are to be the Children of the Rest Center employees. We are having a movie for them. Will get in another letter soon.

All my Love, Mary

Meanwhile, back in Auburn and throughout the United States, families approached the holiday with the same unanswerable questions: Would their loved ones be home by next Christmas? How many more sons and brothers would be deployed? How much more sacrificing would be required? Having endured three years of war and eager to see the conflict end, Americans looked for good news wherever they could find it, and – as 1944 drew to a close – many cheered ongoing progress in the Pacific, where naval and air engagements had put the United States in strategic control of the region. In addition, U.S. forces that autumn had begun retaking the Philippines, with General MacArthur famously declaring "I have returned!"

But encouraging news in that theater had been blunted by jarring developments elsewhere. In the Ardennes forests of northwest Europe, Hitler's army had just launched a surprise counteroffensive, the full extent of which was only starting to be known. Other unsettling news, though entirely different in nature, surfaced in the run-up to Christmas Eve. The popular bandleader Glenn Miller, who left civilian life to entertain troops with his fifty-piece Army Air Force Band, had gone missing in a single-engine plane over the English Channel and was presumed dead. He had been en route to Paris, ready to share his distinctive big-band sound with American soldiers in France, after having given eight hundred performances to troops in England.

Predictably, Mary's letters steered clear of war-related topics. Instead, in two post-holiday letters to her family recapping Christmas Eve and Christmas Day, she focused on the personal and expressed gratitude for her many gifts.

Dec. 27, 1944, Italy

Dearest Mother & Dad –

Another Christmas Day come and gone. I can't believe that a day we have looked forward to for so long passes us by so quickly – But, my day was indeed a happy one. The day before Christmas I worked at the Club until four in the afternoon. It was the Doc's day off as well as Miss Ardith's and Bert's who came back to spend Christmas with us. The three of them really cooked up a surprise for me for when I arrived home my room was all in readiness with a decorated Christmas tree that had me laughing for at least a half hour. Tied on its branches were oranges, gum wrappings, old socks, two empty whiskey bottles, glasses, broken light bulbs, crudely cut-out stars and paper ribbons – but despite the decorations it was very pretty and attractive. All my presents were piled underneath.

At one end of the room they had arranged a table with food – pickles, olives, toast, and all the spreads Doc had received in his packages as well as a few bottles for the party that night. They were as pleased as children that I liked my tree and room. Doc said that as long as it made me smile that was all they wanted.

Our party began after we had a candle light carol sing at the Club. We had a little orchestra to accompany us, Mac [Eileen] read the St. Luke's Christmas story, I sang 'O Holy Night' and then we had records of Dickens 'Christmas Carol.' Most of the officers and the R.C. gals brought their packages into my room and we began the unwrapping. We had a pile of boxes and paper as high as a mountain when we finished but with all the mess it really looked and felt like a Christmas at home. At least several of the men said that just to see us sitting on the floor around the tree was as much like home as anything we could do in Italy. I have so many people to thank for gifts that I'm afraid I'm going to have to make out a form letter.

Speaking of thanking for gifts, yours were lovely. The sweater is beautiful. I wore it Christmas Day. The jumper is darling, and fits. Also it's what I thought a jumper was. Thank you, darlings, thank you. The Doc wants me to thank you, too for the Cigarettes – but where in the world were you able to buy a whole carton. I thought there was a shortage on at home.

I must write Annie, too, so I'll go on from here in her letter.

All my Very Best Love, Mary

[Dec. 27, 1944]

Dearest Annie, George and Bud –

Well, did you have a Merry Christmas? I can well imagine you did – but how I wish we could have been together. I've written Mother & Dad *covering my activities to Christmas Day and shall go on from there in my letter to you. Have to spread these things out, you know.*

First, may I thank you with all my heart for the wonderful Christmas box. The blouse is lovely and fits. The Chop Suey looks wonderful. We'll be whipping it up some of these days along with the Roast Beef. The powder is lovely. I was just ready for another box and wonder of wonders – that was the only one I received. There was quite a bit of duplicating on some things, for example, thirty bars of soap. Some of it I know my Italian friends will appreciate for it costs them $1.50 a cake. Thank you so much for everything.

We had a wonderful dinner in our Mess – turkey and all the trimmings, but of course, nothing like your roast turkeys. In the afternoon we had a little party in our snack bar for the civilian workers. They had Ice cream and cake and were each given a gift of soap, a candle, cigarettes, candy and anything else we were able to give them out of our supply and P.X. Rations. They seemed very pleased but a little bewildered about all the fuss we have been making for Christmas. Our beautiful holly wreaths and laurel garlands have truly shocked them for those they use only for death.

In the evening the Doc and I had another turkey dinner with a Colonel friend of his and his friend at the Colonel's beautiful but cold apartment. He has a good Italian cook but the Italian touch to cooking hardly seems to fit in with our idea of an American Christmas dinner. With ravioli served first and each separate dish and vegetable served as a distinct course we ate until about eleven o'clock. It was good but I was so full and sleepy that we tried to go home almost immediately after eating. I say we <u>tried</u> for when we got outside we found the Colonel's car had been stolen. Cars simply walk away in this city. They are having a terrible time. After a few telephone calls we got another car. I don't know when I've been so glad to get to bed. I had that typical tired but happy Christmas Night feeling when I finally climbed between the sheets.

I received so many beautiful gifts. I'll send the list on to you when I've finished thanking everyone. The Doc gave me a beautiful hand-made silver bracelet. I'm indeed very proud of it.

Again, thank you, for your presents...

All my best wishes for a Happy New Year.

Love, Mary

Two days after her Christmas recaps, Mary celebrated her thirty-fourth birthday. By then she had spent seventeen months working for the Red Cross, with more days of service ahead. Urgent business lay ahead too – the *very* urgent business of writing all her thank-you notes.

Chapter Fourteen
BILL: 1944 - 1945

Christmas Day, 1944
Dear Folks:

For the 3rd straight time I am spending Christmas away from home. I wonder how many more of that kind there will be. We are, at least, having a White Christmas if nothing else – Please send some more good brownies....
Love, Bill

WHILE MARY BRANDON WAS DISPENSING Christmas cheer to U.S. Fifth Army soldiers in Rome in late December 1944, Bill Husselman was more than 750 miles to the north – in a place where neither he nor his fellow soldiers had expected to be.

Weeks before Christmas, Lieutenant General Patton had devised a plan calling for the U.S. Third Army to break out of France and mount an aggressive eastbound offensive to the Rhine River, well inside Germany. The ground operation was to start December 19, preceded by an air bombardment involving three thousand planes. If all went according to schedule, Christmas Day 1944 was to have dawned with Third Army firmly on German soil, trucks and tanks rolling, troops advancing.

But the plan was shelved, the schedule abandoned. Instead, in what would become one of the most remarkable feats in military history, Patton on December 19 ordered the bulk of his 250,000-man army to begin moving north – not east. Days earlier, German forces had launched a surprise attack through the Ardennes forests in Luxembourg and Belgium in a last-ditch gamble by Hitler to regain lost territory. As those German troops hammered the crumbling Anglo-American battle line in that northern region, the line bulged, giving rise to the name "Battle of the Bulge" and underscoring the need for immediate Allied reinforcements. Responding to the crisis, Patton redirected his army toward the Ardennes, commanded his men to travel more than a hundred miles over snow- and ice-covered roads as fast as possible, and ordered them to strike hard against the Bulge's southern flank. He had promised General Eisenhower that his troops would be ready to attack on December 22, and they were ready, lodging the first Allied counterstroke in what became a six-week campaign.

Bill never directly referenced the Ardennes campaign in his letters home that December or in the early days of 1945. Sensitive to censorship, Bill also revealed nothing about the vital work military police units, including his own battalion, performed during the campaign's opening phase. When Patton ordered Third Army to pivot ninety degrees, military police coordinated the complex and dangerous troop maneuver, ensuring that infantry and armored units in more than 100,000 vehicles – jeeps, tanks, half-tracks, and two-and-a-half-ton trucks – moved steadily northward over treacherous roads in wretched weather. Along with ferrying soldiers out of Lorraine, vehicles transported tent hospitals, engineering and communication equipment, stockpiles of fuel and ammunition, and boxloads of maps and other critical supplies. Though the convoys encountered a landslide, enemy strafing, and wrecks that necessitated detours, military police kept traffic flowing, enabling Patton's men to arrive in the Ardennes faster than most military analysts thought possible.

The MPs' contributions didn't go unrecognized. Patton's chief of staff, Brigadier General Hobart R. Gay, would soon commend the 512th MP Battalion and the 503rd MP Battalion for their "extremely efficient and untiring efforts in expediting the recent heavy movement of troops in the Third Army area." Bill's unit, the 512th, would also receive a Meritorious Service Unit Plaque for its efficiency in guiding Third Army operations, the first time an entire battalion was given that high honor.

Constrained as Bill was to keep Third Army's movements a secret, war correspondents had more latitude. Thus, Bill's parents undoubtedly followed newspaper accounts in late December that German troops had encircled a small crossroads town in Belgium known as Bastogne, which the U.S. 101st Airborne Division struggled to defend. On December 22, a German commander ordered American forces to surrender the town, prompting U.S. Brigadier General Anthony McAuliffe to defiantly and famously reply "Nuts!" On that same day, elements of Patton's redirected army poured into the region, and four days later, on December 26, a Third Army armored division barreled through German lines, entered the besieged town, and relieved the embattled Americans. Though the Ardennes campaign was far from over, Third Army's victory at Bastogne decisively blunted the Germans' westward push – and garnered front-page headlines for Patton and his men.

Given the high stakes at the time, for both the Allies and Hitler's forces, Christmas Day 1944 offered no respite from war. Even so, the U.S. military did what it could to dispense its own version of holiday cheer, and Bill relayed that news to his parents in his December 25 greeting. Along with requesting more "good brownies" and reminding his folks what they surely knew – that he was marking his third Christmas away from home – he informed them that every Third Army soldier, whether front-line or rear-echelon, was to have a hot turkey dinner that day. "I've just been down to the kitchen," he wrote, still careful not to divulge his location. "[I] looked at the huge Christmas cake baked by the local baker for the company – all decorated with designs, flowers, writing, etc. It is really a work of art & a shame to cut. The turkeys (1½ lb to the man) were also baked at a bakery. We are having ice cream, candy bars, cigars, coca cola, hard candy, etc. as extras today. It looks like a real feast."

For Bill, the day would include a second feast, his status as a military police officer apparently prompting a nearby family to invite him to dine with them. "What a meal! Steak (mighty good, too), French fries, string beans, soup, two kinds of wine, brandy, coffee and cake," he informed his parents four days later. Those details thus shared, his December 29 letter ended matter-of-factly: "I've been sitting here for over half an hour trying to think of something else to write about. I can't even mention where I am now, so that makes it doubly difficult to write anything. So I guess I'll have to call this a letter. You'll at least know that I'm still O.K."

BILL'S MILITARY-IMPOSED SILENCE as to his location lasted nearly a month – from mid-December 1944 to January 12, 1945. "We are now allowed to say that we are 'somewhere in Luxembourg,' a fact that you have probably already suspected," he wrote his parents on the 12th when making the big reveal. "Of the countries of Europe that I've seen so far, this is much the best. It is very small, but modern and quite a lot like the States. About 65% of the people speak a reasonable amount of English. I'll reserve a description of the country for a later date."

Patton's Luxembourg City headquarters was the Foundation Pescatore. Built as an "old people's home" in the 1890s, the castle-like structure remains a retirement center today. (Photo by author)

In Luxembourg, as in most of Belgium, the Allies had expelled Hitler's occupying forces in September 1944. When German troops roared back into those countries via the mountainous Ardennes a few months later, they reoccupied southeastern Belgium and the northern third of Luxembourg. Remaining free from Nazi control was Luxembourg City, situated farther south. It was there, in that tiny country's capital, that Patton relocated his headquarters in December 1944, even as Germans regularly shelled the city.

If Bill was billeted in or near the capital – and, if so, for how long – his letters do not say. Patton daily took to the roads to assess troop positions in the Bulge before returning to Luxembourg City for his evening lodging. It's possible that Bill, by virtue of his military police duties, motored by jeep in and out of that critical command post and that he lodged there as well. Bill clearly was familiar with the capital. Much later, when censorship eased, he described in detail for his family the city's stone bridges and ancient fortifications.

Meanwhile, just prior to disclosing he was "somewhere in Luxembourg," Bill mentioned his location in general terms, telling his parents on January 11:

The territory where I'm now situated has winter weather just about like Indiana's. There is quite a good sized snow on the ground now, and I suspect the temperature hasn't been much above zero at times. It is probably pretty rough on the tactical troops. We, however, are as comfortable as we would be at home as we are living in a steam heated building. The open jeep is a little more airy than the Dodge was with its heater – but you can't have everything. We are certainly in no position to complain.

Just days prior to that letter, Bill had reported, but not complained about, an injury he received. A combat injury it definitely was not.

2 Jan. 1945
Dear Folks:
... I have an awful shiner. The other night Col. Flynn walked into our billet and gave his steel helmet a careless toss. It landed in my face, smashed one lens of my glasses and scared the Old Man half to death. He insisted that I go to the nearest Evac hospital although I was sure no glass had got into the eye. They did dig quite a bit out from the upper lid & the cheek below the right eye, but I'm all O.K. except for looking like I got the worst end of a brawl. I'm having the glasses repaired.

At mid-month, having been cleared by censors to speak more freely, Bill treated his father to a lengthy letter. Writing from the warmth of his billet, he responded to Oak's query about his work, then shared what he had learned about the "Grand Duchy." As for the ongoing Battle of the Bulge, Allied forces were recovering ceded territory and regaining momentum.

Somewhere in Luxembourg, 15 January 1945
Dear Dad:
I got a great deal of pleasure out of your letter written Christmas Day. I was much interested in your description of prevailing economic

conditions. I was impressed by the wisdom of the Soviet solution of the problem as you outlined it.

You inquired about the functions of the Military Police. Our basic mission is the regulation and control of highway traffic and the maintenance of law and order among the troops. I suppose I cannot more specifically describe our work without violating the rules of censorship. It is about as good a branch of the service as you could pick. It is reasonably safe – my only contact with enemy action has been a little air activity and a few instances of desultory shelling of the area I happened to be in at the time. Its chief advantage is that it permits you to live in relative comfort. In the winter we live in heated billets, and usually have beds to sleep upon. You can well imagine that the tactical troops on the line don't fare so well. It is really Hell up there in the Winter – they can't have so much as a small wood fire because it would expose their position. . . .

The Grand Duchy of Luxembourg has surprised me more than anything I've seen in Europe. I had thought it to be a little, agricultural, picturesque, and backward piece of the Old World, and fully expected to see a little chunk of Europe of the vintage of a century or more ago. Actually it is far and away the most modern and up-to-date territory I've seen since leaving the States – and in many ways is remarkably similar to America. It is very small – only about 200,000 in population, but very wealthy. It is industrial in economy rather than agricultural. You see steel mills that make you think of Gary [Indiana]. It is a rich mining country.

Here you see large automobiles for the first time in Europe – many of them of American make. Of course most have been converted into charcoal burners now. It is highly electrified. They have and use all of the household electrical things made in America – for instance the automatic elevator in one building we occupied was an Otis. The cities, with superficial differences in architecture, remind you of American towns of the same size. I should say that as large a proportion of the buildings are centrally heated here as in America. This is surprising to find in Europe. It is no doubt partly due to the rigors of the winter climate. Winter here is about like it is in Northern Indiana except that they seem to have a trifle more snow here.

The country is quite hilly, and is beautiful when lying under a thick blanket of snow.

The people are a mixture of German, French, Belgian and Holland Dutch. Their language is a bastard one made up of all of the above, but predominantly of the German. The Luxembourg language, oddly, is not taught at all in the schools, which teach instead English, French and German. Most of the people are accomplished linguists and most of the younger ones speak English. Incidentally, they are very proud of their school system – all housed in ultra modern buildings – and claim, perhaps with justification, that it is the finest in the world.

The Luxemburger mixes the culture of France and Germany, with the German side somewhat predominant. They are extremely friendly, and with only a few exceptions are rabidly pro-allied. Many of them were scared stiff when [German Field Marshal Gerd] Von Rundstedt's [Ardennes] drive started. In the section I was then in[,] reinforcements going to the front were so routed that the civilians thought we were retreating instead of sending up men and material. They used to gather by the hundreds along the streets and roads and look upon the traffic with long faces. They'd implore us not to pull out without giving them warning. I don't know whether they wanted to go along, or only wanted a chance to pull in the Allied flags flying from their windows and substitute the swastika.

Their attitude on the war is surprising in view of the fact that many of their sons are in the German Army. The Germans really tried to make this German territory. They drafted the youth for the Army. Many of the young men fled to the mines and hid out – some for years – rather than go to the Army. The Gestapo would deliver an ultimatum to the family – either deliver up the fugitive or the whole family will be packed off to a German Concentration camp. Many families were.

Entertainment includes many English speaking movies. Usually across the bottom of the picture appears a sub-title in French giving the substance of the dialogue. They have cocktail lounges that compare favorably with those in the States. The native seems to like a concoction called schnapps – a colorless liquid that tastes like lighter fluid and has the same general effect as TNT.

I suspect that many men around home of about my age are getting pretty shaky about the draft. They have good reason too, for men drafted now are mighty apt to catch Hell. They seem to give them a course of basic training and shoot them over as combat replacements.

This isn't intended as a book-length feature, so I think I'd better desist before you tire completely of struggling with my penmanship.
  Love, Bill

BILL'S REFERENCE TO FRONT-LINE TROOPS not faring well – "It is really Hell up there in the Winter" – was hardly hyperbolic. Uncommonly bitter weather afflicted northwest Europe in December 1944 and January 1945, with below-zero temperatures forcing inadequately clothed troops to scavenge for dresses and other apparel to wear as shawls and to don bedsheets as capes (the sheets doubled as snow camouflage). Killer-cold temperatures also contributed to frozen radiators and gas tanks, hindering troop vehicle movement. Likewise, heavy snowfall and gale-force winds slowed soldiers' ability to advance on foot.

When digging foxholes, infantrymen tried using pickaxes to break through frozen ground, but often they had to resort to grenades. In and out of those foxholes, soldiers cursed the constant moisture that exacerbated trench foot. Notably, as medical teams strained that winter to treat gunshot, shrapnel, and related wounds, trench-foot cases still outnumbered all other maladies. Bill, ever aware of the brutal front-line conditions, remained grateful he was spared such

Three soldiers hike through snow-covered woods near Wiltz, Luxembourg, mid-January 1945. (National Archives)

suffering, telling his parents on January 22, "I certainly thank my lucky stars that I have a job that permits me to stay warm most of the time. As you will remember, I never could take cold weather very well."

Another of Bill's pronouncements – that newly drafted Americans were "mighty apt to catch Hell" – also was accurate. Facing a mounting shortfall in fighting men, the U.S. Army in late summer 1944 began reassigning cooks, clerks, drivers, and mechanics to combat duties. The Army likewise continued turning to the home front for replacements. By January 1945, the draft levy had been hiked from 60,000 to 90,000 men a month; in March, the number would climb to 100,000. With conscripts' services in high demand, GIs barely finished basic training before they were shipped overseas and assigned to units where few of the men had trained together and where such training, if it existed at all, was inadequate. Lieutenant George Wilson, a rifle company commander fighting in the Bulge, recounted years later in his book *If You Survive* that he received one hundred replacements on December 29: "We discovered that these men had been on the rifle range only once; they had never thrown a grenade or fired a bazooka, mortar, or machine gun." The consequences often were deadly. As the military historian Francis C. Steckel noted in a 1994 article for *Army History,* "Often, more than half the replacements sent directly into combat [in Europe in World War II] became casualties in the first few days of fighting." He further noted, "Occasionally a soldier arrived and died before anybody learned his name."

And die men did that winter of 1944-1945. By January 25, after weeks of ferocious fighting in villages and towns, in fields and forests, the Ardennes campaign ended, with the Allies pushing German troops back to their homeland, exactly where they had been six weeks earlier. Hitler had gambled everything to launch his risky offensive, and in the end it had cost him mightily; by some estimates, the fighting had left as many as 100,000 German soldiers dead, wounded or missing.

Steep, too, were Allied losses, especially for the United States. Altogether, some 600,000 Americans fought in the Ardennes campaign, with the casualty count approaching 90,000. Third Army bore the brunt of the suffering. Patton saw his soldier-and-officer ranks thinned by some 50,000 – men listed as killed, wounded, missing, and non-battle casualties. Of all the U.S. combat casualties during World War II, including those in the Pacific, roughly one in ten took place at the Battle of the Bulge. Notably, even before the campaign ended, British Prime Minister Churchill recognized the sacrifices made by Americans in the Ardennes. Addressing the House of Commons on January 18, 1945, Churchill said "the United States troops have done almost all the fighting and have suffered almost all the losses.... [They] have lost 60 to 80 men for every one of ours."

To his countrymen that day, Churchill added: "Care must be taken in telling our proud tale not to claim for the British Army an undue share of what is undoubtedly the greatest American battle of the war and will, I believe, be regarded as an ever famous American victory."

HAVING EMERGED FROM THE Battle of the Bulge in remarkably fine shape, Bill spent the final week of January and all of February "somewhere in Luxembourg." His military police duties continued to come with perks. "I am going to have dinner at the home of a police chief tonight. Luxembourg dinners are supposed to be really something to remember," he enthused to his parents on February 6.

Two weeks later, he enjoyed more tasty dining: "Last night I had dinner again with the police chief. Really a good meal, with delicious soup, tender roast beef (really veal, I think), french fried potatoes, two kinds of apple pie, red wine and the inevitable schnapps. The chief is quite a character. I am enclosing a couple of pictures he gave me."

The Luxembourg City Chief of Police, far left, befriended Bill during his tour of duty there. The chief gave Bill this photo.

Along with food, Bill counted as another perk his new set of wheels, a photograph of which he included in a February 1 letter. "The sedan isn't standard MP equipment. It is a captured German Opel, which we recovered and had registered. It is certainly a lot warmer to ride in than a jeep. It is named 'Mary Ann' after Capt. Remley's new daughter." In that same letter, Bill offered his parents visual reassurances that he was well-clad. "The rather untidy coat I'm wearing in the pictures is an officer's field coat. It has a detachable blanket-like liner, and a hood to protect the neck, ears & most of the face. In winter it is really a fine piece of equipment."

Bill with "Mary Ann"

Motoring about in the Opel, a bundled-up Bill joined elements of Patton's army that February as it pushed east from Luxembourg City toward the ancient city of Trier, just inside the German border. Much to Patton's dismay, swollen rivers and mud- and ice-covered terrain limited the progress of his tired infantry. Progress was further limited when Eisenhower ordered Patton to slow down his army's movement; Eisenhower wanted to give British Field Marshal Bernard Montgomery adequate time to unleash his forces farther north. Chafing at being reined in, Patton headed to Paris in mid-February for three days of rest and relaxation, his first leave in thirty months. He accorded his troops the same opportunity, and in late February Bill also departed for the French capital, penning a letter on his return.

Somewhere in Luxembourg, March 1, 1945
Dear Folks:

I think I have subject matter enough for a long letter tonight. We'll see how it develops.

First of all, I have already received all four birthday packages, all in good condition. Thanks a lot. The bill fold works pretty well with this foreign money – undoubtedly better than anything you could buy now. The toilet kit came at about the right time. I bought a good one just before coming overseas, but it has had a hard life and is just about worn out.

I am sorry you sent your only nail clip, as I was able to buy one in Paris. I think I'll mail it back when I get time.

I just got your letter of February 15th telling about "Ziggy."[1] She'll be lots of company for you. I'm not so sure you should have named her that. "Ziggy" is a corruption of a naughty German word! However I guess it is corrupted too much for recognition.

My Poker is still on the up and up – and in spite of a trip to Paris I'll be able to send money orders home for $120.00 as soon as I can get them.

That brings us to the story of the big trip to Paris. The Battalion sent fifteen men and two officers on three day passes plus travel time. I was one of the lucky officers, mainly because I was the only one in "A" Company who wasn't stone broke. The other officer was Lt. Peterson of "C" Company. A long time back [the] Battalion obtained a captured German bus of 22 passenger capacity, and we went in that. It was a slow rough ride, but much more comfortable than it would have been in a truck.

You have heard a lot about the Red Cross – some pro, some con, but they are at least doing a good job in Paris. Just one hour after hitting the city limits we had our men homed, the bus put up, and were in our own hotel room, even tho we hadn't the slightest idea of where to go or what to do when we arrived. The Red Cross operates a lot of hotels for men on pass. They are staffed by the regular French staff and are very comfortable (except for lack of heat) and are not more crowded than any busy hotel. You have to stay at one of them, as they are the only places in town where men on pass can eat.

They use regular G.I. rations, but the French chefs can really do something to them.

The hotel only costs the men 60 f [francs] for three nights, and meals are only 10 f. The officers' rates are 120 f for the room and 20 f per meal. You can drink in French cafes, but can't eat there.

My hotel was the [the name was literally cut out of the page] *near the Place de la Concorde, at the end of Champs Elsysee (Sp?) once one*

---

1. Upon acquiring a new dog that winter, Bill's parents named their pet "Ziggy," a nod to the battalion's beloved mascot that had died months earlier in France.

of the most famous hotels in the world, and in the center of everything. At lunch and dinner a very fine Russian orchestra played dinner music. You would have got a big kick out of it.

Paris has been little touched by the war physically, except that most of the many statues on the squares were removed or destroyed by the Germans. About the only means of transportation now is the Metro (subway) which is very fine. In fact it is as efficient as the N.Y. subway.

I took a sight seeing tour which took in, among other places, the Invalides, where Napoleon's tomb is and where the big Army museum is. Napoleon's tomb is beautiful. His influence on France is still strong – they revere his memory. I think he sort of confused his own identity with that of Julius Caesar. He copied Caesar in everything – his triumphal arches, his laurel wreaths, etc. Even in death the practice of the Roman Emperors is copied – like them, he is buried facing North rather than East as is the usual way. The tour also took in the huge triumphal Arch and the Cathedral Notre Dame de Paris. This is one of the seven wonders of the modern world. It is about 700 years old and looks it, as its stones appear quite weather-worn. It has a glamorous history, you know. Napoleon was crowned there; Mary, Queen of Scots was married there, etc. etc. The tour also took in the Louvre, where before the War many of France's art treasures were displayed. It is a huge Palace, started in the 16th Century by Francis the First. The oldest structure I saw was the ruins of a wall of a Roman bath, dating back to 50 B.C.

Another interesting monument is the Church of the Magdeline [sic]. This church is built in the manner of a Greek Temple, with huge pillars or columns running all the way around. I understand it was built by Napoleon so that he'd have a building of this type from which to display his battle flags. Of course I saw the Eiffel Tower – you couldn't avoid that if you wanted.

We were fortunate enough to get tickets for the Folies-Bergere (yes, the French spell it with only one "l"). This is a very elaborately staged and costumed affair, altho very often the costume of the ladies of the chorus consists solely of a G-String. [New York Mayor Fiorello] LaGuardia, I'm sure, wouldn't stand for it on Broadway.

The last night we went to the Opera – the first time incidentally – that I've ever heard top flight Grand Opera. The Opera was Othello – and it was extremely well done. More interesting than the Opera *itself, however, is the Opera House, undoubtedly the largest and most beautiful in the world. It was built by Napoleon III, apparently as a sort of monument to himself. I imagine there are larger Opera houses so far as the auditorium itself is concerned, but here the auditorium proper is only a small part of the great marble structure. It has great stairways, beautiful balconies and many mirrored and gilt rooms of great splendor. It is 75 years old, and looks it on the outside. On the inside it is so well kept up that it might have been built last year.*

I think it is the locale of the "Phantom of the Opera," where the great glass chandelier figured. You should see it. Its terrific weight is supported by about half a dozen heavy steel cables, and it is not hard to imagine the devastation that would follow if it were to drop on the audience in the Orchestra. Speaking of Orchestras, the one that accompanied the Opera must have consisted of eighty pieces.

Dad would get a big kick out of walking the streets – you see many little art shops and galleries where oils and watercolors are displayed for sale. I think I'd have bought one, except that there is too much red tape encountered in sending them home because of censorship regulations. I shopped around for some memento to send you but finally gave up in disgust.

Everything is either junk you wouldn't have around, or else costs at least $100.00. The rate of exchange is very inequitable to the soldier.

On the second page I did the censoring, not the base censor. I thought they might object to the name and exact location of a Red Cross Club.

This indeed did turn into a long letter. I guess I'd better close now before you get too tired trying to decipher it.

Love, Bill

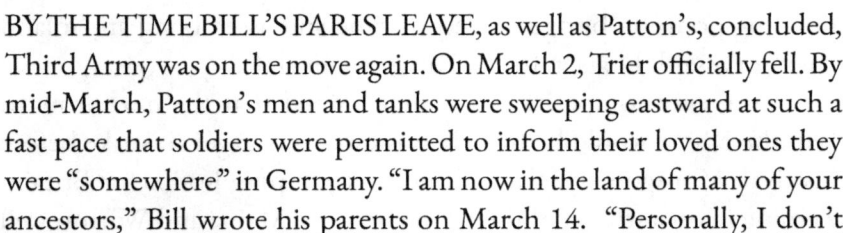

BY THE TIME BILL'S PARIS LEAVE, as well as Patton's, concluded, Third Army was on the move again. On March 2, Trier officially fell. By mid-March, Patton's men and tanks were sweeping eastward at such a fast pace that soldiers were permitted to inform their loved ones they were "somewhere" in Germany. "I am now in the land of many of your ancestors," Bill wrote his parents on March 14. "Personally, I don't blame them for leaving it. I wouldn't trade an acre of [Auburn] for all of it. Of course I'm not seeing it at its best. The American bombers and the artillery of both sides haven't left much but mud."

Days later, Bill elaborated, his words bearing witness to the 130,000 tons of bombs that Allied aircraft had and would continue to drop in March, the heaviest bombing month of the war. "The Germans are getting a real taste of the horrors of war that they wanted to inflict on the rest of the world," he wrote home on March 17. "This country is beat up worse than anything I've ever seen. It even beats Normandy. Many towns are just a heap of rubble, with hardly a building habitable. I'll bet these German farmers will be blowing themselves up for the next hundred years on the mines and unexploded shells in their fields. Well, they asked for it, and they are getting it."

What Third Army was still asking for, and had yet to get, was passage across the strategically vital Rhine. Broad, fast-flowing, and at no point fordable, even at low water, Germany's longest river – fed by glaciers in Switzerland before eventually emptying into the North Sea – had historically been a formidable natural obstacle against invasion from the west. Since the late 1800s, it also had served as a beloved symbol of German nationalism, one that Hitler had used to his advantage by rallying citizens to repel enemy river-leapers at all costs.

By late winter 1945, with Allied forces advancing toward the Rhine across a broad front, Hitler took the dramatic step of ordering bridges up and down the river to be demolished. One span was overlooked, however, and in early March soldiers with the U.S. First Army chanced upon the Ludendorff Railroad Bridge at the resort town of Remagen, roughly thirty miles south of Cologne. Upon capturing the still-intact structure, First Army fought its way across before the bridge collapsed, the result of ferocious German artillery and air bombardment. With no other spans standing, Allied troops from March 17 onward had to use their ingenuity to breach the Rhine, ingenuity that included building pontoon bridges in record time and assembling an "inland navy" of assault boats, rafts, and other water craft.

Patton, ever-competitive, was determined that the next army to leap the Rhine would be his. He was especially eager to strike before his rival, Montgomery, claimed the river-jumping honor for Britain. Zeroing in on a stretch of the Rhine between Mainz and Worms, well to the south of Remagen, Patton ordered an assault late on the night of March 22. A few of his units paddled across in tiny boats near the town of Nierstein. Others slipped across a few miles upstream near the barge-harbor town of Oppenheim. Initially encountering little to no resistance, Third Army troops poured across en masse the next morning, their passage aided by pontoon bridges and safeguarded by antiaircraft gunners who eliminated late-arriving Luftwaffe. Later that day, and much farther north, Allied troops under Montgomery launched their river assaults. But by then, Patton was proudly phoning his superior, General Omar Bradley, and urging him to "tell the world Third Army made it before Monty."

The next day, March 24, Patton commemorated his army's triumphal feat – and simultaneously displayed his knowledge of history – by striding across a pontoon bridge, dropping to a knee on the river's east bank, and digging his hands into German soil, thus imitating the reputed actions of William the Conquerer on his arrival in England from Normandy in 1066. Minutes earlier, Patton had added another flourish – midway across the bridge he urinated into the Rhine, declaring he had been "looking forward to this for a long time."

Bill's crossing was doubtless less dramatic, though he shared no particulars at the time. Before departing Oppenheim, however, he treated himself to a souvenir that he soon sent home. "Tomorrow I am sending out a package," he would write his parents in April. "It contains a German Airman's leather jacket and matching gloves, three flags, a knife and the old family nail clipper." Upon learning the items had arrived in Auburn, Bill sent another letter with a telling detail: "The small flag was obtained at Oppenheim, on the Rhine river."

BY LATE MARCH seven Allied armies – the U.S. First, Third, Seventh, and Ninth, and the British Second, Canadian First, and French First – had catapulted the Rhine and were surging across a 250-mile front, driving deep into Germany's heartland. Frankfurt, thirty miles east of the Rhine, fell to Patton's army on March 29, the collapse coming after days of house-to-house fighting, though months of aerial bombardment already had left the city in ruins. As Bill would soon write his parents: "I went through Frankfurt the other day. Imagine a city nearly as large as St. Louis, with hardly a building intact, and with thousands of them just a heap of rubble. It must have been a most beautiful city at one time. These Germans certainly are damn fools."

Despite all the destruction and waste, Bill admitted that all was not ugliness as the Allies bounded east. The German countryside "is rolling and in places almost mountainous – I think it beats anything I've seen on this side, except Cornwall [England]," he wrote at the end of March. A week later: "Germany is among the most beautiful spots in the world, from a scenic standpoint. There are drives along both the Mosell[e] and Rhine rivers that I have never seen surpassed in beauty." For Bill, the visual delights included castles, one of which he described in detail:

7 April 1945

Dear Folks:

Tonight I am staying in an old castle. There is an ancient stone tower built in the year 1200. The rest of the castle was destroyed in the 30 Years War, and the present house, built on the old foundations and alongside the tower, was erected early in the 17th century. Imbedded in the masonry of the tower are short chains to which are attached iron collars with huge padlocks. Men were chained by the neck with these as punishment or for torture. The ancient timbers of the building are all held together by wooden pegs. The house is full of old chests and cases, handcarved and painted, or inlaid, some of which must date back several centuries. Most of the furniture consists of museum pieces. I made the family that lived in it move out into rooms over the stables. As [U.S. Civil War General William T.] Sherman said "C'est la Guerre."

If residents of that hilltop castle – or, for that matter, dwellers in towns and on farms throughout central Germany – wondered why Wehrmacht troops weren't rushing to rescue them, numbers told the story. The vaunted German army was crumbling. At the start of April, as many as ten thousand German soldiers were surrendering every day, and Patton's army, having already processed 400,000 POWs, would soon process several hundred thousand more. Altogether, Allied forces were capturing so many enemy troops that cages in which to confine them were at a premium; make-do enclosures – a single strand of barbed wire – sometimes had to suffice. That said, even as the overall German prisoner count exceeded 1.3 million at mid-month, die-hard Wehrmacht soldiers refused to give up. More than 10,600 Americans would be killed in action in Europe that April, a number that rivaled GI deaths in June 1944 when the Allies invaded Normandy.

Bill, as his job required, did his part to haul in prisoners. With so many Germans surrendering or preparing to do so, however, he and his colleagues increasingly had the upper hand. "The other day Lt. Sudbury went [deer] hunting and got several shots. He didn't hit anything, but the noise flushed several Jerries [Germans] out onto the highway where they were picked up," Bill wrote home in April. His letter continued:

Several days ago I had a similar experience. I was going down a back road in my jeep with a driver and an interpreter when I met seven Jerries in full uniform coming down the road. I stopped and interrogated them. They said they'd never been captured but had been living in a house in a town that had been bypassed and were trying to get to a German hospital in a certain town. So, I stopped a couple of colored boys driving a truck and put them on it and sent them into the next town where I knew there were troops who would turn them over to a PWE [Prisoner of War Escort]. [The Germans] were not armed – and I was armed to the teeth, with a tommy gun. I followed them in and saw they were taken care of.

Meanwhile, as April 1945 neared its midpoint, the world was rocked by news from the United States. On April 12, an ailing President Roosevelt, who had guided the nation through the Great Depression and steered it through more than three years of war, died at his home – the "Little White House" – in Warm Springs, Georgia. By day's end, Vice President Harry S. Truman had been sworn in as the nation's thirty-third president, the responsibility for bringing the war to a decisive end now squarely on his shoulders.

Earlier that same day, Patton – not yet aware of FDR's death – toured a salt mine at the German village of Merkers, where Third Army troops had recently discovered a half-a-billion-dollar hidden cache of treasure, everything from gold bars and currency to artwork and jewelry looted from homes throughout Europe. That afternoon, Patton, still in the company of Generals Eisenhower and Bradley, embarked on another tour, visiting a newly liberated labor camp near the German town of Gotha.

Inside the camp, Patton vomited, Bradley was rendered speechless, and Eisenhower – when cabling Army Chief of Staff George Marshall in Washington, D.C., a few days later – would declare that "the things I saw beggar description."

Bill would see similar sights – hideous, horrifying, word-defying.

Chapter Fifteen
MARY: 1945

ITALY
JAN. 1, 1945

Dearest Mother & Dad –
Happy New Year and I <u>do</u> mean it. Instead of saying those words we've adopted the Italian phrase "Buon Anno." I came on duty this morning at the club at eight o'clock – there certainly isn't much to do, all the soldiers are sleeping – just myself and the Italian workers seem to be holding forth. Yesterday was my day off and I had a wonderful walk in the high hills back of the Area in the morning, and in the afternoon Doc and I went to the movies in town. We had a very quiet celebration last night but stayed up long enough to wish everybody "Happy New Year" and throw a few paper ribbons. . . .
Again, my dears, Good-bye and God Bless You, Both.

IN THE EARLY WINTER OF 1945, in the days and weeks after Christmas, Red Cross operations at the U.S. Army Rest Center in Rome hummed along uneventfully. "Life has settled down again into a rather uninteresting groove – not much to write about," Mary Brandon informed her parents on January 4. At month's end, she penned much the same: "I actually have very little news to tell you. We do about the same things day in and day out and I don't seem to have anything new to add."

As had been the case since the previous June, when Allied forces liberated Rome, new truckloads of soldiers arrived every five days at the center, and Mary and her Red Cross colleagues followed the same "cheer-and-comfort" regimen. They dispensed coffee and cookies to GIs in the snack bar, helped them write letters to loved ones, laughed at their corny jokes, and listened while they vented. Afternoons featured dancing. "The boys seem to enjoy dancing more than anything we can do for them," Mary wrote home in mid-January. "I assure you, dancing isn't quite the pleasure for me that it once was, but, on the other hand, it isn't too difficult a way to earn one's living."

More difficult was remembering the names and faces of soldiers previously encountered. As Mary noted in a January 24 letter, "We are beginning to have boys again who were with us last winter [at Caserta]. I'm afraid many of them I've forgotten but they remember us and make us feel as if they are seeing old friends again."

The "boys" – Mary's preferred term – were engaged in limited fighting that winter. Harsh weather had made it all but impossible for Allied troops to dislodge entrenched German forces from the highly fortified Gothic Line in Italy's northern Apennine Mountains. With offensive operations halted, Allied commanders used the winter months to rotate exhausted front-line units to rear areas and to hastily train inexperienced, but much needed, replacements. Commanders likewise stockpiled supplies and ordered equipment repaired for what was anticipated to be a massive spring assault.

Overseeing all the Allied ground troops in Italy, a fighting force that eventually included soldiers from more than two dozen nations, was Lieutenant General Clark, who had been named to the post in mid-December. Replacing Clark as head of the U.S. Fifth Army was Lieutenant General Lucian K. Truscott, who had distinguished himself during campaigns in Sicily, at Anzio, and in the invasion of southern France the previous August.

Battle-hardened German troops also took advantage of the winter respite. Ordered by Hitler to hold their position, they began building additional defensive barriers north of the Gothic Line toward the Alps. Even so, morale-crushing realities bore down on them. By January 25 the Third Reich's all-out offensive in the Ardennes – the Battle of the Bulge – had failed, forcing beleaguered German soldiers to retreat to their homeland. By month's end, Soviet troops advancing from the east had pulled to within fifty miles of Berlin.

MARY: 1945

While Mary struggled to find topics on which to write that winter, she nonetheless kept up her correspondence, knowing family members enjoyed her letters as much as she cherished theirs. She assured them that her December 29 birthday had not been forgotten, not even by the Russian artist Vladimir Wolkonsky whose clever Christmas decorations had so amused her. He and his wife had given her a silver vase filled with mistletoe, a kindness she repaid by giving them a gift that seemed oddly mismatched – but much appreciated. "They are such wonderful people and are so hungry these days that I gave them the can of lobster [that Annie sent me]," Mary wrote her parents on New Year's Day. "They said they would save it for their Russian Christmas and that I must come and celebrate it with them. I think it would be interesting, don't you."

Delivering more "all-is-well" updates, Mary reported a week later, on January 6, that she had just undergone a required medical check-up and was "sure they couldn't have found anything wrong with me. I've never felt better – haven't even scored a cold so far this winter." At mid-month, she pronounced herself "snug now as a bug in a rug" for having traded her large, but drafty, room at the Rest Center for one that was smaller but "most comfortable." And in late January, she informed her folks that she had found an outlet for boredom: "We are all going Cribbage crazy around here, playing every minute we have a chance when not at the Club and every opportunity we have while at work. Quite a number of the boys play – so we have plenty of available players."

Meanwhile, her tired feet occasionally received a break, especially when local "Signorinas" occupied the dance floor, as Mary also reported in late January:

We had a floor show this afternoon in place of our usual dance. It is comprised of entertainers from a down town night club. It's typical Italian entertainment with plenty of pretty girls (Signorinas) in not too many clothes all doing about the same kind of shapeless dancing. Some of them flirt shamelessly with the boys but they love it of course. They do it all <u>for free</u> with only a cup of coffee and cookies at the Snack Bar.

That same month an unsettling incident took place outside Mary's room. Her parents likely approved of her follow-up action:

Outside my door this morning [January 21] a workman is putting in new locks and keys due to a little incident last week. Several times we have had people wander into our quarters and didn't feel too safe since we couldn't be locked in. Last week, however, topped the list and we demanded keys. Eileen, Ardith and I were all tucked in bed when I heard loud voices in our hall. When I jumped out of bed to look thru the keyhole I saw them reading our names on the doors and starting my way. I held tightly on to the door handle and pushed but they were pushing too. I think they felt someone was trying to keep them out so they wandered on down the hall and entered Eileen's room. She wakened in time to tell them to get "the hell out" – they went peaceably. They were just two drunken innocent lieutenants but some time it might not be too innocent – hence the precaution. . . .

I've completed my Christmas list of Thank You letters but it's at the Club so I'll send it to you next time.

All my Love forever, Mary

True to her word, Mary sent the Christmas list home a few days later, relieved to have finally finished the time-consuming task of writing thank-you notes. She had been eager for her parents to see the names of everyone who had remembered her during the holiday, and, as her two-page list showed, the gift-givers had run the gamut – from family and Auburn friends to Red Cross colleagues, medics in Doc's dispensary, and Italian civilians with whom she worked.

The list also confirmed what Mary earlier had reported: her Christmas haul was substantial. She had raked in a raft of "personal care" items – soap, toilet paper, tissues, make-up, perfume, nail polish, hair bows, safety pins. She likewise had received much-welcomed clothing and much-needed food, from canned salmon and sardines to smoked turkey and crackers. Even the hometown Girl Scouts sent her a late-arriving Christmas package of cold creams and toothpaste. As Mary readied her list to mail home, she informed her parents on January 24 that a box of taffy – "heavenly" – had just arrived from Mrs. Simmons: "Do thank Mrs. S. for me until I can get a note off to her."

In that same correspondence, Mary lamented that she had not heard from her parents for "about a month." A day later, she repeated that lament to Annie, reporting no "mail for many weeks now."

AMERICAN RED CROSS

Christmas Present List

Tri Kappa (Some of the cards were lost from the individual packages, so these are the things that I'm not sure who sent them.

Mary R. Miller ~~Stationary~~
Cigarettes, Lux Flakes, Kleenix, Hard Candy, 2 Cans Tuna Fish, Hankies.
Frances McCammon - Stationary
Thelma Rieke, Alice Close, Ginny Treesh - Helena Rubinstein Water Lily Cream
Jean Renner - Revlon Polish
Beverly Guild - Can Salmon
Marge Kokenge - Helena Rubinstein Herbal Hand Cream
Lois Kelly y Marjorie Timbrook - Soap, Hankies
Doris and Jean Carmer - Soap
Gloria and Rose Anne Davis - Fruit Cake
Mary Sprott - Candy and Peanuts
Beverly Gonser - Homemade Butterscotch Candy
Helenjane, Joanna, Tip - Jersey Blouse

Lucille Miller - Bath Salts, Candy, Toilet Paper, Soap, Powder Puff, Cards, Aspirin.

Georgia Hines - Elizabeth Arden Make-Up Kit

Janet and Charlotta Sellew - Slip, Lip Stick

Harriet - Pants (2), Perfume, Gardenia Soap.

Ruth Brandon - 2 Pair Stockings

Gladys and Arvada - Cookies, Slip, Pop-Corn, Shrimp, Cream Perfume, Cake Make-Up.

Jessie - Stockings (2), Revlon Polish, Perfume, White Clay Pack.

Mrs. Fink - Stockings (2), Cream Perfume, Cigarette Case, Handkerchief.

Betty Hicks - Magazines, Soap (Dorothy Gray), Kleenix

Gus and Cookie - Ry-Krisp, Smithfield Spread, Shrimp (2Cans), Mexican Candy (Charlie) Smoked Turkey, Anchovies, Sardines, Bouillon Cubes.

Jewell - Peanuts, Soap, Polish, Perfume.

Annie - Blouse, Dusting Powder, Chop Suey, Roast Beef, Hanky, Cigarettes, Candy, Bathrobe, Shrimp, Lobster.

Mr. Schumann - Fruit Cake

Mother - Sweater (I love it), Jumper, Pop Corn, *hankie*

Anna Maude and Janie - Stockings (2)

Ruth Messenger - Hair Bows (Black Horse Hair with all colored velvet bows sewed on) Handkerchief, Shower Slippers, Cologne, Hair pins, Safety pins, Dental floss Face Powder, Powder Puff, Deodorant Cream, Revlon Polish, Eye Cream, Murine, Anchovie Paste, Deviled Ham, Sanitary Belt.

Page 1 of Mary's Christmas gift list

Whatever accounted for the delay, word from home soon arrived. "At last, yesterday there came two letters from you and Annie, dated about the 6th of January," Mary wrote her parents at month's end. Though pleased to have received *some* communication from Auburn, Mary was not entirely satisfied, telling her folks, "But I still don't know what happened in between. I haven't heard a word about your Christmas, where you spent it, what you did, or what Santa Claus brought you." Rather than belabor her point, Mary shifted her letter's focus to a story about a soldier – a narrative in keeping with her earlier accounts of how GIs were homesick for their children and how they enjoyed putting gum and candies into the outstretched hands of Italian youngsters who trailed them in the streets.

Mary's latest story included a twist.

January 29, 1945

Dearest Mother & Dad –

... The other day a soldier who drives for our Commanding Officer came into the Club with a darling baby. I thought, at first, it was some child that belonged to a family around here but gradually he began telling me about it. The baby is really his own, the mother died at child birth and he has it living with a family across the river. He wants to get it home to his parents in New York but it is too small yet (7 months old). I ask[ed] him if he would like for me to bring it home when I come and he seemed very pleased so I'm going to try to begin making negotiations with whatever authorities must be consulted.

I can ask Red Cross to return in June when my eighteen months [overseas] are up – but that doesn't particularly mean I'll be able to make it then. . . . This boy is rather pathetic about the baby – he is simply wild about it and she is as clean as a whistle. Blue eyes, curly hair and such rosy cheeks. He continually wiped her nose or pulled his comb out of his pockets to run it through her little curls. I hope I can manage it – I'd love to bring her home.

It didn't take long, however, for that idea to be quashed, as Mary reported in her next letter.

. . . I'm afraid I won't be bringing the baby home with me after all. The father brings her in the Club about every day and told me that he was afraid he couldn't stand to let her come without him.

He loves her so much but does quite a few things for her that she doesn't appreciate too much. I'm afraid – like bringing her to the dances, so many people and loud noise frightens her – he wakens her from a nap to take her riding and down to the P.X. for a Coke. He bought her a huge Japanese lantern that only made her eyes pop and her mouth pucker. She is such a beautiful little baby . . . .

The child's name was Antoinette.

MARY: 1945

IN EARLY FEBRUARY Mary inherited more responsibility when her snack bar colleague, Ardith Spalding, announced she was returning to the States. Before departing, Ardith doled out advice that an appreciative Mary took to heart. "I've been very busy the last few days learning all the Snack Bar angles for Ardith is leaving very soon now," Mary wrote her parents on February 8. "[The work] involves quite a little but not very complicated book-keeping. Even at its simplest it will probably be hard for me – I certainly hate to see Ardith leave. I shall miss her so much." Six days later, Mary wrote home again: "We are all very sad today. Ardith left and all of the Snack Bar people are in tears. They are going about dripping into the coffee and into their aprons. We will miss her – but it's time she is getting home – she's been overseas for over two years."

Mary barely had assumed her new duties when operations were put on hold so that the snack bar could be repainted. Whether Mary instigated the redecorating isn't clear, but she clearly supported sprucing up the popular soldier gathering spot. In a February 20 letter to her parents, she explained that "because we are below the ground level two flights it is quite dark [in the snack bar] and we are painting it white and sunshine yellow." While hired painters tackled the brushwork, Mary set off on at least one shopping trip to secure supplies. As she noted in that same February 20 letter, the trip included sightseeing:

Eileen went with me this morning to try to find scoops for the Ice Cream. Angelico, our driver, took us to many little out-of-the-way streets in trying to locate them. He knows the city so well so we ask[ed] him to take us to some of the churches we hadn't seen (combining business with pleasure). In one there was the Shrine of a Saint with a child in her arms. She was lighted by candles which made her beautiful golden crown and belt shine as if the sun were on it. Arranged all about her were the gifts that had been given her, sacred hearts, women's jewelry, even the epaulets from Generals' shoulders. In another church the columns on each side that support the roof were from the temples of the ancient Romans.

In this church we saw a lighted casket of an early Saint, dressed in his rich funeral robes but with a fine veil to cover the exposed bones. Angelico ask[ed] one of the Franciscan fathers if we might see the "Bambino" – he led us to a small chapel and as he pressed a button the wall opened and showed us, brightly illuminated, a doll whose entire robe was covered with jewels. For centuries Italy had adorned her churches with such elaborate richness while her people have starved. It has always been hard for me to understand Catholicism but here it is entirely impossible.

Less than a week later, on February 26, Mary updated Annie on the redecorating project and expressed her approval.

The Snack Bar is finished now and in operation again. It looks very nice and fresh and Springlike in its new coat of paint. The walls are yellow and white and the Ice Cream and Serving Bars are in green. The gardener came yesterday to set the plants around – Primroses and Laurel trees in pots give a finished touch. We do a pretty big business and it's really keeping me busy. When you consider that we use 400 pounds of sugar a week just to sweeten coffee you have an idea how many snacks are sold. We hired another Bus boy the other day. He is Egyptian and has such a funny name we call him Tommy. He says he's 16 but he looks about 12. He's a pretty smart little kid, though – speaks six languages.

Mary earlier had shared with her parents, before the snack bar's brief shutdown, what her morning work schedule was like:

We have 23 people working down there and none of us ever stop for a minute in the mornings which is our busiest time. Everyone comes in for their breakfast coffee and rolls. They pass along a bar where they pick up their rolls & cookies and pass on to the Coffee Urns. I try to put the sugar in their coffee in order to keep the line moving faster. We are having Brazilian soldiers now, too, and they really like the sugar – so much as ten and eleven teaspoons in one cup.

Mary's reference to the Brazilians was notable for reasons other than their liking sweetened coffee. Allied troops in Italy reflected a patchwork of nationalities, including – but not limited to – Americans, British, Canadians, French, New Zealanders, South Africans, Greeks, Indians, Poles, Italians, Czechs, Algerians,

Senegalese, and Moroccans. Among the U.S. troops was an African-American combat division, the 92nd Infantry, an anomaly at a time when the vast majority of black U.S. servicemen were not allowed to take up arms and instead were assigned to segregated construction or supply units. The 92nd was known as the Buffalo Soldiers, its infantrymen adopting a name that Native Americans had bestowed on black cavalrymen after the Civil War. Even as the 92nd fought in Italy, however, Army hierarchy still reflected the prejudices of the time: White officers commanded the unit.

U.S. troops in Italy also included "Nisei" – Americans of Japanese ancestry. Initially prohibited from enlisting in the military on grounds they were "enemy aliens," Nisei soldiers contributed from the very outset of the Italian campaign, storming Salerno's beaches in September 1943 and then fighting valiantly during the murderous attempts to capture Monte Cassino. Organized as the U.S. 100th Infantry Battalion, the segregated Nisei unit received reinforcement help in the spring of 1944 from another all-Nisei force, the 442nd Regimental Combat Team (RCT). That unit, as noted earlier, had trained at Camp Shelby when Bill Husselman was stationed there, prompting him to tell his parents at the time: "I would feel safe in saying that they are far and away the best troops on the post."

By late winter 1945, this diverse Allied army, stalled by harsh weather and restless to get moving, understood that a spring offensive was in the offing. Plans for a final push had been drafted, preparations were underway, and General Clark was expected to give the go-ahead as soon as ground and air conditions permitted. April was pegged for the launch – the earlier, the better.

BUT APRIL WAS STILL WEEKS AWAY and, for Mary, the month of March brought no respite from long work hours and ramped-up responsibilities. As she wrote her parents on March 1, "The days slip by so fast that I suppose it is a long time again since I've written. I'm working longer and harder now . . . I begin at 8:30 in the morning and must come back at night to open the Snack Bar for the evening. By the time I get back to our quarters it is seven and then after dinner it is almost too late to do very much."

In that same letter, Mary acknowledged that war itself offered no respite, especially not from death or loss or heartbreak. She recently had learned that two students she taught in her music classes at Auburn High School had become casualties: "Annie wrote me that Kent McKenney had been killed and that Dick Thomas is missing. I'm so terribly sorry – they were two of my favorites. I'll try to write their Mothers."

Dick Thomas, 1940 yearbook photo

Like thousands of other young American servicemen who fought in the Battle of the Bulge in late December 1944 and early January 1945, both Richard (Dick) Thomas and Kent McKenney paid dearly for their service. Thomas had been serving in the medical detachment of the 423rd Infantry, 106th Division, when he was reported missing in action on December 21, 1944, soon after German troops barreled through the Ardennes. Thomas' family would learn later that he had been captured and was in a German POW camp. He would survive, with his release coming at the war's end.

Kent McKenney, 1940 yearbook photo

McKenney – like Thomas, twenty-two years old in December 1944 – was a staff sergeant in the 501st Infantry, 101st Airborne Division. A paratrooper who had survived Normandy and *Operation Market Garden* in the Netherlands, he was killed in action on December 23, just days before General Patton's Third Army relieved the besieged town of Bastogne. McKenney and two others died when a large artillery shell exploded outside their platoon command post in Bizory, a Belgian village near Bastogne. Buried in Arlington National Cemetery, McKenney was the son of H.L. McKenney, superintendent of Auburn's schools and Mary's boss during her teaching career, thus giving her a double link to the family.

Two weeks after receiving that painful news, Mary addressed another cost of war – its psychological toll on troops. In a March 14 letter to her parents, she relayed what she often observed while sitting outside Doc's office at the Army Rest Center: "It's indeed strange how conditions [affect] human behavior. I have sat many times in the Doc's room which is next door to the Dispensary while he has gone in to take care of a boy temporarily out of his mind through the stress and strain of combat. When [soldiers] get here the tension relaxes enough to begin thinking. It is then that one can tell the fibre of a personality. Sometimes it takes all six of Doc's boys and himself to get them quiet."

Around that same time, Mary also alluded to ongoing hardships experienced by the Italian people, especially in Rome where the population had nearly doubled since the war's start. Fueling the city's growth were refugees desperately in need of shelter.

March 13, 1945

Dearest Mother & Father –

The week has been a busy one. First, I had a frantic telephone call last week from the woman who lives upstairs in my [Rome] apartment to tell me that the Italian police had broken in and were moving in a Refugee family. I called our Military authorities who sent an officer out. He found that they had moved every stick of furniture into the dining room and had begun living in the other rooms.

He also noticed that I hadn't been living there (which is true I hadn't slept there since November, too cold) and asked me to give it up. Since I was still responsible I had to have everything moved back to its place, and cleaned and another inventory made. Needless to say, that took my entire day off. I was not sorry to give up the place but will miss having the fun of cooking over there occasionally. . . . It seemed a shame not to let the family, a father & mother & six children stay on there but our army has the apartment requisitioned – so it will go to an Officer.

While addressing serious topics in her March letters, Mary made sure to sprinkle in snippets of cheer. Early in the month, she mailed home a photograph of "sweet baby" Antoinette and commented that the child and her father "are most touching together – he plays with her like a boy with a puppy." A week later she informed her parents that Doc had been promoted to major, a cause for cocktail celebrating at the commanding officer's residence. Not long afterward, Mary wrote Annie and, along with asking her sister to send brassieres and other necessities, mentioned having spent a pleasant afternoon getting schooled in a British team sport.

. . . Yesterday afternoon we watched a big Rugby match, the British football. It was played in the Stadium here [at the Rest Center] and seemed awfully good – the atmosphere of a big game was in the air and it reminded me of a big football game at home. It's quite like our football in many respects but very different in others. We would have been entirely at a loss without the explanations a British officer sitting beside us came out with at our probably foolish questions.

They have a kind of a huddle called a <u>Scrum</u> (horrible word) where everybody pushes with the shoulders. When all the players are firmly pushing each other in the scrum the ball is tossed into the middle and then kicked out with the feet. They never must pass a ball forward, always back and must kick it to the side.

In a somewhat ironic twist, Mary found herself trying to comfort her parents at month's end. They had written to her about stateside shortages due to increasing amounts of food being shipped overseas – for troops as well as for growing numbers of German POWs and civilian refugees. Acknowledging the situation, Mary wrote home on March 26: "I'm most sorry to hear that it is hard for you to get food. Our rations too have been cut considerably and we are now eating Spam and Vienna sausages again. I suppose it will be a long time before any of us will be able to get big thick steaks[,] for with each new mile gained by our army [that] means many more civilians to feed."

Closing on a hopeful note, she added: "I do miss you but it won't be long now, I'm sure."

APRIL'S ARRIVAL COINCIDED with Easter Sunday. Mary marked the day by attending worship services in the Rest Center's movie theater, where religious gatherings took place every week. An improvised altar with a white cross, accented with calla lilies and potted plants, had been set up for the occasion, and, as Mary wrote her parents three days later, "It looked lovely." As for herself, "I didn't have a new hat but I did have a corsage from my Snack Bar people. They also gave me a huge bouquet of red carnations for my room."

Mary also informed her parents in that same April 4 letter that she and Red Cross colleagues, along with military staff, had lunched recently with U.S. Ambassador Alexander Kirk in his apartment in one of Rome's "pretentious" palaces. The ambassador, whom Mary had met the previous November as he prepared to assume his official duties, had insisted his guests were "family" and had entertained them lavishly, in keeping with his reputation and despite wartime privations. Declared Mary: "The lunch was delicious, the service beautiful, all and all we were most impressed."

Some two hundred miles north of Rome, the April countdown was underway for the long-awaited spring offensive. Preliminary battles already had taken place, notably in late February when the U.S. 10th Mountain Division, America's elite Alpine fighting force, had ousted Germans from the summit of the 3,800-foot Mount Belvedere in the North Apennines – an ouster that weakened the enemy's ability to control Italy's agriculturally and industrially rich Po River valley. The 10th Division had continued its peak-to-peak assault in March, capturing ten mountains and taking 1,000 prisoners in three days, all the while securing thirty-five square miles of territory.

Other units had also been active. In late February and early March, the Brazilian 1st Division had attacked alongside the 10th Division's "Mountain Men," though at less demanding altitudes. On March 21, Allied aircraft had savaged German shipping operations in Venice's harbor. And at the start of April, elements of the 92nd Infantry (Buffalo Soldiers), in concert with the 442nd RCT (Nisei), had begun diversionary advances up Italy's western coast.

When the full-blown offensive began on April 9, kicked off by massive Allied aerial and artillery bombardments, Mary and her colleagues closely monitored the news. They tracked troop breakthroughs across northern Italy as well as breathtaking advances by Allied forces in Germany. As Mary told her parents a week later, on April 16: "The war in Europe, I'm sure, can last only a few more weeks. We keep our ears glued to the radio and follow every move of the armies with our maps. Everybody, everywhere is on the move. We have so few boys here now that it is practically like a vacation. Our Snack Bar seems as empty as a tomb."

In that same April 16 letter, Mary also shared her reaction to stateside news – the death of President Roosevelt on April 12.

The President's death has been a great shock to everyone here. All our dances, and activities have ceased and Saturday afternoon at 4:00 we observed a five minute silence, every head bowed both American and Italian.

All the schools here are closed and every flag is at half mast. From the pictures we saw of him at the Yalta Conference he looked like a doomed man and I wasn't too much surprised to hear of his death.

I learned of it in a rather strange manner. I was awakened early in the morning by the loud speaker outside my window which ordinarily doesn't waken me for it is always on at that time to instruct the troops who are arriving to tell them where they will be quartered, the various programs, rules, etc. I thought I heard the speaker saying something about the President, Warm Springs Ga, but thought I was only dreaming and went back to sleep, to learn the actual truth at breakfast.

Mary had more to say that day, choosing to write to Annie's family about the leisurely pace of her life. So, too, did she address the eerie juxtaposition between the peacefulness of a golf course and the intense fighting to the north, where her "boys" risked their lives.

[Monday] April 16, 1945

Dearest Annie, George & Bud –

If anyone would have told me that my life in Red Cross would be so civilized that I would be playing Golf on Sunday morning in Italy I would have thought they were crazy but that is exactly what we did yesterday and have plans to do it other Sundays in the future. I won't even mention what a terrible game I played but it was wonderful just to be out on a course again. The Italians aren't as addicted to the sport as we are so this course which is quite close to us is one of the few in the whole country. Only the <u>ultra ultra</u> [rich] play so the Club House and grounds are beautiful.

Our Special Service here at the Rest Center has stocked itself with clubs and balls for the use of the Military personnel and Eileen and I were invited to play with two other Special Service officers and the Doc. The greens were in fine shape but the fairways were as high as the roughs at home and practically impossible to find a ball. Instead of having dandelions the grass is filled with tiny African daisies and buttercups and although it looks beautiful it's very difficult to play in. It was so peaceful and lovely it seemed as if we were thousands of miles from a war except squadron after squadron of heavy bombers flew overhead flashing bright and silver in the sunlight on their way to bombing missions. It was hard to think looking at their beautiful wings that some people would not be having the happy day we were enjoying.

The Course itself has the same aspect as one would at home, with its streams, its knolls, its dog leg holes except that across the road are some ruins of an ancient Roman aqueduct.

The Cocktail party the other afternoon for the personnel of the coaching school was quite successful. There are some very famous people in their own line here – Isbell from Purdue, Dr. Staley from Illinois and a Mr. Cavanaugh who was, I thought, the most colorful. He has been the boxing instructor at West Point for years and is supposed to know more Generals by sight than most anyone in this man's army, but he says he can never remember their names. . . .

All my Love, Mary

The school Mary mentioned was the "Central Sports School" operated by the army's Special Services branch. Confident that hostilities in Europe would end soon, the U.S. military had begun making postwar plans, with the understanding some troops would be sent home and others would be shipped to the Pacific or redeployed as an occupying force. During the reshuffling – whenever it might begin – the Army believed many of the nearly three million men in Europe would benefit from "morale-building" athletic activities. Thus the Army Rest Center in Rome – with its two stadiums (one unfinished), two indoor swimming pools, tennis courts, gymnasiums, athletic fields, and classrooms, all courtesy of the deposed Mussolini – was tapped as the host site. The first of the civilian instructors arrived in April, with a cocktail party to welcome them.

Recruited by the Army, the instructors were to teach officers and enlisted men how to set up sports programs and promote mass participation within their units. As Mary's letter correctly noted, the teaching roster boasted many well-known current and former college football, basketball, soccer, and track coaches, as well as professional baseball players and boxers. Cecil Isbell, whom Mary cited, had played football for Purdue University in the 1930s, helped lead the Green Bay Packers to the NFL Championship in 1939, and since 1944 had been Purdue's head gridiron coach. Dr. S. C. Staley, whom Mary also mentioned, was director of the School of Physical Education at the University of Illinois and a leading organizer of the overseas training program. In coming weeks, new arrivals were to include Hoosier-born Everett Dean, who had been Indiana University's first basketball All-American in 1921, head coach at his alma mater from 1924-1938, and the bench general who guided Stanford University to its first NCAA basketball title in 1942.

Meanwhile, the Army made sure the sports school was well-equipped. The groundwork already had been laid, with the military – from D-Day onward – shipping massive amounts of sporting goods to Europe. Troops in the Mediterranean Theater alone had received more than 117,000 baseballs, 96,000 softballs, 89,000 bats, 18,000 footballs, 14,000 basketballs, and nearly 4,000 sets of boxing gloves, not to mention fishing tackle, swimming trunks, and other supplies. So much athletic gear had been sent overseas that, by 1945, civilians in the United States experienced shortages.

Needing gear herself, Mary reached out to Annie in late April. By then, having little or no work to do, Mary was playing golf regularly with Doc and friends, and even though the war's end was in sight, she surmised that her Red Cross duties would keep her overseas in the coming months. Thus, envisioning a summer of golf, Mary entreated Annie "to send my golf shoes. I slip and fall continually in the only shoes I have to wear."

Her entreaties went further: "Golf balls are very hard to get, too, so if I have any left in my bag will you send those along with some golf tees and <u>ankle</u> socks."

HAVING BEEN UNLEASHED TO FINISH their work in Italy, Allied soldiers – a million-and-a-half strong under the command of the U.S. Fifth and the British Eighth armies – moved quickly and decisively in April to crush a rapidly disintegrating German army. Aided by air and armored support, the Allies booted Germans from Apennine ridges, chased them across flatlands, and encircled them at Bologna. Hurtling ever-northward, they secured river crossings, advanced across lakes, drove resisters from towns, and roared up highways, capturing prisoners by the tens of thousands, many of whom simply laid down their arms. From the French border on the west to the famed Brenner Pass on the Austrian frontier to the Adriatic on the east, the Allies left no doubt – they were in control. On April 29, after weeks of secret discussions, the utterly routed German army in Italy unconditionally surrendered, the ceasefire to take effect at noon on May 2.

Four days before the April surrender, Mussolini and his mistress, Clara Petacci, fled the northern city of Milan and joined up with a German convoy heading for Switzerland. Near the border on April 27, the convoy was stopped by Italian partisans who recognized Mussolini, despite his having donned a German military overcoat and helmet. A day later, Il Duce and Petacci were summarily executed by machine-gun fire, with their bodies – as well as the bodies of at least a dozen fellow Fascists – taken by van back to Milan and unceremoniously dumped in a public square. Kicked and spat upon by a gathering crowd, the corpses were hung upside-down from a rusty girder outside a gas station, with angry citizens inflicting even more abuse. In an April 30 letter to her parents, Mary skipped the sordid details of the dictator's demise and instead let three sentences suffice: "Most of the Italians seem to be celebrating Mussolini's death. All the flags are out down town [in Rome] and tomorrow is a big Holiday. It is the first they have been able to celebrate the first of May since before the Fascist Regime."

In raw numbers and by mere observation, there was little to celebrate. The war had laid waste to Italy, ravaging its countryside, decimating its infrastructure, and destroying its cultural treasures. During the 608 days that the Allied and German armies had battled – from September 1943 to April 1945 – lives and livelihoods had been chewed up in untold ways. The German casualty count, by some estimates, exceeded 530,000. On the Allied side, the total number of dead and wounded stood at 313,000. Factoring in civilian losses of nearly 153,000, the Italian campaign's overall casualty count approached or likely topped one million.

Military historians continue to debate the wisdom of the Allies' decision to fight in Italy. Prime Minister Churchill had argued vigorously in 1943 that attacking Europe from the south could help launch Allied armies into Austria and Germany. Churchill also had argued that an Italian campaign would – at the very least – draw enemy forces away from upcoming battles on the continent's interior. American war planners had demurred, believing all manpower and resources should be reserved for the 1944 invasion of northern France. But in the end, the United States grudgingly acceded to Churchill's wishes, and Italy became a war theater, albeit a largely forgotten one after D-Day.

For Mary, there was – and there would be – no forgetting the soldiers who slogged up Italy's boot. Admittedly, she could not always recall their faces. Admittedly, too, their names did not always roll easily from her tongue. And of course, she never met them *all*.

Even so, Mary took pride in knowing and remembering the "boys" collectively – the GIs who loved smelling her perfume and spinning her around the dance floor and bragging about their hometowns, the soldiers who played pianos with blackened hands and walked with limps and battled demons in their heads. They were boastful, scared, hardened, weary. Like her, they had come to Italy to do a job. To the very end, they did it.

On May 3, 1945, one day after the ceasefire took effect, General Clark hosted the formal signing ceremony. A German representative surrendered the remaining Reich forces in northern Italy, thus ending World War II in the Mediterranean. The history-making ceremony took place not in Rome but farther south at Caserta, the site of Allied group headquarters and in the same drafty palace that Mary knew so well.

Mary would not romanticize the palace, not in 1944 when she worked there nor in 1945 when the war ended. But she would embrace her association with it, writing her parents on May 9: "The palace where I lived . . . was mighty cold and uncomfortable, but I'm proud now to say that I lived in the same place as where the Surrender in Italy was signed."

General Mark Clark, center, addresses a German commander at Caserta Palace, finalizing Germany's unconditional surrender of its forces in Italy and West Austria, May 1945. (Imperial War Museums via Wikimedia Commons)

Chapter Sixteen
BILL: 1945

*G*ERMANY
21 APRIL 1945

Dear Folks:
We've been moving about so much that I haven't been able to write for several days. I haven't had a letter from you in more than two weeks.
You have read about Nazi concentration camps where they kept Jews, political prisoners, etc., and probably like me figured that the stories were colored by propaganda. Take it from me, they couldn't be colored. Nothing could be worse than they actually are....

EARLY IN WORLD WAR II the American press had begun publishing reports of the Hitler regime's ongoing slaughter of European Jews and other "undesirables" in concentration camps. The public, preoccupied with military victory, largely had overlooked those dispatches or dismissed them as hyperbole, recalling that exaggerated claims of atrocities also had circulated in World War I. In July 1944, the unsettling reports received more notice when Soviet troops overran a Nazi concentration camp near Lublin, Poland and found ample evidence of mass murder and criminality. More monstrous evidence surfaced in late January 1945 when the Soviets, having freed a string of camps in occupied eastern Europe, liberated the notorious Nazi killing center known as Auschwitz in southern Poland.

Even then, however, the full extent of the Reich's depravity remained unknown. It would take until April 1945, when American and British armies swept across Germany, for the colossal scale of Nazi evil to be exposed. The U.S. Third Army, with Bill Husselman's 512th MP Battalion still attached, would be the first of the Western Allies to liberate camps within the Fatherland and to thoroughly document – for the entire world – the horrors within.

April 4 marked the start of discoveries. Third Army troops were looking for a Nazi communications center near the German town of Gotha when they came, unexpectedly, upon a labor camp of enslaved Jews and other targeted groups. Inside the compound, from which German guards had just fled, GIs found sick and starving prisoners and thousands of naked and decomposing corpses. Eight days later, on April 12, Lieutenant General Patton arranged for Generals Eisenhower and Bradley to join him in inspecting the facility, and it was there that the notoriously hard-nosed Third Army commander vomited, repulsed by the grotesque scenes of cruelty.

Eisenhower was equally horrified, and before departing Ohrdruf, as the camp was known, ordered all nearby troops not on the front lines to tour it. Having seen with his own eyes evidence of the "Final Solution," the Nazi policy to exterminate Europe's Jewish population, Eisenhower also urged Army Chief of Staff George Marshall to send a delegation of American lawmakers and newspaper editors to Germany to witness the barbarism firsthand.

On April 11, the day prior to the generals visiting Ohrdruf, Third Army soldiers made yet another discovery. Thirty miles to the east, near the culturally renowned city of Weimar – home to the composer Franz Liszt and writers Johann Wolfgang von Goethe and Friedrich Schiller – Patton's men came upon Buchenwald, one of Germany's largest concentration camps and one that administered dozens of satellites, including Ohrdruf. Since Buchenwald's opening in 1937, more than 250,000 prisoners had passed through the main camp and subcamps, and more than 56,000 inmates had succumbed to disease, malnutrition, beatings, and executions.

When Third Army troops, including the 512th MP Battalion, entered Buchenwald's barbed-wire confines, they entered a hellish world of corpses, cremated remains, piles of bones, and sunken-eyed survivors, many bearing little resemblance to human beings. The 21,000 survivors included children, among them sixteen-year-old Elie

Wiesel, a future Nobel Peace Prize winner who would detail his Holocaust experiences years later in his acclaimed memoir *Night*.

Precisely when Bill reached Buchenwald isn't known. But as he informed his parents in his April 21 letter, he arrived soon after the camp was liberated "while the [victims] were still there and before it was cleaned up." With military censorship relaxed – Eisenhower by then had made clear that he *wanted* troops to tell their families what they saw – Bill served up a searing account of Buchenwald's horrors. Weeks later, he would send home photos taken at the camp. For the time being, he relied on whatever words he could muster.

... What I saw left me physically and mentally sick. I saw men in every stage of starvation – some so weak that they could move no part of their bodies save only their eyes. I saw a big six oven crematory where they daily disposed of about 250 bodies of men killed or starved to death. In the ovens were the charred and half burned bodies of men. Stacked like cords of wood outside of the building were the naked bodies of sixty or seventy men awaiting cremation. Some had died of malnutrition, some had been knocked in the head.

There was one room which they had used for hanging. Around the walls were ordinary iron hooks, about eight feet off the floor. Men were hanged from there by very short ropes, with their feet just a few inches off the ground. You could see the imprint of the ribs of the victims on the walls under the hooks.

There had been a large factory nearby where the prisoners had been worked. They were given only three hours of sleep a day. The factory part had been completely destroyed by the Air Force. The camp where the men lived, which was very close, was completely untouched – quite a tribute to the accuracy of our bombers, I thought.

I didn't go into the hospital of the camp, but those that did said that the sadistic doctors stationed there had a huge lamp shade made out of human skin, and made ladies hand bags of the same material.

Outside of the crematorium, in addition to the bodies, was a stack of small bits of human bones that hadn't burned and had been raked out of the ovens. This pile, about the size of a jeep, was the residue from the cremation of about 250 bodies.

Words cannot describe the human misery – nor the bestial nature of those who operated the place. It could better be termed an "extermination camp" than a "concentration camp." *The stories you got from the prisoners – those who were still physically able and could speak English acted as guides – about the treatment they received would make your hair stand on end. They say they intended to kill all the prisoners – and there must have been 35000 of them – before the Americans came, but the army came through so fast they didn't have time to do more than save their own hides....*

Love, Bill

Not surprisingly, Patton conducted his own inspection of Buchenwald on April 15. Angry and sickened, much as he had been at Ohrdruf, Patton ordered one thousand residents of nearby Weimar to march to the camp the following day and confront the atrocities perpetrated by their government. Some townspeople refused to look, others wept openly, still others fainted. Most professed not to have known what took place inside, the smoke from the crematory ovens and the stench of death notwithstanding.

Before long – and in keeping with Eisenhower's request – U.S. congressional delegations and prominent publishers, as well as British parliamentarians, showed up at Buchenwald. War correspondents from around the globe also arrived, and their firsthand accounts and gut-wrenching photographs soon flooded the pages of newspapers and magazines. In addition, the Army soon released film footage that flickered across movie screens in the U.S. and elsewhere, the damning visual images confirming what Bill and others tried to communicate by letter.

Throughout April and into May, Allied armies would throw open the gates to other camps, and names such as Bergen-Belsen, Flossenburg, Dachau, and Mauthausen would enter the public lexicon. From those slaughterhouses and filthy prisons would emerge more photos of gallows and whipping blocks and obscene instruments of torture, more documentation of heinous medical experiments, more gruesome testimony from skeletal survivors of the burial pits they had been forced to dig and the degradations they had endured.

"Take it from me," Bill had urged his parents in his April 21 letter, hoping to disabuse them of any notion that camp "horror" stories were overblown. "Nothing could be worse than they actually are."

"I am enclosing some pictures taken at the Buchenwald concentration camp," Bill wrote his parents on June 2, weeks after he first entered the prison. "They show a pile of bodies ready for the crematorium, the ovens of the crematorium, with skeletons showing, a pile of bones - the residue from the ovens, and a typical case of malnutrition." Bill's letter did not indicate whether he took the photos or acquired copies from someone else.

THOUGH IN NO WAY COMPARABLE to the suffering in the camps, Allied soldiers saw misery of another kind that spring. Trudging along the sides of roads and in ditches were millions of displaced persons (DPs), many swaddled in rags, many with bundles on their shoulders, many others lugging a suitcase or pushing a cart.

The DPs included hundreds of thousands of slave laborers – sick, weakened, and newly abandoned by their Nazi captors as the Allies bombed factories and overran camps. Other DPs – again, hundreds of thousands – were refugees from ravaged cities in central Europe. Determined to escape what remained of Hitler's army, most headed west hoping to find sanctuary somewhere other than in the Soviet Union, a place many feared.

In the sector of Germany through which Bill and fellow Third Army soldiers traveled, Allied officials estimated that the shambling masses topped four million, with DPs representing as many as forty-seven nations. "You should see the backwash of war – the displaced persons who you find wandering about," Bill had written home on April 7. "There are Russian & Pole slave laborers, freed Prisoners of War of all nationalities, German refugees. People in America don't know what the word 'war' means, and I hope they never find out."

Amid this human "backwash," tens of thousands of U.S. military vehicles – trucks, jeeps, armored personnel carriers, self-propelled artillery – rolled deeper into the country's interior, forcing Germany's civilian population to witness what it had hoped *not* to see: a display of Allied mobility and might so overwhelming that the war's outcome was little in doubt. The vehicles traveled over roads unknown in the United States and viewed by troops as a marvel. "And you should see the Autobahn highways!" Bill informed his parents in that same April 7 letter. "Beautiful four lane concrete roads, with the directional lanes separated. . . . It was really darn nice of Hitler to build these roads for us, don't you think? They are of extra thick concrete, built especially for heavy military traffic."

Whether troops advanced along those "dream" highways or on less modern byways, they sometimes spotted more than refugees along the routes. Hitler's army relied heavily on horse-drawn transportation, and by that spring U.S. firepower literally was crippling enemy movement. "When one of these [horse-drawn] outfits would be caught on the road by our aircraft or tanks, the carnage was total, and we would frequently pass a mile-long string of unfortunate animals lying beside the road still attached to the equipment that they were pulling," a fellow Hoosier and Third Army officer, Captain Maurice Biggs of the 177th Field Artillery Battalion, recorded in his memoir years later.

Meanwhile, Bill had become something of an authority on jeep travel. Official business had routinely sent him motoring across stretches of Europe, and, without disclosing many details in letters sent home, he occasionally referenced trips he had taken or was about to take. He wrapped up an April 13 letter by telling his parents "I have to travel a round trip of 250 miles tomorrow by jeep, so I think I'd better turn in." A few weeks later, he quantified his travels by reporting that his vehicle had logged 20,000 miles. "My jeep . . . is probably the best in the company. Allen [the driver] makes the mechanics fix every rattle and squeak as soon as one appears, so it is about as tight as a new vehicle." Emphasizing his good fortune, Bill added:

One of the best features of being an M.P. is to have your own vehicle and driver used for nothing but your own transportation. Mighty few junior officers in the ETO [European Theater of Operations] have that. The whole set-up is quite a deal. We've seen more of Europe than any tourist could, and have been paid for it. If I had my choice and could do it over again, I'd choose the same outfit.

If German civilians were inclined – in the face of so much Allied power – to treat newly arrived troops amicably, U.S. commanders forbade any type of fraternization; violators, including soldiers caught "ogling" girls and women, were subject to $65 fines. As a military police officer, Bill was granted more leeway with the locals, especially since his duties at times required him to converse with mayors and town officials. Dusting off German language skills rarely used since his college days – and aided by a fellow officer – Bill managed throughout the spring to carry out needed interactions, most of which were cordial. In a late March letter to his parents, he noted "I haven't as yet run into any hostility from civilians. Many of them smile and obviously try to be friendly. Many, if given a chance, profess anti-Nazi sympathy. One tried to tell one of our officers that we were liberators!" Charm-offensives notwithstanding, Bill was by no means naive: "All of this is very obviously just an attempt to make the best of a bad situation. Germany could not possibly have fought the war without the all-out support of nearly all the population, so we treat all friendly overtures as hooey."

Cordiality had its limits, however. As Allied troops heard tales of atrocities in concentration camps and personally witnessed the scenes within, soldiers had little stomach for extending niceties to citizens who had tolerated such butchery. In an early May letter to his parents, Bill made that clear:

This morning I decided I didn't like the billets of one of our detachments, so I found another building and cleared it by ordering its twenty some German occupants out, giving them an hour and fifteen minutes to move. Boy, you should have heard the women squall. These Jerries are really getting a taste of the medicine they used to prescribe.

After seeing German concentration camps I have no scruples whatever, and rather enjoy tossing them out of their homes. You should see their faces when you go through their houses and then tell them to get out. They never question your orders – they are too familiar with the methods of their own Gestapo to take any chances.

Right now I'm living in the sumptuously furnished owner's apartment of the best hotel in this town. On the whole, these people are paying plenty for their delusions about the Master Race and all that.

IN THE SECOND WEEK OF APRIL 1945, Eisenhower revealed to his generals that the Soviet army – not the Western Allies – would be tasked with capturing Berlin. Patton thought the decision wrongheaded, not least because he had hoped to lead his Third Army to the German capital and fight the war's climactic battle there. British Field Marshal Montgomery also objected, having set his own sights on taking what had long been considered the war's main prize. But Eisenhower, having based his decision on practical considerations as well as a political one, was not to be dissuaded.

The political considerations stemmed from a February 1945 conference attended by the three chief Allied leaders – Roosevelt, Churchill, and the Soviet Union's Joseph Stalin. Meeting at the Crimean resort town of Yalta on the Black Sea, those "Big Three" had agreed at the weeklong gathering that the Allies would divide Germany into four zones of occupation at the war's end, with Berlin also to be divided into four sectors. The occupying nations would be the Soviet Union, the United States, Great Britain, and France.

Churchill, Roosevelt and Stalin in February 1945. An ailing Roosevelt would be dead two months later. (National Archives)

Guided by that agreement, Eisenhower had surveyed the battlefield in late March and observed that Soviet troops were only thirty miles from Berlin, with more en route for a massive offensive. Western Allies, in contrast, were more than two hundred miles from the capital, and while their armored divisions could have reached Berlin quickly, the city's postwar partition did not hinge on who captured it.

Moreover, Eisenhower understood the need to conserve American troops, given that U.S. forces were still needed to fight the Japanese. If Eisenhower had ordered Western Allies to take Berlin, his commanders had estimated that American casualties alone could range from ten thousand to one hundred thousand.

Weighing on Eisenhower's mind as well were reports of resistance fighters in the mountains of southeastern Germany (Bavaria) and Austria. Allied intelligence had been warning for months that, upon the Third Reich's imminent collapse, Hitler and other high-level Nazis planned to retreat to a last-stand stronghold in the Alps. Thus, as April began, Eisenhower resolved to send two American armies, the Seventh and the Third, into Europe's Alpine region. The Seventh Army was to advance southwest, with Patton's forces – on April 21 – to slash southeast along the German-Czechoslovakian border and then into Austria's Danube Valley.

As for Bill and his fellow soldiers, the intense spring campaign came with a notable downside: Mail delivery suffered. "The mail situation is terrible. Nobody has had any to speak of for a week. I suppose the big push on now has set up transport priorities that leave nothing to haul mail. It's O.K. if it ends this business any quicker," Bill wrote his parents in mid-April. He repeated his mail woes when writing home days later, his frustration clearly mounting but remedies beyond his control. When word from Auburn finally came, Bill sent home a swift reply: "Last night [April 23] I received three air mails and a V-mail from you. . . . It was quite a relief to receive them as I hadn't had a letter in over two weeks, and one can't help but worry. I hope my letters aren't reaching you so irregularly."

If news from the home front was slow in coming, not so with war news. The Soviets, having begun their heavy bombardment of Berlin on April 16, finally managed after days of fierce resistance to surround the city and fight their way block by block to the Reich Chancellery, where Hitler had lived on and off for months in an underground bunker. On April 30, with Berlin but a shell of its former self, Hitler and his mistress, Eva Braun, took their own lives – the Führer by a bullet to the head, Braun by cyanide. Their bodies were carried upstairs by guards, doused with gasoline, and incinerated, though such details at the time were not made public, prompting officials in Washington and London to be skeptical.

Two days later, on May 2, a negotiated ceasefire took effect in Italy, marking the German army's collapse in southern Europe and enabling Bill to trumpet the back-to-back developments in a letter he composed that evening: "Well the news is looking up, what with the death of der Fuhrer and the surrender of the German Italian Army. While I personally take the news of Hitler's alleged demise with a good-sized grain of salt, he at least seems to be out of the picture now." As he wrote, Bill admitted to enhancing his jovial mood by "imbibing a sort of cordial" and suggested even his mother might enjoy the liqueur. Continuing, he confessed: "[I] am getting slightly addled, so if this doesn't make sense, it isn't my fault. Liquor is free in Germany, too. We can sometimes draw many cases of it with class I rations (food)."

Around that same time, Eisenhower ordered Patton, whose troops were astride the Czech border, to halt his army's march, yielding to a request from the advancing Soviets. On May 4, Patton was cleared to send his troops as far as Pilsen, an industrial and beer-making center less than fifty miles inside the Czech border. When word came that Pilsen fell quickly, Patton desperately wanted his men to keep heading east and liberate Prague, the capital. Even Churchill urged that Third Army be allowed to take such a prize. But Eisenhower again ordered Patton to halt, aware that the Soviets had honored Allied requests to limit their advance into eastern Germany at the Elbe River. Seeing no strategic benefit to capturing another European capital and unwilling to risk American lives strictly for political purposes, Eisenhower stood by his order. In the postwar era, especially when Czechoslovakia became a Soviet satellite state, Eisenhower's decision to halt Patton's army would be sharply criticized. But the supreme commander's concern at the time – and as he would affirm afterwards – was to end the war quickly.

And quickly it did end. On Monday, May 7, with Patton's troops in Pilsen and with German soldiers throughout Europe laying down their guns en masse, Colonel General Alfred Jodl, a longtime Hitler loyalist and top Wehrmacht commander, agreed to an unconditional surrender. He did so at a brief signing ceremony at Eisenhower's headquarters in Reims, France, prompting a ceasefire to take place immediately. To allow time to send word to German troops garrisoned in Norway and to U-boat crews in the Atlantic, the surrender did not officially take hold until the following day, May 8, which the Allies declared as V-E Day, or Victory in Europe Day. By then, celebrations already had begun in cities such as Paris and London, and jubilant throngs soon would mass in other parts of the world, including in New York City's Times Square.

But even though a war that had lasted five years, eight months, and six days was over, even though a halt had been called to steady bloodletting across the continent, not everyone was inclined toward wild partying and huzzahing. For many, especially those in uniform, a subdued mood accompanied the surrender. The war with Japan raged on, leaving many servicemen to assume they soon would be shipped to the Pacific Theater. Moreover, with European battlefields now quiet, soldiers had time to reflect on buddies who never would go home, on bodies broken and spirits crushed, on wreckage and wastage and innocence lost. As for his thoughts on the war's end, Bill shared a few musings with his parents. But first, he did what in many ways came easier than cheering or crying: He got "stinko" drunk.

Germany, May 8, 1945
Dear Folks:
V-Day. Strange how apathetic the soldiers are toward it. The official announcement has been anti-climax. The captain and I used it for an excuse to get gloriously stinko last night with some major from a finance office on our monthly liquor ration. When we heard the news last night Captain Remley unfurled a huge Nazi Victory flag and hung it from our hotel window just to see the civilian reaction. There wasn't much. One said "Nix, nix, no good, kaput" but that's all.

I think all of us have our attention drawn to the Pacific too much to greet VE Day with the enthusiasm that you would expect. VJ [Victory over Japan] Day will be the one.

I was just thinking how few blonde blue-eyed German men of the type Hitler called typical I've seen. I suppose they are dead. All but those who are prisoners in England or the States. A day or two ago I was in Nürnberg, which was the very heart of Nazi ideology. It is laid flat as are practically all of Germany's large cities. Germany really is "Kaput" this time.

What the damn fools wanted to hang on so long for is a mystery. I know a town about the size of Peru, Indiana or Napoleon, Ohio, that was practically untouched by war two weeks ago. Now it is just a pile of rubble with more than a thousand stinking bodies under the heaps of blasted brick and stone. If one generation is capable of taking a lesson from another, these people may think twice before setting the world on fire again a quarter of a century from now....

I see it is nearly supper time, so I'll end this rambling missile and eat. Because I'm hungry.
Love, Bill

HOWEVER ANTICLIMATIC Bill judged V-E Day to be, he was not to be denied a celebration. He soon was sent to Domazlice, a small city in western Czechoslovakia that Third Army troops recently had freed and where Czech citizens – having endured Nazi rule since 1938 – raucously greeted their American liberators. The welcome lasted for several days and included parades, pageants, and dances. Bill savored every minute of the rollicking reception and, as he would write his parents, he swelled with "a little bit of pride" in having done his part, however small, in freeing his appreciative hosts from Nazi oppression.

Somewhere in Czhko-Slavacia, 13 May, 1945.
Dear Folks:
The name of the country is unquestionably misspelled, but I think you can get the idea. We have an absolutely unbelievable set-up. We are temporarily relieved of all duty and have been sent over here solely to permit fraternization with civilians during the rest period. We officers are living in a fine hotel, each with his separate room. The men are quartered in two other hotels. Our mess is set up in one of them. We have a fine dining room with music by a seven piece orchestra during dinner and supper. Supper is followed by a dance until 9 PM each night.

We are in a town just a little bigger than Auburn, and the people have been wonderful. When our convoy arrived, thousands of them lined the streets. Elements of the Czhk Army formed an honor guard and there was speech making. – All for a single company of Military Police.

Last night a big dance was thrown for us and AMG [Allied Military Government] lifted the civilian curfew. I guess it lasted all night (I didn't). About thirty women attended in the National dress and gave exhibitions of the folk dances. It was very, very colorful. It was the second dance here in seven years – the first was held when the first allied troops came through.

This morning they put on a huge pageant for us – their first in eight years. Thousands of men, women, and children in the national dress from miles around participated – there was much parading and dancing of folk dances in the street. Major Allgier, the battalion commander, was visiting us and accepted the hospitality of the people in an ancient ceremony wherein he had to cut a piece from a loaf of bread, salt it, and then eat it.

The native or national dress I've mentioned above is the most colorful thing you've ever seen. The garments are all hand embroidered, in smashing colors.

This was strictly the stuff of which Paramount Pictorials are made. I doubt very much if in the entire history of American arms so elaborate a demonstration was ever made before for a unit so small as a company. The whole town is a riot of color anyway, with the flags of this country, the U.S., England and Russia flying everywhere.

After the pageant this morning we all attended a mass at the 400 year old church. This, the first I ever attended, was also replete with color. They had a small choir of about thirty voices, that was wonderful – hearing them accompanied by organ and orchestra you might have thought you were listening to top-flight opera.

There are plenty of girls for all of the men – and this old beat up lieutenant has come through with about the cream of the crop. I've been playing two sisters both of whom are choice – I can't make up my mind which to concentrate on!

Their dance orchestra plays mostly American music – except for the demonstrations of folk dances. The one that plays for our mess has three young girl singers who are very good. It is amusing to hear them sing lyrics in the native tongue to American swing.

Our arrangements are made mostly through a peppery little Jew who somehow survived the Nazi occupation, and who lived in Chicago for seven years. His mixture of American and local idiom in his speech is something to hear, but he has been going on the run for us practically 24 hours a day to have everything run smoothly, to see that we never run out of beer, etc. This beer is the best I've had since I left the States.

All of my conversation with my girl friends is carried on in German, as they speak no English at all. My German is very limited, but we can still carry on considerable talk, so long as we don't try to express an abstract idea.

These people have had a long and interesting history. And I suppose no event will loom larger in it than their liberation from the Nazi yolk [sic]. During the ceremonies this morning I couldn't but feel a little bit of pride in having played even a very small and remote part in it.

I think you'll agree with me that the war is giving me a pretty complete tour of Europe. I have, several days ago, several times crossed the river that inspired Strauss – the Beautiful Blue Danube. (It was muddy when I saw it, and not blue at all.)

I received the box with the hair oil, chocolates and nuts in good condition. Many thanks. Love, Bill

Citizens of Domazlice, Czechoslovakia, welcome and thank U.S. soldiers with the 512th MP Battalion.

Germany

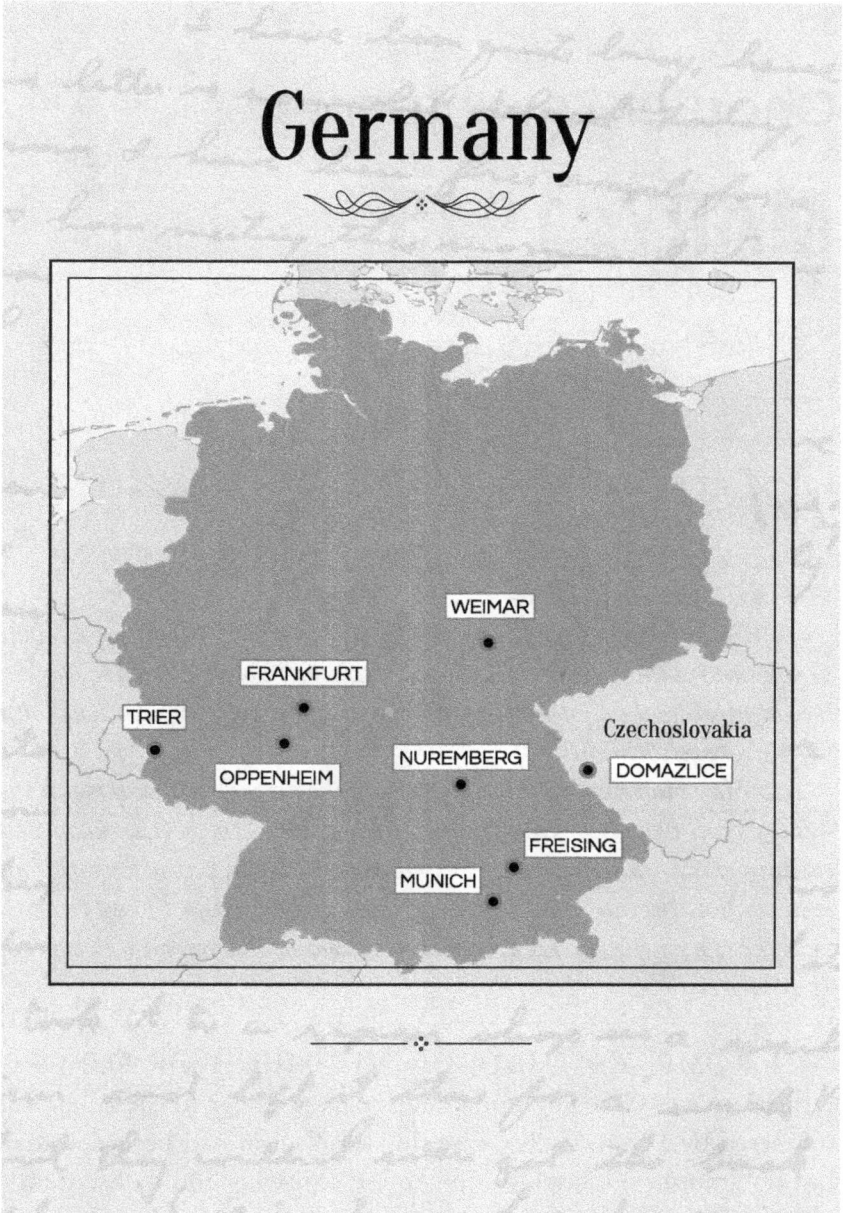

When censorship was relaxed, Bill wrote his parents about having spent time in the German cities listed above and in Czechoslovakia, where he and his battalion were welcomed as liberators at the war's end.

Chapter Seventeen
MARY: 1945

*M**AY 9, 1945*
ROME, ITALY

Dearest Mother & Dad –
... We are on our third day of celebration (of V-E Day) and by now, as you can imagine we are all more or less worn down. We have worked like mad, since the first inkling of news, making our preparations for a big Victory celebration.
Yesterday morning we spent putting up the decorations we have made – flags of all the nations and murals for the walls. In the afternoon and evening was a dance complete with a grand march, paper ribbons and even confetti that we made ourselves. Everything was very gay but still with the sobering influence of still having another enemy and Theatre of War to overcome. . . .

IN ROME, AS THROUGHOUT MUCH OF EUROPE, jubilation over Germany's unconditional surrender to the Allies was tempered by a stark reality. Fascism and Nazism had been defeated, but no amount of dancing and confetti-throwing could obscure the obvious: The world was not yet at peace; Japanese Imperialism still had to be vanquished.

Even so, Mary Brandon began her May 9 letter, one day after the "official" V-E Day and one week after German forces surrendered in Italy, on a wholly upbeat note. To her parents, she declared, "At last, I can say what you must have known all along that I am in Rome and have been since last June 10th ... Censorship is lifted and I will be able to tell you many things that have been restricted before."

Embracing her unmuzzling, Mary immediately launched into a story both timely and personal. Dr. G. Bromley Oxnam, president of DePauw University when Mary was a student there, had traveled recently to Rome in his new capacity as American Bishop in the Methodist Episcopal Church. Days earlier, Mary had managed to reconnect with him, as her May 9 letter explained:

Dr. Oxnam is in Rome on his way to Greece – Sunday he gave the sermon in one of the down town American churches. It was wonderful hearing him again. He looks and speaks exactly the same. I talked to him after the service – He said he remembered me but I'm sure he said it the same way that I say I recognize some of the thousands of soldiers I have met since being here.

Dr. Oxnam, c. early 1930s

After noting that Bromley's son was a chaplain stationed at Caserta, Mary then relayed another reunion story, this involving two colleagues who had just completed a nerve-jangling road trip.

Fritzie Houghland [sic] and Liz Elliott, two of our old friends of Capri and Washington [D.C.] days, stopped in to see us for a few minutes last night. They are Club-mobile girls attached to the 3rd Division. They drove by themselves in a jeep down from Austria. Some of the little towns they passed through were still occupied by the Germans. No one had had the chance yet to make them surrender their arms. They said they weren't sure whether they would get a bullet in their back or not. They had driven solidly for two days and a night and I've never seen anything more bedraggled or <u>smellier</u>. They have certainly seen a lot of Europe and much of this war. They even went to one of the German prisons and said that things are quite as bad as everyone says and reads.

Before concluding her May 9 letter, Mary mentioned that the many troops who had surged north in April soon would make their way back to the Rest Center: "Of course, for the last few weeks ever since the push started we have had no combat men, only rear area groups, but now with hostilities ended [the army] will be sending them back again for leave either before going home or on their way to the Pacific." As her letter also noted, Mary and coworkers fully expected "to get very busy here again."

Doc on beach outside Rome.

But truckloads of soldiers did not immediately return; the Rest Center, in turn, continued to experience a lull. With little choice but to make the best of her leisure time, Mary played extra rounds of golf and spent one afternoon with Doc at nearby Lido Beach, where his little dog Stubs got her "first taste of salt water and I'm afraid she didn't like it as much as we did." During the lull, Mary also vacationed on the Isle of Capri, traveling there with Doc sometime after May 14. How long her trip lasted isn't known, but Mary was back in Rome by month's end.

May 28, 1945

Dearest Mother & Dad –

The long absence in writing is due to my vacation. You know, one can't possibly do the usual things on a vacation so I didn't write a line – I hope you will forgive me.

The Doc and I went to Capri. I was so eager to go back and find out if the Island still had the fascination for me that it held when I was first there. It was every bit as beautiful as I thought and we had a wonderful time, climbing the mountains, swimming in the most azure water one could imagine. There is a cave there that I visited before but was unable to describe to you then called the "Blue Grotto." It is approached in a Row Boat and one must lie down in the boat to enter. A good wave washes the small boat into the cave where the light enters from under the water changing the whole cavern into an eerie blue. The water looks like blue fire and as the oars splash across the water it looks as if an iridescent blue rain of fire is falling. Another day we climbed the highest mountain to the site where Tiberius, an old Roman Emperor, had his castle. The ruins are still there with the walls standing enough to show its palatial rooms and dining halls. At one point on the hill is a sheer drop to the sea where he is supposed to have pushed his political enemies. The little towns on the Island are so quaint and unique. Some of the streets are so narrow that one can touch the buildings on both sides. We took some good pictures. I hope they turn out well....

Since I have several more days of leave accumulated Fay[e] Smith, our director wants me to go with [colleague] Eileen on a little jaunt. Right now we are trying to get a Jeep and will head for Northern Italy – we'd like to see Lake Como and Venice. I think perhaps we will be leaving in a week or two.

I'm sorry I've not written to Annie. Twice before my vacation I started letters to her but was interrupted both times so gave up the attempt. Tell her not to lose faith in me – I will get around to it one of these days....

Must stop and at least act like I'm busy. We've not much work these days. Do be good and remember I send all my love. Oh yes, I bought some Flower seeds in Capri for your garden next summer. Everything else was so expensive I couldn't afford to buy a thing.

Mary with her easy smile

Days after that letter's posting, the calendar jumped to June, and Mary continued to wait for the predicted swell of soldiers. As snack bar manager, she also wrestled with problems largely out of her control. "The Snack Bar isn't doing too well of late," she wrote home on June 4. "We are having a terrific sugar shortage which limits our out-put of cookies and cakes (I'm being bothered, Eileen is trying to take my picture) and only one teaspoon for a cup of coffee. Too, the Ice Cream factory has been closed and then the out-door Festival hasn't helped any. However, we are expecting a large group of 5th Army men in this week so business may pick up again."

The festival Mary referenced had begun just days earlier and was to last all summer. Organized by the army's Special Services branch, it featured stage shows, dance bands, and carnival-style games. The "action" began near the Rest Center's entrance and extended across a vast open space that, with censorship lifted, Mary was free to describe at length. She did so enthusiastically in her June 4 letter, adding details about the entire campus and its history.

Dearest Mother & Dad –

... We've had a most exciting week with the opening of a summer festival. There is a built-in stage for U.S.O. shows and the dance orchestra. It is arranged in cabaret style with tables and chairs[,] and booths on either side for Rifle ranges, pin ball machines, photographers shops – the only booths lacking are blanket and hamburger stands. The whole business is placed in an area between a giant marble obelisk constructed by Mussolini and with his name on it[,] and a huge Marble ball fountain. The booths are placed between great blocks of marble on all of which were inscribed excerpts from Mussolini's speeches. To really understand the whole Rest Center and its layout I can now tell you what this place was before. It was called the Mussolini Forum and was a school for Fascist youth. They were instructed in Music, sports at the same time with Fascist doctrines and in this beautiful place and its wonderful buildings a young boy was bound to be impressed. The approach to the Rest Center[,] which is now called the "Foro d'Italia" by the Italians[,] is directly across a wonderful expanse of new bridge on the Tiber river.

As one crosses the bridge the buildings are on both the left and right of the marble obelisk I have already described. Sitting here on our terrace which is the farther building to the right of the obelisk I can see the bridge, the apartments across the river, if I lean out far enough on my right is the stupendous dome of Saint Peters and on the left the smoky blue mountains in the distance. This is truly a beautiful city. But to get back to the festival – the opening was Friday night [June 1] complete with the official opening by General McNarney and the crowning of a Wac [Women's Army Corps] queen. We had a dinner for the official

Mary on the rooftop terrace

party before with the Doc in charge. It kept him sweating to know which General to put where, but everything went off perfectly....
All my Love, Mary

Mary wasn't alone in highlighting the festival's opening. The June 3 edition of *The Stars And Stripes* devoted a page to the Friday night activities, with a headline that trumpeted "Lots Of Fun For Everybody" and with photographs showing an overview of the stage, a female bass fiddler performing before a crowd of GIs and their dates, and a "prominent figure" wheeling around the dance floor. The figure was General Joseph T. McNarney, the army's top brass in the Mediterranean Theater who within months would succeed General Eisenhower as overall commander in Europe.

In a hastily written V-Mail a few days later, Mary alluded to a different type of fun. She informed her mother that she and colleague Eileen McEown were finalizing plans for their much-anticipated "jaunt" north of Rome. Mary also shared two starkly contrasting images – that of nature's bounty, as evidenced by fresh fruit and flowers, and the pinched, if not dire, circumstances of a local family.

June 6, 1945
Dearest Mother –
I've just had your letter telling me you have received the hats. I'm so glad you got them and like them too.

The seasons here are so much more advanced than at home. All ready, the grain has been cut, we are having bouquets of zinnias and this morning I had my first peach of the year. The fruit is wonderful, huge red sweet cherries and lemons as big as melons. This noon I am going to see a boy who works in the Snack Bar who hurt his foot the other day. He is just a young boy, 14 years, but doing a man's work. He has a sick father and many brothers and sisters. I'm taking him my candy rations for the past few weeks and some money for the poor little fellow.

Eileen and I are busy making plans for our trip next week, pouring over maps and counting miles. We've decided on Lake Como, Verona and Venice. So much for now. Will write more later.

Mary followed up on June 12, confirming that her trip would begin the next morning and that she and Eileen were traveling light: "We're not taking any fancy clothes just mostly clean underwear, plenty of cold cream and sun-tan oil for we have no top on the jeep, not much money but plenty of camera film." Shifting the letter's focus, Mary told her parents that "I think of . . . all of you a thousand times a day and am counting the weeks until I see you all again." Addressing Winnie directly, Mary then brought up a delicate matter – her desire to keep working for the Red Cross postwar: "Mother, my job with Red Cross isn't finished. I feel that there is still much to do and the visit [to Auburn] you will have to consider as only a furlough from the Army. I won't know where they will want to send me next . . . ."

What prompted Mary to speak frankly at that moment isn't clear. She simply may have decided it was time to prepare her parents for her next career step. She had informed them weeks earlier that she filed paperwork to return to the States in September, but she had avoided offering specifics. Her June 12 letter made clear that she wished to remain employed by the Red Cross and that any visit to Auburn would be short-term – or so she hoped.

MARY AND EILEEN PACKED in as much sightseeing and socializing as they could in the second half of June. They traveled on roads and highways over which Allied troops had moved, witnessing for themselves the destruction and death the war had wrought. They likewise encountered military personnel not seen in months, including soldiers with a Special Services unit that had performed at Caserta and Rome, with one of the soldiers none other than Joyce Gregory's fiancé, Bill. Near their trip's end, they even saw Ardith Spalding, who had gone home to Utah in February, leaving Mary to take over snack bar operations. Ardith had returned in May to new duties in Pisa, where she was in close company with her beau, Bert Arnberg.

Amid all the reconnecting, the two travelers also absorbed recent history. They stopped at picturesque Lake Garda, where Mussolini had set up his puppet government in a neo-Gothic villa, only to abandon it as the U.S. Fifth Army approached in the war's final days. They visited the gas station in Milan where the bodies of the Fascist dictator and his mistress had been ignominiously displayed. They traveled along Italy's northwest coast where cliffs still bore white paint spelling the disgraced strongman's title.

At journey's end, Mary shared her travelogue with her family, a day-by-day account packed with information. Among the details Mary shared was a telling clue about Italy's still-suffering economy. A bar of soap, in some places and under some circumstances, was worth its weight in gold.

Thursday, June 27, Rome
Dearest Mother & Dad –
We've been so busy since our return Sunday night from our trip that I've just not had a minute to get a letter off to you. Such a wonderful and beautiful trip we had, I feel so inadequate to try to describe it to you. We were gone twelve days and each one of them filled with beauty and pleasure. Since I owe Annie a letter too perhaps I shall tell you of the first six days and Anne the last six, then you two will have to get together to complete our trip by Jeep through Northern Italy. We took roll after roll of pictures which will help to show you some of the wonders we have seen.

June 13 – Wednesday.
Left the Rest Center in Rome at 9:00 A.M. We drove on Highway 2 to Florence on which still contains the broken wrecks of vehicles left from the German retreat last summer. Along this road are many American Military cemeteries, all neatly planned and worked in contrast to a grave here and there, some even crudely covered with stones which mark the graves of the Germans. We ate a picnic lunch which had been packed for us at the Rest Center beside a little stream under an olive tree.

In Florence we stopped only for gas (supplied entirely free by the army) and drove on to Montecatini, a small resort town filled with Hotels. In peace time the town compared to our White Sulphur Springs where people go to drink Sulphur Water. It has been used by the Army all winter and spring as a Rest Center. It was here that we saw again many old friends of mine who are in the 21st Special Service Co. They were with us in Caserta and then in Rome. They are the ones who give special stage shows and Bill, Joyce's beau, is the star of the show. It was his last night's performance for he was to leave the next day to join Joyce in New York and be married. Thanks to their hospitality we stayed in their hotel and left the next morning for Verona.

June 14 – Thursday.

We drove over one of the highly contested roads of the war, Highway 64, to Bologna where we stopped for lunch. The mountains are very high before the city but beyond fall immediately into the fertile and beautiful Po Valley. We arrived in Verona, which is badly shattered, in time for dinner at the Red Cross billets where we spent the night. Before going to bed we drove out beyond the river to the camp of a Trucking outfit that had been stationed with us for several months. The boys were lonely and very glad to see us again. We were extremely lucky to have found them for we stopped in to see them again on our way home from Venice when we were having our only trouble with the Jeep.

June 15 – Friday.

We started for Venice in the morning over a good and one of the only flat roads we found. We arrived in the outskirts of the city about noon, parked our car in a garage and took a Military Ferry into the city, there are no vehicles of any kind, of course, because every street is a canal. We stayed in a British Hotel which was very comfortable for a startling price of 30 lire a day which included three meals and tea in the afternoon, if we wanted it. After dinner we walked about for a bit of exploring with no idea where we were going, a turn left here and right there until we came into the Piazza of St. Marks, the most astonishingly beautiful square I have ever seen. It is entirely surrounded by high arcaded buildings and at the far end the brilliant Byzantine Cathedral of St. Marks. The square was filled with people, all out for their evening walks and literally thousands of pigeons flying about or peacefully eating out of the hands of the children. The bell tower and the Doges Palace just beyond the square are too much for my feeble description but we got some good pictures which I will be able to show you soon.

June 16th – Saturday.

In the morning we poked around in the shops, looked at beautiful expensive Venetian lace and glass all beyond our poor pocket books, however I did pick up a few doilies for you and a collar for me and some rings for friends at home. In the afternoon we took a Gondola and went to another Island where the famous glass is made. I could have had a beautiful hand painted bottle if I'd only had some soap with me. The woman who was making it wanted to trade but my only legal tender was in lires which I gave a few for a little piece of glass instead. In the *evening after a dance at the hotel we rode in gondolas to cool off a bit with musicians in the same boat with us. There was a moon, the night was soft and the music made it just as romantic as you have ever read that Venice could be. As we drifted down the Grand Canal we noticed a large Gondola in the middle entirely covered with lights and surrounded by other Gondolas that were all listening to the music from it. I suppose it was their idea of a Saturday night band concert, a little more beautiful and romantic than the Auburn variety, I think.*

June 17th – Sunday.

We left Venice about 8:30 A.M. for Verona again. The little old Jeep would cough and spit when we went under 40 M.P.H. and if we stopped it was impossible to start it again. We hailed another Jeep who pushed us and stayed behind us until we reached the Trucking Company where they tightened the points and stopped our only car trouble of the entire trip. They also gave us lunch and we started out again for Lake Garda and Fifth Army Headquarters. We found the Red Cross there which is a Beach Club and had a dip in the beautiful lake. Believe me, it was most refreshing after our hot dusty ride. After dinner at the Fifth Army Mess, which incidentally was the best dinner I've had since I left home, (a half a head of lettuce with Russian dressing, hot rolls, and chocolate sundaes were the high lights) we were taking a little drive to look about and spotted another of our old friends Lt. [Edward S. Kubisek] who had been with the Rest Center. He is under Lt. Col. [Samuel M.] Fletcher, another of our old friends, in planning and executing all the Fifth Army Hotels in Italy. Kuby called ahead to Milan and engaged the best room in the Hotel for us and we saw Col. Fletcher again in Alassio where he made sure we were well taken care of. We have been so lucky everyone doubled over backwards to be good to us and we certainly appreciated it.

June 18th – Monday.

After breakfast Kuby, Eileen and I drove up to the top of the Lake so we could see a project the Germans had been working on during the war. The road was a beautiful one which was built through miles and miles of tunnels cut into the heavy rock. In the tunnels themselves (there were 65 of them) the Germans had an airplane motor factory. The machines, the lathes and motors are still there on one side of the road where they were completely protected from our Bombers. After dropping Kuby and having lunch we went on to Milan and arrived in time for dinner. They were expecting us at the Hotel, thanks to Kuby and we did have a wonderful room. In the evening with the sun shining golden on the beautiful Gothic Cathedral we got some wonderful pictures of Il Domo. Its stone spires are fine and delicate and with the sun looked like a heavenly design of golden lace. The famous stained glass windows have been removed but its greatest beauty is in its spires and statues which are all intact.

This takes me to the end of half of our holiday – so I shall go on with the rest to Annie. So happy to hear about [next door neighbor] Marian [Kaylor]'s new brother. I wish I were there to help bring him up, but I'll be seeing him soon. I do hope you are both well and don't overdo when you have your summer visitors.

Two days later, Mary penned as promised the remaining account of her trip.

Rome, Italy, June 29, 1945
Dearest Annie, George & Bud –
I have written Mother and Dad the first six days of our vacation and shall go on with the last six for you. I hope you can get together, for the whole thing was twelve days of the most wonderful trip possible. I forgot to say that on our way to Florence we stopped in Siena and bought Geo. a pipe in the factory where the famous Siena briars are made. I don't know much about pipes but a Major who was there buying pipes too helped me pick it out – so if you don't like it, Georgie, you will have to blame the unknown Major.

Tuesday – June 19th, Milan
This is a city more like an American one. The people are well dressed and traffic is similar to that at home. But we noticed as we shopped in the morning that the people stared at us with a look of more than curiosity in their eyes. It gave us a most strange feeling. Prices are much cheaper than Rome and I was able to buy a silver plate for one of the boys in Doc's dispensary who was married the Saturday before for $10.00 while in Rome the same thing would have been about $50.00. In the afternoon we found the square where Mussolini and his gang were displayed and took a picture of the abandoned filling station where their names are printed above the girders where they hung by their heels. We took our swimming suits and drove up to Lake Como expecting a nice dip. The

lake is beautiful but nothing compared to Lake Garda where we stayed on Sunday, and is so completely built up that we couldn't find a single spot to swim and had to be content to dip our hot feet in the water. We came back for a few hot games of Cribbage and to bed.

Wed. – June 20th

We drove over one of Mussolini's prize roads to Genoa. The first part of the way is through the valley where most of the bridges are still blown – one Bailey Bridge (put together with steel Girders like a Tinker Toy) is called the Ernie Pyle Bridge, in Memory of the Dough Boys Friend and another pontoon variety. But in the mountains before Genoa the road is excellent and still advertising Duce, Duce, Duce, written in white paint on all of the cliffs. The road from Genoa on up the coast is the most scenic I've ever witnessed. It followed the coast all the way to France, over hair pin curves, with the ocean on one side and the mountains on the other, and through fragrant pine groves, one of which we stopped to eat [our] K-Ration lunch.

The first person we saw in Alassio was Colonel Fletcher when we arrived late in the afternoon and he made sure we had a good place to stay. This is a perfectly marvelous little town on the Italian Riviera. The whole place is being used for a Rest Center for 5th Army troops, where they use all the Hotels and even some of the Villas. There are side walk Cafes and Clubs, Beach Clubs, everything all for the G.I.'s. No officers are allowed in the town except those who are connected with the place like Col. Fletcher.

Eileen and I had a suite of rooms in the Villa (more like a Palace) of the Marquise Farrara. She was young and sweet and most hospitable and we were waited on hands and feet by two of her servants! Maria washed our many dirty clothes and Emilio, our dusty Jeep. We were just a couple of yards from the beach where [we] spent the whole of ---

---Thurs. – June 21st

This day was just about the most fun and relaxing of our whole trip. The minute we stepped on the beach, 6 GI's took us in hand. The breakers were very high and we spent the whole afternoon playing in the waves and returning up to the Beach to drink ice cold Champagne to get the salt taste out of our mouths. Gosh – that was the Life. These kids had spent a hard winter of Combat and were really grateful for our company. We went dancing with them in the evening.

Fri. – June 22nd

We drove on up the Coast to San Remo another Resort town and were then only a few miles from France. We could have gone over on a Red Cross tour and have seen Blenda (remember her?) who is working in Nice, but we decided we had so much fun the day before on the Beach that we would go back to Alassio and do it again. We did, but the waves weren't so high and so we missed half the thrill of it.

Sat. – June 23rd

This hot long day was spent entirely in driving from Alassio back to Leghorn, over a beautiful but hair raising road. We stopped in Pisa and took pictures of the Leaning Tower and on to Leghorn where we spent the night at the Red Cross billets. Here we found too that Ardith and Bert were at Pisa so ---

---Sun. – June 24th

We went back to find Ardith working in a hot outdoor camp (a Staging Area) and had lunch with her before starting back to Rome. We arrived home about 8:30 and I found my room filled with flowers from the Doc who said he missed us no end. Tommy and Bill (our Poker playing friends) were just home too from a trip to Cairo (they brought us some Egyptian Cigarettes and scarabs) and we all talked until late into the night comparing the merits of our trips. The poor Doc [who] had been so lonely with all of his friends away could only add to the conversation the bit of news of Frankie Sinatra's singing here at the Rest Center while we were all gone. We had a wonderful time but it was fun getting back too and I've been busy as a bee since returning picking up the threads of work.

It has taken the entire morning to get these letters off to you and I must stop. My room looks as if a cyclone had gone through it.

Mary's "Ernie Pyle (Bailey) Bridge" reference, which her travelogue cited on June 20, was notable for two reasons. Developed during the war by the British, the Bailey was a portable, pre-fabricated, truss bridge that Allied engineers used, along with pontoon bridges, to quickly replace bombed-out spans. The Bailey played an especially important role in the Italian campaign, where German and Italian armies destroyed bridges as they retreated. By the war's end, the Allies had built more than 3,000 Baileys in Sicily and Italy, with the spans collectively stretching fifty-five miles. As British Field Marshal Montgomery noted in a 1947 tribute, "Bailey Bridging made an immense contribution toward ending World War II."

Also making an important contribution was the syndicated newspaper columnist Ernie Pyle, who embedded himself with military units wherever the action was heaviest, reporting first from North Africa, then Sicily and Italy, then France and eventually the Pacific. Throughout the war, Pyle – a Hoosier from the state's mid-section – described the work and lives of individual soldiers, and in so doing he helped bridge the gap between those serving overseas and those waiting for loved ones to return home. On April 18, a mere two months before Mary penned her travelogue, Pyle was killed by a sniper's bullet during the Battle of Okinawa. That soldiers half a world away would so quickly name a bridge, albeit a temporary one, after him signified how much America – its fighting corps *and* its civilians – loved the gritty foxhole correspondent.

Ernie Pyle (Library of Congress)

WITH HER ITALIAN HOLIDAY BEHIND HER, Mary jumped back into her regular duties at the Rest Center. She was happy to see more soldiers returning to Rome and delighted that she could serve them tastier ice cream. On America's birthday, she stepped away from the snack bar long enough to engage in some swimsuit silliness.

July 9, 1945
Dearest Mother & Dad –
Did you see the eclipse of the sun today? It was so bright here that I could only sneak one little tiny peek and see the eclipse in the after-image. Our weather is right hot now, in fact. I'm writing this with my shoes off and my feet on the cool marble. Marble floors are fine in summer but so cold in winter. We had a wonderful day on the 4th with a Bathing Beauty

Contest at our club in the afternoon. Some of the Italian girls who come to dance wore their suits while the Red Cross gals rented old fashioned suits from a costumers and I'm afraid we rather stole the show. We paraded around the pool, we interspersed between the Bathing Beauty queens. While they were called Miss Napoli, or Miss Roma we called ourselves Miss Podunk, and Fran [Hennessy] and I (for we are the same height) went as the Toonerville Twins. We had some pictures made which should be dillies. In the evening there was a dinner dance complete with fire works shot from the mountain behind the Rest Center.

We have had a lot of boys in the Rest Center lately and our Ice Cream draws them in the Snack Bar like a bunch of flies. It really is very good. The mix comes from home and so it tastes just like that in the States. Yesterday afternoon we took in $145.00 (At a nickel a snack that means quite a few tickets sold). . . . I do hope you are well and getting all you need to eat.

Mary, with a cigarette in her hand and hives on her leg, relaxes at band picnic with an unidentified friend.

In a letter begun that same day, and resumed a week later, Mary wrote to Annie about a picnic that the Red Cross staff arranged for the club's two dance bands. The picnic took place in Tivoli, about twenty miles northeast of Rome, at a 16th-century villa famous for its Renaissance gardens and profusion of fountains. Long a cultural attraction, the Villa d'Este had undergone major restoration after World War I, but Allied bombings in 1944 had caused considerable damage, leaving most of the fountains inoperable. Mary noted as much to Annie, though the place – today a UNESCO World Heritage site – still managed to impress her.

Taking up more pressing business at the letter's end, Mary confided to Annie that the mere thought of resuming her teaching career filled her with dread and even provoked nightmares. Clearly conflicted about her future – and wondering if, for her parent's sake, she should remain in Auburn – Mary sought, per usual, her sister's advice.

Rome, July 9, 1945
Dearest Annie –
I feel as if I'd just had a little visit with you for your July 2 letter arrived after dinner. It's good to hear that Bud is working but he shouldn't complain about "Lettuce Again." I only wish I could have some.

Did you have your usual house full of company on the 4th. We had quite –

July 16
This is as far as I got the other day without being interrupted and now it seems like such a long time ago to tell you about the 4th. Nevertheless we had a good old fashioned day complete with fire works. I've told Mother about it so you have probably read the letter. Last week we had a picnic for the two dance bands who play at our club every day. We went to an abandoned villa in a little town not far from here. The place is one of the most beautiful I've ever seen. The gardens [and] fountains are magnificent. In its hey-day thousands of fountains were in operation but now only a few are working. The whole fountain system ends in a series of pools where the boys went swimming. They really enjoyed themselves, those kids, because we had a wonderful picnic for them.

Faye, our director, found someone (in the Army, of course) who gave her some chickens and had them fried down-town (wonderful crispy brown and more than they could eat). We made a huge kettle of potato salad in the Snack Bar as well as a crate of deviled-eggs, besides we had rolls and potato chips, tomatoes and a whole container of Chocolate Ice Cream. They are still talking about it and want another but it's a pretty big job to make a picnic for seventy-five.

This weather is really waxing itself into the "good old summertime." Besides being hot I have hives and a Ring worm on my leg – merely minor annoyances.

We haven't heard anymore about our request to come home in September but I'm sure it will be granted. They are flying Red Cross people home now so perhaps we will get in on a quick trip. I hope so, for once I get started back I'd like to get there in a hurry. Don't do too much *talking during August so that you can have your voice all rested to give me all the dirt when I get home. Do you think I'd better plan on staying home now and if so – is there <u>anything</u> I can do besides teaching school? You and George give a good look-around for me. I have night-mares about coming home and teaching again. I've realized since I've been gone just how unhappy I was and if it means staying home I've just got to find something different to do.*

Say Hello to everyone for me. Be good, dearie –

Despite her reluctance to return to teaching, Mary, somewhat ironically, reported two days later that she had organized and was supervising a music-themed class for the "boys."

July 18, 1945

Dearest Mother and Dad –

… I have started a little Opera Review at the Club for the boys who wish to attend a performance. We have it three days a week and includes a review of the story with illustrations on the phonograph and by two of the musicians we use ordinarily in the Snack Bar. They are a funny looking pair but can play anything from Swing to Opera so they are very popular with the boys. One doubles on the Marimba and believe it or not, on a musical <u>saw</u> (but the boy's good) and the other one a most peculiar looking gent nearly blind, always squinting through thick lensed glasses plays the piano and accordion. Despite their funny appearance they do play well and know everything from all the operas, so they are a great help to me.

I have gone to several of the operas last winter and spring and people tell me who have seen opera in New York that the staging and scenery are better here. This summer however, because of the heat, the performances are being given out-doors in a most interesting and novel place, the ancient ruins of the Baths of Caracalla. Here the old Romans gathered, to play, bathe and gossip all at the same time. The present stage and seating arrangement are placed right in the ruins which form a perfect amphitheatre.…

A week later, Mary wrote not of opera but of a new furry pal.

Dearest Mother & Dad –

This is a dull morning in the Snack Bar. We are closed down to allow the paint to dry on our counters but will begin "business as usual" this afternoon. Netty, the Scottish lady, is out buying peaches so we can give the boys fresh peach sundaes this afternoon. Sound good? Beginning next month we are to stop charging for the snacks so it will [eliminate] quite a bit of work including Book-keeping.

Eileen and I have a new puppy. She is all black with just a spot of white on her bosom and the tips of her toes. I'm afraid she isn't any special kind – just dog, but she's very cute. She has been having a little tail trouble [so] the Doc cut it off the other night – but she looks much better without that little black garter snake tail wagging behind her. We found her wandering about in the club one day just about to be shooed out by one of the cleaning women. She was filled with fleas, but after a good dusting with flea powder, a bath with G.I. Soap and another dose of powder she hasn't done too much scratching of late.

Have you read that phone calls could be made from Rome to the States? I've been thinking about giving you a ring but don't know whether I'd be able to say much once I got you. I'm afraid the tears would choke me too much, so I guess I'd better wait till I get home.

We are certainly having some hot days here and I'm reading in the paper that you are having a heat wave, too. I believe our Snack Bar is the coolest place in Rome because it is so far underground. The only disadvantage is the dampness, but then you can't have everything.

I had a letter the other day from Ed Kingsbury [an acquaintance from Auburn]. All winter he was stationed near Leghorn which isn't too far from here but is [now] at Bari, way down near the heel, however he said he might be able to fly up to Rome sometime to see me. He told me he has a daughter he has never seen.

Anne tells me that Brother [Charles] has been to see you. I know what a nice visit you must have had. I do hope you are well and not minding the heat too much....

Familiar topics – the stifling heat, her "peppy" puppy – filled a letter Mary wrote her family eleven days later. Included was a fresh concern she tried to articulate: "I am having such a mixed feeling of emotions these days – now that coming home is drawing near. I'm most anxious to see you all but sorry too, to be leaving so many good friends here. We've all been through a lot together and it's hard to think of never seeing many of them again, but, that's life, isn't it."

AT 1:16 A.M. ROMAN TIME on August 6, 1945, a U.S. B-29 Superfortress dropped a nearly 10,000-pound bomb over Hiroshima, Japan. Three days later, a second atomic bomb was detonated over the city of Nagasaki, making Japanese surrender all but certain – as indeed it was on August 15 when Hirohito, that island nation's emperor, told his subjects by radio that the war was over.

The Japanese foreign minister signs the surrender document aboard the U.S.S. Missouri on Sept. 2, 1945. (Library of Congress)

The official surrender-signing ceremony would take place a few weeks later aboard the U.S. battleship *Missouri* anchored in Tokyo Bay. But as news of the nuclear explosions grabbed the world's attention, Mary – six thousand miles away from the devastation in Japan – received a letter from her father, something that pleased her immensely given that he rarely wrote. Not surprisingly, her letter back to him mentioned the powerful, and "horrible," new weapon.

August 13, 1945
Dearest Pappa –
Well you <u>did</u> surprise me and I <u>did</u> almost faint to have a letter from you. It seems awfully good and I was so proud and pleased. I know you think of me but it is hard to write letters, isn't it?

We are all in a flurry of anticipation around here as everyone must be the whole world over. No one, of course, can be happier than most of the boys we have around here as they have been "sweating out" (as the Army calls it) going home only to be sent to the Pacific. I'm only sorry though that the surrender had to come as a climax to this horrible atomic bomb. I feel that we may be sorry some day our scientists ever discovered such power.

Yesterday I packed up a few trinkets I've had around my room and expect to send them off this morning. I hope they reach home safely for most of them are breakable. I still have more to send but will wait a few days until I can find another box.

I still don't know the exact date of my departure and think I may wait now until October in order to get a trip into Switzerland next month. They are sending excursions daily for an eight day leave and all the people I have talked to say it is a wonderful trip. They leave by air from here to Milan where they take an electric train thru the mountains to Switzerland. I hate to postpone my homecoming but I know I'll never get back here and feel I should take advantage of it. When could I go to Switzerland again for $35.00 including passage, food and the best hotels?

Our Summer Festival is still very active and we are having bands from the European Theater now. Imagine my surprise to see Meredith Van Zile Saturday in the Snack Bar. He is playing in the band that is here at present. You may not remember him but Anne and George will for he and his wife lived in the other half of their apartment. He seemed well and felt a wonderful relief to be playing in a band after going thru combat.

I do hope you are both well and I'll be seeing you soon.
Love, Mary

Eight days later, Mary confirmed that she had booked her trip to Switzerland. She also pegged October as the date for her return to Auburn, saying she hoped her homecoming would entitle her to longed-for foods and leisurely family drives. On a more serious note, she urged her parents to "please be patient" as she adjusted to a "future that has nothing planned in it."

August 22, 1945

Dearest Mother and Dad –

Well the time is really growing short now, although I've heard nothing definite about when I'm to leave. The word will probably come one day and I shall have to be ready to leave the next.

I do know that I am going to Switzerland next week for 8 days and it will be any time after I return from the trip. October should find me in Auburn Indiana after 26 months away from home. There are going to be some things I want to eat, like cherry pie, a glass of ice cold milk and a real baked potato. Do you think your ration card could hold for a big family dinner[?]

I've read that the gas rationing has been lifted so we'll be able to do a little tooting about. Then tell Bud to get my golf clubs all slicked up and we'll have some golf games. That baby, too, is going [to] have to be played with as well as making the acquaintance of his sister [Marian] all over again [another reference to the neighbor family, the Kaylors].

I may feel pretty restless and rather lost for awhile so please be patient with me. It's hard to think of a future that has nothing planned in it.

We have so many little mice in our Supply Room in the Snack Bar that yesterday I borrowed from Sgt. Lee (the Mess Sgt in one of the buildings) his mother cat and four kittens. We can't get regular mouse traps but she is supposed to be better than six of them anyway. The kittens are darling – young enough to be playful but not old enough to catch mice.

I'll write again before leaving for Switzerland. I may know a little more then.

All my Love, Mary

Making the most of what remained of her time in Rome, Mary spent the following evening in Doc's company. Writing Annie the next day, Mary reported that he also was to return home soon. Noticeably absent from the letter was any sign of sentimentality, suggesting that Mary wished, for the time being at least, to keep her true feelings about Doc to herself.

August 24, 1945
Dearest Annie –
... Last night Doc and I had another fling at the opera. He's not much of a fan but it was his suggestion last night, perhaps because it's our last chance. He probably will be gone by the time I get back from Switzerland. The operas in summer are held out doors in the ruins of the old Roman Baths of Caracalla. Great high arches from the old buildings form the immense stage. It's truly beautiful sitting out there under the stars and a bright moon. Lucky there was one last night for the lights failed for awhile and threw all the Italians into a panic. We had a little Fiat from the Rest Center motor pool waiting for us but that was about all the good it did us for after going about a block we had a flat tire. And believe me that's not like having a flat tire at home where you can drive into a filling station to have it fixed. Since the Fiats use Jeep tires they are too small to carry a spare [so] we had to walk about a mile to Rome Area Command to a telephone (which incidentally is across the square from the famous Mussolini balcony). A British sergeant gave us tea while we waited for an hour until some help could come from the Rest Center.

It's awfully hard these days keeping my mind on my work and I'll be awfully glad to get started home. Get Bud to have those clubs all polished for a game of golf. And why don't you play, too. Are you making plans for building your new house? Well, let's get at it.

All my Love, Annie, Mary

MARY DEPARTED FOR THE SWISS ALPS on Tuesday, August 28. When she wrote home again on September 7, her alpine tour was over, and she was back in Rome, single-mindedly focused on wrapping up loose ends, knowing her return to the States could take place at any time. She had been given the option to depart by plane; she preferred to wait for a ship.

Dearest Mother & Dad –
The tour of Switzerland is over and a beautiful memory. Now it's just a matter of waiting a few days to start home. The Naples office called yesterday to say that I was to come down immediately in order to fly home

but I shied away from that offer. I don't mind a short trip in the air but a solid 18 hours is too much. I may now have to wait for a boat but at any rate it won't be long now. Eileen left the morning I arrived home from Switzerland – she called me last night from Naples to give me a few tips about packing. Every single item must be inventoried, so I'm going to have a busy day beginning my packing.

I know that I will be seeing you soon enough so I won't write you much about the Swiss trip. I didn't get to Berne where your family are from but did go to Geneva and many other smaller but interesting villages in the mountains. The beauty of the country is indescribable but I have some pictures and travel folders to show you. I bought a few presents for all of you but not much for although prices are low we were allowed only $35.00 to take into the country. This was changed for us in Milan to Swiss francs. If I start telling you more I could write all day and I haven't time for that. Start dusting off the old "Welcome Mat"....

A week later, in her last letter from Rome, Mary described tender farewells from coworkers and friends. She also was the recipient of unexpected generosity.

September 15, 1945
Dearest Mother & Dad –
At last, my bags are all packed and I've said most of my Goodbyes and am ready to leave for Naples tomorrow morning. Just how long it will be waiting there I haven't the vaguest notion, it may be a few days or could even be a few weeks but I truthfully hope the time will be short. I shall have to report to Washington before coming home but that will be only a matter of a day or two.

Everyone has been so wonderful to me that it is almost as sad as it was leaving home in the beginning. The Snack Bar people had a surprise party for me the other day. There was a huge cake with the words "Lest you forget us, Miss Mary" on the icing. There was a beautiful corsage of roses and some lovely hand [made] Italian jewelry. Everybody sang and cried and we had a wonderful time.

Then yesterday, the artist [Vladimir] Wolkonsky, the Russian Prince ... invited me to his apartment and presented me when I left with a Red Cross decoration the Czar had given his mother for her work with Red Cross during the Japanese-Russian War. It's very attractive and

I'm most proud to wear it. Even our laundress sent a huge bouquet of gladioli.

We have had a gay festive week. One of our girls was married Wednesday in a beautiful American Church down town. It was a lovely wedding with a reception afterwards at the Rest Center. I have some pictures that I'll be bringing with me. I do hope everyone is well and start getting out that fatted calf. I know there will be some time in Naples so I shall write you again before I leave from there.

All my Love, Mary

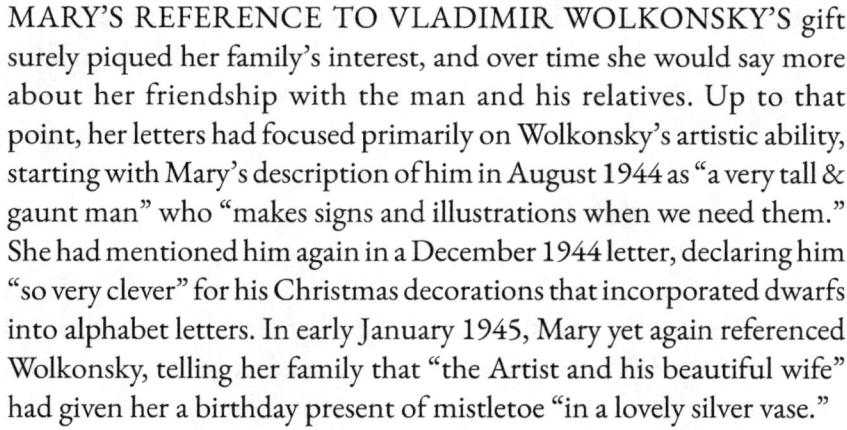

MARY'S REFERENCE TO VLADIMIR WOLKONSKY'S gift surely piqued her family's interest, and over time she would say more about her friendship with the man and his relatives. Up to that point, her letters had focused primarily on Wolkonsky's artistic ability, starting with Mary's description of him in August 1944 as "a very tall & gaunt man" who "makes signs and illustrations when we need them." She had mentioned him again in a December 1944 letter, declaring him "so very clever" for his Christmas decorations that incorporated dwarfs into alphabet letters. In early January 1945, Mary yet again referenced Wolkonsky, telling her family that "the Artist and his beautiful wife" had given her a birthday present of mistletoe "in a lovely silver vase."

It was not until May 1945, after V-E Day, that Mary's family learned the artist was "a Russian prince." The revelation came when Wolkonsky's sister, Mary Paschkoff, wrote Mary's mother. Paschkoff was living outside New York City at the time and wanted the Brandon family to know about Mary's good deeds.

Valley Cottage, N.Y., P.O. Box 315
May 14, 1945
Dear Mrs. [Winnie] Brandon,
I am taking the liberty of writing you though I do not have the pleasure of knowing either you nor your daughter – Miss Mary Brandon, who is at present in Rome. But since the end of last year I have been corresponding with your daughter who in this way has helped me to keep in touch with my brother – Prince Vladimir Wolkonsky.

The other day I received a letter from him, which took months to come, in which he speaks of Miss Brandon's extraordinary kindness and great capacity to help everybody around her. I'm writing primarily at his request and would like to quote from his letter: Tell Mrs. Brandon what kind of a "wonderful being she has brought into the world."

In these days of suffering, selfishness and cruelty – encountering such personalities – revives ones faith in Christianity and the human race. I would like to join my brother in expressing to you my deep gratitude to your daughter for the help she has given us in our troubles.

Sincerely yours, Mary Paschkoff

Two weeks after Paschkoff penned her letter, Mary wrote her parents and mentioned that Annie "told me that you had heard from Mary Paschkoff and were curious about who she is." Mary continued:

She is the sister of our artist that I'm sure I've written you about. He is a Russian prince – his sister and I have written frequently exchanging news of him. The civilian mail is so uncertain and he was anxious to let her know that he was safe but badly in need of clothes and money. I am curious to know what she said to you.

However much Mary knew about Wolkonsky's and Paschkoff's ties to Russian aristocracy, she shared – in that letter – no additional information. What Mary may have pieced together, based on conversations with the artist, is that his father, Alexandr Wolkonsky, had been a Russian military diplomat with postings in Italy and other countries prior to the Bolshevik Revolution (1917-1923). After the revolution, Alexandr and some family members remained in Rome in exile. As Europe braced for war in the 1930s, Mary Paschkoff immigrated to the United State. Vladimir remained on the continent.

In 1992, Mary was asked by Rachel S. Roberts, an Auburn writer, to say more about her friend Vladimir, who – despite his lofty title – barely managed to eke out a living:

I know it all sounds terribly romantic. But it wasn't that way. He was married and he needed a job, so he applied to work at the Red Cross club. Since he was an artist, we put him to work. He painted signs and made props. He did all sorts of creative displays and painted Christmas and Easter scenes on mirrors for us. He was very tall, slim, and had a kind of square face, but he was blond. He had courtly manners, and each time he saw or met me, he would bow stiffly and say, 'Good morning, Miss Mary.'

Mary also recalled, in that same interview, that Vladimir's wife suffered from tuberculosis and was very ill: "Times were hard and medicine scarce, so I gave the Prince my vitamins to give to his wife."

It was against this backdrop, and in the context of an unlikely friendship, that Wolkonsky passed along to Mary a gift given to his mother, Eugenia, from Nicholas II, the last of the Russian czars. Imperial Russia had had a Red Cross "society" since the late 1860s, funded largely by the aristocracy, and Eugenia's contributions during the 1904-1905 Russo-Japanese conflict apparently were enough to earn her a "decoration."

The attractively designed pin, made of enamel and silver, was shaped like a shield with a crown atop. It featured a bright red cross on a white background with Cyrillic characters along the edge spelling out the phrase "Love Your Neighbor as You Love Yourself" in Russian. Mary kept the Prince's gift her entire life and, as she said in her 1992 interview, it helped remind her that she shared a connection with people from "opposite sides of the world," a connection forged in the midst of war's sorrows and suffering.

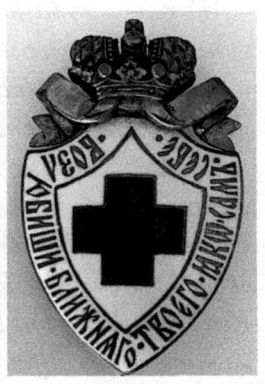
Wolkonsky's gift

The pin remains in her family today.

NOT LONG AFTER HER MID-SEPTEMBER farewell party, Mary wrote home again – this time from Naples, where she waited to board the Italian ship *Vulcania* for her voyage to the United States. Life in Naples had improved since Mary's earlier visits there, but the city still suffered and she found it tolerable only because of Doc's presence. The two had driven down from Rome together, with his overseas departure also imminent. During the next few days, they walked the dirty but rubble-cleared streets, shared meals, and counted down the hours. In her last letter penned from Europe, Mary still betrayed no emotion about separating from Doc.

Sept. 22, 1945, Naples, Italy

Dearest Annie –

We have been in this horrible city nearly a week now but are practically ready to sail. Our boat came in yesterday and our "B" luggage (that for the hold) left this morning. We probably will board tomorrow or the next day. The trip should take from 8 to 10 days and then to Washington for a few days and then to Auburn, Indiana.

Gosh, it just doesn't seem possible yet, and probably won't until I actually set my feet on home soil again.

We have very little to do here. It took only a few hours on the first day to be processed – we still have to receive our Travel Orders and have our money changed – but outside of that there is nothing to do but eat, and sleep and an occasional movie.

The Doc is here too waiting to go home. We drove down together from Rome. He, of course, is in his Replacement Area outside of town. But he comes in every afternoon and we either walk around the filthy streets or play Cribbage or Ping Pong in the Officers' Club, have dinner at the Red Cross Mess, but he must leave at 9:30 for his area so it doesn't give us much Night Life. It is good, though, having him here. There would be nothing to do without him.

We are staying in the same place in Naples (Headquarters) as when we first arrived in Italy but believe me, the picture has changed. All the glass is in the windows, there is water and it's hot, too, although it is turned off at 5:30 P.M. and everyone makes a mad scramble for a bath, the streets are cleaner, the rubble has been piled neatly away and then there isn't that nightly fear of bombings.

We have a beautiful view of the harbor from our windows and it certainly is a contrast too from our first view of the Bay of Naples. The Barrage balloons are gone and the lights at night are wondrously beautiful. Last night there was a full moon peeking over Vesuvius and the little harbor lights twinkled from all the little towns down the coast. Naples is all right at night, but my Gosh, it's awful in day time.

Quite a few of the same people who came over with me are going home too. Some I've not seen since we left them on departing and others like Eileen I've seen frequently so it's going to be a pleasant trip, I'm sure. But I'm awfully anxious to be getting home and will be seeing you soon.

All my Love, Mary

Three days later, on September 25, the *Vulcania* sailed from Naples, with Mary among the thousands of American passengers aboard. The diesel-powered luxury liner, which Mussolini's government had used to carry troops to North Africa and which the German navy later commandeered, had since been refitted as an Allied troopship, ready to repatriate uniformed men and women to the United States. Unlike Mary's Atlantic crossing two years earlier, when German submarines prowled the waters, the seas were safe for passage, torpedoes no longer a threat.

As for what transpired during her homeward journey, Mary left no record. But one can imagine the stories she and fellow Red Cross workers traded – about who served the most doughnuts or danced with the most soldiers, who experienced the greatest danger or ventured nearest to battle zones, who was rushing home to a job or a marriage proposal or both.

Conversations also may have drifted to General Eisenhower. Months earlier, on June 18, 1945, he had had kind words for their organization and, by implication, each of them. Addressing a joint session of Congress, he told lawmakers that day that the Red Cross "stands high in [soldiers'] admiration. The Red Cross, with its clubs for recreation, its coffee and doughnuts in the forward areas, its readiness to meet the needs of the well and help minister to the

Mary, left, on the Vulcania's sundeck with a Red Cross colleague.

wounded . . . has often seemed to be the friendly hand of this nation, reaching across the sea to sustain its fighting men."

The shipboard talks and deck mingling ended on October 4. The *Vulcania*, at sea for nine days, steamed into New York Harbor along with ten other troopships, altogether bringing home some 18,500 uniformed service members in that one day at that one port. Although dockworkers were on strike, the president of the International Longshoremen's Association had promised that the labor stoppage would not keep the returnees from disembarking – a promise kept. Joining Mary and her Red Cross colleagues in walking down the *Vulcania's* gangplank were nearly 4,600 troops, including the 486th and 832nd Medical Hospital ship platoons, the 40th Station Hospital, and 547 WACs.

Upon leaving New York, Mary spent some time in Washington D.C., getting "debriefed" by Red Cross officials. From the nation's capital, now a peacetime capital, she headed by train for Auburn. The exact date of her arrival isn't known, though by mid-October she was back under her parents' roof, presumably basking in her family's attention, relaxing in her old bed, and enjoying her favorite foods. As for her recently unpacked bags, an item in the neighboring town's newspaper suggested they would be repacked soon – quite soon.

> *Miss Mary Brandon, who is spending a leave with her parents, Mr. and Mrs. Ora Brandon of 208 East Fifth street, Auburn, after nearly two years of service with the Red Cross overseas, expects to continue in Red Cross work. She will report on Nov. 25 at St. Louis, Mo., to continue recreational work in hospitals for veterans in the United States. – The Garrett Clipper, October 15, 1945*

Chapter Eighteen
BILL: 1945

MAY 6, 1945
No MAN or woman, no matter how long he or she has been in service, overseas or in combat, will be released from the Army if his or her services are required in the war against Japan. . . . In the meantime, don't write home and tell your mother or sweetheart that you'll be home next week or next month. For most of you, it just ain't so.
— Don Williams, Staff Correspondent, The Stars And Stripes

23 May, 1945
Dear Folks:
I suppose you've been wondering how many "points" I have. . . . At present I have three battle participation stars and may get two or three more on the new deal that has just been announced covering the Ardennes, Rhine, & central Germany.
But even that would leave me a couple of points short. So, I guess I won't be in civies for some time.
It's late and I'm tired, so Good Night.
Love, Bill

IN THE AFTERMATH OF V-E DAY, few questions weighed more heavily on the minds of men and women in uniform than that of "What's next?" Would they redeploy to the Pacific for the invasion of Japan? Spend more time in Europe as part of an occupation army? Or might they be released from military service, the GI version of "hitting the jackpot"?

The answer hinged on a point system the U.S. War Department devised for reducing troop strength in Europe. Known as the Adjusted Service Rating (ASR) Score, the system awarded soldiers points for their length of service, time spent overseas, battle stars or decorations earned, and the number of dependent children at home. So-called "essential" soldiers, as defined by their duties, were not eligible for immediate release. Neither were soldiers with insufficient points. Of the Army's nearly three million troops in Europe in May 1945, the majority did not have 85 points, the magic number for going home.

Bill Husselman was among those shy of the requisite number. Like most of his colleagues, he had wondered for some time how swiftly demobilization – military parlance for the disbanding of troops – would take place. As early as February 1945, as Allied victory seemed increasingly likely, he had told his parents that "speculation [among soliders] runs high as to what will be done with us after V-E day." Weeks later, when he informed his folks that he was racking up military decorations, he summarized his "gadgets" but said nothing about how they might speed his release:

Incidentally this unit has been awarded the Presidential plaque for Meritorious Service. If I ever get back home I'll be able to wear a lot of gadgets on my uniform – the ETO ribbon with three campaign stars, three overseas service stripes (at least!), the insignia of the Presidential plaque, and probably they'll issue a new ribbon for the Rhine campaign. Look like a Christmas tree, won't I?

Even as he jested, Bill took point-tallying seriously, and by V-E Day he was factoring every star and stripe into his calculations. He was entitled to – and the Army eventually awarded him – 36 points for three years of service, 16 points for 16 months overseas, and 25 points for five battle participation stars (Normandy, Northern France, the Ardennes, the Rhineland, and Central Germany). His total came to 77 points, eight short of the all-important 85. Faced with that reality, he resigned himself to spending more time in uniform and to reminding his parents not to look for him anytime soon. He had used the word "guess" in his May 23 letter, as in "I guess I won't be in civies for some time." By June he was clear-eyed: "Don't count on me getting out of the Army. I wouldn't give two whoops in Hell for my chances."

Reasonably confident that Europe, not Japan, would be his home for the foreseeable future (Third Army had been designated an occupation force), Bill applied in early June for "detail" to the Judge Advocate General's Department. That was the same military branch to which he had sought admittance before becoming an MP officer. He didn't regret having served in the military police; to the contrary, he believed he had made a wise choice given his options at the time. As it turned out, in the war's final months he worked as both an MP officer and as a military prosecutor – namely, as a Trial Judge Advocate of a General Court. Liking the trial work, he decided after V-E Day to pursue more opportunities to sharpen his courtroom skills. On June 10, from his new base in Munich, Germany, he informed his parents that he had formally submitted his JAG application. He also reported that "I am currently at work preparing to try a murder case. I've just returned from a two day trip of nearly 500 miles to interrogate witnesses."

That Bill's legal expertise would be needed in the final months of the war and in the postwar period wasn't surprising. Although the overwhelming majority of Allied troops in Europe conducted themselves honorably, criminal behavior within the ranks was by no means an anomaly. By November 1944, GIs were committing infractions and serious offenses at such a rate that General Eisenhower recorded in his diary that "disciplinary conditions are becoming bad." By December, Eisenhower was telling his subordinates that "the large incidence of crimes such as rape, murder, assault, robbery, housebreaking, etc., continues to cause grave concerns." Those concerns spilled into 1945, not least because of large-scale looting by Allied troops in Germany and the Netherlands. Military authorities meted out justice throughout the war, with accused soldiers subject to trial by court-martial (tens of thousands of courts-martial would be convened), and with guilty servicemen facing a range of sentences – up to years of imprisonment or, in cases of rape, murder or desertion, death by firing squad or public hanging. At least ninety-six U.S. servicemen in the European and Mediterranean theaters were executed for wartime crimes, including Private Eddie Slovik, the only American put to death for desertion – his case, then and now, the only desertion execution since the Civil War.

Bill had no expectation that his application for JAG detail would be approved swiftly; military service had long schooled him in the need for patience. Indeed, in his June 10 letter, he reminded his parents that his request "has to go all the way to Washington, and I couldn't possibly hear... in less than a couple of months." Much to his surprise, however, he was immediately reassigned, though the move was not an official transfer to the department. As he explained in a later letter:

I think they are just making a job for me because they don't want to lose a lawyer whom they can have handy for trial work, etc. when needed. I think it is a definite break in my favor. I'll live quite comfortably – a hotel room all to myself – eat well – dress in a class A uniform, and get back to working in purely legal channels. If the discharge business pans out, all well and good. If not, this may be a good spot to be in for awhile.

The reassignment required Bill to move from southern Germany – where newly promoted four-star General Patton oversaw the region's military occupation – to Reims, France, eighty miles northeast of Paris. Renowned for its majestic Gothic cathedral and for underground caves where champagne fermented, Reims had served as Eisenhower's headquarters in the final months of the war. It was there, in the "war room" of a technical school building, that Germany unconditionally surrendered on May 7. Nine months earlier, Patton's Third Army had liberated Reims in its drive across France, after which the city and its environs became an assembly area for newly arrived and refitted U.S. troops. After V-E Day, Reims became a depot in reverse, a staging area for troops heading home or to the Pacific.

Bill liked his new location. Though Reims had suffered severe damage during World War I – its outskirts still bore signs of "old rusty, rotted down barbed wire entanglements, old caved-in trenches, old shell craters etc."– major rebuilding had taken place between wars, and the city, in Bill's words, had survived the latest conflict "virtually untouched." Its gargantuan cathedral, long the coronation site of French kings, was in Bill's estimation "the most impressive church I've seen in Europe, including Notre Dame de Paris." He likewise was impressed with the city's ancient monuments, including a well-preserved third-century Roman arch. Adding to his pleasure was the staging of live opera. "Last night 'Carmen' was sung here in Reims

– and it was surprisingly good for a provincial town," he wrote home on July 1. Good, too, was the champagne, as noted in another July letter:

> *I went through one of the world's largest champagne plants today – Pommery & Greno, here in Reims. The underground caves where it is aged were made 2000 years ago in the quarrying of chalk rock, probably by the Romans. There are eleven miles of underground passageways, 100 feet under the surface, where the present stock of 10,000,000 bottles is stored and aged. One of the sights was a 16000 gal. keg. After the tour I had two glasses of Pommery 1928 vintage, which is supposed to be about the last word in champagne. . . . I noticed on a souvenir menu they had, that the 1928 vintage was the champagne served at a dinner given some years ago by the President of the French Republic for the King & Queen of England. The best is none too good for me!*

While opera and champagne-sipping proved satisfying, work did not. More precisely, what most frustrated Bill was the *lack* of work. "I am an accomplished loafer, but eight hours a day in an office with absolutely nothing to do is beyond even my capabilities," he wrote home on June 23, just days after arriving in Reims. A week later: "My work is still too light for comfort. I have reviewed the proceedings in a few inferior court cases, processed a few sets of charges, etc., but I'm not busy enough to keep time from growing heavy." He repeated that sentiment on July 6: "I don't have anything to do here and certainly am not earning my pay. We're like a big firm all set up with lots of lawyers and fancy offices – and no business." On July 13, the same: "Business here is still slow. I'm not doing a thing."

Even at month's end, he could report no change. "Here," he wrote on July 30, "I don't do one actual day's work a week, altho I did try several cases last week. The Army surely wastes manpower."

FRUSTRATED AS HE WAS by slow-paced legal work, Bill expressed no desire to return to Germany. There, U.S. soldiers were overseeing the discharge of German POWs, coordinating care for millions of displaced persons, sealing borders to prevent the escape of high-ranking Nazi Party members, and – not least – patrolling the region between American and Soviet occupation zones, necessitated by mounting tensions between the two newly emerged world powers. Assuming he had any interest in those duties, Bill had spent enough time in Germany to know he had seen enough – enough Reich cities reduced to smoldering ruins, enough bridges and other infrastructure blown to smithereens, enough human misery and despair. More than five million German servicemen and 2.4 million civilians had lost their lives in the nearly six years of war, roughly ten percent of the country's prewar population. Put differently, one-third of all German boys born between 1915 and 1924 were dead or missing. Though Bill's reassignment to Reims was less than ideal, he preferred working in France rather than in a country he labeled "kaput."

British Prime Minister Clement Attlee, left, at Potsdam conference with Truman and Stalin. (National Archives)

Moreover, Bill's undemanding work schedule had at least one upside. It gave him time to monitor the still fast-moving international developments. In late July, British Prime Minister Churchill, Soviet Premier Stalin, and President Truman met at Potsdam, outside Berlin, to finalize earlier agreements for administering postwar Germany. While there, Churchill learned he would not retain his post due to his party's defeat in an election, and he was replaced immediately at the conference by Britain's new prime minister, Clement R. Attlee. "It was just announced today about the Labor victory in Britain and the resignation of Churchill," Bill wrote his parents on July 27. "Of the leaders of the powers at the beginning of the war [Roosevelt, Churchill, Stalin], now only Stalin remains."

Potsdam would be a hub for other news, though not all of it immediately made public. Upon arriving at the conference, Truman received word that an atomic bomb test in the New Mexico desert had been successful and, without giving specifics, he discreetly informed Stalin that the United States had developed a powerful new weapon. Also during the conference, three nations – the U.S., Britain, and China – issued a statement warning Japan to surrender unconditionally or else face destruction. Ignoring the warning, Japan fought on, and thus on August 6 a single uranium bomb fell from the belly of the B-29 Superfortress *Enola Gay*, detonating over Hiroshima, killing tens of thousands, and officially ushering in the Atomic Age. On August 9, a day after the Soviet Union declared war on Japan and invaded Manchuria, the U.S. dropped a larger bomb over Nagasaki, annihilating everything within a mile of impact.

"Even I, pessimist that I am, am beginning to see a chance that the war won't last too much longer," Bill wrote his parents that very day, reacting to the momentous news. Unease accompanied his budding optimism, however: "I don't know that I am too enthused about this bomb business. It is O.K. as long as the U.S. is the only country that has it but that won't be for long, I'm afraid. Think what the next war will be like. I'm going to spend that one in DeKalb County."

Six days later, on August 15, President Truman announced Japan's surrender. On August 17, as the military gave soldiers a day off to celebrate victory, Bill wrote home and cautioned his parents against getting their hopes up regarding his return: "I suppose you are wondering how soon you can expect me home now that it is over. I really don't know. Not very soon, I'm afraid. I really think it will be inside of a year though. It takes a long time to get everyone home and I don't have many points."

A week later, Bill again tamped down expectations.

23 Aug. 1945, Reims
Dear Folks:
I just received your letter of the 15th describing the reception of the V.J. [Victory over Japan] news. I can well imagine the excitement that prevailed in America. Soldiers are surprisingly apathetic about such things, altho they were much more demonstrative than they were over V.E. day.

Most of us have no immediate prospects of getting home, which is a sobering factor. I really believe I'll be home within the next several months tho, and that isn't long in comparison with the nearly three years and a half already spent.

I, along with all other officers and soldiers in France, have had quite a substantial increase in pay. The French are going to pay each American stationed here $17.00 per month, you know. I suppose this is to deter the U.S. from revaluing the franc in terms of dollars.

Everybody is getting leaves now. I may take one, probably to Switzerland, one of these days. I haven't applied for one because I really have no desire to go thru the effort of making any more long trips under present travel conditions. Maybe they'll open up Italy for leaves from France. I'd really rather go there – to Rome in particular. I'd like to visit the Ditchfields, but don't think I'd do that as I ought to go somewhere I've never been before.

An officer isn't under the necessity to get his leaves as an enlisted man is to get his furloughs. Whatever leave time you have at separation from the service is given to you as terminal leave. In other words, you are not formally discharged after you go home until your leave is used up, and you continue to draw your pay.

I suppose there will be an awful scramble for commodities as rationing is lifted. How does it feel to say "fill her up" at a filling station?

I'm working on the defense of a robbery case, and should be doing that instead of writing this letter, so I'll close now.

While Bill's overall workload remained light, spurts of legal activity energized him, notably in early August. "Well, I'm a little keyed up now," he wrote home on August 9. "I have just finished defending two field grade officers before a high ranking General Court against the Chief Trial Judge Advocate of the office, and got them both off scot free in a rather bitterly contested law suit. That doesn't happen very often in the rather discouraging business of being defense counsel. We usually get our ears pinned back." A week later he also reported being "pretty busy – out of town the last three days trying cases. Tried five and got two acquittals, so it has been a pretty successful week."

Soon, however, he was back in the doldrums, writing his parents on August 26: "I wish my turn to go home would speed up. Life here is becoming awfully boring. Same old routine, day after day." Two days later, the same refrain: "I am writing this at the office, where I'm having a tough time putting in the day as I haven't anything to do. Just got back from lunch. Have been in the officers' Red Cross Club for an hour listening to my associate defense counsel play the piano, which he does beautifully."

Less than a week later, as Japanese representatives signed a surrender statement aboard the US battleship *Missouri* in Tokyo Bay, marking Sunday, September 2 as the official end of World War II, Bill reported an uptick in office business. "Tomorrow, Labor Day, is a day off but I shan't be able to take advantage of it," he wrote his parents. "I have a number of cases coming up this week, some of more than usual importance, and shall have to spend the day touring the camps in a command car interviewing witnesses." A week later, on September 9, he shared the results of his trial work: "Yesterday I defended an officer charged with burglary. He was found not guilty. Just before that we tried a negro for murder and I was scared that I would lose my 'patient,' but managed to get him off with a life sentence on the theory that he was drunk when he did it. Both cases were difficult to try as they involved the interrogation of French witnesses through an interpreter and I was dead tired when I got back to Reims last night."

The increase in cases continued. "You remember I was complaining some weeks ago about having nothing to do. I'm still complaining, but for the opposite reason. I'm awfully busy now," began his letter of September 16. A week later, on September 23, he reported that he once again had just finished trying five cases, won two of them, and hoped he would not have to try many more. But his schedule remained full, and, at month's end, legal work sent him east of Reims to Metz, the fortress city where – just a year earlier – Third Army had struggled to dislodge German troops.

Metz, France, Date? I've lost track [Postmarked Oct. 1, 1945]
Dear Folks:

I've come to Metz for about 10 days to try cases. Lt. Gergen, the other member of the trial team, and I have a beautiful room in the best hotel in town. There aren't many troops here so we ought to have a pretty good time.

Germans are certainly methodical workers. I was in the room all morning. A couple of P.Ws [prisoners of war] wanted to clean it up so I let them work while I was present. They proceeded slowly and methodically to make the beds, without a wrinkle, to clean the lavatory and sweep and dust everywhere. They work without fanfare but get things done thoroughly and pretty quickly at that. We came here yesterday in a command car. The roads were terribly slippery with mud and once we turned completely around in the road and ended up in the ditch. No damage was done, except to our nerves. The rainy fall season has definitely set in.

I caught a head cold yesterday and don't feel so hot today. It's the first cold I've had in a long, long time.

I had the first Martini I've had in almost two years last night. They have a swell bar here in the hotel, operated by an Officers' Club, where you can get almost anything. It is a fancy cocktail lounge, with the girls who serve the tables decked out in fancy suits. Last night I tried to cure my cold with the soda in Scotch & sodas. It didn't do the cold much good, but it was fun trying!

Gergen and I are about to take a walk to look Metz over, so I'll close now. I have no more information on when I'm likely to start moving West.

Bill never reported the outcome of his trial work in Metz or the number of cases, if any, he litigated there. Instead, he dashed off a letter on October 6 that undoubtedly thrilled his parents: "On receipt of this stop writing because your letters won't reach me anymore. I am on my way home. Don't know how long it will take, but I should make it before Thanksgiving anyway. I am leaving Reims tomorrow."

True to his word, Bill did leave Reims, writing his parents on October 9 that he had arrived in a "repple depot" where he expected to remain a week before proceeding to a staging area close to a shipping port. The repple depot – military shorthand for replacement/redeployment – was a tent camp, likely one of the many that the U.S. Army operated in the vicinity of Reims. As Bill's letter explained, "I am living in a tent again for the first time in a year. Haven't a thing in the world to do. We've been killing some time playing bridge."

His October 9 letter announced other major news, albeit untimely:

By the way I am a 'JAG' now instead of an MP. I had a letter from Gen. Cramer, the J.A.G., informing me that he had approved my application and that orders would issue within the next few days. I hope the orders never catch up with me, but don't think it will affect my release.

I don't think – at least I hope – that no branch will keep an officer from being released who has the critical score.

Exactly when Bill wrote home again isn't clear. His next – and final – letter from Europe bore no date. As for the ever-critical ASR score, he recently had been awarded eight additional points for service between May 12 and September 2, making him fully eligible for discharge and a one-way ticket to Indiana.

Dear Folks:

I am at Camp 'Twenty Grand,' one of the staging area camps for the port of LeHavre, [France] patiently (?) awaiting a ship.

The shipping shortage has caught us, but I really don't think the situation is as black as it is painted in the papers and I think I'll get out of here within the next few days.

I am scheduled to be separated at Camp Atterbury which I believe is about 35 miles east of Indianapolis. If transportation from there is too tough you might get a call to take a trip.

Obviously if you don't hear from me for an unreasonable time you'll know I'm on the high seas.

ON OCTOBER 28, 1945, the USS *General J.C. Breckenridge* departed LeHavre, a major seaport northwest of Paris and a hub through which an estimated three million American troops either entered or left Europe in 1945-1946. The shipping shortage, which Bill's letter referenced, was all too real that autumn. Millions of military personnel – in Europe, Asia, and the Pacific – were eligible for return home but the number of vessels available to transport them was inadequate, this despite the fact that ocean liners, cargo ships, and even warships were being converted to troop carriers.

To what extent, if any, the shortage delayed Bill's departure isn't known. But by October 28, when the *Breckenridge* sailed into the English Channel and out into the Atlantic, Bill was among the 5,187 troops aboard. By then, he had seen enough of Camp Twenty Grand, its distinctive name – and that of other staging camps – reflecting

1940s-era brands of popular American cigarettes. By that October date, too, Bill had heard enough soldier slang, eaten enough army grub, and "killed" enough time. Home is what he wanted, and that's where he was headed.

On Sunday, November 4, after an eight-day journey, the *Breckenridge* arrived in Boston's harbor. After setting foot on American soil, filling out paperwork at a repatriation center, and checking rail schedules, Bill boarded a train that eventually delivered him to Camp Atterbury, southeast of Indianapolis. Established in 1942 as an army combat training base, the camp had since become a center from which enlisted men and officers separated from the military.

Waiting at Atterbury for Bill were his parents, Oak and Blanche, who had motored downstate to escort their son home. On Thursday, November 8, with Bill and his bags in the car and with spirits buoyed, the three returned to Auburn. There, by all accounts, Bill planned to stay put.

Oak and Blanche, 1945

> *Mr. and Mrs. Oak Husselman of east of Auburn went to Camp Atterbury Thursday and were accompanied home by their son, Lt. Wm. H. Husselman, who was released from the army. Lt. Husselman, a former prosecuting attorney of DeKalb county, was in the military service three and a half years and was in Europe 21 months. He will resume the practice of law with his father. – [Auburn] Evening Star, November 8, 1945*

Chapter Nineteen

BILL AND MARY

*M*ORE THAN 56 PERCENT of the 8,300,000 men who were in the army on V-E day will be back in civilian life by Jan. 1, the war department estimated today.
– Wire service, [Auburn] Evening Star, November 20, 1945

LIST OF DISCHARGES RECORDED IN AUBURN:
Total of 232 in DeKalb County Released from Armed Services in November, an Increase of 35 over October
– Headline, [Auburn] Evening Star, December 4, 1945

IN THE AUTUMN OF 1945, as global leaders confronted a raft of political, social, and economic postwar issues, uniformed Americans zeroed in on the personal and practical. Most soon would be civilians again. Out of uniform, what would they do?

For Bill, the question was not particularly vexing. His father, Oak, had kept the family law practice afloat, and Bill – upon his return home that November – slipped back into his "partner" role in the second-floor Husselman & Husselman office above the Auburn State Bank. There, Bill re-immersed himself in real estate law, the firm's specialty, and resumed management of a related business, DeKalb Abstract & Title Company. He also recommitted himself to public service, eventually becoming town attorney for the nearby community of Waterloo and, later, city attorney for Auburn, a position he would retain for twelve years. He also would accept, in due course, an appointment to Auburn's Board of Public Works.

Husselman farmhouse on the Auburn-Butler road

Always at ease around his family, Bill immediately resettled himself on the homestead east of Auburn. There, his mother, Blanche, still raised Leghorn chickens, and his feisty eighty-five-old grandmother, Lydia Cattell, still worked in the garden. The barn had received a fresh coat of paint during Bill's absence, but the modest farmhouse had changed little. Inside, the furnishings and items that had defined the place as home – the stacks of books and the drop-leaf table, the wash tubs and the treadle sewing machine – remained as before.

Oak with his telescope

New to Bill's eyes was the telescope that Oak, an amateur astronomer, had built during the war. New, too, was a black cocker spaniel. Bill's parents initially had named the pooch Ziggy, in memory of the dog their son and his fellow soldiers had adopted in Europe. But Oak and Blanche had rechristened the spaniel when they learned, in a letter from Bill, that the German name had a naughty connotation. Thus Bill was introduced to "Mickey."

Unlike Bill, Mary entered postwar life on less sure footing. The October 15, 1945 account in the *Garrett Clipper*, stating that she would continue her Red Cross work at a St. Louis hospital in late November, was inaccurate, for reasons not entirely clear. What is known is that Mary, having returned only recently to Auburn and having no desire to resume her teaching career, had dashed off a letter on October 15 to American Red Cross Headquarters in Washington, D.C. She soon received the following:

American Red Cross
National Headquarters, Washington 13, D.C.
October 18, 1945
Dear Miss Brandon:
In reply to your letter of October 15, addressed to Mrs. Brookings, we can appreciate your state of restlessness. All of us experience the same lack of adjustment to normal civilian lives. Your family is perfectly justified in that you spend your leave resting.

Regarding your request for hospital recreational work in the Midwestern Area, as soon as your personnel folder is complete we will transmit it to Mrs. Margaret Lewis, who is in charge of domestic assignments, and she will prepare a transcript for the Midwestern Area Office. After their perusal you will undoubtedly hear from them if they have an opening suitable to your talents. This will take a matter of a month or more, so enjoy your rest to the fullest.

We take this opportunity to inform you that your evaluations from your theatre are excellent. It must be gratifying to know that your efforts have been rewarded.

Sincerely yours,
Martha R. Harrold
Personnel Counsellor

Forced to bide her time as she awaited further directives, Mary likely tried to do what the letter instructed, which was to enjoy her rest. Her parents and Annie undoubtedly welcomed the chance to pamper her and to catch her up on family news. Likewise, Mary's many friends – former teaching colleagues, Tri Kappa associates, literary and music chums – no doubt clamored to hear about her adventures and to share local gossip. Among neighbors who visited was the then-teenaged Retha Manon [Butler], who lived across the street and who had spent the war years listening to Winnie Brandon read aloud many of Mary's letters. To Retha's delight, Mary bestowed gifts on family and friends, with the teen receiving a lapel pin shaped as a guitar.

If Mary yearned to hear from wartime acquaintances, she didn't have to wait long. A British ordnance soldier wrote her that October, apologizing for not writing sooner and explaining that he had been hospitalized for three weeks, followed by a month's leave back in England. He had since been reassigned to southern Italy, where he was "miserable" and counting down the days until his release from six years of military service. "I suppose you've called me all you can think of, but honestly I hadn't, haven't and never will forget you and your kindness," began the soldier, whose letter the Red Cross forwarded to Auburn. After addressing a range of topics – from their mutual friends to the scarcity of food and coal in England – the soldier indulged in some postwar editorializing: "All I do hope is that the friendships our blokes formed in the services are not wasted or forgotten . . . It should always be 'WE' won the war now let 'US' win the peace. The <u>whole</u> United Nations!!!" He closed with "Cheerio, Mary, thanks for everything. All the best of luck."

Not long afterwards, postcards and letters from other parts of the country and from overseas began arriving at the Brandon home. In early November, a Red Cross colleague, who had returned to the States with Mary on the *Vulcania*, wrote to say she had been doing some "speechmaking" in her home state of Iowa. In mid-December, an Italian snack bar worker at the U.S. Army Rest Center in Rome wrote to say how much she missed Mary and to report her own misfortune; she had been laid off due to a lack of business. Two weeks later, on Christmas Eve 1945, another Italian snack bar employee confirmed that major staffing changes had taken place:

We have again in the Snack bar a Christmas tree, again St. Nicolaus, but . . . I feel your absence, Miss Ardith's and Miss Eileen's. [Now] in the Bar are working 6 German prisoners instead of our men. You know also that all the evening shift including Netty [the Scottish woman] are no more working? These are all things that have changed the Bar's harmony.

That letter writer, Vittoria de Riso, wished Mary "all what you desire for a happy life. You are good and God will always bless." After apologizing for her limited and fractured English, De Riso concluded with a touching plea: "You remember me, dear Miss Mary, please do not forget me as I love you."

Meanwhile, assuming the Red Cross followed up on Mary's request for reassignment, no record has been found. The organization may have notified Mary that it had no immediate need for her services or no openings suited to her talents. It's possible, too, that Mary turned down a Red Cross offer because the work or the location did not appeal to her. Whatever the case, family obligations consumed Mary's time and weighed heavily on her mind as the weeks went by. Her seventy-nine-year-old father, Ora, had grown more frail, and his lameness – he could barely walk – had become increasingly burdensome on Winnie. At age seventy-four, Winnie battled her own health issues, with migraines still sending her to bed for long stretches.

Annie's health was also problematic. She continued to suffer from diabetes, and her health took a bad turn sometime before Christmas 1945, causing her temporarily to move back into the Brandon home to be cared for by Winnie and Mary. After the holidays, Mary accompanied her sister to St. Louis, where Annie sought additional medical advice. The two stayed at the home of their brother, Charles, a reunion that Winnie celebrated from afar.

"All of you together it must seem nice. Annie tells me how good you all have been to her," Winnie wrote her son on January 27, 1946. While Winnie lamented that her elder daughter had "such an awful afliction [sic]," she told Charles in that same letter how grateful she was that Mary had rejoined the family: "[Annie] and Mary are such lovers. Mary came home just at the right time to take care of Annie." Heaping more praise on the returnee, Winnie reminded Charles that Mary knew her way around the kitchen: "She's some good cook, too. Haven't you tried her out?"

When the St. Louis visit was over and the sisters were back in Auburn, Mary appears to have carried on as before – helping her parents with household chores, visiting with hometown friends, trying to chart a career path. She remained in contact with Red Cross colleagues and received a postcard that winter from Eileen McEown, whose updates on former coworkers may have stirred Mary's wanderlust. Eileen, who was vacationing in California, reported that one colleague already had headed back to Italy. "Guess she had a 'pull' to get back – but then she would!!" quipped Eileen, her cryptic remark suggesting romance.

SOMETIME IN THE LATE WINTER or early spring of 1946, Bill and Mary met for cocktails at the Auburn Hotel, a downtown establishment that doubled as a food-and-drinks gathering spot for the city's business and professional class. In the preceding months, the two likely had met there on other occasions to discuss their overseas experiences and to reminisce about prewar times. They likely also had begun taking stock. Both were in their mid-thirties and single with no immediate prospects for marriage. Both were responsible for the care of aging parents. Both, for better or worse, had longstanding ties and attachments to people in their hometown.

Mary and Bill, July 1946

Thus, according to family lore, Mary got right to the point over cocktails that evening. "Bill," she said, "Don't you think it's about time we got married?" Still reserved, especially in the presence of women, Bill needed no arm-twisting. The pretty girl he had known since his childhood, the vivacious teenager and intelligent young woman he had long admired, was proposing. She was practical; so was he. Their engagement was soon announced.

Down through the years, family members would repeat that story, and Mary and Bill always vouched that it was true. The couple's parents approved of their children's marriage plans, and by late June, Mary's friends were hosting a bridal luncheon at the Auburn Country Club. A month later, on Saturday, July 20, 1946, Bill and Mary exchanged vows. Opting for little fanfare, the couple chose to be married in the neighboring community of Butler, in the parsonage of the Rev. George Hubbartt, a Methodist minister who formerly had served Mary's home church in Auburn. Following a short wedding trip, the newlyweds moved into an apartment, a block from the Brandon homestead on North Cedar Street. They purchased their first home a year later.

The marriage, if not born out of passion and romantic flourishes, endured. It also produced a family. A son, Daniel Oak Husselman, was stillborn seventeen months later, in December 1947. Two healthy babies followed – Anne Brandon Husselman in May 1951 and Ellen Elizabeth Husselman in November 1953. Throughout the next two-and-a-half decades, Bill tended to his successful law practice, and Mary supervised the home and their daughters, in accordance with that era's defined gender roles. Mary also remained active in Auburn's literary and social clubs and oversaw the family's calendar, arranging – among other things – vacations, holiday gatherings, and parties with friends. When Bill retired in 1975, Mary had looked forward to the couple sharing more time together, recording in her memoir that "I never felt as some wives do that having a husband at home all day might be a problem. . . . He was a dear sweet man to live with."

Mary with her young daughters, Anne and Ellen

But shared time together ended in 1977. Suffering from heart disease and lung cancer, Bill died on September 26 at age sixty-six. The local newspaper reported his death on its front page, leading with the words "Prominent Auburn Attorney William H. Husselman" and mentioning his academic achievements, military service, civic contributions, and surviving family members, which at that point included two grandsons.

Mary carried on, eventually selling the family's Midway Drive home in an older, well-heeled Auburn neighborhood and moving to a smaller residence a block away – before eventually downsizing yet again to a condominium. Daughter Anne remained in Auburn for most of her adult life, making it easy for Mary to stay in touch with her eldest child and to enjoy Anne's sons, by then totaling three. Though Ellen lived in California, mother and younger daughter spoke weekly by telephone. Mary also traveled west to see Ellen every few years, and Ellen, in turn, made frequent trips home.

Mary died on May 13, 1994, at age eighty-three, her health relatively good until near the end. With her passing, the generation of Brandons and Husselmans who had lived through World War II was gone. Ora Brandon had died in September 1946, seven weeks after Mary and Bill wed. More deaths had followed in the next decade – George Olinger, husband to Mary's sister Annie, in 1951; Oak Husselman in 1953; Bill's grandmother, Lydia Cattell, in 1954; and Blanche Husselman in 1957. Winnie Brandon passed away at age ninety in 1961. A decade later, in 1972, Mary's brother, Charles Brandon, died.

Mary's beloved sister, Annie, died in 1985.

LIKE SO MANY WORLD WAR II VETERANS, Bill did not boast about his military service or talk incessantly about it. But neither was he silent. His daughters recalled playful sessions in their childhood when their father taught them how to march, Bill counting out military cadence in the family's living room, they responding as he barked out commands learned in his soldier days. Older daughter Anne also recalled her father obliging when she pressed him for stories. She especially remembered his accounts of how he transported a German boy with appendicitis to a hospital, how he saw a soldier die stepping on a land mine, how he witnessed horrors at Buchenwald.

In his old footlocker, in the family basement, Bill stored war memorabilia. Inside was a German airman's sheepskin-lined leather jacket and a German labor corps dagger. Inside, too, was Bill's olive-drab army shirt and his wool jacket. As a high school student in the late 1960s, Ellen sometimes wore the jacket, old military uniforms by then having become a trendy youth fashion. Bill, meanwhile, made use of another souvenir. When gazing at the night sky, he peered through the pair of high-powered German field glasses he had acquired indirectly from a Frenchman, who had traded them for cigarettes.

As for Mary, stories of wartime service spilled out easily. "When I was little, my mother talked constantly about the war years – how wonderful Rome was, how much fun she had, her friendship with the Russian prince," recalled Anne. Ellen did not remember those stories to the extent her older sister did, but as a child she was aware that the Red Cross had factored prominently in her mother's life: "It was just part of who she was. . . . We knew that she had been there [overseas], and that she had stuff." The "stuff" included the foot-high ceramic Madonna, as well as a still-fragrant ring box made from orange peels from Capri, a gondola-shaped trinket from Venice, a bracelet with Italian-themed charms, and, of course, the Russian Red Cross medal. Wartime friendships also had remained important to Mary. Ellen recalled that on one occasion Blenda Larson, with whom Mary worked overseas, had visited their Auburn home and been warmly welcomed.

In her advancing years, Mary continued to discuss her Red Cross service, remembering both the work and the times as exhilarating and demanding. In her 1992 interview with Rachel Roberts, which subsequently appeared in the northern Indiana publication *Mature Living,* Mary reminisced at length about her various overseas assignments. Perhaps most striking was what accompanied the article

Mary, age 81, wearing her Red Cross hat and uniform

– a photograph of Mary modeling her decades-old uniform, which still fit her petite frame perfectly. Several years earlier, she also had donned the uniform, this time for a World War II-themed party where she raked in compliments for still looking so professional and where a younger generation admired her for answering the call to duty.

Urged by family members, Bill and Mary each took stabs at writing their memoirs. Bill took up pen and paper on July 5, 1976, inspired – according to Mary – "by the celebration the day before when we watched the great displays on television of the 200th Anniversary of our country, the tall ships sailing up the Hudson, the bands, the speeches and the general outpourings of patriotism." Bill began his account with generations of Husselman family history and then worked his way forward to his childhood when, after completing twenty-two pages, he stopped, unable to continue due to ill health.

Mary took up her pen in 1982. Along with offering her thoughts on Bill's retirement and illness, she recounted how the two of them had first met as seventh-graders. Giving no explanation, Mary stopped writing after completing only a page and a half. More than a decade passed before she resumed the project, and when she did – in January 1994, just months before her death – her focus was solely on sharing Brandon family history. After five pages, she ended with "It's been refreshing to think back on these stores [sic] – my memory is certainly not as agile as it once was. I should have started it earlier – but, then you might have been bored."

Like Bill's memoir, hers recorded no World War II stories.

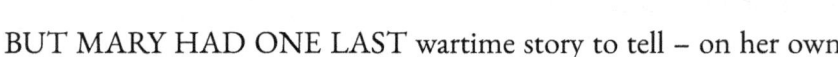

BUT MARY HAD ONE LAST wartime story to tell – on her own terms, in her own time.

Waiting until she was in her eighties and at that point long widowed, she chose to speak up one day when Ellen was home visiting from California. Deciding the occasion was suited for candor and perhaps sensing that death might preclude other opportunities, Mary entered a room where Ellen was relaxing, said she wanted to talk, and held up two photos of a dark-haired soldier in uniform. The man, Mary told Ellen, was someone with whom she had been intimate during the war. "Why didn't you marry him?" Ellen had asked. "He already was married," Mary replied.

Unprepared for her mother's confession, Ellen wasn't sure exactly what to make of it or why it was being offered. She listened as Mary gave the soldier's name and shared that he was a doctor. Ellen listened, too, as her mother remarked that "times were different then. War made things different." Eventually Mary shifted to talking about Bill – how he was a good husband who had loved his daughters very much – and Ellen, her mind still trying to process what she had just heard, remained largely silent. Generating little reaction from her daughter, Mary finally said, "Well, okay, then," and left the room. As Ellen later recalled: "I remember she seemed kind of put out that I wasn't more interested."

Ellen *was* interested. But her interest would not pique until later – after her mother's death, after she had read and pored over all of Mary's wartime correspondence. By then, Ellen understood that Mary, during that awkward mother-daughter conversation, had wanted to say in her own words what would be revealed on the written page. Mary could have chosen to destroy her letters; she could have shielded that part of her history from her daughters – in the same way that women for generations had hid their stories of premarital sex or of intimate relations with married men. But Mary had wanted the letters to survive her. And she had not wanted her daughters to be caught unawares.

The name Mary revealed to Ellen that day in Auburn was Wyman E. Jacobson. Later, when reading her mother's wartime letter dated March 13, 1945, Ellen found that exact name on an invitation tucked inside the envelope. The invitation was typed on a prescription pad and requested Mary's attendance at the March 10, 1945 cocktail party celebrating Doc's promotion to major. Doc had signed it "WEJacobson Major."

"Doc" - Major Jacobson

"I thought you might like to see the invitation to Doc's cocktail party on Saturday night . . . We all received one written on the Prescription blanks that he uses in the Dispensary," Mary had written Winnie and Ora at the time.

That confirmation of Doc's name – and Ellen's growing curiosity – led her to debate whether she should try to learn more about the major, of whom she knew virtually nothing. Would her mother approve? Was it proper? Concluding that her mother had not slammed the door on further sleuthing and had "left it up to me," Ellen, skilled at research and aided by the internet, eventually began pulling together threads of Jacobson's life. The threads included his date of birth and rearing in the upper Midwest, his graduation from medical school in 1939, his enlistment in the Army in 1941, his shipment overseas as a medical corps captain in April 1942, and his tours in North Africa and Italy.

After the war, Jacobson's story – as Ellen also came to learn – mirrored that of so many returning veterans. He returned to his native state, resumed practicing medicine, raised a family, and contributed to the well-being of his community. He died in 2002 at age eighty-six. If Doc and Mary ever corresponded after the war, if they ever reconnected before their deaths, no evidence has been found.

While Mary's story had taken Ellen completely by surprise, it likewise surprised Anne, though to a lesser extent. During Anne's teenage years, she recalled hearing her mother mention that she had a friend in the war who was a doctor. But no details were given, no elaboration offered. In Anne's case, no suspicions were aroused.

Eventually, Ellen's research led her to Jacobson's daughter, the two women separated by only a year in age. The daughter, Laura Jacobson McCammon, knew nothing about Mary Brandon or her father's wartime relationship with the Red Cross worker from Auburn. McCammon also said that, while her father wrote about his military service in two volumes of his memoirs, neither volume referenced Mary or any other woman. That written record aside, McCammon said Jacobson rarely spoke about his war years, keeping them to himself and regarding them for what they were – the past.

As for reckoning with that past, McCammon said she could understand Mary and Doc's relationship on at least one level: the need for people to forge connections. The pandemic of 2020 – a time of stay-at-home orders, enforced shutdowns, and monthslong separations from family and friends – gave her insight into loneliness and lonesomeness, the kind of emotional isolation that she could imagine servicemen and women experienced in World War II. Cut off from familial and familiar ties, they formed new ones. As McCammon put it: "People need people."

Ellen, too, could understand how Mary and Doc's relationship bloomed within the context of the times. More broadly, Ellen was grateful for what the war-era letters taught her about each of her parents. By no means saints, Bill and Mary had their shortcomings and made mistakes. But when their country asked them to commit to saving the world from maniacal dictators, they came forward, made the required sacrifices, and followed through with their assignment until the mission was accomplished. For Ellen, the opportunity to come to know Bill and Mary not as her parents but as *people* – as young, interesting, goal-driven people – was a gift she had not expected to receive.

But receive it she did, in their handwriting, in their voice. And Ellen received it for what it was: a window into their humanity.

Mary and Bill, 1974 (Photo by Ellen England)

Epilogue

UNDER A TOWERING MAPLE in Woodlawn Cemetery south of Auburn rests the polished gravestone of Mary E. and William H. Husselman. Etched into the granite are two sets of dates: 1910-1994 for Mary, 1911-1977 for Bill. Some quick math reveals that Mary lived nearly five decades after the end of World War II. During those decades, she married, had children, enjoyed friends, traveled widely, welcomed grandchildren, and grew old gracefully. What Mary was granted – a half-century of postwar living – was not a privilege accorded to all American Red Cross workers. Seventy-eight died while serving overseas in World War II, including one who hailed from Mishawaka, Indiana, not far from Auburn.

Bill Husselman also enjoyed a postwar life, long enough to marry, experience fatherhood, advance his career, meet two of his grandsons, and retire. More than 400,000 U.S. military personnel were not so fortunate. Their World War II service cost them their lives – lives that in many cases had barely begun, with some dying while still in their teens, others having barely reached their twenties. In Indiana, the war dead totaled nearly 12,000. In Bill's home county, DeKalb, the number approached one hundred. To honor lost sons, citizens of Auburn and neighboring towns banded together in 1947 to erect an eight-foot-tall memorial in the rotunda of the county courthouse. The monument stands today, the fallen collectively identified as "heroes."

The generation to which Bill and Mary belonged had been asked by President Franklin D. Roosevelt, in 1936 amid the Great Depression, to continue waging war at home "against want and destitution and economic demoralization," with FDR arguing the "survival of democracy" was at stake and declaring Americans had "a rendezvous with destiny." Within a few short years, Bill and Mary's generation mobilized for another "rendezvous with destiny," this time fighting despots on far-flung shores. Perhaps not surprisingly, this demographic group found itself singled out again at century's end. In recognition for having proven itself so resilient through the Depression and so committed and patriotic during World War II, a new label – "The Greatest" – was affixed to it. Members had not sought the label. Nor did they coin it or consider it entirely accurate, knowing as they did their own blemishes. But "The Greatest Generation" label, popularized by television journalist Tom Brokaw in his 1998 book by the same name, lives on. And it looks to have staying power.

Not so with the generation itself. Up and down the rows from Bill and Mary's gravestone in Woodlawn are markers bearing the names of the couple's generational peers. On holidays such as Memorial Day and the Fourth of July, when miniature American flags adorn the grassy gravesites of veterans, one can easily identify those who grew up in the pre-World War II era, put on military uniforms, and at war's end returned to raise families and build communities. Here one finds the resting place of an army captain, over there a staff sergeant, here and there a private first class and a lieutenant colonel. Here and there, too, rests a merchant marine man and a Pacific airman and a navy lieutenant commander. Nearby, gravestones point to Americans who, judging by birth and death dates, spent the war years at home, their service to country taking place perhaps in factories and on farms or in myriad other ways that aided the troops.

The letters in this book obviously do not reflect the wartime experiences of every member of the so-called Greatest Generation. Neither do they mirror the experiences of every uniformed man or woman who served or marched or fought on foreign soil. But these letters, tucked away for decades, still retain the power to instruct future generations. And they reveal a truth to which many, regardless of generation, can relate.

Bill and Mary left home to defend their country. Always, always, they kept home in their heart.

Acknowledgments

I NEVER WOULD HAVE EMBARKED on this project had Ellen England not reached out to me years ago and encouraged me to read some of her parents' World War II letters. Knowing my love of history, she suggested I might find the letters interesting, which – upon my reading a few – I did. Might the letters make for a good book? Might she and I work together? Ellen posed those and other questions, and as I warmed to the idea, she began delivering to my house jumbo-sized notebooks filled with her transcriptions of the letters and numerous other printed materials. Ellen's solid grasp of the subject matter impressed me. So did the amount of research she already had undertaken.

Hence, our project was launched, and together we worked to bring the story of Bill Husselman's and Mary Brandon's war service to life. Ellen was an ideal partner, always open to suggestions yet able to defend her viewpoints at critical junctures, dogged in her determination to track down missing information, candid in providing feedback when reading early drafts, sharp-eyed in spotting errors. A talented photographer, she also lent her expertise by poring through Husselman and Brandon family albums, then selecting and editing the personal photos that appear in this book. In short, working with Ellen was both instructive and a pleasure, and I am indebted to her for allowing me to be her collaborator.

Ellen and I were helped throughout this project by people who knew Bill and Mary and who kindly shared their recollections. When first contacted, most of the interviewees were in their seventies and eighties and, in the ensuing years, a number have died. Their deaths sadden

ACKNOWLEDGMENTS

me on many levels, not least because I wish I could thank them again for plumbing their memories for rich nuggets of information. All their names are listed in the bibliography.

Laura Jacobson McCammon deserves a special thanks. She graciously consented to a lengthy interview about her father, World War II veteran Dr. Wyman E. Jacobson. McCammon's remarks were informative, thoughtful, and much appreciated.

Kimberly Guise, senior curator and director of curatorial affairs at The National WW II Museum in New Orleans, also deserves special mention for fielding my questions and helping me better understand the significance of wartime correspondence. I highly recommend her article, "Mail Call: Letters from the Archives" (March 7, 2018), accessed through the museum's website (see bibliography).

At Eckhart Public Library's Willennar Genealogy Center in Auburn, the staff – particularly Jane Feyl and Karen Nesius Roeger – aided me in gathering valuable primary source material. Staff at numerous other institutions also assisted me, especially in my hunt for photographs. My thank-yous extend to Leslie Nellis, associate archivist for digital initiatives and records management, American University Library; Patricia Fiorilla, assistant curator, Boca Raton Historical Society; Susan Gold, archives and collections manager at Beaches Museum, Jacksonville Beach, Florida; Laura Peters, director of archives at "The Muny" Theatre, St. Louis, and Jessica Judd, librarian at Willard Library, Battle Creek, Michigan.

To that list, I add Dusty Mercier, archivist at the Mississippi Armed Forces Museum, Camp Shelby, and Justin M. Batt, director/curator at Harbor Defense Museum, USAG Fort Hamilton, Brooklyn, New York. Special thanks, too, to archivists with the still picture reference team at the National Archives & Records Administration.

Sharon Zonker, whose research specialties include DeKalb County history, helped clarify information regarding Mary Brandon's home church, today known as First United Methodist of Auburn. Railroad historian and author Craig J. Berndt helped inform me about rail service in DeKalb County.

Ray Boomhower, senior editor at the Indiana Historical Society Press and author of many books, including several on war correspondents, remained generous – as always – with editorial advice.

Finally, I thank my husband Doug. He's my trusted partner in all things, and he was at my side as we toured the Churchill War Rooms in London, the D-Day Landing Beaches at Normandy, General George S. Patton's "Battle of the Bulge" headquarters in Luxembourg City, and the many towns and cities in Germany through which First Lieutenant Bill Husselman traveled. Likewise, Doug accompanied me as we followed Mary Brandon's wartime footsteps – in Naples, on the Isle of Capri, at the Royal Palace in Caserta, and at the Foro Italico in Rome. As much as I appreciated Doug's companionship abroad, I also valued his special reservoir of knowledge: He's my go-to expert on World War II movies, classic or otherwise.

– Barbara Olenyik Morrow

I will be forever indebted to Barbara Olenyik Morrow for her considerable talent, determination, and hard work in bringing my parents' stories to light. Barb readily embraced the challenge of weaving the two stories together along with the unfolding history of the war. She threw her vision and extraordinary energy into the project, building a unique account of the war in Europe told from the vantage points of two Hoosiers, their families waiting anxiously at home.

Before embarking on this project, I knew Mary and Bill only as "Mother" and "Papa." Their letters were magic in showing me what interesting lives they led before they were "just my parents." I deeply appreciate getting to know them as vital and engaging young adults who set out for destinations unknown, eager to defend their country and the world from tyranny. I am indebted to my grandmothers who lovingly saved their letters so future generations could benefit from their legacy. Indeed my forebears saved a trove of family history – scrapbooks, photo albums, Bibles, letters, books, documents, and other mementos – telling the story of our roots, firmly planted in the soil of northeast Indiana; roots that were deep enough to pull me back home after thirty years in California.

I am grateful to my mother who loved and trusted me enough to share her secret with me, one that she no doubt struggled over. As she

ACKNOWLEDGMENTS

said, things were different during the war. But things are different now in the twenty-first century than they were in the 1940s when young women were meant to save themselves for marriage. I hope I have not betrayed her trust by sharing her secret, but I believe her frankness and willingness to confess to her daughter are more noteworthy than the fact that she engaged in an affair before she was married.

My sister, Anne Thomas, being two years my senior, was a valuable resource for her memories of our parents' stories from the war years and beyond. It is priceless to have a sibling to reminisce with about bygone years.

Finally, I owe a debt of gratitude to my husband, Bruce, whose patience, love, and encouragement sustained me through this project, and always.

– Ellen England

Selected Bibliography and Index

PRIMARY SOURCES

The letters of Mary Elizabeth Brandon and William "Bill" Henry Husselman, the primary source material for this book, are in the possession of Ellen Husselman England. Also in England's possession are family ancestry records, the unpublished memoirs of her parents, the unpublished diary (1916-1920) of Anne L. Brandon, relevant high school and college yearbooks, printed materials that Bill and Mary collected during the war, postwar correspondence to Mary from Red Cross colleagues and Italian workers, and two scrapbooks filled with local newspaper articles about Mary and Bill, the latter compiled by Blanche Husselman.

Essential information about Bill Husselman's military career is in his personnel file supplied, upon the family's request, by the National Personnel Records Center, National Archives, St. Louis.

The William H. Willennar Genealogy Center, a branch of Eckhart Public Library in Auburn, provided helpful resources such as city directories, local history books, Auburn High School yearbooks, photographs, maps, and microfilmed newspaper articles that shed light on life in Auburn in the first half of the twentieth century.

Oral history interviews with people who knew Mary Brandon and Bill Husselman in the pre-World War II years also were helpful. Among those the authors interviewed were Retha Manon Butler, Marilyn

Kail Carr, Nancy Western Derrow, Dorothy Cattell Hefty, Beverly Gonser Kelly, Donald Mefford, Elizabeth Brandon O'Herin, Joyce Rohm Springer, and Roger Wertenberger.

Anne Husselman Thomas shared insights about her parents, Mary and Bill, in the postwar years. Also sharing postwar recollections were Susan VanHorne Fischer, Frances R. Mefford, and Rachel S. Roberts.

Laura Jacobson McCammon shared stories about her father, Dr. Wyman E. Jacobson.

Linda Petrie, archives assistant in the Wabash College Archives, provided pertinent information on Herman Berns. The family of Maurice Biggs, an Indiana native and a World War II captain (177th Field Artillery Battalion, U.S. Third Army), shared his unpublished memoir.

SECONDARY SOURCES

Books

Allen, Robert S. *Lucky Forward: The History of General George Patton's Third U.S. Army*. New York: MacFadden-Bartell, 1965. Copyright 1947 by Robert S. Allen, published by arrangement with The Vanguard Press.

Ambrose, Stephen E. *Citizen Soldiers: The U.S. Army from the Normandy Beaches to the Bulge to the Surrender of Germany, June 7, 1944 to May 7, 1945*. New York: Simon & Schuster, 1997.

Atkinson, Rick. *An Army at Dawn: The War in North Africa, 1942-1943*. New York: Henry Holt and Company, 2002.

_____. *The Day of Battle: The War in Sicily and Italy, 1943-1944*. New York: Henry Holt and Company, 2007.

_____. *The Guns at Last Light: The War in Western Europe, 1944-1945*. New York: Henry Holt and Company, 2013.

Blumenson, Martin. *Patton: The Man Behind the Legend, 1885-1945*. New York: William Morrow and Company, 1985.

Boomhower, Ray E. *The Soldier's Friend: A Life of Ernie Pyle*. Indianapolis: Indiana Historical Society Press, 2004.

Brighton, Terry. *Patton, Montgomery, Rommel: Masters of War*. New York: Crown, 2010.

Brinkley, David. *Washington Goes to War*. New York: Knopf, 1988.

Brokaw, Tom. *The Greatest Generation*. New York: Random House, 1998.

Brooks, Thomas R. *The War North of Rome: June 1944-May 1945*. Edison, N.J.: Castle Books, 2001.

Cox, LeOna Kriesel, and Kathleen Cox. *Destination Unknown: Adventures of a World War II American Red Cross Girl*. Lexington, Kentucky: Kathleen Cox, 2009.

D'Este, Carlo. *Patton: A Genius for War*. New York: HarperCollins Publishers, 1995.

Dickson, Paul. *The Rise of the G.I. Army 1940-1941: The Forgotten Story of How America Forged a Powerful Army Before Pearl Harbor*. New York: Atlantic Monthly Press, 2020.

Dulles, Foster Rhea. *The American Red Cross: A History*. New York: Harper & Brothers, 1950.

Edsel, Robert M. *Saving Italy: The Race to Rescue a Nation's Treasures from the Nazis*. New York: W.W. Norton & Company, 2013.

Forty, George. *Patton's Third Army at War*. London: Arms and Armour Press, 1976.

Gannon, Michael. *Operation Drumbeat: The Dramatic True Story of Germany's First U-Boat Attacks Along the American Coast in World War II*. New York: Harper & Row Publishers, 1990.

Goodwin, Doris Kearns. *No Ordinary Time. Franklin and Eleanor Roosevelt: The Home Front in World War II*. New York: Simon & Schuster, 1994.

Gillis, Susan, Richard A. Marconi, and Debi Murray. *Palm Beach County During World War II*. Charleston, South Carolina: Arcadia Publishing, 2015.

Green, Michael, and James. D. Brown. *Patton's Third Army in World War II: A Photographic History*. New York: Crestline, an imprint of The Quarto Group, 2017.

Hastings, Max. *Armageddon: The Battle for Germany, 1944-1945*. New York: Knopf, 2004.

Henderson, Bruce. *Sons and Soldiers: The Untold Story of the Jews Who Escaped the Nazis and Returned with the U.S. Army to Fight Hitler*. New York: William Morrow, 2017.

History of DeKalb County, Indiana. Indianapolis: B.F. Bowen and Company, 1914.

Holland, James. *Italy's Sorrow: A Year of War, 1944-1945*. New York: St. Martin's Press, 2008.

Isserman, Maurice. *The Winter Army: The World War II Odyssey of the 10th Mountain Division, America's Elite Alpine Warriors*. Boston: Houghton Mifflin Harcourt, 2019.

Johnson, Paul. *Eisenhower: A Life*. New York: Viking, 2014.

Korda, Michael. *Ike: An American Hero*. New York: HarperCollins Publishers, 2007.

Larson, Erik. *The Splendid and the Vile: A Saga of Churchill, Family, and Defiance During the Blitz*. New York: Crown, 2020.

LeCouturier, Yves, and Isabelle Bournier. *The Beaches of the D-Day Landings*. Rennes, France: Editions Ouest-France, 2011.

Ling, Sally J. *Small Town, Big Secrets: Inside the Boca Raton Army Air Field During World War II*. Charleston, South Carolina: The History Press, 2012.

Madison, James H. *Slinging Doughnuts for the Boys: An American Woman in World War II*. Bloomington and Indianapolis: Indiana University Press, 2007.

Madison, James H. *World War II: A History in Documents*. New York and Oxford: Oxford University Press, 2010.

Meacham, Jon. *Franklin and Winston: An Intimate Portrait of an Epic Friendship*. New York: Random House, 2003.

Patton, George S., Jr. *War As I Knew It*. Annotated by Paul D. Harkins. Boston: Houghton Mifflin Company, 1947.

Peckham, Howard H., and Shirley A. Snyder, Editors. *Letters from the Greatest Generation: Writing Home in WWII*. Bloomington and Indianapolis: Indiana University Press, 2016. Originally published as *Letters from Fighting Hoosiers* by Howard H. Peckham and Shirley A. Snyder, Indiana War History Commission, 1948.

Perret, Geoffrey. *Eisenhower*. New York: Random House, 1999.

Petesch, Angela. *War Through the Hole of a Donut*. Madison, WI: Hunter Halverson Press, 2006.

Province, Charles M. *Patton's Third Army: A Chronology of the Third Army Advance, August, 1944 to May, 1945*. New York: Hippocrene Books, 1992.

Pyle, Ernie. *Brave Men*. New York: Henry Holt and Company, 1944.

Reynolds, David. *Rich Relations: The American Occupation of Britain, 1942-1945*. New York: Random House, 1995.

Rose, Kenneth D. *Myth and the Greatest Generation: A Social History of Americans in World War II*. New York: Routledge, Taylor & Francis Group, 2008.

Silveri, Umberto Gentiloni, Andrea Di Stefano, and Stefano Palermo, Editors. *Rome: 4 June 1944*. Rome: Palombi Editori, 2011.

Sisson, Frank, with Robert L. Wise. *I Marched With Patton: A Firsthand Account of World War II Alongside One of the U.S. Army's Greatest Generals*. New York: William Morrow, 2020.

Smith, Bruce C. *The War Comes to Plum St.* Bloomington and Indianapolis: Indiana University Press, 2005.

Stevenson, Eleanor, and Pete Martin. *I Knew Your Soldier*. New York: Penguin Books, 1945.

Smith, John Martin. *Auburn: The Classic City*. Charleston, South Carolina: Arcadia Publishing, 2002.

Smith, John Martin. *History of DeKalb County, Indiana: Volumes One and Two*. Auburn, IN: NATMUS, Inc., 1992.

Tobin, James. *Ernie Pyle's War: America's Eyewitness to World War II*. New York: The Free Press, 1997.

Winik, Jay. *1944: FDR And The Year That Changed History*. New York: Simon & Schuster, 2015.

Articles

Ambrose, Stephen E. "Ike, Beetle, and D-Day: The Hoosier at Supreme Headquarters." *TRACES of Indiana and Midwestern History*, Summer 1996.

Beck, Lee. "The Cord That Binds." *TRACES of Indiana and Midwestern History*, Spring 1994.

Crawford, Kenneth. "Furlough in Heaven." *Newsweek*, November 15, 1943.

Dixon, Kenneth L. "Dixon with the AEF: Finds Good Bed and Comforts of Isle of Capri Too Much." *The Indianapolis Star*, January 21, 1944.

Dixon, Kenneth L. "Dixon with the AEF: Let's Have Another Cup of Coffee." *The Indianapolis Star*, January 22, 1944.

"Don't Visit Your Husband in an Army Town." *LOOK,* September 7, 1943.

"Fifty Years Later: Hoosiers Remember WWII." Collection of articles in a special issue of *TRACES of Indiana and Midwestern History,* Fall 1991.

Fine, Benjamin. "Private Pete Learns to Read." *Liberty,* August 28, 1943. Excerpted in *The Reader's Digest,* October 1943.

Gellhorn, Martha. "Cracking the Gothic Line." *Collier's,* October 28, 1944.

Gellhorn, Martha. "Postcards from Italy." *Collier's,* July 1, 1944.

Gellhorn, Martha. "Treasure City – The Fight to Save Florence." *Collier's,* September 30, 1944.

Gervasi, Frank. "Battle at Cassino." *Collier's,* March 18, 1944.

Gervasi, Frank. "Rome Lives Again." *Collier's,* September 9, 1944.

Kinkead, Katherine Theobald. "Miss Latimer and Her Kit." *The New Yorker,* November 11, 1944.

McNeel, John. "A Question of Leadership: The 5th Army in Italy." *Virginia Quarterly Review: A National Journal of Literature and Discussion,* Winter 2000.

Pratt, Sara E. "March 17, 1944: The Most Recent Eruption of Mount Vesuvius." *EARTH Magazine,* March 15, 2016.

Roberts, Rachel S. "Despite War's Horrors, Red Cross Service Was Rewarding." *Mature Living,* February 1, 1992.

Rhoads, Joanna. "Red Cross Bundle for American Pilots." *The Cross Keys: The Magazine of Tri Kappa,* July 1944.

Steckel, Francis C. "Morale Problems in Combat American Soldiers in Europe in World War II." *Army History,* Summer 1994.

"Teacher Education in Rome." *The Journal of Health and Physical Education,* June 1945.

Wissing, Douglas. "Mr. Selective Service: General Lewis B. Hershey." *TRACES of Indiana and Midwestern History,* Winter 2016.

Miscellany

MP: The Story of the Corps of Military Police. Booklet, one of a series of *G.I. Stories* published by *The Stars And Stripes,* Paris, 1944-1945.

The United States Army Rest Center, Foro D'Italia, Rome 1944-45. Booklet. Rome: Casa Editrice Dalmatia, 1945.

Websites
Good sources of information on soldiers and Red Cross workers referenced in Bill Husselman's and Mary Brandon's letters:
https://www.ancestry.com
https://www.newspapers.com
https://www.e-yearbook.com
https://www.findagrave.com

Organizations with helpful websites:
American Red Cross
https://www.redcross.org

The National WW2 Museum
https://www.nationalww2museum.org

United States Holocaust Memorial Museum
https://www.ushmm.org

U.S. Army Heritage & Education Center
https://ahec.armywarcollege.edu

Photo Credits
Unless otherwise noted, all images are the property of Ellen England.

SELECTED BIBLIOGRAPHY AND INDEX

INDEX

Alexander, Harold, 176
American Red Cross, 2, 84-87, 210, 222, 389, 400. See also *Mary* chapter 6
American University, 3, 90, 104
Anzio, 167, 172, 176, 179, 199
Ardennes, 254, 288, 293, 320
Arnberg, Bert, 268, 274-75, 285, 289, 352, 358
Attlee, Clement, 380
Auburn Automobile Co., 9, 80
Auburn Courier, 9-10
[Auburn] Evening Star, 72, 82, 386-87
Auburn High School, 12, 77-78, 81-82
Auburn Methodist Church, 80

Baker, Edith, 86
Bastogne, 294, 320
Battle of the Bulge, 254, 293-301,312, 320
Baxter, Jessie, 190-91
Berg, Phil, 178, 265
Berlin, Irving, 96, 196-97
Berns, Herman, 82-84, 144, 263
Berns, Jack, 263
Biggs, Maurice, 335
Boca Raton Army Air Field, 41-44
Bogart, Humphrey, 151, 156-57
Bradley, Omar, 138, 215, 229, 310, 331
Brandon, Anne [Olinger], 74-87, 391, 394. See also all *Mary* chapters
Brandon, Charles, 74-84, 163, 391, 394. See also all *Mary* chapters
Brandon, Mary, ix-xii, 2-4, 14, 144, 225, 229, 387-401. See also all *Mary* chapters
Brandon, Ora, 74-86, 193, 391, 394. See also all *Mary* chapters
Brandon, Russell, 74
Brandon, Winnie, 74-87, 193, 391, 394. See also all *Mary* chapters
Browand, 276, 283
Buchenwald, 331-34, 394
Butler, Retha Manon, 389
Buffalo Soldiers/92nd Inf, 319, 323

Camp Atterbury, 385
Camp Lee, 108, 110
Camp Patrick Henry, 118-19
Camp Pickett, 108-09
Camp Polk, 137
Camp Shelby, 124-26, 210
Carnegie, Andrew, 10
Capri, 278, 348-49. See also *Mary* chapter 8
Casablanca, 123, 150, 278
Casablanca, film, 150-51, 156
Caserta, 173, 176-77, 255-56
Caserta, Royal Palace, 328-29. See also *Mary* chapter 9
Cassino, 167, 172, 176, 179, 189, 199, 256, 319
Cattell, Lydia, 131, 388, 394
Central Sports School, 325
Chamberlain, Neville, 224
Chester, England, 212
Churchill, Winston, 150, 159, 173, 207, 228, 300, 328, 337-38, 340, 380
Clark, Mark, 138, 176, 198, 201-02, 312, 319, 328-29
Crosby, Bing, 58, 246
Crosby, England, 207, 213

D-Day, x, 215, 217, 222, 226-28, 239, 255, 269
DeKalb Abstract & Title Company, 7, 387
DeKalb County Courthouse, 1, 10, 400
DePauw University, 79, 347
Derrow, Nancy Western, 81
Dewey Thomas, 282
Dietrich, Marlene, 249
Dillinger, John, 81
Ditchfield, Catherine, 206, 209, 225, 232, 382
Ditchfield, Dave, 206, 210, 212, 227-28, 232
Ditchfield, John, 206, 208, 212
Ditchfield, Tony, 206, 227-28, 232
Dunham, Elmer, 135
Dyer, Gertrude, 266
DeRiso, Vittoria, 390

Eckhart, Barbara, 75
Eckhart, Charles, 10, 75, 80

INDEX

Eckhart Public Library, 10
Edward VIII, 223
Eisenhower, Dwight, 18, 50, 138, 159, 196, 207-19, 251, 293, 310, 331-33, 337-38, 373, 377
Elizabeth II, 224
Empress of Japan, 122
Empress of Scotland, 120, 122, 150
Enola Gay, 381

Ferguson, Jo, 27
Fink, Richard, 184-86, 195, 287
Fletcher, Samuel, 355, 357
Florence, 269, 280-81
Flynn, Thomas, 131, 135-36, 144, 146, 227, 296
Forester, C. S., 225-26
Foro Mussolini/Italico, 257, 264, 350
Fort Belvoir, 94
Fort Benjamin Harrison, 1, 5, 17-19, 143
Fort Custer, 62, 124
Fort Hamilton, 147
Fort Lauderdale, 46-50, 52
Fort Meade, 99-100, 102-03
Fort Oglethorpe, 65
Fort Sam Houston, 144-45
Foundation Pescatore, 295
Fowler, Phillip J., 236, 246
Frank, Anne, 219

Gable, Clark, 46-47
Garrett, 7, 87,
Garrett Clipper, 374, 388
Gay, Hobart, 293
George VI, 224
Gothic Line, 269, 281, 283, 312
Great Depression, 13, 80, 401
Greenock, 205
Gregory, Joyce, 255, 272, 281, 352-53

Harrison School, 12, 78
Haugland, Fritzie, 169, 337
Haugland, Vern, 169
Hebel, Bill, 6, 8

Hebel, John, 7
Hershey, Lewis, 58
Hiroshima, 364, 381
Hitler, Adolf, 1, 15, 81, 222, 258, 339
HMT *Rohna,* 150
Hodges, Courtney, 125
Hotel Benedict, 114
Hotel Campo Imperatore, 275-76
Husselman, Anne [Thomas], x, 393-95, 398
Husselman, Blanche, 78, 265, 386, 388, 394. See also *Bill* chapters
Husselman, Daniel, 393
Husselman, Oak, 386-88, 394. See also *Bill* chapters
Husselman, William, ix-xii, 1-4, 78, 173, 387-401. See also *Bill* chapters

Indiana University, 6, 13-14, 77
Irons, Bob, 31, 145
Ischia, 255, 278

Jacobson, W.E. (Doc), 396-98. See also *Mary* chapters 9, 13, 15, 17.
Japanese-American 442nd RCT, 125, 133-34, 272, 319, 323
Jefferson Barracks, 18-23, 30, 54, 126
Jodl, Alfred, 340
Judge Advocate General's Department, 15, 23, 30, 37, 39, 56, 70-71, 377

Kappa Alpha Theta, 79
Kaylor, Marian, 106, 356, 366
Kingsbury, Ed, 363
Kirk, Alexander, 284, 323
Knott, Opal, 13, 78
Kubisek, Edward, 355

Larson, Blenda, 171, 178, 183-84, 192-93, 266, 358, 395
Lash, Don, 81
Leesville, 138-43
Liberty, 126
Life, 89
Look, 139
Louisiana Maneuvers, 137-38

INDEX

MacArthur, Douglas, 154, 169, 288
Manon, Katie, 190, 195
Marshall, George, 20, 137-38, 310, 331
Martin, Miriam, 273-74, 279
McAuliffe, Anthony, 294
McCammon, Laura Jacobson, 398
McEown, Eileen, 278, 282, 289, 317, 349, 351-58, 363, 368, 373, 390-91
McKenney, H. L., 73, 320
McKenney, Kent, 320
McNarney, Joseph, 350-51
Mefford, Donald, 83, 87
Messenger, Ruth, 85
Methot, Mayo, 156
Metz, France, 242, 251, 383-84
Miami Beach, 46-47
Military Police, Officer Candidate School, 30, 62, 65-72
Military Police, 512th Battalion, see *Bill* chapters 7, 10, 11, 12, 14, 16, 18
Miller, Glenn, 288
Montgomery, Bernard, 302, 306-07, 337
Mount Vesuvius, 187-89, 199, 200
Munford, Mary, 273, 277
Muny Theatre, St. Louis, 28-29, 35
Mussolini, Benito, 257-258, 260, 262, 275-76, 327, 350, 352, 356-57

Nancy, France, 242, 247, 295
Naples, 142, 156, 167, 169, 174. See also *Mary* chapters 9, 17.
Newsweek, 31, 137, 157, 159
Northwestern University, 82

O'Herin, Elizabeth, 84
Oklahoma! 3
Olinger, Buddy, 86, See also *Mary* chapters
Olinger, George, 86, 394, See also *Mary* chapters
Operation Avalanche, 142
Operation Dragoon, 269
Operation Drumbeat, 46
Operation Market Garden, 320

Operation Market Garden, 207, 215, 221
Operation Torch, 50, 150
Oppenheim, Germany, 307
Ohrdruf, 331
Owens, Jesse, 81
Oxnam, G. Bromley, 79, 347

Paris, 231, 235, 302, 305
Paschkoff, Mary, 369-70
Pas de Calais, 215, 218, 222
Patton, George, Jr., 138, 207, 215-17, 222, 225, 228, 230-31, 238-39, 241, 270, 292, 300, 331, 333, 337-38, 378
Patton, film, 216
Pearl Harbor, 2-4, 15, 45, 84, 137-38, 156
Petacci, Clara, 327
Pompeii, 188, 200-01
Pope Pius XII, 260-61, 266
Potsdam, 380-81
Purdue University, 145, 326
Pyle, Ernie, 239, 351, 357-59

Queen Elizabeth, 147-48, 205
Queen Mary, 147-48

Raut, Frederick, 15
Raut, Mary Ashleman, 75
Reagan, Ronald, 96, 134
Red Ball Express, 241
Reims, 340, 378-81, 383-384
Remagen, 306
Remley, Robert, 223, 227, 233-35, 237, 301
Rhine River, 241, 292, 306-08
Rhoads, Joanna, 160, 170, 178, 265
Richardson, Elizabeth, 158, 266
Richmond, VA, 107-13
Rieke Metal Products, 4
Riley School, 78
Rome, 390. See also *Mary* chapters 13, 15, 17
Rommel, Erwin, 31
Roosevelt, Eleanor, 117
Roosevelt, Franklin, 4, 14, 20, 35, 97, 150, 202, 207, 282, 309, 324, 337-38, 380, 400-01

INDEX

Roberts, Rachel, 370, 395
ROTC, 13

Sacco, Tony, 200
Saint-Dizier, 231, 245
Salerno, 142, 156,
San Carlo Opera Company, 195-96
San Carlo Opera House, 196
Saturday Evening Post, 85
Sawtelle, Eleanor, 278, 281
Scott Field, 22-40, 126
Seabiscuit, 99
Selective Service Act, 15, 57
Sicily, 100, 136, 138, 207, 215
Siegfried Line, 231, 241
Sigma Chi, 6-7, 67
Simpson, Wallis, 223
Skorzeny, Otto, 276
Slovik, Eddie, 377
Sorrento, 156, 198
Smith, Faye, 249
Spalding, Ardith, 268, 274-75, 279, 285, 287, 289, 317, 352, 358, 390
Springer, Joyce Rohm, 82
Stalin, 337-38, 380-81
Stars And Stripes, 351, 375
Steinbeck, John, 167
Stimson, Henry, 251
Summersby, Kay, 210
Switzer, Carl, 200
Szymanski, 51-52

Thomas, Richard, 320
Tiberius, 167, 172, 348
TIME, 31, 208
Truscott, Lucian, 312
Truman, Harry, 309, 380-81
Tuttle, Dorothy Groscop, 94, 115, 118

U.S. Army Rest Center, see *Mary* chapters 13, 15, 17
USO (United Service Organization), 15, 29-30, 92, 97, 99
USS *General J.C. Breckenridge,* 385-86
USS *Missouri*, 364, 383

Utah Beach, 228

V-E Day, 340-42, 346, 375-78
V-J Day, 341
Van Buskirk, 28, 34-35, 38
Van Nuys, Frederick, 15-16
Vatican City, 260, 268, 275
Victor Emmanuel III, 258, 260, 284
Villa d'Este, 360
Vitry-le-Francois, 245
Vulcania, 371, 374, 390

Wabash College, 84
WAC (Women's Army Corps), 2, 85, 374
Ward, Sterling, 178, 265
Washington, D.C., 77, 85-86. See *Mary* chapter 6
Watson, Marianna, 105-06, 115, 118
Watson, Myron, 105-06, 115
WAVES (Women Accepted for Volunteer Emergency Service), 2, 85
Wiesel, Elie, 332
Wilkins, Robert, 133
Winsberg, Bill, 206, 210, 212, 227
Wolkonsky, Vladimir, 270, 287, 313, 368-371

Yalta, 337

Ziggy, 236-37, 246, 251, 303, 388

About the Authors

BARBARA OLENYIK MORROW is the author of seven books, most focusing on Indiana history. A former journalist, she has been a Pulitzer Prize finalist for editorial writing. Her previous books include two youth biographies published by the Indiana Historical Society Press: *Hardwood Glory: A Life of John Wooden* and *Nature's Storyteller: The Life of Gene Stratton-Porter*. Morrow lives in northeast Indiana.

ELLEN ENGLAND has a master's degree in Library and Information Studies from UC Berkeley. Now retired, England worked as a programmer analyst for the University of California's systemwide library automation project. She has since moved back to her hometown of Auburn, Indiana. Her parents were the source of letters for this book.

www.ingramcontent.com/pod-product-compliance
Lightning Source LLC
Chambersburg PA
CBHW071959150426
43194CB00008B/936